Discoveries

A Step-by-Step Guide to Writing Paragraphs and Essays

Kate Mangelsdorf
Evelyn Posey
University of Texas at El Paso

BEDFORD / ST. MARTIN'S
Boston ◆ New York

For Bedford/St. Martin's

Senior Developmental Editor: John Elliott
Production Editor: Bernard Onken
Senior Production Supervisor: Dennis J. Conroy
Senior Marketing Manager: Rachel Falk
Art Direction and Cover Design: Lucy Krikorian
Text Design: Wanda Kossak
Copy Editor: Denise Quirk
Indexer: Riofrancos & Co. Indexes
Photo Research: Martha Friedman
Cover Photo: Royalty-Free/CORBIS
Composition: Stratford Publishing Services, Inc.
Printing and Binding: R.R. Donnelley & Sons Company

President: Joan E. Feinberg
Editorial Director: Denise B. Wydra
Editor in Chief: Nancy Perry
Director of Marketing: Karen Melton Soeltz
Director of Editing, Design, and Production: Marcia Cohen
Managing Editor: Erica T. Appel

Library of Congress Control Number: 2004108333

Manufactured in the United States of America.

1 0 9 8 7 6
f e d c b a

For information, write: Bedford/St. Martin's, 75 Arlington Street, Boston, MA 02116 (617-399-4000)

ISBN: 0-312-39065-3 (Student Edition)
0-312-41383-1 (Instructor's Annotated Edition)

EAN: 978-0-312-39065-5
978-0-312-41383-5

Acknowledgments
Acknowledgments and copyrights are continued at the back of the book on pages 663–64, which constitute an extension of the copyright page.

Preface for Instructors

As writing teachers for over twenty years, we have worked with many talented students, instructors, reviewers, and editors who have helped shape our thinking and answer important questions about teaching developmental writing. How do we provide opportunities for students to discover their own ideas, their own voices, while at the same time giving them sufficient structure so they aren't overwhelmed by a college writing assignment? How do we encourage students to write texts that are personally meaningful and also appropriate for academic and workplace contexts? How do we help students master standard written English, while still showing respect for their diverse cultural experiences? With *Discoveries: A Step-by-Step Guide To Writing Paragraphs and Essays,* we share what we have learned, what we know works best, and what ensures that students understand the value of writing in their lives.

Developed from sound classroom practices, *Discoveries* provides a user-friendly approach to writing that helps students succeed. Every assignment chapter in Parts One and Two guides students step by step through the process of writing a paragraph or essay using one of the standard rhetorical patterns. We know that this step-by-step approach works because we've used it in our own classrooms and in our first textbook, *Choices: A Basic Writing Guide with Readings,* whose users across the country — both students and instructors — have confirmed its benefits. The most significant benefit, we believe, is that because students are guided throughout the process, their confidence increases and they begin to realize that they have important ideas to share.

Organization

Discoveries is divided into four sections: Part One, "Reading and Writing Paragraphs"; Part Two, "Reading and Writing Essays"; Part Three, "Other Kinds of Writing"; and Part Four, "Handbook with

Exercises." In "Reading and Writing Paragraphs," students are introduced to important writing concepts such as audience, purpose, patterns of development, and the writing process. After writing a variety of paragraphs — there is a paragraph chapter for each of the nine rhetorical patterns — students progress to "Reading and Writing Essays," which includes chapters for four of the most common patterns. "Other Kinds of Writing" provides instruction in several other writing tasks students encounter in their college classes: journal writing, essay exams, writing summaries, and using sources. The "Handbook with Exercises" provides clear, easy-to-follow instruction and exercises on paragraph and essay format, sentence grammar, word choice, spelling, punctuation, and mechanics. This part ends with a Guide for Multilingual Writers, which focuses on language issues common to students from language backgrounds other than English.

Features

A Secure Structure for Developmental Writers

Step-by-step guides. Each assignment chapter introduces a rhetorical pattern with a definition and two examples and then poses a writing assignment that engages students in selecting and narrowing their topics. Students next explore their audience and purpose so that they can apply these concepts to their writing. They continue the process by gathering ideas and drafting, revising, and editing their work. Finally, they share what they have written with their readers. Specific skills and strategies — such as clustering, adding examples, or using progressive order — are taught in the context of individual steps.

"How To" boxes. Every assignment chapter includes easy-to-find guidelines for every step of the writing process. These bulleted lists, designed to provide a quick review, help students check their understanding and remember important points.

Student examples as ongoing models. Every assignment chapter follows a student model through the writing process, showing how one student completed the chapter assignment and providing material for students to analyze as they write on their own topics. Early drafts accurately mirror students' work, including surface errors, to demonstrate the importance of revising and editing.

Peer review guidance. Each assignment chapter includes customized prompts and questions to guide students as they review their classmates' writing. Through peer review, students learn the value of working within a community of writers and see the effect their ideas have on their readers.

Grammar Help Students Need — When They Need It

Integrated sentence-level coverage. The step-by-step guide in each assignment chapter concludes with an Editing section that addresses one sentence-level problem likely to occur in that rhetorical pattern, such as sentence fragments in exemplification or comma splices in narration, and provides practice exercises along with a cross-reference to the appropriate section of the handbook.

Comprehensive handbook. The comprehensive handbook in Part Four covers sentence grammar, word choice, spelling, punctuation, and mechanics. Plenty of exercises help students learn to write clear, coherent sentences and paragraphs, improve their word choice, and eliminate common errors.

Extensive Preparation for Writing in College and Beyond

Real-life writing assignments. Each assignment provides a practical reason for writing either for school or work, connects that purpose to students' lives, and encourages students to share their writing with an audience beyond the classroom. For example, in Chapter 14, "Writing an Essay That Tells a Story," the assignment asks students to provide a writing sample in the form of a narrative essay as part of the application process for an internship offered by the career services program at their college. The topic of the essay can be either an event in the student's life that interested him or her in a certain profession or a job that changed him or her in a particular way, and students are encouraged to save their finished essays to use in their own applications for internships, jobs, and so on.

Help with other academic writing. Part Three gives advice on dealing with writing situations students encounter in other college courses as well as their developmental writing class: keeping journals, taking essay exams, writing summaries, and doing research. The chapter on journals explains how to keep three different kinds: a personal journal, a dialogue journal, and a learning log. The research chapter explains what sources are and when to use them, how to find them in the library and online, how to evaluate them, how to take notes and avoid plagiarism, and how to use and document them in an essay.

Integrated computer advice. Throughout the text, boxed tips offer students specific advice about using computer technology to support their writing. In addition, Web tips direct students to online writing resources, additional online assignments, and grammar practice specifically designed for students using *Discoveries*.

Collaborative activities. More than forty group activities encourage students to work with classmates as they develop ideas and address challenges. Through collaboration, developmental students get not only help with their specific writing tasks but confidence from learning how other students handle the same issues.

Content that Reflects the Diversity of the Developmental Classroom

A variety of authors. With examples and models from a culturally diverse group of student and professional writers, students discover the range of styles and voices available to them in their own writing. Additional readings for each of the nine rhetorical patterns are available in a free ancillary, *Readings for* Discoveries.

Extensive ESL coverage. Part Four offers thorough coverage of ESL issues in a separate section, Guide for Multilingual Writers, as well as in Multilingual Writers boxes in the other sections of the handbook.

Ancillaries

Print

The Instructor's Annotated Edition offers marginal teaching and resource tips that include discussion prompts, strategies for teaching ESL students, ideas for collaborative learning, and more. It also contains answers to all exercises and suggestions for using the other ancillaries.

***Resources for Instructors Using* Discoveries,** by Sandra Blystone, contains information and advice on working with basic writers, facilitating collaborative learning, teaching ESL students and speakers of nonstandard dialects, and assessing student progress. It also offers sample syllabi.

***Readings for* Discoveries** offers two brief professional essays to illustrate each of the nine rhetorical patterns, with headnotes and reading activities that complement the approach in *Discoveries*.

***Diagnostic and Mastery Tests to Accompany* Discoveries,** by Bruce Thaler, offers diagnostic and mastery tests complementing the topic coverage in *Discoveries*.

***Supplemental Exercises to Accompany* Discoveries,** by Bruce Thaler, provides additional grammar exercises (including material from the Exercise Central online exercise collection).

***Transparency Masters to Accompany* Discoveries**, which help instructors reinforce key concepts from the book in the classroom, are available both as a printed package and as files downloadable from the book's Web site, bedfordstmartins.com/discoveries.

The Bedford/St. Martin's ESL Workbook, by Sapna Gandhi-Rao, Maria McCormack, and Elizabeth Trelenberg, provides ESL students with a broad range of exercises covering grammatical issues for multilingual students of varying language skills and backgrounds.

Teaching Developmental Writing: Background Readings offers more than two dozen professional articles on topics of interest to developmental writing instructors, accompanied by suggestions for practical applications to the classroom.

Electronic

The *Discoveries* Web site, bedfordstmartins.com/discoveries, gives students free access to Exercise Central, a large collection of interactive grammar exercises; Re:Writing, a comprehensive set of resources for writing, research, grammar, and more; and sentence combining exercises and links to sites that are useful to ESL students. For instructors, the Web site offers online versions of the *Resources for Instructors Using* Discoveries and of other ancillaries, alternative writing assignments, and a preview of the *Discoveries* content developed for use with course management software (such as Web CT and Blackboard).

Exercise Central to Go: Writing and Grammar Practices for Basic Writers is a CD-ROM containing hundreds of exercise items for writing and editing skills, drawn from the Exercise Central collection.

The Testing Tool Kit CD-ROM provides a comprehensive and easy-to-use test bank that allows instructors to create secure, customized tests and quizzes from a pool of nearly 2,000 questions.

Acknowledgments

We are indebted to many people whose inspiration and hard work helped us complete *Discoveries,* but especially our students, many of whose writing samples enliven these pages. We also thank our colleagues Kathy Stein and Donna Loudon, who provided material for Parts Three and Four. Sandra Blystone wrote the excellent *Resources for Instructors* with her usual grace, humor, and intelligence. Cecy Rhymes, Janet Davis, and Lluvia Rodarte copied and mailed manuscript pages, helping us to meet our deadlines.

Since publishing our first book with Bedford/St. Martin's over ten years ago, we have discovered the joy of working with a group of truly dedicated and talented professionals. The thoughtful suggestions and patient encouragement of each and every person form the basis of our growth as authors. We want now to extend our sincere thanks to those at Bedford/St. Martin's who contributed to the development of *Discoveries;* their attention to detail and insistence on excellence have helped us produce a textbook we are proud of.

We will probably never know the name of everyone who contributed to this effort, but we want to thank those we have worked with closely and have had the pleasure to know well. Ben Morrison and Marcia Muth were both patient and cooperative in shaping an early draft of *Discoveries*. Ellen Kuhl made significant contributions to the final manuscript, finding the common threads and weaving them into a cohesive whole, and Bernie Onken tactfully kept us on deadline throughout the production process. John Elliott's unwavering dedication to finishing this project, down to the final editing, has been a great source of strength to us. With John, we knew the book was in the best possible hands.

Working with Nathan Odell was a pleasure; his lighthearted e-mails, continually urging us on, were a joy. Nick Carbone and Eric Crump enthusiastically helped us with the digital aspects of the book, encouraging us to stretch our technical skills, while Rachel Falk, one of the many people at Bedford/St. Martin's who seems to have boundless energy, is responsible for getting the word out to the Bedford/St. Martin's sales force about this book. We are elated with the momentum she has brought to the project.

Simple words fail us when we try to thank Joan Feinberg, Denise Wydra, and Nancy Perry. It goes without saying that their unflagging support of *Discoveries* is responsible for its publication. What's more, their impeccable leadership skills, mutual respect, and eye for editorial talent have created the positive work environment that we have come to appreciate so much. We will do our best to continue to merit the trust they have placed in us.

We'd also like to express our deep appreciation to the following instructors whose reviews of various stages and parts of *Discoveries* provided invaluable help in shaping the book: William Abernethy, Washtenaw Community College; Elizabeth A. Butts, Delaware County Community College; Ann D. Ecoff, Lambuth University; Annmarie Chiarini, Community College of Baltimore County; Scott Fisher, Rock Valley College; Anthony C. Gargana, Long Beach City College; Linda Gilmore, Carroll Community College; Karen N. Gleeman, Normandale Community College; Marie Heim, Mississippi Gulf Coast Community College; Patsy Krech, University of Memphis; Mary Likely, Nassau Community College; Alpha McMath, Triton College; Rosie M. Soy, Hudson County Community College; Ted Walkup, Clayton College and State University; and June Wenzel, Parkland College.

Finally, as always, we thank our families, especially Bob and Bruce, for their continued support and encouragement.

Kate Mangelsdorf
Evelyn Posey

Brief Contents

Contents

Discoveries

A Step-by-Step Guide to
Writing Paragraphs and Essays

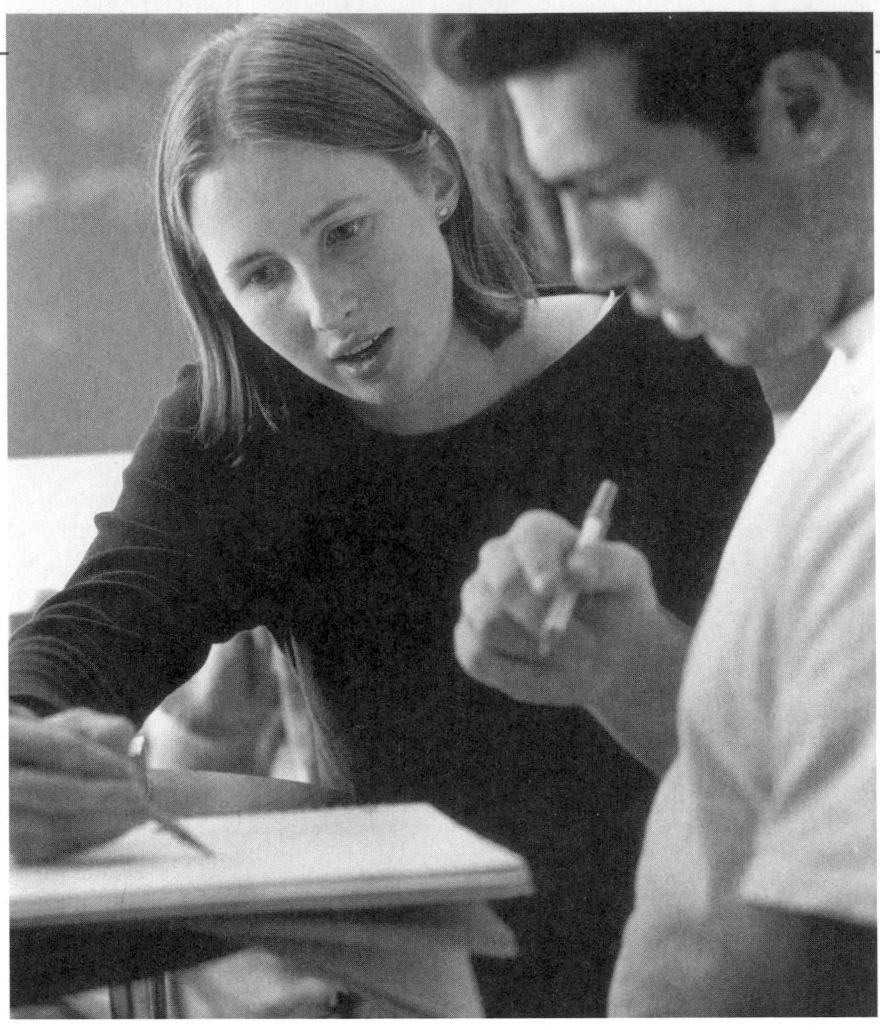

How have you grown as a writer? You have probably become better able to explore your ideas and express them to others. Writing has probably become more rewarding to you even if it remains challenging. In this chapter, you will think about your writing experiences and consider how you can become an even stronger writer.

CHAPTER

1

Discovering Writing

In this chapter, you will

- write about your experience as a writer.
- learn how reading can improve your writing.
- explore patterns of writing.
- discover the composing process.

What comes to mind when you think about writing? Perhaps you recall keeping a journal or instant-messaging a close friend, where all you needed to do was express your thoughts and feelings. Perhaps you remember more challenging writing activities, such as staying up late to finish a research paper, taking an essay exam, or working overtime to complete a report. However, even these difficult writing tasks have their rewards — a well-written paper, a good grade, a job well done.

This book will help you appreciate the rewards of writing. It will take you step-by-step through writing assignments, starting with paragraphs and advancing to essays. It will help you shape your writing according to your audience and purpose. Finally, it will help you see writing as a process of discovery. Through writing you can explore ideas about important aspects of your life. Through writing you also can communicate your ideas so that others understand and appreciate them. Writing helps you discover your ideas — and helps your readers discover you.

Writing Assignment

Your first assignment is to describe yourself as a writer. You can get your ideas flowing by writing for a few minutes in response to each of the following questions:

- What three words best describe you as a reader?
- What three words best describe you as a writer?
- What was the most important writing event of your life? Consider not only assignments for school or work, but also letters, reports, and e-mail messages.
- Can you recall any times when you felt unsuccessful as a reader or writer? What was the event? Why did you feel this way? What changes did you make as a result?
- Do you think your reading and writing skills can improve? How? Why?

Use your best ideas to write a description for your classmates and instructor of how you view yourself as a writer and how you plan to develop your reading and writing skills.

READING TO IMPROVE YOUR WRITING

Many of us read a newspaper or visit a favorite Web site to keep up with current events, and it's always fun to read a novel and compare it with the movie version of the same story. Some people read during their commute to and from work to make the ride pass more quickly. At times, reading occupies a particularly special place in our lives. Reporter Neely Tucker, who grew up in a very poor region of Mississippi, explains in the following passage how reading helped him imagine a better life for himself.

> **On the long summer days and endless evenings, on rainy winter afternoons, with nowhere to go and not much to do, I began to lose myself in books and stories, imagining a world far from our sleepy pastures. I would start turning the pages and our house would fade away, replaced by another world that came from nowhere. . . .**
>
> **Those worlds seemed as real and important as anything going on in our little town — and a lot more exciting. I longed not just to watch the train go by our house, but to catch an armload of the next freight train running and ride it out of there, traveling to some of the places I read about.**
>
> — **Neely Tucker, from *Love in the Driest Season: A Family Memoir***

The advantages of reading multiply when you read the way writers read — to learn how to improve their writing. When you examine a piece of writing to learn how the author communicates a certain idea, you're like an athlete who watches a game to observe the moves of the players. Examining other people's writing strategies helps you use these strategies in your own writing. If you read like a writer, you can learn ways to organize, develop, and express your ideas in your own writing.

Suppose you can't decide how to begin a paper for your ethics class. Around the same time, you read an article in *Newsweek* about the environmental costs of the development boom. Here is its beginning paragraph.

> **Seeing a bald eagle in one of your trees is like running into a movie star on the street. After years of viewing two-dimensional images, there's a conspicuous shock in encountering the thing in the flesh, looking just like its pictures. Or like the back of a quarter. Majestic white head, curved beak, a wingspan to die for: yep, that's the national bird eating one of those trout bought and paid for at the hatchery. It's so thrilling you want to ask for an autograph, perhaps a scrawled "E Pluribus Unum."**
>
> — **Anna Quindlen, from "Put 'Em in a Tree Museum"**

From this paragraph you learn two strategies for beginning an essay. First, a surprising comparison is a good way to get your audience's attention. Second, opening with a personal example can make a topic that could be boring more engaging.

HOW TO Be an Active Reader

1. Preview the text.
   - Think about the title and what it means to you.
   - Think about whether you recognize the author's name.
   - Read any headings, captions, charts, and lists.
2. Read the text.
   - Read carefully, underlining the most important points.
   - Circle and look up the meanings of words you don't know.
   - Briefly list the main points in the margin.
3. Write to comprehend and remember.
   - List or outline the most important points.
   - Write your personal reactions to what you have read.
   - Review these notes before class.

ACTIVITY 1: Sharing Favorite Readings

Make a list of your favorite books or magazines. You might want to list them in different categories. For example, you could classify popular novels as science fiction, romance, or horror, and magazines as music, fashion, or sports. As a class, compile a list of recommended readings.

Reading can also improve your vocabulary. Suppose that you enjoy reading suspense novels. Here's an excerpt from the first page of Michael Crichton's best-seller *Timeline*:

> Dan Baker winced as his new Mercedes S500 sedan bounced down the dirt road, heading deeper into the Navajo reservation in northern Arizona. Around him, the landscape was increasingly desolate: distant red mesas to the east, flat desert stretching away in the west. They had passed a village half an hour earlier — dusty houses, a church and a small school, huddled against a cliff — but since then, they'd seen nothing at all, not even a fence. Just empty red desert. They hadn't seen another car for an hour.

The word *desolate* might not be familiar to you, but from the context of this passage you can guess that it means "lonely" or "deserted." From this passage you can also guess that *winced* means "frowned" and that *huddled* means "crowded." Check your guesses by looking up unfamiliar words in a dictionary.

HOW TO Make Vocabulary Cards

- As you read, circle words you don't know and can't guess from the context.
- Look up each word in a dictionary.
- Write one word each on one side of a three-by-five-inch index card.
- On the other side, write the definition and a sentence using the word.
- Review regularly, using these vocabulary cards to test your memory.

ACTIVITY 2: Collecting New Words

Read an article that interests you in your campus or local newspaper. Circle any words that are unfamiliar to you. Based on your understanding of the article, guess the meaning of each unfamiliar word. Then, test your accuracy by looking the words up in a dictionary.

Keep a list or make vocabulary cards of new words and their meanings so you can refer to them when you read and write. Try to add at least five words a week to your list or cards.

Online Dictionaries
The *Discoveries* Web site includes dictionaries. Go to **bedfordstmartins.com/discoveries** and click on "Annotated Web Links," and then choose one of the online dictionaries.

PATTERNS OF WRITING

The more you read, the more you'll notice that writers make their paragraphs and essays interesting and convincing by developing them in detail. Supporting details increase interest, help readers understand a writer's thoughts, and support the writer's main ideas.

Writers use specific methods, or patterns, to develop the details in their paragraphs and essays. The most common of these patterns are example, narration, description, process explanation, classification, comparison and contrast, definition, cause and effect, and argument.

Example

Chapters 3 and 13 explain how to use examples in your writing.

In writing, *examples* can explain and support a writer's point. Examples may include names, dates, numbers, statistics, ideas, and any other information relevant to your topic or idea.

Narration

You will learn more about narration in Chapters 4 and 14.

Narrative writing tells a story, either true or made up. Writers use *narration* when they want to develop ideas by relating a series of events. In most cases, they organize events in chronological order — the order in which the events happened. Writers might also use dialogue to make a narrative feel more vivid and real.

Description

Chapter 5 shows you how to write a descriptive paragraph.

Using *description* in writing allows readers to become more involved. In descriptive writing, writers use the five senses to create an image of their main point. As a result, readers can mentally see, hear, touch, smell, or taste what is being described.

Process Explanation

You will have a chance to explain a process in Chapter 6.

Writers use a technique called *process* to explain how something works or how to do something. Cookbooks and repair manuals come to mind when we think of process writing, but bookstore shelves are filled with all sorts of other books describing processes — from explanations of how wind is used to make electricity to advice on how you might arrange your closet.

Classification

Classification is explained in detail in Chapter 7.

Writers use *classification* to organize ideas and help readers understand them. Paragraphs and essays that classify organize a number of things into categories on some particular basis. For example, cars might be classified by size (compact, midsize, full-size, and SUV), by country of origin (Kia and Hyundai from Korea; Volkswagen and Mercedes from Germany), or on any other basis a writer considers important.

Comparison and Contrast

Comparison and contrast makes relationships clear: How are people, places, or ideas alike? How are they different? To *compare,* writers identify the similarities between two or more things; to *contrast,* they identify differences. Sometimes the focus is on one or the other, but at other times both similarities and differences are included.

To learn more about comparison and contrast, see Chapters 8 and 15.

Definition

Writers use *definition* to explain and make clear what something means. A good definition has two parts: first, the term being defined is placed in a general category, and then, an explanation of where it fits in that category — a discussion of its distinguishing features — follows.

For more information on definition, see Chapter 9.

Cause and Effect

Cause and effect explains why something happened (the cause) and says what the result (the effect) was. Writers use cause and effect to show a necessary or logical connection between two or more things.

Chapter 10 will walk you through the process of writing a cause-and-effect paragraph.

Argument

Argumentative, or persuasive, writing uses one or a combination of the eight other patterns to change a reader's opinion or convince a reader to take a particular action. Newspaper editorials and advertisements are two types of argumentative writing.

You will practice using argument in Chapters 11 and 16.

Choosing a Pattern

When you write, selecting the appropriate pattern will help you get your ideas across. Imagine that your supervisor has asked all employees to write a paragraph about their most important achievement in the past year. She will use these paragraphs to help her decide who will get year-end bonuses. You've achieved many things throughout the year — how do you select one to write about?

HOW TO Choose a Writing Pattern

- Select an idea you're interested in and examine it from different angles: give examples of it, tell a story about it, describe it, tell how to do it, put it into groups, compare it with other things, define it, explain its causes or effects, or persuade somebody to think about it the way you do.
- Choose the pattern that makes for the most interesting way to develop your idea.

Student writer Andrea used the following ideas to choose her topic.

List examples of my achievements at work

I trained two new employees.

I took over the duties of Fred, who moved to another department.

I reorganized the old files.

Tell a story

I could talk about some of the problems I ran into doing Fred's job as well as my own and how I solved them.

Describe one of the achievements

I could describe the way I reorganized my work space to make room for Fred's work.

Explain how to do one of the achievements

I could explain how I helped the new employees.

Classify (or put into groups) the achievements

I could classify the types of work I trained the new people to do.

Compare and contrast the achievements

I could compare taking over someone's job with hiring a new person.

Define the achievements

I could define Fred's duties.

Give the causes and effects of the achievements

I could explain how I saved the company money by taking over Fred's job.

Make an argument about the achievements

I could try to persuade my boss that I deserve a raise because of all the extra work I did.

After Andrea wrote down these ideas, she discovered that her most important achievement had been taking over Fred's job. Knowing that her supervisor was most interested in results and that she would be impressed that Andrea saved the company money, Andrea chose to write a paragraph that detailed the causes and effects of her achievement.

ACTIVITY 3 (Group): Identifying Patterns of Writing

With your classmates, identify the pattern of writing used in each of the following paragraphs as example, narration, description, process explanation, classification, comparison and contrast, definition, cause and effect, or argument. Some patterns may overlap.

1. American colleges are unbelievably varied. There are thousands of institutions of post–high school instruction in the United States: more than 2,300 four-year colleges, more than 1,800 two-year colleges, and an unknown but large number of trade schools, technical institutes, art or music centers, and other specialized schools. There are night schools for people with jobs; online or written correspondence courses for people in remote locations; universities in big cities and on secluded campuses in Oregon and Maine. There are technical institutes — for music, nursing, forestry, aviation — and colleges that emphasize the classics. The American higher-education establishment includes the Air Force Academy and Juilliard, Bob Jones University and Caltech.

   — *The Atlantic Monthly,* from "Our First Annual College-Admissions Survey"

   Pattern of writing: ______________________________

2. I wandered across to the station and found him bent over the engine of his car, an ancient Chrysler convertible from the forties. I circled the car, taking it in. The convertible top was rotten and riddled with holes. The rubber grips on the running boards were so buckled that they could trip you if you weren't careful. Lakes of rust had formed on the body where the paint had worn away. The leather seats were webbed with cracks. The rumble seat was split outright, with stuffing thrust up through the hole. That the car was up on blocks emphasized the devastation.

   — Brent Staples, from *Parallel Time: Growing Up in Black and White*

   Pattern of writing: ______________________________

3. Dennis was the eldest sibling and the family pioneer. He was an artist who drew pictures that told incredible stories about the places he'd been and the people he'd met. He had money in his pocket, actual dollars and cents, with change to spare. He was a giant among us, casting a huge, oblong shadow that hung over us children like the Lincoln Memorial, which he had visited — twice. His great achievements, spoken of in his absence because he came home only for holidays, were glowingly recounted,

dissected, rumored, enhanced, extolled. The heights he had attained, heights we puny mortals could only dream of achieving, were trumpeted and crowed about by Mommy in every corner of the house. Dennis had finished college. Dennis had gone to Europe. And now, for his crowning achievement, Dennis, oh glorious Dennis, oh mighty Dennis — Dennis! *Dennis!* — sought the highest, most wonderful, most incredible achievement any human being, any son, could hope to achieve.

— James McBride, from *The Color of Water: A Black Man's Tribute to His White Mother*

Pattern of writing: ______________________________

UNDERSTANDING THE WRITING PROCESS

The writing process refers to the way you go about writing, whether you're e-mailing a friend, composing a job-application letter, or producing a report for your biology class. Some writing processes are short. For instance, when you e-mail a friend, you might think for a few minutes about what you want to say and then quickly type the message. At other times, your writing process will be longer and more complicated. When applying for a job, for example, you want to appear intelligent, mature, and capable, so you might write several drafts, or versions, of the letter before mailing it. And when you write for your college courses, you'll want to be careful to shape your ideas and communicate them as clearly and effectively as possible, to demonstrate to your teachers that you understand the material.

HOW TO Use the Writing Process

- Step 1. Gather ideas: Get your thoughts down on paper.
- Step 2. Draft: Take your best ideas and write them in paragraph or essay form.
- Step 3. Revise: Make your ideas more convincing and easier to understand.
- Step 4. Edit: Correct errors in grammar, punctuation, and spelling.
- Step 5. Share: Show your writing to your readers.

In this book you will practice a writing process that will enable you to master writing assignments step-by-step. These steps will work whether you write a paragraph or an essay. The steps in this writing process consist of gathering ideas, drafting, revising, editing, and sharing. Even though these steps are presented in a particular order, you can go back and forth among them as you complete a writing project.

ACTIVITY 4: Comparing Your Writing Process

One way to become a better writer is to exchange ideas about how people write. Compare your answers to the following questions with your classmates' answers. What can you learn from your classmates' writing processes?

1. In the writing I have done in the past, did I gather ideas, draft, revise, edit, and share my work? If not, what were the steps in my process?
2. What would I like to change about my writing process?

Explore the *Discoveries* Web Site
The *Discoveries* Web site contains helpful tools and interesting activities that accompany the assignments in this book. Go to **bedfordstmartins.com/discoveries**.

ADDITIONAL WRITING ASSIGNMENTS

1. Write a paragraph for your instructor and classmates about a previous writing experience. It could be an important letter, a class assignment, or a work report. Who was the audience, and what was the purpose? How successful was the piece? Is there anything that you would do differently?
2. Write a paragraph for your instructor and classmates about something you have enjoyed reading — a book, play, poem, magazine article, newspaper article, Web site, and so on. In your paragraph, give the title and author of the piece, and briefly explain what it was about. Then, explain why you enjoyed reading it.
3. Write a paragraph in which you introduce a classmate to the rest of the class. First, ask your classmate about important aspects of his or her life, such as career goals, school schedule, hobbies, family life, and so on. Then, write a paragraph saying what you learned about this person. Finally, read your paragraph to the rest of the class.

PART ONE

Reading and Writing Paragraphs

The women on this U.S. team took gold in the World University Games held in Beijing, China, in 2001. What have you achieved? Your achievement might not have appeared in newspapers, but it may have meant a lot to you personally. Perhaps you did well in your classes despite juggling demands from home and work, or perhaps you overcame a fear of speaking in public. In this chapter, you will write about one of your achievements or long-term goals as you continue to learn about the writing process.

CHAPTER

2

A Step-by-Step Guide to Writing Paragraphs

In this chapter, you will

- discover how paragraphs work.
- write about an achievement or a long-term goal.
- learn how to gather ideas.
- learn how to write a discovery draft.
- learn how to revise.
- learn how to edit.
- share your writing.

UNDERSTANDING PARAGRAPHS

Think for a moment about the kinds of writing you are familiar with reading. Perhaps you enjoy relaxing with a novel or a biography. You might like to read magazines about news, sports, or lifestyles. Maybe you have a collection of letters from your loved ones. Although books, articles, and personal correspondence are very different kinds of writing, they have one important thing in common: They are usually broken down into paragraphs that help you follow the writer's ideas.

A paragraph is a group of sentences that focuses on a single topic. This topic is announced in the *topic sentence.* The rest of the paragraph presents information, or *supporting ideas,* that explain the topic and make it interesting. Often a concluding sentence summarizes the topic. Most paragraphs are about three to ten sentences long, depending on the writer's topic, audience, and purpose. Consider the following example:

topic sentence

supporting ideas

concluding sentence

The names that children call each other can have harmful effects that last through adulthood. Children who are called "fatso" or other derogatory terms relating to their bodies can grow up to feel self-conscious about their looks. Being called "dumb" or "stupid" can make people assume they aren't smart enough to go to college. Names such as "clumsy" or "nerdy" can make people believe they aren't good enough to play sports. Many adults spend years trying to rid themselves of the self-images these names gave them.

Paragraphs have three major characteristics — focus, support, and order. That is, a well-written paragraph makes a single point; it provides information that explains that point; and it arranges sentences in a way that helps readers move from one idea to the next.

Writing Assignment

Many schools assign advisors to help students navigate their way through college. Imagine that you are going to meet with your advisor for the first time and that he or she has asked you to bring along a brief explanation of what's important to you.

- Write a paragraph about your most important achievement during the past year. This achievement can be related to school, work, or your personal life.

OR

- Write a paragraph about one of your goals, such as saving money for a vacation, succeeding in a particular profession, or being faithful to a certain set of beliefs.

STEP 1: DISCOVER IDEAS FOR WRITING

The first step of writing a paragraph is to think about what you are going to write about. You'll want to consider your topic, your audience and purpose, and what information you can share with your readers. Don't worry if you can't think of anything to say: There are lots of ways to discover ideas for writing. The next few pages will introduce you to some of them.

Choosing a Topic

Sometimes a topic will be given to you. For instance, your biology instructor might ask you to write a definition of photosynthesis or your supervisor at work might ask for a brief report on last month's sales figures. In such cases, you'll know what to write about, although you may not always be interested in the topic.

Often you'll have more choice. A history exam, for example, might ask you to write a paragraph on one of the protest movements of the 1960s; or you may have to write a paragraph about television commercials for your communication class. In cases like these, you have a general subject but you need to choose a topic, such as the 1969 Stonewall riots or the commercials on Saturday morning cartoon shows. (For this chapter's assignment, you can write about something you've done or something you'd like to do, but that gives you endless options for a topic.) It's always best to find something that interests you personally. No matter how you arrive at your topic, you'll need to write about it in a way that is unique to you.

HOW TO Choose a Topic

Make a list of possible topics. Then, answer the following questions:

- How much does this topic interest me?
- How much do I know about this topic?
- Is the topic focused enough to be explained in a paragraph?
- How well does this topic satisfy the assignment? Use your responses to these questions to decide on a good topic.

Considering Your Audience

Almost everything you write — with the exception of what you say in a diary or journal — will be read by someone else. Family, friends, co-workers, supervisors, classmates, or instructors might read your letters, reports, evaluations, or papers. Even subscribers to a newspaper or magazine may at some time read your writing.

Whenever you write, try to understand what your readers expect and what they already know and feel about your topic. For example, if you're writing an e-mail to a close friend, you know that she will be interested in what you say and will probably know something about your topic. Therefore, you don't need to attract her attention, give her background information, or pay a great deal of attention to grammar. On the other hand, if you're writing a letter to the editor of your local newspaper, you can assume that your readers don't know you, may not be interested in your topic, and may not know much about it. As a result, you'll need to write carefully, being sure to explain the importance of your topic, give useful background information, and avoid errors.

HOW TO Consider Your Audience

Ask yourself these questions:

- What might my readers already know about my topic?
- What do my readers not know about my topic?
- What opinions might they have?
- How interested will they be in my topic?
- How concerned will they be that I write correctly?

DISCOVERY PRACTICE (Group): Get to Know Your Classmates

Some of the most important readers of your writing will be your classmates. Pair up with someone in your class and ask each other the following questions. Then, introduce your classmate to the class by summarizing his or her responses.

1. What is your name? Do you know why you were given that name?
2. What do you plan to do after you graduate?
3. What three words best describe you?
4. If you were given a million dollars, how would you spend it?

Considering Your Purpose

There are three main purposes, or reasons, for writing: to express, to inform, and to persuade. Although a paragraph can be written for all three purposes, one of them will usually dominate.

HOW TO Identify Your Purpose

- *To express:* Communicate your thoughts, feelings, or personal history.
- *To inform:* Share something you know.
- *To persuade:* Convince others of your opinion.

Writing to Express

When you write to *express,* you convey your thoughts, feelings, or personal history. Diaries, journals, letters to friends or family, and essays that tell a story about your life are examples of this type of writing.

In the following paragraph the writer explains her love of chocolate:

> **Even as an adult, I do not have a great deal of restraint when it comes to chocolate. Delayed gratification has never been a strong goal for me. As a child I had almost no restraint. Every year my mother gave me a huge basket full of candy, and every year my mother took it away from me again at least by noon because I saw no reason to have a huge basket of Easter candy unless I could sit right down on the floor and eat the whole thing. I do not have a "full" button that lights up and tells me to quit eating. I do not have an "enough" button that ever lights up for anything. As a child or an adult, I can literally eat until whatever I am eating is gone. I may be uncomfortable later, but at the time there is nothing to warn me of the coming consequences.**
>
> **— Cheryl Peck, from "The Chicken Coupe"**

Writing to Inform

When you write to *inform,* you explain something using facts, statistics, and examples. Informative writing includes textbooks, nutrition labels, directions, encyclopedias, most newspaper articles, and much of the writing you do in college, such as lab reports.

The following paragraph, for instance, uses facts to inform readers about Bruce Springsteen's concert schedule.

> **Bruce Springsteen was 45 minutes late when he arrived at rehearsal at the Continental Airlines Arena in East Rutherford,**

N.J., on Thursday afternoon. He was limping, his hand was bandaged, and he was clearly exhausted. In several hours, he would be performing the last of his record-setting 15 sold-out concerts at the arena. In the last five months he had already logged two public rehearsals in Asbury Park, a 36-show European tour, and 14 performances at this arena. One would think he wouldn't have to rehearse anymore.

— Neil Strauss, from "Necessary Springsteen Keeps the Faith"

Writing to Persuade

When you write to *persuade,* you attempt to convince readers to change their minds or take a certain action. Newspaper editorials, college applications, and letters of complaint to companies about their products are examples of writing intended to persuade. Often phrases such as *should* or *need to* are used in persuasive writing, as in "We *should* abolish the death penalty" or "Schools *need to* enforce dress codes."

The following paragraph from a student essay tries to persuade readers that colleges should pay more attention to dormitories.

Where a person lives is important to his or her well-being. Since so many students live in dorms, the college should try to make them attractive. The rooms should be clean, the walls painted an uplifting color, and the furniture fairly new. A dorm should also have updated facilities so that students can plug into the college computer system in their own rooms. How else can students examine the library records or talk to their instructors on e-mail? Because many students are away from home for the first time, a dorm should also offer opportunities for students to meet other people. Finally, a dorm should be a good place to study.

— Jody Albert, from "Avoid Dryden Hall"

DISCOVERY PRACTICE (Group): Identify Purposes for Writing

Bring to class a paragraph-long sample of each of the three purposes for writing. Exchange them with several classmates, and discuss why they express, inform, or persuade. Share your conclusions with the rest of the class.

WRITING ACTIVITY 1: Analyze Your Audience and Purpose

For this chapter's writing assignment, your audience will be your college advisor, whom you have not met. Keep that in mind as you answer the following questions.

1. Will you write about an important achievement or a long-term goal? What is your tentative topic?

____

____

____

2. What does your reader already know about your topic? What does he or she not know about it?

____

____

____

3. What opinions might your reader have about your topic?

____

____

____

4. How interested will your reader be in your topic?

____

____

____

5. How concerned will he or she be that you write correctly?

____

____

____

6. What is your purpose in writing this paragraph?

____

____

____

Gathering Ideas

Once you have thought about your topic, audience, and purpose, you're ready to begin gathering ideas for your paragraph. The following techniques can help you find ideas worth writing about.

HOW TO Gather Ideas

- *Brainstorm* by listing thoughts about a topic.
- *Freewrite* by writing nonstop for a set period of time.
- *Cluster* by drawing a map of your ideas.
- *Ask questions:* who, what, where, when, why, and how?
- *Interview* others about your topic.
- *Outline* your thoughts to see how they fit together.

Brainstorming

When you brainstorm, you list all the thoughts that come into your head on a topic. You don't consider whether your ideas are good or bad; you just write them down.

Here is how student writer Krikor brainstormed about his long-term goals:

Acting

My main goal

So impractical, my dad says.

Don't waste your college degree on acting!

It's what I want to do.

Maybe I should try something else?

A business degree?

Freewriting

When you freewrite, you write without stopping for a certain period of time or until you reach a given page limit. You don't pause, go back, or make corrections. You can focus on one topic or go on to new ones as they come into your mind. If you get stuck, write about being stuck. The point is to keep writing.

Here is Krikor's freewriting on his long-term goals:

> Goals. Long-term goals. What are my long-term goals? Well, my whole life I've wanted to be an actor. I know it's really hard, but that's what I've wanted to be since I was five years old. Being in plays in high school made me think I had made the right choice. Other goals? Well, I'd like a family but not until my career is stable. And of course I'd like to be a good person. Do unto others as you'd want them to do unto you, that's my motto that I try to live by. When I think of goals, my first thought is always acting.

Clustering

When you cluster, you draw a picture of your ideas as they come to mind. Write your subject in the center of a blank page and draw a circle around it. Then, as ideas about the topic come to mind, write them down, put circles around them, and draw lines to the center circle. As you think of more details, circle them and connect them to the main ideas.

Here is Krikor's cluster on his long-term goal of acting.

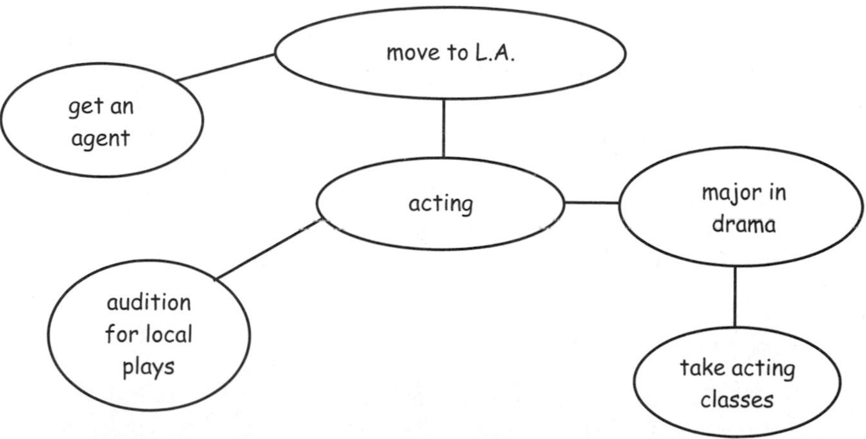

Asking Questions

The six questions that journalists use to gather information can help you discover ideas for your own topic.

- Who?
- What?
- When?
- Where?
- Why?
- How?

Krikor used these questions to gather more ideas for his paragraph about acting.

Who	Me
What	My goal of being an actor
When	During college, I'll major in drama. After college, I'll begin my career.
Where	I'll probably move to L.A.
Why	Since I was a child, I loved to watch actors. In high school, I was in some plays and I felt totally involved and happy.
How	It's a difficult career because it's hard to find work. But I'll never give up.

Interviewing

Talking to someone knowledgeable about your topic can give you facts and details for your paragraph. If you use information from the interview in your writing, be sure to tell your readers where the information is from.

Krikor decided to interview his high school drama teacher about being an actor. Here's part of what his teacher told him.

> **"Acting is a hard profession to break into. Most actors at the beginning have other jobs like waiting tables. The best thing is to get an agent who will find jobs for you. You pay the agent a percentage of what you make. The more people you know in the acting industry who can help you, the more jobs you'll get."**

Outlining

If you have a general idea of what information you'll include in your paragraph, creating a rough outline can help you decide if you're on the right track. List your main ideas and then put additional information — such as examples and details — under them. Then, look over your outline to see if there are places where you need more information.

Krikor prepared the following outline:

I. Main goal in life: To be an actor.
II. Inspiration: Watching other people act.
   a. movies
   b. television
III. Acting experience
   a. high school
   b. college
IV. Future plans
   a. go to Hollywood
   b. audition
   c. never give up

WRITING ACTIVITY 2: Gather Ideas for Your Paragraph

First, decide whether you want to write about an achievement or a goal. Then, use at least three of the prewriting strategies — brainstorming, freewriting, clustering, asking questions, interviewing others, and outlining — to discover ideas for your topic. You might want to gather ideas about several achievements or goals at first, then choose one to gather more ideas about.

Narrowing Your Topic

Because a paragraph is short, you need to narrow your topic so you can develop your ideas in detail. A good way to narrow your topic is to move from the general to the specific. For example, "television shows" is general; "cable TV shows" is more specific; *The Sopranos* is even more specific; and "the character of Carmela on *The Sopranos*" is still more specific.

As you narrow your topic, keep your readers in mind. Their attitudes, knowledge, and interest in your topic should guide you. Krikor, for instance, decided to narrow his ideas from "acting" to "how to become an actor" because he thought his advisor would be most interested in how he planned to achieve his goal.

DISCOVERY PRACTICE: Narrowing Ideas

Narrow the following topics by going from general to specific. The most specific topic should be suitable for a paragraph to be read by your classmates and instructor.

EXAMPLE Voting

Voting ⟶ Importance of voting ⟶ Making voting easier ⟶ Voting day should be changed to Saturday

1. Nutritious Eating

____

____

____

2. Buying a House

____

____

____

3. The Best Television Shows Ever

____

____

____

4. Types of People

____

____

____

5. Country Music

____

____

6. Crime

____

____

____

7. My Favorite People

____

____

8. Computers

____

____

9. Smoking

____

____

____

10. College

____

____

____

WRITING ACTIVITY 3: Narrow Your Topic

Read over the information you have gathered and circle the ideas that you might want to use for this chapter's assignment. Then, narrow your ideas by going from general to specific.

STEP 2: WRITE YOUR DISCOVERY DRAFT

Once you have gathered ideas for your paragraph, the next step is to write a discovery draft with a topic sentence, supporting details, and a concluding sentence. The discovery draft is just your first try at putting your ideas in paragraph form. Concentrate on getting your thoughts down on paper. You'll have plenty of time to improve things like grammar, spelling, and punctuation in the later stages of the writing process.

Save and Number Your Drafts
Because you'll be rewriting your draft, number and save each version as you complete it.

Drafting a Topic Sentence

The topic sentence tells readers what the main point of a paragraph is and why it's important. Usually, the topic sentence comes first so the reader immediately knows what to expect from the rest of the paragraph. Look again at the first sentence of the paragraph that opened this chapter:

> **The names that children call each other can have harmful effects that last through adulthood.**

This is the topic sentence because it identifies what the paragraph is about (names that children call each other) and why it's important (they have harmful effects). The topic sentence is then followed by a series of examples that support this main idea.

HOW TO Write a Topic Sentence

- Review the ideas you've gathered about your topic.
- Focus the topic so it can be explained in a single paragraph.
- Write a sentence that expresses the main point you want to make.
- Explain what you think is important about the topic.

DRAFTING PRACTICE (Group): Topic Sentences

With several classmates, write a topic sentence for each of the following topics. Be sure that you include a main point and explain why the topic is important.

EXAMPLE

TOPIC	Applying for financial aid
TOPIC SENTENCE	Applying for financial aid is easy if you follow these three steps.

1. Topic: Overcrowded classes in high school

   Topic Sentence: ______________________________

   ____

2. Topic: Parents who become violent at children's sporting events

   Topic Sentence: ______________________________

   ____

   ____

3. Topic: My grandmother

   Topic Sentence: ______________________________

   ____

4. Topic: Difficult college classes

   Topic Sentence: ______________________________

   ____

5. Topic: New Year's Eve

   Topic Sentence: ______________________________

   ____

WRITING ACTIVITY 4: Draft Your Topic Sentence

Check that your topic is focused enough to develop in one paragraph. Then, draft a topic sentence that says what your main point will be and explains why it is important. Don't worry about getting your topic sentence perfect just yet: Your goal right now is to come up with a statement that will help guide your discovery draft.

Adding Support

Once you have a topic sentence, you need to provide support for it. Supporting ideas explain a topic sentence by providing examples, facts, reasons, and other information that give information about your topic.

Good supporting ideas have three characteristics:

- They provide information about your main point.
- They stay on the topic of the paragraph.
- They are specific.

In the paragraph about name calling, for example, the topic sentence is supported by three examples of name calling: names about body shape, names about intelligence, and names about physical ability. The writer includes specific examples of names, such as "fatso," "stupid," and "clumsy," and explains how they affect people. Notice also that the supporting ideas stay focused on the topic: A sentence about the names adults call each other would not fit because the paragraph is about the effects of names *children* call each other.

HOW TO Add Support

- Use the methods for gathering ideas — brainstorming, freewriting, clustering, asking questions, interviewing, and outlining — to find supporting details.
- Select examples, facts, reasons, and other information that help explain the main idea of the paragraph.
- Make the support specific and focused on the main idea.
- Remember that your support might change as you revise your paragraph.

Student writer Krikor planned to use the following supporting ideas to explain his goal of becoming an actor:

FACT	I've wanted to be an actor since I saw *Back to the Future* when I was five years old.
EXAMPLE	I liked being in *Charley's Aunt* in high school.
REASON	When you act, you can pretend to be someone else.
FACT	When I'm on stage, I forget about my own problems.
FACT	I focus on just becoming the character.

DRAFTING PRACTICE (Group): Adding Supporting Ideas

With several classmates, think of at least three supporting ideas for each of the following topic sentences. Use examples, facts, reasons, and any other information that you can come up with.

EXAMPLE

TOPIC SENTENCE	One of the best jobs I've ever had is waiting tables.
SUPPORT	I made good money from tips.
	I met interesting people, including my wife.
	My work hours were flexible, allowing me to finish college.

1. Topic Sentence: The day I graduated from high school was one of the best days of my life.

   Support: ______________________________

   ____

2. Topic Sentence: Registering for classes is easy if you follow these steps.

   Support: ______________________________

   ____

3. Topic Sentence: Time management is one of the most important skills a college student needs.

   Support: ______________________________

   ____

   ____

4. Topic Sentence: Sports fans can be divided into three different types.

   Support: ______________________________

   ____

   ____

   ____

5. Topic Sentence: By establishing a day-care program for students' children, college administrators can improve the quality of students' lives.

   Support: ______________________________

   ____

   ____

WRITING ACTIVITY 5: Add Support for Your Paragraph

With your narrowed topic in mind, use at least one of the methods of gathering ideas — brainstorming, freewriting, clustering, asking questions, interviewing others, or outlining — to develop additional ideas for your paragraph. The more ideas you gather, the more you'll have to choose from for your discovery draft.

Writing a Concluding Sentence

A *concluding sentence* lets readers know that a paragraph is finished. If your paragraph is a part of an essay, the concluding sentence can prepare the reader for the main idea in the following paragraph. If your paragraph stands alone, the concluding sentence should refer back to the main idea of the topic sentence, either by restating the main point, summarizing the supporting details, reminding readers why the topic is important, or suggesting something they can do about it.

Consider the concluding sentence of the paragraph about name calling:

> **Many adults spend years trying to rid themselves of the self-images these names gave them.**

This concluding sentence refers back to the main point — that name calling has lasting effects — and emphasizes how deeply people can be hurt by the names children use.

HOW TO Write a Concluding Sentence

- Refer back to the main idea stated in the topic sentence.
- Emphasize a particular aspect of the topic, summarize the supporting ideas, point out the topic's importance, or suggest that something be done.
- Remember that you can change your concluding sentence as you revise your paragraph.

Student writer Krikor drafted these possible concluding sentences for his paragraph:

> Becoming an actor is difficult, but I know I can do it.
>
> One day you might see me at the Oscars, accepting my award for best actor.
>
> I don't need to be famous because I just want to act.

When he wrote his discovery draft, Krikor selected the third sentence because it emphasized his main point that acting is important to him.

DRAFTING PRACTICE (Group): Concluding Sentences

The concluding sentence has been omitted from the following student paragraph. With several classmates, read the paragraph out loud and compose a concluding sentence that explains the writer's main point.

> Of all the times I went with my father to the ball games, one stands out. It was a warm afternoon when my father asked me to go with him. When we got there, it began to get very cold and the wind was blowing. I remember that I was just wearing shorts, so my legs were freezing. I told my father that I was cold, but I didn't want to leave. He then suggested we move to another place where the wind didn't blow as hard. But when we moved to the new place, it was still cold, so my father sat in back of me and asked me to bend my knees toward my chest and lean back. Then he put his warm hands on my legs, like a duck protecting his duckling from a predator that might hurt him.

____

____

____

WRITING ACTIVITY 6: Draft Your Concluding Sentence

Look again at the topic sentence and supporting ideas that you have drafted for your paragraph. Compose three possible concluding sentences: one that restates your main point, one that summarizes your supporting details, and one that emphasizes why your topic is important. You can decide which one works best when you write your discovery draft.

Krikor's Discovery Draft

After drafting his topic sentence, supporting details, and concluding sentence, Krikor wrote this discovery draft about his goal of becoming an actor. Like most first drafts, it includes some errors. That's okay: Krikor will fix them later.

> Since I was five years old, my main goal in life has been to be an actor. I saw <u>Back to the Future</u> when I was five, even though I was

too young to really understand it, I wanted to be just like Michael J. Fox. As I got older I learned that I could be anyone I wanted to be by acting. I'm majoring in acting and hope to be in plays here. In high school I was in three plays, my favorite was Charley's Aunt, it was funny. I'm already taking an acting class. I don't like the teacher as much as I liked my high school teacher. When I graduate I plan to go to Hollywood and do some auditions. I know its hard and I won't make much money at first. I'm pretty stubborn and will keep at it until I get some parts. I don't need to be famous because I just want to act!

HOW TO Format a Paragraph

- Indent the first sentence by leaving five blank spaces (or one-half inch) in the left margin.
- Use one-inch margins on all sides.
- Double-space all of the lines.
- If you are writing on a computer, choose an easy-to-read font (such as Times New Roman, Garamond, or Courier) and use 10- or 12-point type.

WRITING ACTIVITY 7: Complete Your Discovery Draft

Using the material you have written so far, write a discovery draft. Be sure to include a topic sentence, supporting details, and a concluding sentence. Focus on what you want to say, not how you'll say it.

Use Color to Analyze Your Paragraph

To make sure that your paragraph contains a topic sentence, support, and a concluding sentence, use a different color for each element. For instance, type the topic sentence in red, the support in blue, and the concluding sentence in green.

STEP 3: REVISE YOUR PARAGRAPH

Nobody writes perfectly on the first try. Writing is a process of discovery: You learn what you want to say as you put your ideas on paper. Most writers revise their discovery drafts several times, each time making their writing clearer, more interesting, and easier to follow.

Once you have finished your discovery draft, put it aside for a while — a few hours at least, preferably a few days or a week. Looking at it with fresh eyes will help you see ways to strengthen your focus, build your support, and improve the order of your points.

Cut and Paste

Use the cut-and-paste function of your word processor to move sentences or blocks of text. Print different versions and compare them to decide which is more effective.

Strengthening Your Focus

Paragraphs stick to one topic, which is usually expressed in the topic sentence. Paragraph focus, or unity, makes your ideas easier to follow because your thoughts are organized around a single point.

You may have noticed that Krikor's discovery draft had one sentence that was not related to his main point about wanting to become an actor:

> I don't like the teacher as much as I liked my high school teacher.

How much he likes his teachers has nothing to do with Krikor's goal of acting, so he deleted this sentence when he revised.

HOW TO Strengthen Paragraph Focus

- Check that your topic sentence expresses a main point.
- Review the paragraph. Make sure that every supporting sentence refers directly to the topic sentence.
- Delete any sentences that are off topic.

Sometimes a lack of focus in a paragraph means that you haven't yet decided what your main point should be. In this case, use one of the methods of gathering ideas — brainstorming, freewriting, clustering, asking questions, interviewing others, or outlining — to help you figure out what point you want to express.

REVISION PRACTICE: Strengthening Focus

The following paragraph is a student's discovery draft about the voting process. Read it closely and underline any sentences that don't support the writer's main point.

> Because fewer than half of registered voters actually vote, we need to make the process of voting easier. First, people should be able to register to vote on the Internet. This change would save people the inconvenience of having to pick up registration cards, fill them out, and mail them. I registered to vote at an Earth Day festival. Also, people would be more likely to vote if information about the candidates were easier to obtain. Therefore, all candidates should have their own Web sites that spell out where they stand on the issues. I wish they would spend less time insulting each other. Negative campaigning hurts everybody. Finally, the voting day needs to be changed from Tuesday to Saturday so that people would have more free time to go to the polls. Because voting is so important in a democracy, we need to do everything possible to help people vote.

Building Your Support

In your discovery draft, you used examples, facts, and reasons to explain your main idea. Now, read your paragraph from your audience's point of view. Did you provide enough information to help them understand your point? When you revise, improve your support to make your paragraph clearer and more convincing for your readers.

HOW TO Build Support

- Review your discovery draft and decide if you need to include more information to explain your main point.
- Use one of the following methods to gather new ideas: brainstorming, freewriting, clustering, asking questions, interviewing others, or outlining.
- Select examples, facts, and reasons that give more information on your topic. Add them to your draft.

When Krikor's classmates read his discovery draft, they told him they wanted to know more about how he was going to accomplish his goal. He realized he needed to add information about the process of becoming an actor to answer his classmates' questions.

REVISION PRACTICE (Group): Building Support

With several classmates, add facts, examples, and reasons to the following paragraph to make it more interesting and informative. Read your revised paragraph out loud to the class.

> Last Saturday was exhausting but fun. My family and I went to a park for a picnic. On the way home, we decided to see a movie. By the end of the day I was very tired. I fell asleep as soon as my head hit the pillow.

Organizing Your Points

When you write a discovery draft, you may be too busy getting your thoughts on paper to consider how you organized them. Your ideas should move easily and logically from the first sentence to the last. How you organize your points will depend on your topic, your purpose, your audience, and your support. There are, however, a few patterns that writers find especially useful.

Topic-Illustration-Explanation Order

Topic-illustration-explanation (TIE) order is useful when you're giving examples to make your point. To use TIE organization:

- State the topic sentence.
- Give examples.
- Explain how the examples relate to the topic sentence.

The following paragraph uses TIE organization:

> **Although our nation professes a growing commitment to cultural egalitarianism, we consistently oversimplify and misunderstand our rural culture. Since the 1960s, minority groups in America have fought for acknowledgment, appreciation, and, above all, respect. But in our increasingly urban society, rural Americans have been unable to escape from the hillbilly stigma, which is frequently accompanied by labels like "white trash," "redneck" and "hayseed." The negative stereotypes are as unmerciful as they are unfounded.**
>
> **— Rebecca Thomas Kirkendall, from "Who's a Hillbilly?"**

Chronological or Sequential Order

When you're telling a story or explaining how something happens, it's usually best to write things in the order they happened. Using chronological (sometimes called sequential) order helps your readers follow the course of events.

Writer Andre Dubus uses chronological order to describe a significant moment from his childhood:

> **In the spring of 1948, in the first softball game during the afternoon hour of physical education in the dusty schoolyard, the two captains chose teams and, as always, they chose other boys until only two of us remained. I batted last, and first came to the plate with two or three runners on base, and while my teammates urged me to try for a walk, and the players on the field called Easy out, Easy out, I watched the softball coming in waist-high, and stepped and swung, and hit it over the right fielder's head for a double. My next time at bat I tripled to center. From then on I brought my glove to school, hanging from a handlebar.**
>
> **— Andre Dubus, from "Under the Lights"**

Progressive Order

Writers who want to convince readers of something or leave them with a strong impression often arrange their supporting ideas (examples, facts, and reasons) from least to most important, persuasive, or startling.

In the following paragraph, Irina Groza uses *progressive order* to describe how the Romanian government of the 1950s denied its citizens religious freedom.

> **In another attempt to suppress the people and to destroy their spirit, the government began a campaign to discourage church attendance. Celebrations of religious holidays were prohibited, and people who openly expressed their faith put themselves in jeopardy. One day a police officer stopped me and ridiculed me in front of my friends because I was wearing a cross around my neck. I felt embarrassed and angry, but there was nothing I could do. I had heard that many people had been beaten by the police, and we lived in constant fear of them. Those who continued to oppose the system were thrown into jail or put into mental institutions.**
>
> **— Irina Groza, from "Growing Up in Romania"**

Directional Order

When you use *directional order,* you describe something by moving from one location to another, such as left to right, top to bottom, or near to far.

Directional order is used in the following description of a house.

> **Let me tell you about our house. If you entered the front door and turned right you'd see a small living room with a couch along the east wall and one along the west wall — one couch was purple, the other tan, both bought used and both well worn. A television set was placed at the end of the purple couch, right at arm level. An old Philco radio sat next to the TV, its speaker covered with gold lamé. There was a small coffee table in the center of the room on which sat a murky fishbowl occupied by two listless guppies. If, on entering, you turned left you would see a green Formica dinner table with four chairs, a cedar chest given as a wedding present to my mother by her mother, a painted statue of the Blessed Virgin Mary, and a black trunk. I also had a plastic chaise lounge between the door and the table. I would lie on this and watch television.**
>
> **— Mike Rose, from "I Just Wanna Be Average"**

Question-and-Answer Order

Question-and-answer order is another method for organizing ideas in a paragraph. It involves asking a question at the beginning of the paragraph and then answering that question in the rest of the paragraph. In the following paragraph, a business writer asks and answers a question about restaurants' used frying oil.

> **What makes cooking oil a hot opportunity? More than half of the 878,000 restaurants in the United States are equipped with deep fryers, which collectively pump out 3 billion pounds of waste oil each year. Handling the grease is a slippery business. Dumping used oil down the sewer is illegal in many cities, and fryer-related burns are a leading cause of injury among restaurant workers.**
>
> **— Brian Caulfield, from "How to Turn Grease into Gold"**

Regardless of what order you use, the ideas in your paragraph should be connected with transitional words and phrases. Transitions show your readers how one idea relates to the next, making your paragraph easy to follow.

HOW TO Connect Ideas

Here are some of the most commonly used transitions:

- *To add ideas:* also, and, additionally, in addition, too, however, although, or
- *To show differences:* in contrast, but, on the other hand
- *To show similarities:* in the same way, similarly, in comparison
- *To show time:* then, since, when, while, soon, after, before, now, first, second
- *To show cause and effect:* because, therefore, as a result
- *To introduce examples:* for example, for instance
- *To add emphasis:* in fact, obviously, clearly, of course

REVISION PRACTICE (Group): Ordering Points

The sentences for the following paragraph are out of order. With several classmates, read all of the sentences out loud. Decide what organizational pattern would work best, then use the blanks to number the sentences in the correct order from 1 to 9.

_____ On the day of the climb, light snowflakes swirled around us, and the ground was muddy and slick.

_____ Spending time with my friend Marissa has allowed me to see new people and places.

_____ But Marissa talked me into going.

_____ The scent of pine trees filled the air.

_____ I didn't want to go because I thought the climb would be too difficult.

_____ When we finally reached the top, we gazed at the beautiful vista of purple mountains and turquoise sky.

_____ This climb was just one of the things I've done with Marissa that have made me more self-confident.

_____ One of the best times we ever had was climbing to the highest point in the Organ Mountains, about 9,000 feet above sea level.

_____ I was proud of myself for reaching the top of the mountain.

Krikor's Revised Draft

Before you read Krikor's revised draft, reread his discovery draft. Notice the changes he has made in this revised draft. You will still see some errors; these will be corrected when Krikor edits his paragraph later on.

My main goal in life, to be an actor, will be difficult to acomplish, but I know I can do it. When I'm acting, I feel as if I'm in a different world. Which makes me feel happy and fulfilled. I've already had some experience acting in plays in high school, but I know I need to do much more. My first step will be to major in acting. In addition to taking acting classes for my major, I hope to be in plays the drama department puts on. Also, I'll try out for small parts in movies that are filmed in this area. My next big step will be after I graduate, when I'll move to Los Angeles and begin to audition for parts. At first I'll audition for anything I can get such as commercials and small parts in TV shows and movies. My final step will be to have a good enough reputation to be considered for larger parts. I don't want to be famous because I just want to be a good actor. I know becoming an actor is hard, but I'm determined to make it!

GROUP ACTIVITY: Analyze Krikor's Revised Draft

Use the following questions to discuss with your classmates how Krikor has revised his draft.

1. Compare Krikor's original topic sentence with the topic sentence in his revised draft. How has he improved it?

____

____

____

2. How has Krikor strengthened his focus?

____

____

____

____

3. How has Krikor provided support for the topic sentence?

____

4. How has Krikor improved the organization of his points?

____

5. How has Krikor connected his ideas? Give an example.

____

6. Compare the concluding sentence of Krikor's revised draft with the concluding sentence of his discovery draft. How has Krikor improved it?

____

____

7. What else can Krikor do to improve his draft?

____

____

____

WRITING ACTIVITY 8 (Group): Peer Review

Form a group with two or three classmates and exchange copies of your drafts. Read your draft aloud while your classmates follow along. Take notes on your classmates' answers to the following questions.

1. What do you like best about my paragraph? What interested you the most? What do you want to know more about?
2. Were you ever confused while you read?
3. How clear is my topic sentence? How can I improve it to better explain what I am writing about?
4. Is my paragraph focused? What sentences should I consider deleting?
5. Evaluate my supporting ideas. Are they consistent with my topic sentence and with each other? Are there enough of them?
6. Are my points well-organized? How can I improve my organization?
7. Does my concluding sentence restate my topic sentence or summarize my main points?

WRITING ACTIVITY 9: Revise Your Draft

Using your classmates' responses to your draft in previous activities, revise your draft. In particular, strengthen your focus, build your support, organize your points, and connect your ideas.

STEP 4: EDIT YOUR PARAGRAPH

Because you have spent a great deal of time and energy on communicating your ideas, you don't want errors to make your ideas hard to follow. When you edit, you check your revised draft for errors in spelling, punctuation, and grammar. You can look up words in a dictionary, read about rules for writing in the Handbook in Part Four of this book, or receive advice from a writing tutor, your instructor, or a classmate or friend.

Spell-Check
The spell-check on your word-processing program will catch many spelling errors. However, it won't catch words that sound the same but are spelled differently, such as *there, they're,* and *their.* Be sure to check your writing yourself for this type of error.

Keeping an Editing Log

As you edit, keep an editing log to record and correct your errors.

HOW TO Keep an Editing Log

- Date your entry.
- Copy the sentence with the error.
- Identify the type of error.
- Rewrite the sentence, correcting the error.

Add to your editing log whenever you check your writing for errors. With practice, you'll learn to recognize the mistakes you're most likely to make. Keeping a record of them will help you avoid making them in the future.

Krikor's Edited Draft

With help from a writing tutor and the Handbook in Part Four, Krikor corrected the errors in his paragraph. His corrections are underlined here. Then, he recorded these errors in his editing log.

My main goal in life, to be an actor, will be difficult to accomplish, but I know I can do it. When I'm acting, I feel as if I'm in a different world, which makes me feel happy and fulfilled. I've already had some experience acting in plays in high school, but I know I need to do much more. My first step will be to major in acting. In addition to taking acting classes for my major, I hope to be in plays the drama department puts on. Also, I'll try out for small parts in movies that are filmed in this area. My next big step will be after I graduate, when I'll move to Los Angeles and begin to audition for parts. At first I'll audition for anything I can get, such as commercials and small parts in TV shows and movies. My final step will be to have a good enough reputation to be considered for larger parts. I don't want to be famous because I just want to be a good actor. I know becoming an actor is hard, but I'm determined to make it!

Krikor's Editing Log

September 2, 2004

INCORRECT	acomplish
ERROR	spelling
CORRECT	accomplish
INCORRECT	Which makes me feel happy and fulfilled.
ERROR	Sentence fragment
CORRECT	When I'm acting, I feel as if I'm in a different world, which makes me feel happy and fulfilled.
INCORRECT	At first I'll audition for anything I can get such as commercials and small parts in TV shows and movies.
ERROR	No comma
CORRECT	At first I'll audition for anything I can get, such as commercials and small parts in TV shows and movies.

WRITING ACTIVITY 10: Edit Your Paragraph

Referring to a dictionary and the Handbook in Part Four of this book, edit your paragraph for errors in spelling, punctuation, and grammar. Record your errors and corrections in an editing log.

STEP 5: SHARE YOUR PARAGRAPH

Sharing, the final stage of the writing process, is a rewarding experience. You have worked hard on your paragraph, so give your finished draft to someone to read. In addition to your instructor, your classmates, friends, family members, or colleagues at work will be interested in what you have to say. Even a simple letter to the editor of your local newspaper can give you a wide audience — and a chance to express your views about an important topic.

Krikor shared his paragraph with several classmates, who told him they'd be sure to see him when he began acting in plays and movies. Krikor also pinned a copy of his paragraph over his desk to remind him of his goal whenever he got discouraged.

ADDITIONAL WRITING ASSIGNMENTS

1. Write a paragraph for your instructor and classmates in which you describe a photograph that is important to you. Use directional order.
2. Write a paragraph for your campus newspaper to explain how something about your college can be improved. Use the most appropriate order for your sentences (topic-illustration-explanation, chronological, progressive, directional, or question-and-answer). Edit the paragraph carefully for the newspaper audience.
3. Write a paragraph for your instructor and classmates about your most treasured memory. First, imagine what that memory looks like. Then, write about the memory, explaining what happened and why you treasure it so much.

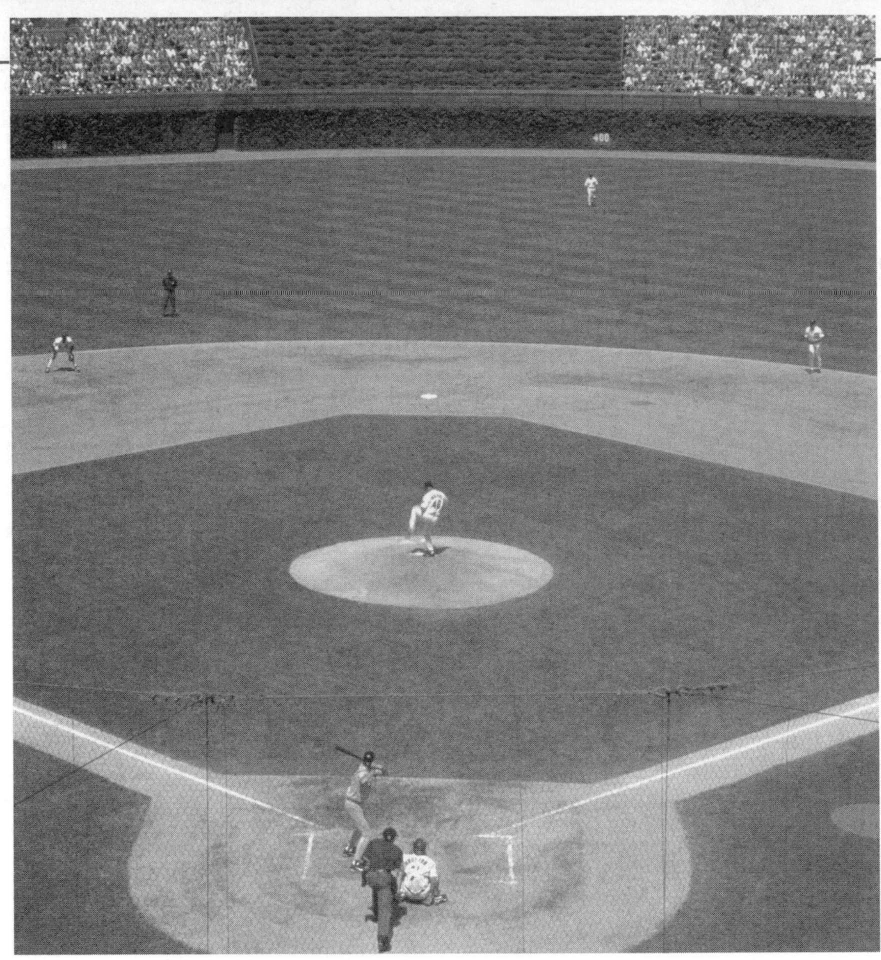

In this chapter, you will read Lara Flynn Boyle's description of the childhood Sundays she spent watching the Cubs at Wrigley Field, pictured here, and you will use examples to describe something memorable from your own experience. What place or event from your past stands out in your mind?

CHAPTER

3

Writing a Paragraph That Gives Examples

In this chapter, you will

- discover how examples work.
- brainstorm to gather ideas.
- write about a memorable place or event.
- use topic-illustration-explanation to order your points.
- edit for sentence fragments.
- read your finished paragraph to a classmate.

UNDERSTANDING EXAMPLES

Imagine that this is your first day of class. You are excited, but also a little bit nervous. You don't know any of your classmates and you wonder if any of them are from your neighborhood. You are trying to get up the nerve to ask the name of the person next to you when, to your surprise, your instructor asks all of you to write a paragraph to introduce yourselves. You can help your classmates get to know you by giving them examples of things that matter to you.

Examples are facts and specific cases that support a statement by illustrating it or providing a clearer picture of it. Examples answer questions like these:

- Can you explain that to me?
- Can you be more specific?
- Can you show that to me?

The following statements are followed by examples. Notice how facts and specific cases in the second sentences help you understand the first ones:

STATEMENT I have several classes this term.

EXAMPLES I'm enrolled in English, calculus, American history, and biology.

STATEMENT College football games make a great deal of money.

EXAMPLES Our last game against State made $400,000 for the athletic department.

READING PARAGRAPHS THAT GIVE EXAMPLES

The paragraphs that follow show how two writers use examples to explain, support, and make clear their ideas about what is important to them.

A Memorable Place

Sometimes a place is memorable because it is unusual. In this paragraph, food critic Jonathan Gold gives examples to show what is special about Singapore's Newton Circus Hawker Center.

JONATHAN GOLD

from "The World's Greatest Street Food"

Almost everybody you meet in Singapore will try to talk you out of going to the Newton Circus Hawker Center: the clerk at your hotel, a new business associate, the cabbie who drove you in from the airport. But the very things that make many native Singaporeans avoid the place also more or less explain why you should eat at Newton on your very first night in the city. The hawkers are a little forward — they're used to tourists — but almost before you know it, they will find you a seat, ply you with iced sugarcane juice, and try to sell you a nice plate of fried cuttlefish. And though you will end up spending a bit more than you should, you will also, almost without trying, end up outside on a warm night, a little tipsy on Tiger beer, surrounded by platefuls of grilled lobster, beef *saté,* crispy oyster omelets, barbecued stingray, fresh durian, and fried Hokkien *mee* with prawns. And isn't this what you came to Singapore for in the first place?

READING ACTIVITY 1: Build Your Vocabulary

Try to determine the meanings of the following words from Jonathan Gold's paragraph. Then, check their meanings by looking the words up in a dictionary.

hawkers ______________________________

forward ______________________________

ply ______________________________

READING ACTIVITY 2: Read to Improve Writing

Read and answer the following questions about Jonathan Gold's paragraph.

1. Which sentence in this paragraph states Gold's main point?

____

____

____

2. What examples does Gold use to illustrate his topic sentence?

____

____

____

____

____

____

3. Why do native Singaporeans discourage tourists from eating at the Newton Circus Hawker Center?

____

____

4. What are some of your most memorable places?

____

A Memorable Day

Many of us have fond memories of special days during our childhood. In this paragraph, actress Lara Flynn Boyle explains why Sundays were a favorite time for her.

LARA FLYNN BOYLE

from "My Favorite Day in Chicago"

Growing up in Chicago, my favorite times were Sundays during baseball season. My mom and I lived in a part of town called Wrigleyville, the area that surrounds Wrigley Field, long before it became fashionable to live there. Our day began with us putting on our "NO LIGHTS" T-shirts — because that is the only way baseball should be played — followed by the long walk down Belmont to Halstead to Wrigley Field with the rest of our neighborhood baseball fans, especially my uncles, Wayne and Tom, who are the world's biggest Cubs fans. During the game, my mom and I would eat hot dogs while we cheered on the Cubs. After the game, we would always head to our favorite dinner spot, the El Jardin Mexican restaurant on Clark Street. There we would dine on tacos and the world's best flan. . . . After having our fill of flan, we would go home, light candles, sit on our glider, listen to the Bee Gees in the breezeway, and enjoy the evening.

READING ACTIVITY 3: Build Your Vocabulary

Try to determine the meanings of the following words from Lara Flynn Boyle's paragraph. Then, check their meanings by looking them up in a dictionary.

fashionable ______________________________

flan ______________________________

breezeway ______________________________

READING ACTIVITY 4: Read to Improve Writing

Read and answer the following questions about Lara Flynn Boyle's paragraph.

1. Boyle's topic sentence states where and when she spent her most memorable days. Why is this important to her reader?

____

____

____

2. What examples does she use to support her main idea that Sundays during baseball season were her most memorable days?

____

____

____

3. Do you agree with Boyle that baseball should not be played at night? Why or why not?

____

4. What are some of your most memorable days?

____

Writing Assignment

Introduce yourself to your classmates by writing a paragraph about yourself.

- Write a paragraph in which you use examples to show why a particular place is special to you.

  OR

- Write a paragraph in which you use examples to show how you spent a memorable day or days.

STEP 1: DISCOVER IDEAS FOR WRITING

Many people find it difficult to select a topic to write about. The decision is a little easier if you consider who is going to read your paragraph, why you're writing, what examples you have, and what you want to focus on.

Choosing a Topic

For more advice on how to choose a topic, refer to p. 19.

A paragraph's topic is what it is about. Jonathan Gold's topic, for example, is street food; Lara Flynn Boyle's topic is her favorite day in Chicago. For this chapter's assignment, you have a choice of writing about a memorable place or a memorable day (or days). The first thing you need to do, then, is pick one of those options.

Ask yourself if any places or times have been especially memorable for you. Maybe something comes to mind right away, or maybe you're stuck. Don't worry too much about which choice is better: You can always change your mind before you start writing.

Explore Re: Writing Links Libraries
To help you brainstorm topic ideas, go to the Re: Writing Web site at **bedfordstmartins.com/rewriting** and click on "Links Libraries."

Considering Your Audience and Purpose

Read more about audience and purpose on pp. 20–22.

You're using examples because you want the other students in your class to know you better. Your classmates, then, are your readers. Before you write for this audience, consider what you know about them as well as what they already know about you.

In addition, you need to understand why you're writing about a memorable place or day. Perhaps you want to express your thoughts and feelings about a special place, or inform your classmates of something you have learned, or persuade them to think differently about something that matters to you. Understanding your purpose will help you write a paragraph that accomplishes that goal.

WRITING ACTIVITY 1: Analyze Your Audience and Purpose

Answer the following questions to help you think about your audience and purpose.

1. What things will your classmates likely already know about you? What might they not know?

___

___

___

2. Of those things they don't know about you, what might interest them most or help them understand you better?

___

___

___

3. What do you hope to achieve? Do you want to express your thoughts and feelings, inform your readers of something that you know and they may not, or persuade them to change their minds?

___

___

___

Brainstorming to Gather Ideas

Now that you've chosen a general topic and thought about your audience and purpose, it's time to begin gathering ideas for your paragraph. Maybe you have a lot of ideas and aren't sure which examples will work best. Or maybe you're still not sure what you want to write about. A good way to gather ideas is to use brainstorming, quickly listing words or phrases on a topic.

Learn more about brainstorming on p. 24.

HOW TO Brainstorm Examples

- Write your general topic at the top of the page.
- In words or in phrases, list all of the facts about the topic and specific cases of it that come into your head.
- Don't worry about whether these examples are good ones or not. Just write down everything you think of.
- Don't worry about grammar, spelling, or punctuation.

Student writer Naresh chose to write about how he spends memorable days. He used brainstorming to help him decide on a specific topic. Here is the list he came up with.

My Memorable Days

reading science fiction

going to the amusement park

flying an airplane

volunteering at the retirement home

walking my dog

When he looked back at his list, Naresh noticed that two of his ideas stood out as more interesting than the rest: flying an airplane and volunteering at the retirement home.

WRITING ACTIVITY 2: Brainstorm Your Topic

Write either "my most memorable places" or "my most memorable days" on the top of a blank page, then brainstorm whatever comes to mind. Aim to write down at least five ideas. Look over your list and decide which idea is the most interesting topic for your paragraph.

For more information on narrowing a topic, see pp. 27–29.

Narrowing Your Topic

Because you're drafting only one paragraph, you must focus your topic so that you can provide enough details to make it interesting without overwhelming your readers.

Suppose your most memorable days have been spent restoring old cars. You could provide examples of every part you have ever worked on, but your readers probably wouldn't be interested in such a list. It also would be difficult to describe them all in one paragraph. Instead, you might choose two or three of your favorite projects to use as examples.

HOW TO Narrow a Topic for a Paragraph That Gives Examples

- Select a general topic.
- List facts, ideas, and specific cases to serve as examples about the general topic.

- Decide which of these examples interest you.
- Decide which of these examples will interest your readers.
- Decide which of these examples are most related to your topic and to each other.

Student writer Naresh decided to write on the topic of flying airplanes. He thought his fellow classmates might not know much about his hobby and would be eager to learn more. He narrowed his topic by brainstorming another list, this time using flying as his topic:

Flying Airplanes

my first time in an airplane

freedom, mystery, sense of control

how to fly

all the instruments on the control panel

my first solo flight

pride, challenge, accomplishment

thrill, danger

airplanes I have flown: Aronica Champ, Piper Pacer, Cessna 150, Navaho, Pitts S-2

spirit of life

self-confidence

WRITING ACTIVITY 3: Narrow Your Topic

Choose a topic from your brainstorming list and brainstorm again. This time brainstorm for facts and specific cases that relate to your topic. Aim to write down five to ten examples.

STEP 2: WRITE YOUR DISCOVERY DRAFT

You have now chosen and narrowed a topic for your paragraph and brainstormed examples. It's time to move to the stage of the writing process where you put your ideas together so that you can share them with your readers.

At this point you just want to get your ideas down on paper, so don't be too concerned with exact wording, grammar, spelling, or punctuation. Focus on your ideas.

Drafting a Topic Sentence

For more ideas about topic sentences, see pp. 30–31.

A topic sentence helps your readers understand your paragraph right away. It tells them what you're writing about and why. Usually, the topic sentence begins the paragraph, and then all of the sentences that follow help explain it.

For example, Lara Flynn Boyle's topic sentence is the first sentence in her paragraph:

> **Growing up in Chicago, my favorite times were Sundays during baseball season.**

She continues with examples of what made Sundays special.

Here are some examples of topic sentences written by student writers on how they have spent memorable days:

> My most memorable days were spent restoring an old Volkswagen Beetle that my uncle gave me for my sixteenth birthday.

> Bungee jumping is an exciting way to spend a day.

Here are topic sentences written by student writers on memorable places:

> Stonehenge is the most mysterious place I've ever been.

> I enjoy going to Mission Bay, California, because of the variety of activities there.

Notice how all of these topic sentences identify both a subject (for example, bungee jumping) and why the author is writing about it (it's exciting).

HOW TO Write a Topic Sentence for a Paragraph That Gives Examples

- Identify your topic.
- Express the main point you want to make.
- Be sure that you can add examples to show or explain this topic sentence.

WRITING ACTIVITY 4: Draft Your Topic Sentence

Decide what you want to say about your narrowed topic and draft a topic sentence for your paragraph. Use the sample student topic sentences as models if you wish.

Adding Examples for Support

Now that you have a topic sentence, you are ready to support it with examples. Refer to your brainstorming notes and write down in sentence form some facts and specific cases that provide information about your topic.

Read about other ways of adding support on pp. 31–34.

Student writer Naresh wrote the following topic sentence:

> I enjoy flying small airplanes because it gives me a sense of control over what is happening to me.

He then wrote his first example. Notice how it explains what it means to be in control.

> When I'm the only person aboard the airplane, everything depends on my skill to control the airplane so that I can go where I want to go and how I want to get there.

Use a Word Processor
If at all possible, use a word processor to draft. This will make revising your paragraph quicker and easier.

WRITING ACTIVITY 5: Gather Examples

Write down several examples that support your topic sentence.

Drafting a Concluding Sentence

A concluding sentence sums up what you want your readers to remember. In other words, you end with an important thought about your topic. One way to do this is to restate why a special place or day is memorable.

Let's look again at the concluding statement of one of the examples we read earlier. Jonathan Gold's paragraph about the Newton Circus Hawker Center concludes:

> And isn't this what you came to Singapore for in the first place?

Learn more about concluding sentences on pp. 34–35.

By ending this way, Gold refers back to his topic sentence without repeating himself.

WRITING ACTIVITY 6: Draft a Concluding Sentence

Write a sentence that summarizes the main point of your paragraph. Compare it with your topic sentence to be sure that you have stayed on the same topic.

Naresh's Discovery Draft

After Naresh wrote his first example, he provided more examples of why flying is important to him. He then put everything together into the paragraph below. You might notice that Naresh's discovery draft includes some errors. That's okay; he will correct them later.

The Freedom to Fly

I enjoy flying small airplanes because it gives me a sense of control over what is happening to me. If I make it to my destination I have succeeded, I have always succeeded! When I'm the only person aboard the airplane, everything depends on my skill to control the airplane so that I can go where I want to go and how I want to get there. No one else is in control of my life. Flying a new airplane gives me a sense of challange and eventually a sense of accomplishment. Other challanges I have faced are when I moved to Maryland and when I took calculus. Each airplane is the same but each is different. For example, in order to have the nose rise. I must pull on the control. How much? Each airplane is different. It is very much like trying to tell someone how much pressure to put on the brake in order to stop exactly at the right spot. When I'm not flying an airplane, I'm driving my car, a canary yellow Mustang.

WRITING ACTIVITY 7: Complete Your Discovery Draft

Using the topic sentence, examples, and concluding sentence that you wrote in Activities 4, 5, and 6, write your discovery draft. Concentrate on what you want to say. You'll have time to improve your paragraph later.

STEP 3: REVISE YOUR PARAGRAPH

When you revise, you improve your discovery draft so that your reader will fully understand your paragraph and be interested in reading it. You'll look at what you have said and how you have organized it. When revising, you will want to consider three things: your focus, your support, and your organization.

Strengthening Your Focus

To strengthen your focus, you make sure that each example in your paragraph supports and develops your topic sentence, and that each detail develops or supports an example. You may have noticed that two sentences in Naresh's draft did not specifically relate to his topic sentence:

For other ideas about paragraph focus, turn to pp. 37–38.

```
Other challanges I have faced are when I moved to
Maryland and when I took calculus.

When I'm not flying an airplane, I'm driving my car,
a canary yellow Mustang.
```

When revising his paragraph, Naresh removed these two sentences, so that every sentence in his paragraph would be focused on his love of flying.

Building Your Support with Stronger Examples

A key part of revising is making sure your examples provide enough support for your topic sentence. Your paragraph should have enough examples and details to help your readers understand your main point. In addition, your examples should be clear, believable, and interesting for your audience.

Naresh reviewed his paragraph on flying airplanes and thought that all of his examples were believable and that they would interest his readers because they provided new information for them. But he decided that one example — "Each airplane is the same but each is different" — wouldn't be clear for people who haven't flown, so he deleted it.

Naresh also decided that to express fully his enthusiasm for flying he needed to add more examples and more specific details. When he revised, he wrote some new supporting sentences, such as this one:

```
My favorite airplane to fly is the Pitts S2. It's a
very small biplane, fully aerobatic, with a tail
wheel, and it can do any maneuver I want.
```

HOW TO Build Stronger Examples

- Decide if your examples are clear, believable, and interesting. Revise or delete any that are not.
- Check that you have provided enough examples to help your reader understand your main point.
- If necessary, write new examples.
- Add details where needed to develop your examples.

Using TIE to Organize and Connect Your Points

When you drafted your paragraph, you probably did what most people do and wrote your examples down without thinking too much about the order you put them in. As you revise, you want to organize your examples and details so that they relate to each other in a way that makes sense for your readers.

Other ways to order paragraphs are described on pp. 39–42.

For a paragraph using examples, *topic-illustration-explanation (TIE)* order is a good way to develop your ideas. To use TIE order, start with a topic sentence. Then, give each example (illustration) and explain how it relates to the topic sentence. Finish with your concluding sentence.

You can find more information about using transitions on p. 42.

To help your readers recognize and understand your examples, use transitions, such as *for example* or *to illustrate.* Transitions help connect your ideas so that readers can follow them when you move from one to another.

HOW TO Connect Ideas in a Paragraph That Gives Examples

The following phrases tell your reader that you are providing an example:

- For example,
- For instance,
- To illustrate,
- In particular,
- First, second, third, etc.

When Naresh revised his paragraph, he moved some of his sentences so that they followed TIE order. He also added an explanation for one of his examples:

Example

```
Flying a new airplane gives me a sense of challange
and eventually a sense of accomplishment.
```

Explanation

```
When I take on that challange, I must study the
problems and come up with creative solutions and
learn from those challanges that have gone before.
```

Naresh's Revised Draft

In his revised draft, Naresh strengthened his focus, added and reordered examples, and added transitions. This draft still contains some errors in grammar, spelling, and punctuation that he will correct when he edits.

```
                   The Freedom to Fly
  I enjoy flying small airplanes because it gives me
a sense of freedom and control over what is happening
to me. When I'm the only person aboard, everything
depends on my skill to control the airplane so that
I can go where I want to go. If I make it to my
destination. I have succeeded, and I have always
succeeded! Flying a new airplane gives me a sense of
challange and eventually a sense of accomplishment.
When I take on that challange. I must study the
problems and come up with creative solutions and
learn from those challanges that have gone before.
Another example of a challange is human and machine
against nature. Every time I go flying, the weather
is different and sometimes challanging. I have to be
up to it. My favorite airplane to fly is the Pitts
S2. It's a very small biplane, fully aerobatic, with
a tail wheel. Can do any maneuver I want. I enjoy
flying small airplanes because flying sets me apart
from most other people.
```

GROUP ACTIVITY: Analyze Naresh's Revised Draft

Use the following questions to discuss with your classmates how Naresh improved his draft.

1. Compare Naresh's topic sentence in his discovery draft with the one in his revised draft. How did he improve his topic sentence?

   ____

   ____

   ____

2. What examples did Naresh add in his revised draft? Do they improve it? Why or why not?

   ____

   ____

   ____

3. In his revised draft, Naresh deleted some sentences. Is this an effective change? Why or why not?

   ____

   ____

4. What could Naresh do to further improve his draft?

   ____

WRITING ACTIVITY 8 (Group): Peer Review

Form a group with two or three classmates and exchange copies of your drafts. Read your own draft aloud while your classmates follow along. Take notes on your classmates' answers to the following questions about your draft.

1. What do you like best about my paragraph?
2. How clear is my topic sentence? Do you have any suggestions for revision?
3. Evaluate my examples. Is each example clear, believable, and interesting? Are there things you would like to know more about?
4. How well do I build support for my topic sentence? Where would you like more information?

5. Are my points in the best order? Which sentences would you suggest I move?
6. Where should I add transitions to help you follow my thoughts?

WRITING ACTIVITY 9: Revise Your Draft

Before you revise, review Naresh's draft, his revision, and your analysis of his work for ideas. Then, using your classmates' peer review suggestions, revise your draft. Add examples and explanation where needed, and delete any sentences that are not related to the topic. Consider reordering your sentences if necessary.

STEP 4: EDIT YOUR PARAGRAPH

Since you have worked so hard to express your ideas, you don't want to distract readers from them with errors in grammar, spelling, or punctuation. To edit your draft for these errors, you'll need a dictionary and the grammar Handbook in Part Four of this book.

In this chapter you will focus on eliminating sentence fragments, but you should be alert for other errors in grammar, spelling, and punctuation as well.

Online Writing Centers

A number of college writing centers offer online tutoring. Tutors will answer your editing questions electronically. To find one of these writing centers, go to the *Discoveries* Web site at **bedfordstmartins.com/discoveries** and click on "Annotated Web Links."

What Is a Sentence Fragment?

A sentence fragment is an incomplete sentence: It looks like a sentence, but something is missing.

A complete sentence has both a subject and a verb and expresses a complete thought. The subject tells who or what is doing the action. The verb explains the action or links the subject to the rest of the sentence.

To learn more about correcting sentence fragments, turn to pp. 548–54.

At times, writers use fragments intentionally for special effects or in dialogue. But in writing you do for college classes or at work, it is best to avoid sentence fragments because they may be considered errors.

Correcting Sentence Fragments

If your sentence is missing a subject or a verb (or both), it is actually a fragment. Here are examples of sentence fragments that have been corrected with the addition of a subject or a verb.

FRAGMENT The Grand Canyon a beautiful place.

SENTENCE The Grand Canyon *is* a beautiful place.

FRAGMENT Spend all of my spare time studying!

SENTENCE *I* spend all of my spare time studying!

Other sentence fragments have a subject and a verb, but they don't express a complete thought. These fragments are usually dependent clauses that begin with subordinating conjunctions such as *after, although, because,* and *unless,* or with relative pronouns such as *that, who, whoever,* and *which.* Sometimes a fragment like this can be combined with the sentence before or after it to create a complete sentence. Other times you may need to add information to the fragment to complete your thought. Often, simply deleting the conjunction or pronoun at the beginning will turn a fragment into a complete sentence.

Here are examples of dependent clauses that have been turned into complete sentences.

FRAGMENT I like to go to the gym. After I finish class.

SENTENCE I like to go to the gym after I finish class.

FRAGMENT Unless you help.

SENTENCE I can't do this unless you help.

FRAGMENT Which makes sense.

SENTENCE It makes sense.

HOW TO Correct Sentence Fragments

- Check that each sentence (1) has a subject, (2) has a verb, and (3) expresses a complete thought.
- Revise a fragment without a subject and/or verb by adding the missing subject and/or verb.
- Revise a fragment that is a dependent clause by (1) combining it with another sentence, (2) adding information to make it a complete thought, or (3) deleting the conjunction or pronoun at the beginning.

EDITING PRACTICE: Correct Sentence Fragments

Correct the sentence fragments in the following items. Some of the sentences are correct.

EXAMPLE

FRAGMENT I never learned to swim. Because I didn't really try.

CORRECT I never learned to swim because I didn't really try.

1. I gave Janet the money. Before she left.

____

2. My favorite pastime dancing.

____

3. Since I began painting.

____

4. Guess I'll give up scuba diving until my leg heals.

____

5. Unless you know someone.

____

6. Although I can't afford to buy them, I have always loved vintage motorcycles.

____

7. I'll go back on my diet after the summer.

____

8. Barbara Morgan is an astronaut. Who came to my school.

____

9. That I never liked.

____

10. A lot of fun.

____

Exercise Central
The *Discoveries* Web site includes additional practice exercises in correcting sentence fragments. Go to **bedfordstmartins.com/discoveries**, click on "Exercise Central," and select "Sentence Fragments."

Naresh's Edited Paragraph

Naresh's revised paragraph contained some errors in grammar, spelling, and punctuation. He edited his paragraph to eliminate the errors. (The underlining indicates where he corrected errors.)

The Freedom to Fly

I enjoy flying small airplanes because it gives me a sense of freedom and control over what is happening to me. When I'm the only person aboard, everything depends on my skill to control the airplane so that I can go where I want to go. <u>If I make it to my destination, I have succeeded, and I have always succeeded!</u> Flying a new airplane gives me a sense of <u>challenge</u> and eventually a sense of accomplishment. <u>When I take on that challenge, I must study the problems, come up with creative solutions, and learn from those challenges that have gone before.</u> Another example of a <u>challenge</u> is human and machine against nature. Every time I go flying, the weather is different and sometimes <u>challenging</u>. I have to be up to it. My favorite airplane to fly is the Pitts S2. <u>It's a very small biplane, fully aerobatic, with a tail wheel, and it can do any maneuver I want.</u> I enjoy flying small airplanes because flying sets me apart from most other people.

WRITING ACTIVITY 10: Edit Your Paragraph

Using a dictionary and the Handbook in Part Four of this book, edit your paragraph. As you edit, focus in particular on eliminating sentence fragments. Add corrections to your editing log.

Editing logs are explained on pp. 45–46.

STEP 5: SHARE YOUR PARAGRAPH

Naresh and one of his classmates were asked to read their paragraphs to each other. They then introduced each other to the class by telling what they had learned from listening to each other's paragraph. Other classmates asked Naresh to tell them more about his love of flying and asked if he ever took passengers with him when he flew.

ADDITIONAL WRITING ASSIGNMENTS

1. Write a paragraph to a close friend explaining why you value his or her friendship. Give examples from your personal experience to support your topic.
2. Write a paragraph to your classmates explaining why you chose to attend college. Give examples of what you think college has to offer.
3. Write a paragraph to your instructor explaining what makes you a truly unique person. Give examples to show what sets you apart from other people.
4. Write an editorial to the school newspaper explaining your views on whether students should work while attending college. Give examples to support your view.

What makes a friend a friend? In this chapter, you will answer that question by telling a story about a time when a friend helped you, or about an experience that you and a friend shared that brought the two of you closer. You will add details and dialogue to bring your story to life.

CHAPTER

4

Writing a Paragraph That Tells a Story

In this chapter, you will

- discover how narration works.
- freewrite to gather ideas.
- write about a friend.
- use chronology to order your points.
- edit for comma splices.
- post your paragraph to a personal Web page.

UNDERSTANDING NARRATION

Everyone likes to hear a good story. Children are fascinated by ghost stories that keep them awake at night. Elders often enjoy telling stories about their younger years. Friends share stories about their feelings and thoughts. Stories help us remember important events and understand our lives.

Stories, also called narratives, are based on a series of events. They can be either fact or fiction, as long as a book or as short as a paragraph. Stories answer questions like these:

- What happened?
- When and where did it happen?
- Why did it happen?
- What did it mean to you?

Good stories include colorful details, and often they contain dialogue in which people's actual words are quoted.

READING PARAGRAPHS THAT TELL A STORY

Later in this chapter you will write a story about a significant experience you shared with a friend. The following paragraphs show how two writers have narrated stories on this topic.

A Friend's Help

Blind and deaf from the age of eighteen months, Helen Keller was an activist for the disabled. In this paragraph, she tells about the moment her teacher and friend Anne Sullivan helped her understand the meaning of language.

HELEN KELLER

from **The Story of My Life**

We walked down the path to the well-house, attracted by the fragrance of the honeysuckle with which it was covered. Someone was drawing water and my teacher placed my hand under the spout. As the cool stream gushed over one hand she spelled into the other the word *water,* first slowly, then rapidly. I stood still, my whole attention fixed upon the motions of her fingers. Suddenly I felt a misty consciousness as of something

forgotten — a thrill of returning thought; and somehow the mystery of language was revealed to me. I knew then that "w-a-t-e-r" meant the wonderful cool something that was flowing over my hand. The living word awakened my soul, gave it light, hope, joy, set it free! There were barriers still, it is true, but barriers that could in time be swept away.

READING ACTIVITY 1: Build Your Vocabulary

Try to determine the meanings of the following words from Helen Keller's paragraph. Then, check their meanings by looking the words up in a dictionary.

well-house ____________________

spout ____________________

gushed ____________________

consciousness ____________________

barrier ____________________

READING ACTIVITY 2: Read to Improve Your Writing

Read and answer the following questions about the paragraph from *The Story of My Life.*

1. What is the author's main point in this paragraph?

 ____

 ____

2. What details does Keller give in telling her story?

 ____

 ____

 ____

3. Why is it so important that Helen learn the connection between the letters spelled into her hand and the water?

 ____

4. What can you remember about a time when one of your friends helped you?

 ____

An Event Shared with a Friend

Shared experiences can make friends closer. In the following paragraph, Steve Tesich writes about a time he and his best friend raced each other.

STEVE TESICH

from "Focusing on Friends"

The best friend I had in high school was Louie. . . . We were both athletes, and one day we decided to "run till we drop." We just wanted to know what it was like. Skinny Louie set the pace as we ran around our high-school track. Lap after lap. Four laps to a mile. Mile after mile we ran. I had the reputation as being a big-time jock. Louie didn't. But this was Louie's day. There was a bounce in his step and, when he turned back to look at me, his eyes were gleaming with the thrill of it all. I finally dropped. Louie still looked fresh; he seemed capable, on that day, of running forever. But we were the best of friends, and so he stopped. "That's it," he lied. "I couldn't go another step farther." It was an act of love. Naturally, I said nothing.

READING ACTIVITY 3: Build Your Vocabulary

Try to determine the meanings of the following words from Steve Tesich's paragraph. Then, check their meanings by looking the words up in a dictionary.

reputation ______________________________

gleaming ______________________________

capable ______________________________

READING ACTIVITY 4: Read to Improve Your Writing

Read and answer the following questions about the paragraph from "Focusing on Friends."

1. What are three words or phrases that describe the friendship between the author and Louie?

   ____

2. Tesich ends his paragraph by writing, "It was an act of love. Naturally, I said nothing." Why doesn't he say anything to Louie?

   ____

3. Tesich's paragraph contains two sentence fragments, or incomplete sentences: "Lap after lap. Four laps to a mile." Why do you think the author chose to use sentence fragments to describe this part of the race?

____

____

4. What are some memorable experiences you've had with a friend?

____

Writing Assignment

Imagine that you want to create a personal Web site that will feature photographs, video, music, and factual stories. One section will be devoted to the topic of friends. Write a paragraph for your Web site on one of these topics.

- Tell a story about a time when one of your friends helped you.

OR

- Narrate a memorable experience that you shared with a friend.

STEP 1: DISCOVER IDEAS FOR WRITING

Most of us have so many friends and memories that selecting one to write about seems impossible. Instead of picking something at random, think about who is going to read your paragraph and what they might not know about your friends. It also helps to experiment with different ideas before settling on a final topic.

Choosing a Topic

Before you begin, you need to decide whether you will write about a time when a friend helped you or about something you and friend did together. The sample paragraphs you read each take on one of these topics: Helen Keller tells about the day her friend helped her understand language; Steve Tesich narrates a memorable moment he shared with his best friend.

For more advice on how to choose a topic, refer to p. 19.

Who are your closest friends? Think back and see if you can remember a time when one of them helped you. If the support was important to you, that might be a good choice for your paragraph. But if you can't think of any examples, or if the experience doesn't seem very interesting, consider telling a story about something memorable that you did together. You don't need to know exactly what story you're going to tell yet. The following activities will help you figure that out.

Explore Re: Writing Links Libraries

To help you brainstorm topic ideas, go to the Re: Writing Web site at **bedfordstmartins.com/rewriting** and click on "Links Libraries."

Read more about audience and purpose on pp. 20–22.

Considering Your Audience and Purpose

Anybody with Internet access can read your Web site. In addition to your instructor and classmates, then, your audience will consist of family members, friends, and even complete strangers. Since people you don't know will be able to read your paragraph, avoid revealing information that you consider private. At the same time, be sure you provide enough detail so that a person who doesn't know you and your friend will be able to make sense of your story.

In addition, you need to understand what you want to accomplish with your paragraph. Because you're writing a personal story about a friend, you'll most likely want to express your thoughts and feelings.

E-mail a Friend

Ask your friend what he or she remembers about the first time you met. Also ask your friend to recall a special moment or event you experienced together. Your friend's memories may trigger memories of your own.

WRITING ACTIVITY 1: Analyze Your Audience and Purpose

Pick a friend to write about, then answer the following questions about your audience and purpose.

1. What do your readers already know about you and your friend?
   Readers who know you well

   ____

   ____

   ____

Other readers

______

______

______

2. What will your readers *not* already know about you and your friend?
   Readers who know you well

   ______

   ______

   ______

   Other readers

   ______

   ______

   ______

3. What story will be most interesting to your readers?
   Readers who know you well

   ______

   ______

   ______

   Other readers

   ______

   ______

   ______

4. What is your purpose in writing this paragraph — to express, to inform, or to persuade?

   ______

   ______

   ______

Learn more about freewriting on p.25.

Freewriting to Gather Ideas

At this point, you need to gather ideas for your paragraph. Freewriting is an excellent way to gather ideas because it allows you to explore your thoughts without worrying about details like organization, style, or grammar.

HOW TO Freewrite for a Story

- Write a topic idea at the top of the page (for example, "Celia Saved My Life" or "The Emergency Room Visit").
- Write about that topic, without pausing, for ten minutes.
- Don't stop, go back, or correct your writing.
- Follow your ideas. Don't worry if they're good or bad.
- Don't worry about organization, grammar, spelling, or punctuation.

Student writer Zoe knew she wanted to write about her best friend, but she couldn't decide on a story. To help herself think, she freewrote on both of the suggested topics. Here's what she wrote about the time he helped her through a difficult experience:

> I'll never forget when Ben and I got suspended together. In senior English we had a brand new teacher who was only a few years older than us. He made us write a sonnet. I loved poetry, so I spent a lot of time on it. Next day the teacher says I copied the poem! He said it was too good for me to have written it. Ben got up from his desk and told the teacher he didn't know what he was talking about. It was a big deal. Our parents got called in, and everyone wanted me to prove I'd written it, but I couldn't because I'd thrown the other drafts away. We got suspended for a few days, but it was worth it to find out what a good friend Ben is.

WRITING ACTIVITY 2: Freewrite

Freewrite on both possible topics for your paragraph: (1) a time a friend helped you, and (2) a memorable moment or event you shared with a friend.

Narrowing Your Topic

For more information on narrowing a topic, see pp. 27–29.

Now that you have freewritten on two possible topics, you need to choose one for your discovery draft. You have only one paragraph to tell your whole story, so you need to pick something that you can narrate in detail with just a few sentences.

Suppose, for example, that you're writing about the time that you and a friend took a three-day backpacking trip. You had many memorable moments together, such as getting lost, being swarmed by mosquitoes, watching beautiful sunsets, and talking by the campfire. However, you can't narrate all of these events in a single paragraph. Instead, select one event so you can focus.

A technique called "looping" can help you narrow your topic. Looping is a type of freewriting that helps writers focus their ideas.

HOW TO Use "Looping" to Narrow a Topic

- Freewrite on your topic for about ten minutes.
- Take a minute or two to read your freewriting.
- Find an idea that you'd like to write more about. This idea should be more focused than your original topic. Write this idea down on paper.
- Freewrite on the idea you have selected.

Student writer Zoe decided to do some more freewriting about how her friend stood up for her. She began her "looping" with this paragraph:

> I'd always been a good student, so I couldn't believe it when I got suspended. It wasn't fair. I feel I got punished for working really hard on an assignment. I could tell my parents didn't believe me. Without Ben being there for me I don't know how I would have gotten through it. He knew I had worked really hard on that poem. He didn't care that he got punished, too. I've never had a friend who was that loyal.

When Zoe read her looping, she realized that she had found a focus — Ben's loyalty. In her next bit of freewriting, Zoe wrote more about how Ben had defended her when she had been accused of cheating.

WRITING ACTIVITY 3: Narrow Your Topic

Use looping to narrow your topic. First, freewrite for about ten minutes. Then, read the freewriting to find a good idea. Write that idea down and freewrite about it for another ten minutes. Circle ideas you might be able to use in your paragraph.

STEP 2: WRITE YOUR DISCOVERY DRAFT

A paragraph that tells a story has the same parts as any other kind of writing: a topic sentence, support, and a concluding sentence.

Drafting a Topic Sentence

For more ideas about topic sentences, see pp. 30–31.

A topic sentence usually comes first in a paragraph. Sometimes, however, it comes at the end. For instance, in the paragraph from *The Story of My Life,* Helen Keller states her main point in the next-to-last sentence:

> **The living word awakened my soul, gave it light, hope, joy, set it free!**

Keller's paragraph before this sentence showed how she came to understand "the living word."

In a paragraph that tells a story, the topic sentence should express an attitude or idea about your story. When Zoe re-read her topic sentence, she realized that it didn't explain her main point. She rewrote it to express her idea about Ben's loyalty:

> I never really knew what a good friend Ben was until he defended me when I was unfairly accused of cheating.

Here are other examples of topic sentences for paragraphs that tell a story.

> My sister is my best friend because she helped me through the most difficult time of my life, my back surgery.

> I didn't realize how well my friend Chon and I got along until we spent three hours stuck in a traffic jam.

Notice how all of these examples not only identify a topic (for example, getting stuck in a traffic jam), but also state an idea about that topic (for example, how well the writer and her friend got along).

HOW TO Write a Topic Sentence for a Paragraph That Tells a Story

- State what your story is about.
- Express an attitude or idea about your story.
- Make sure that the topic sentence will lead to a paragraph that can contain details and, possibly, dialogue.

WRITING ACTIVITY 4: Draft a Topic Sentence

Using the ideas you gathered in your freewriting, draft a topic sentence. Be sure your sentence expresses the point of the story you'll be telling about your friend.

Asking Questions to Add Support

A good way to come up with ideas for a paragraph that tells a story is to ask yourself the six questions often used by news reporters:

Read about other ways of adding support on pp. 31–34.

- *Who* was involved?
- *What* happened?
- *When* did it happen?
- *Where* did it happen?
- *Why* did it happen?
- *How* did it happen?

Here is how Zoe responded to a few of these questions:

> *What happened?* Ben defended me when I was accused of cheating. We were both suspended for three days.
>
> *Why did it happen?* We had a new teacher who didn't know that when I worked hard I was a good writer. Ben knew I'd never cheat. He was a good friend so he stood up for me.
>
> *How did it happen?* I wrote a really good poem. The teacher accused me of cheating. Ben told everyone I hadn't done it.

Zoe used some of these ideas when she wrote her discovery draft.

WRITING ACTIVITY 5: Ask Questions

Gather details for your discovery draft by answering the six reporter's questions: *who, what, when, where, why,* and *how.*

Drafting a Concluding Sentence

The conclusion to a story can sum up your main point, explain why your point is important, or look toward the future. Whatever strategy you use, be sure that the concluding sentence makes your readers feel the story is over.

Learn more about concluding sentences on pp. 34–35.

Zoe drafted three possible concluding sentences:

Because of this experience, Ben will always be special to me.

Even though being unfairly accused of cheating is a terrible experience, it made me realize what a good friend Ben is.

I hope that one day I'll be able to help Ben the way that he helped me during this terrible time.

When she wrote her discovery draft, Zoe chose the second sentence because it best expressed the main idea of her paragraph.

WRITING ACTIVITY 6: Draft a Concluding Sentence

Write three possible concluding sentences for your paragraph. Select the best one for your discovery draft.

Zoe's Discovery Draft

When Zoe wrote her discovery draft, she added details to the ones she had already gathered. Her draft contains some of the errors typical of this stage of the writing process, but that's okay. Zoe will correct the mistakes when she edits.

Loyalty

I never really knew what a good friend Ben was until he defended me when I was unfairly accused of cheating. It happened my senior year of high school. We had a new teacher who had never taught before, he was only a few years older than us. He sent us both to the principal's office. Anyway, he gave us an assignment to write a sonnet, which is a type of poem with fourteen lines. I love poetry. At the end of senior year, I had some poems published in a literary magazine. So I spent hours on it. The next thing I know, he calls me up in front of class, he waves my poem in front of me. He says I copied it from someplace! I'm so shocked I don't say anything. Then I hear Ben yell, no way. He and the teacher start fighting. We got suspended for three days. Krazinky

```
always supports the teachers. But I didn't care, I
knew I was right. Even though being accused of
cheating is a terrible experience, it made me realize
what a good friend Ben was.
```

WRITING ACTIVITY 7: Complete Your Discovery Draft

Referring to the topic sentence, supporting details, and concluding sentence you have already written, write a discovery draft. Focus on your ideas; you'll have a chance to improve grammar, spelling, and punctuation later.

STEP 3: REVISE YOUR PARAGRAPH

When revising, you focus on clearly communicating your ideas to your audience. For this chapter's assignment your audience is very broad, ranging from your instructor and classmates to friends, family members, and strangers. Keep your varied readers in mind when you strengthen your focus, build your support, and order your points.

Strengthening Your Focus

To make your story easy to follow, be sure that all of your sentences not only relate to your topic but also support your main idea. Zoe's discovery draft, for example, included two sentences that were related to her story but not to her point about her friend's loyalty:

For other ideas about paragraph focus, turn to pp. 37–38.

```
At the end of senior year, I had some poems published
in a literary magazine.

Krazinky always supports the teachers.
```

Zoe decided that these details would distract readers from her point, so she took them out.

Building Your Support with Dialogue

In a paragraph that tells a story, you can build support by including dialogue, or quotations of people's actual words. If your paragraph includes an encounter between people, putting what they say in dialogue form will make the story livelier.

Steve Tesich uses dialogue at the end of his paragraph about running with his best friend.

> **"That's it," he lied. "I couldn't go another step farther." It was an act of love. Naturally, I said nothing.**

The quotations emphasize the main point of the paragraph — that friendship was more important than winning.

HOW TO Build Support with Dialogue

- Quote people's actual words to emphasize an idea.
- Put the speaker's exact words in quotation marks.
- Put any commas or periods inside the quotation marks.

Using Chronology to Organize and Connect Your Points

Has anyone ever told you a story and forgotten or mixed up the order of events? Perhaps the storyteller jumped back and forth or corrected details as he or she spoke. As a listener, you were probably confused, frustrated, and maybe even annoyed.

You don't want to lose your readers' attention, so be sure to tell your story in a logical way. In most narrative paragraphs, ideas are ordered *chronologically,* which means the events are presented in the order they actually happened.

Student writer Zoe, for example, started her discovery draft by describing how she was sent to the principal's office. When she revised, she moved that detail to a later point in the story so that it followed the exact order of events. She also added transitions to make her narrative easier to follow.

Other ways to order paragraphs are described on pp. 39–42.

HOW TO **Connect Ideas in a Paragraph That Tells a Story**

- To show time, use transitions like these: *then, meanwhile, at that time, during, when, soon, after, before, first, next, finally*
- To add information: *and, also, too*
- To show differences: *but, in contrast, however*
- To introduce an example: *for example, for instance*
- To show cause and effect: *because, therefore*

You can find more information about using transitions on p. 42.

List Your Points

To check that your ideas are ordered effectively, press the "enter" key after each sentence. The sentences will now be in a list. Read this list to determine if the sentences are correctly ordered, and move them around as necessary.

Zoe's Revised Draft

In her revised draft, Zoe improved her focus, added dialogue, reordered some ideas, and used transitions to make her writing clearer. Her revised draft still contains errors that she will correct when she edits her paragraph.

Loyalty

I never knew the true meaning of friendship until my good friend Ben defended me when I was unfairly accused of cheating. It happened my senior year of high school. We had a new teacher who had never taught before, he gave us an assignment to write a sonnet. I love poetry, I spent hours on it. The day after I handed it in, the teacher began class by accussing me of cheating. "There's no way a seventeen-year-old could write a poem like that," he said. "It's to good." I was stunned, all I could do was stare at the freckles on his face. Suddenly I hear Ben yell, "she wrote it herself"! However, the teacher just shook his head and told me to go to the principal's office. When I stood up to leave, Ben did, too. We were both suspended for three days. Without

Ben, I don't know how I could have gotten through that experience. Even though being accused of cheating is a terrible experience, it made me realize what a good friend Ben was.

GROUP ACTIVITY: Analyze Zoe's Revised Draft

Use the following questions to discuss with your classmates the ways that Zoe has improved her draft.

1. How has Zoe strengthened her focus?

   ____

   ____

2. How well has Zoe used details and dialogue to build her support?

   ____

   ____

   ____

3. In her revised draft, Zoe omitted the part about being published in a literary magazine. How effective was this change?

   ____

   ____

4. What transitions has Zoe added in the revised draft? How do these transitions improve her writing?

   ____

   ____

5. What can Zoe do to make her revised draft better?

   ____

WRITING ACTIVITY 8 (Group): Peer Review

Form a group with two or three classmates and exchange copies of your drafts. Read your draft aloud while your classmates follow along. Take notes on your classmates' answers to the following questions about your draft.

1. What do you like best about my draft?
2. How well does my topic sentence state the main point? Do you have suggestions for how to improve it?
3. Where can I strengthen my focus?
4. Where can I add dialogue?
5. Are my ideas arranged in the best order? Can you suggest an improvement?

Peer Review Online
If your class has a Web site, you may be able to do peer review online. Access the peer review questions and send your responses to the writer's e-mail box.

WRITING ACTIVITY 9: Revise Your Draft

Before you revise your draft, review Zoe's drafts and your analysis of her revision. Then, take your classmates' peer review suggestions into consideration. Revise your draft. In particular, delete unnecessary details, reorganize your sentences to be in chronological order, and consider including dialogue to emphasize your main point.

STEP 4: EDIT YOUR PARAGRAPH

You're now ready to edit your paragraph to correct errors in sentence structure, word choice, grammar, spelling, and punctuation. In particular, concentrate on correcting comma splices. Remember — the fewer errors you have, the more impressed your readers will be.

What Is a Comma Splice?

A *comma splice* is a type of error that happens when two complete sentences are joined *only* by a comma. (Keep in mind that a sentence must contain a subject and a verb, and must express a complete thought.) Here are some examples of comma splices:

COMMA SPLICE Sarah has been my best friend for years, we first met in kindergarten.

COMMA SPLICE My best friend is my dad, I can tell him anything.

COMMA SPLICE People who live a long time usually have lots of friends, they stay active in their communities.

Correcting Comma Splices

How do you correct a comma splice?

To learn more about correcting comma splices, turn to pp. 561–66.

1. *Break the comma splice into two sentences:*

   CORRECT Sarah has been my best friend for years. We first met in kindergarten.

2. *Use a comma and a coordinating conjunction:*

   CORRECT My best friend is my dad, and I can tell him anything.

3. *Replace the comma with a semicolon.* You may follow the semicolon with a conjunctive adverb (such as *however, in addition, also, therefore, furthermore*) and a comma if you like:

   CORRECT People who live long lives usually have lots of friends; they stay active in their communities.

   CORRECT People who live long lives usually have lots of friends; *in addition,* they stay active in their communities.

HOW TO Correct Comma Splices

- Break the comma splice up into two sentences. OR
- Use a comma and a coordinating conjunction (*for, and, nor, but, or, yet, so*). OR
- Use a semicolon instead of a comma.

EDITING PRACTICE: Correcting Comma Splices

Selecting the method that works the best, correct the comma splices in the following items. Use each method of correction at least once. Two of the sentences are correct.

1. One of the most unrealistic shows on television was *Friends,* the characters were so good looking and had so much time on their hands.

   ____

   ____

2. The actresses on the show were very thin, I wonder if they had an eating disorder.

3. All of the characters wore the latest styles, their hair was perfectly done.

4. They seemed to spend all their time in Monica and Rachel's apartment, didn't they have jobs?

5. Sometimes you see them working, they all seemed to make mistakes on the job.

6. For instance, Ross once dated one of his students.

7. Rachel dated her assistant, Joey lost his job on a soap opera.

8. I wonder how they managec to pay thc rent on their expensive apartments.

9. I know *Friends* is just a TV show, its lack of realism still bothers me.

10. It doesn't bother me too much, I watch reruns whenever I can.

Exercise Central
The *Discoveries* Web site includes additional practice exercises in correcting comma splices. Go to **bedfordstmartins.com /discoveries**, click on "Exercise Central," and select "Comma Splices."

Zoe's Edited Paragraph

When she edited her paragraph, Zoe improved her sentence structure, word choice, grammar, punctuation, and spelling. The corrected errors are underlined.

Loyalty

I never knew the true meaning of friendship until my good friend Ben defended me when I was unfairly accused of cheating. It happened my senior year of high school. We had a new teacher who had never taught before; he gave us an assignment to write a sonnet. I love poetry, so I spent hours on it. The day after I handed it in, the teacher began class by accusing me of cheating. "There's no way a seventeen-year-old could write a poem like that," he said. "It's too good." I was stunned. All I could do was stare at the freckles on his face. Suddenly I hear Ben yell, "She wrote it herself!" However, the teacher just shook his head and told me to go to the principal's office. When I stood up to leave, Ben did, too. We were both suspended for three days. Without Ben, I don't know how I could have gotten through that experience. Even though being accused of cheating is a terrible experience, it made me realize what a good friend Ben was.

To improve your spelling, study the spelling rules on pp. 584–90.

To learn more about how to punctuate dialogue, study the punctuation rules on pp. 621–25.

WRITING ACTIVITY 10: Edit Your Paragraph

Edit your paragraph, consulting a dictionary and the Handbook in Part Four of this book as necessary. Pay particular attention to comma splices. Add your corrections to your editing log so you won't make the same errors in the future.

Editing logs are explained on pp. 45–46.

STEP 5: SHARE YOUR PARAGRAPH

After sharing her paragraph with her classmates and instructor, Zoe put her paragraph about Ben on her personal Web page and asked him to read it. Although he didn't say much, Zoe could tell he was touched. Other friends and family members also read the paragraph on Zoe's Web site.

ADDITIONAL WRITING ASSIGNMENTS

1. Select a photograph that shows a special event in your life. Write a paragraph that tells the story of that special event.
2. Write a paragraph that tells the story of what you have done today. Try to make the paragraph interesting to someone who doesn't know you.
3. Write a paragraph that tells the story of a disagreement that you had with someone. Use dialogue and details to make the disagreement interesting. How was the disagreement resolved? What, if anything, did you learn from it?
4. Memorable events are often accompanied by music. Select one of your favorite pieces of music and write a story about an event that took place when you were listening to it.

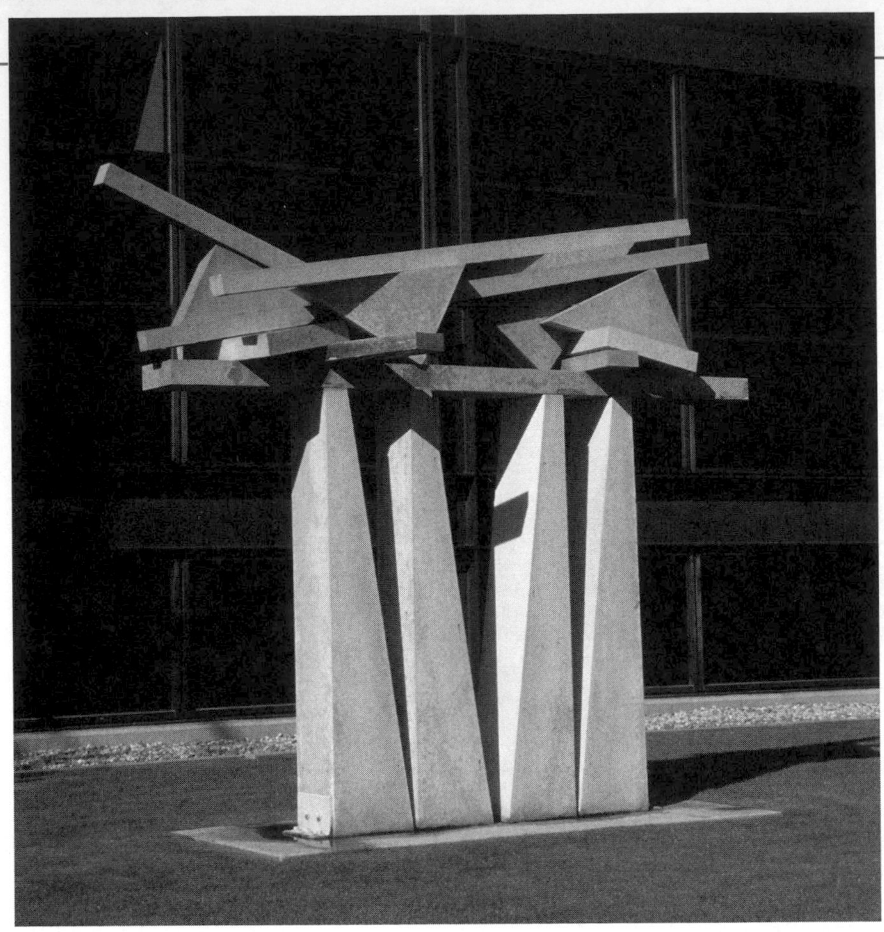

How would you describe this sculpture to someone who cannot see it? You might start by saying that its four concrete columns are close to one another and are leaning a bit, like four people in line who have just been pushed by the crowd and are trying to keep their balance, and that the columns are narrower on top than on bottom. In this chapter, you will use words to help someone imagine what you see.

CHAPTER

5

Writing a Paragraph That Describes

In this chapter, you will

- discover how description works.
- cluster to gather ideas.
- write about something interesting on or near your campus.
- use directional order to organize your points.
- edit for run-on sentences.
- submit your paragraph to your campus newspaper.

UNDERSTANDING DESCRIPTION

Imagine that you have just returned home from playing softball with some friends at the park. As you pull into the driveway, you realize that you left your glove behind. You're in a hurry because you're late for work. You call to your brother, "Hey, Dan, can you go get my glove?"

"Yeah, but where exactly is it?" Dan replies.

You tell him where to find the glove: "It's on a bench at Ponder Park. Ponder Park is the one next to the old amusement park where we used to ride that rickety roller coaster. The bench is the broken one on the hill near the stream. You'll know you're getting close when you can hear the water and see the huge oak tree with the tire swing."

What you have done is used description. Describing is like painting a picture. Just as an artist uses colors and brushstrokes to show a scene, a writer uses words to show a person, a place, an animal, or an object. Description answers the following kinds of questions:

- What do you see?
- What do you hear?
- What do you feel?
- What do you smell?
- What do you taste?

When you write a paragraph that describes, your goal is to create an image that your readers can picture in their minds as clearly as if they were right there with you.

READING PARAGRAPHS THAT DESCRIBE

The following two paragraphs show how other writers have used description to write about animals or places that interested them.

An Interesting Animal

You have probably noticed many interesting people and animals around your own college campus. In this paragraph, Jane and Michael Stern describe an unusual creature they saw at a dog show held in a local park.

JANE AND MICHAEL STERN

from "Dog Show"

Even though the sky is blazingly blue and it is T-shirt weather, Randall, a Chinese Crested dog, is shivering outside of ring 21, where he is scheduled to be judged at 9:50 A.M. It is no wonder he is cold: except for a leonine tuft of hair on the top of his head, and a few fluffs from the knees down, Randall is hairless. He is sitting on his owner Lee Bakuckas's lap as she rubs his bare skin with Nivea cream and fluffs his mane with a comb. He is a spectacularly weird-looking creature. His naked skin is bright pink with big mauve polka dots that make him look like something Dr. Doolittle created as a whim, and he is smaller than a house cat. A handful of gawkers gather to watch Randall being groomed.

READING ACTIVITY 1: Build Your Vocabulary

Try to determine the meanings of the following words from Jane and Michael Stern's paragraph. Then, check their meanings by looking them up in a dictionary.

blazingly ______________________

shivering ______________________

leonine ______________________

tuft ______________________

fluffs ______________________

spectacularly ______________________

mauve ______________________

whim ______________________

gawkers ______________________

READING ACTIVITY 2: Read to Improve Your Writing

Read and answer the following questions about the paragraph from "Dog Show."

1. What are the authors describing in the paragraph? In which sentence is their topic revealed?

____

____

2. Where do the authors use description to increase interest and help their readers imagine what they are describing?

 ____

 ____

3. Why do people gawk at the way Randall is being groomed?

 ____

 ____

4. Where on or near your campus would you be most likely to spot an interesting person or animal?

 ____

An Interesting Place

Interesting natural landscapes are all around us. In this paragraph, a ninety-year-old grandmother who walked from Los Angeles to Washington, D.C., describes the Mojave Desert on the first day of her journey.

DORIS HADDOCK

from Granny D

To begin a day's walk in California's Mojave Desert is like stepping into a child's drawing. Odd, Dr. Seuss-style cacti interrupt a dot pattern of endlessly repeating gray bushes; the sky is crayoned a solid, royal blue with a brilliant sun; layers of purple hills extend in endless vistas to the next valley and next again. There are no sounds but the mesquite-scented breezes whishing lightly across the brittlebush and the occasional flinch of some tiny, prehistoric creature under dry sticks a few paces ahead.

READING ACTIVITY 3: Build Your Vocabulary

Try to determine the meanings of the following words from Doris Haddock's paragraph. Then, check their meanings by looking the words up in a dictionary.

vistas ____

mesquite ____

whishing ____

brittlebush ______________________________

prehistoric ______________________________

READING ACTIVITY 4: Read to Improve Your Writing

Read and answer the following questions about the paragraph from *Granny D.*

1. What is the main idea of Doris Haddock's paragraph?

   ____

2. How does Haddock use description to increase interest and help her readers imagine what she is describing?

   ____

   ____

   ____

3. Why does Haddock describe the desert animals as "prehistoric"?

   ____

   ____

   ____

4. Where on or near campus would you be most likely to spot an interesting place or object?

   ____

Writing Assignment

The campus newspaper is publishing a series on campus life. You and your fellow classmates decide to submit your writing for consideration.

- Write a paragraph in which you describe an interesting person or animal on or near your college campus.

  OR

- Write a paragraph in which you describe an interesting place or object on or near your campus.

STEP 1: DISCOVER IDEAS FOR WRITING

You can write a descriptive paragraph on just about anything. As you look around for a topic, then, try to find something that not only interests you but will also interest your readers. Look, also, for something that you can describe in detail.

Choosing a Topic

For more advice on how to choose a topic, refer to p. 19.

In the sample paragraphs you read earlier, the authors wrote about things that were interesting because they were unusual: Doris Haddock described a strange place, and Jane and Michael Stern described a funny-looking animal. But you might find something interesting for other reasons: Maybe it's beautiful (or ugly), mysterious, surprising, new (or old), or overlooked, for example.

For your paragraph, you can write about a person, an animal, a place, or an object. Start with where you're sitting right now: Do you notice anything interesting? You can also find a topic by asking yourself some of the following questions: Who fascinates you? Do you have a favorite animal, maybe a pet? Is there a special place you like to go to? What is your most prized possession? Whatever you decide to write about, be sure it is something that will interest both you and your readers.

Explore Re: Writing Links Libraries
To help you brainstorm topic ideas, go to the Re: Writing Web site at **bedfordstmartins.com/rewriting** and click on "Links Libraries."

Considering Your Audience and Purpose

For more information on audience and purpose, see pp. 20–22.

Since your paragraph might be published in the school newspaper, your audience will consist mostly of other students at your school. How much do they already know about what you will describe? What will they need to know to be able to picture it? Could a fellow student point out the person, animal, place, or object after reading your paragraph?

Consider, also, your purpose for writing this paragraph. Is your purpose to share your feelings about this person, place, animal or object, to inform your readers of something you have learned about it, or to persuade them to look at it differently? Paragraphs that describe can do any of these things, but choosing one purpose over the others will make it easier to focus.

WRITING ACTIVITY 1: Analyze Your Audience and Purpose

Keeping in mind your audience of fellow students, answer the following questions about your readers.

1. What are you going to describe?

____

____

____

2. What will your audience likely already know about the person, animal, place, or object you describe?

____

____

____

3. What might they not know?

____

____

____

4. How interested will your audience be in the person, animal, place, or object you describe? What can you focus on to make it more interesting?

____

____

____

5. What is your primary purpose for writing this paragraph?

____

____

____

Clustering to Gather Ideas

Learn more about clustering on p. 25.

Clustering is a useful technique that can help you gather and organize your thoughts. Especially if you're a visual thinker, drawing connections can open your eyes to fresh ways of looking at something.

To begin clustering, write your topic in the center of a blank page and draw a circle around it. Then, as ideas about the topic come to mind, write them down, put circles around them, and draw lines from them to the center circle. As you think of ways to describe your ideas, write the descriptions down, circle them, and join these circles to the ideas they describe.

HOW TO Cluster for a Paragraph That Describes

- Write the name of a person, an animal, a place, or an object in the center of the page. Circle this topic.
- Use your five senses — sight, hearing, touch, smell, and taste — to think of ways to describe your topic.
- Circle these words or phrases and draw a line to connect them to the main idea circle.
- Add details to describe these ideas.
- Circle these details and connect them to your idea circles.

Here is how student writer Herminia clustered on the topic of an interesting object she found on campus.

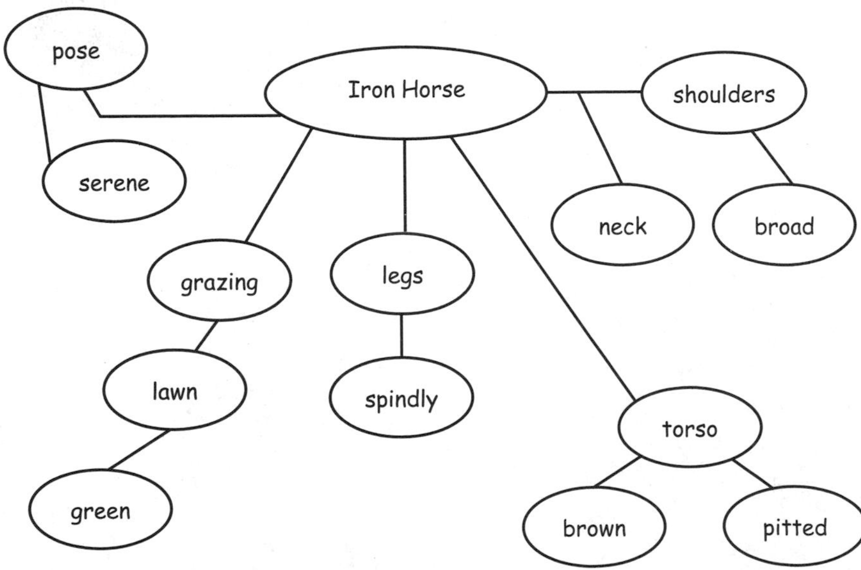

Cluster on the Computer
Use the drawing or picture option of your word-processing program to create your cluster.

WRITING ACTIVITY 2: Cluster Your Topic

Create a cluster that describes an interesting person or animal you have seen on or near campus. Then create a cluster that describes an unusual place or object. Use the five senses — sight, hearing, touch, smell, and taste — to help you. Decide which cluster would work better as a paragraph.

Narrowing Your Topic

Imagine taking a photograph of the ocean. The lens is wide open so that you see the water for miles. Now imagine zooming in on the same scene. The close-up lets you see details — the gulls swooping over the water, the colors of the waves. When you write your paragraph, you zoom in on a topic so your reader can picture the details.

To find out more about narrowing a topic, turn to pp. 29–29.

Be sure that you have selected a topic that you can describe well in one paragraph. If, for example, you decide to describe older students on your campus, you can't describe all of them well in one paragraph. You can narrow this topic by selecting one interesting older student and describing him or her in detail.

HOW TO Use Clustering to Narrow a Topic

- Select a person, an animal, a place, or an object to describe.
- Create a cluster for this topic.
- Notice which part of the cluster is most crowded with ideas. What topic is it on?
- Create a separate cluster for that topic.
- Decide if your new cluster contains the right amount of detail to include in one paragraph.

WRITING ACTIVITY 3: Narrow Your Topic

Look again at the topic you have chosen in Writing Activity 2. Is it narrow enough to describe well in one paragraph? If necessary, create another cluster to narrow your topic further.

STEP 2: WRITE YOUR DISCOVERY DRAFT

With your topic in hand, you're ready to move to the next stage of the writing process. Drafting gives you an opportunity to make sense of your ideas and put them together for your readers.

Drafting a Topic Sentence

To review writing topic sentences, see pp. 30–31.

For a paragraph using description, the topic sentence identifies what you are going to describe and states why it is interesting.

For example, in the paragraph from *Granny D,* Haddock's topic sentence explains that the Mojave Desert is interesting because it is unusual:

> **To begin a day's walk in California's Mojave Desert is like stepping into a child's drawing.**

By comparing the desert to something most people are familiar with, Haddock helps her readers see the desert the way she sees it. This topic sentence also lets her readers know that she will describe what makes the Mojave Desert seem like a child's drawing.

In "Dog Show," the Sterns use their topic sentence to identify their topic and describe the surroundings. By beginning this way, they help their readers imagine the scene:

> **Even though the sky is blazingly blue and it is T-shirt weather, Randall, a Chinese Crested dog, is shivering outside of ring 21, where he is scheduled to be judged at 9:50 A.M.**

This topic sentence lets the Sterns' readers know that the topic of the paragraph will be Randall and that he is interesting because he is an unusual kind of dog.

Here are examples of topic sentences written by student writers about an interesting person or animal:

> As I dug my books out of my pack, a very young couple with an eighteen-month-old girl caught my attention.

> A feral cat that students have named Cougar has the run of our campus.

Here are examples of topic sentences, also written by student writers, about an unusual place or object.

> The Fitness Center shocks visitors with its daring architecture.

> My room has the weirdest desk you have ever seen in a college dorm.

HOW TO Write a Topic Sentence for a Paragraph That Describes

- Identify the person, animal, place, or object that you will describe.
- State briefly what makes your topic unusual or interesting.
- Consider describing the surroundings where your subject is located.
- Be sure that you have enough information to describe your topic in detail.

WRITING ACTIVITY 4: Draft a Topic Sentence

Look again at your narrowed topic. Write a topic sentence that identifies what you are going to describe and states why it is interesting or unusual.

Adding Support with Descriptions

Look back at your clustering. Select the sights, sounds, sensations, smells, and tastes that will bring your topic to life. Turning these words and phrases into sentences will create the support you need for your paragraph. The details you select should also help your readers understand why you think the person or place is interesting or the animal or object unusual.

Read about other ways of adding support on pp. 31–34.

Using the cluster she created, Herminia prepared the following descriptions to include in her paragraph:

> The iron horse stands in the middle of a small patch of green lawn.
> The legs support a boxy torso.
> His shoulders hold and brace the body and balance the neck and head.
> Together they extend full-length down to the nourishing grass.
> The shoulders of this sculpture, broad and jagged, come together to a single point and reach for the sky.

WRITING ACTIVITY 5: Develop Details

Looking again at the cluster you created for your topic, select the words and phrases that create a clear image of the person, place, animal, or object you are describing. Turn them into sentences.

Drafting a Concluding Sentence

To review the characteristics of an effective concluding sentence, see pp. 34–35.

For a paragraph that describes, the concluding sentence sums up what you have described or leaves your readers with a lasting impression of the person, animal, place, or object you wrote about.

Look again at the concluding sentence of one of the paragraphs you read earlier. The Sterns end their paragraph with this sentence:

> **A handful of gawkers gather to watch Randall being groomed.**

This conclusion provides a lasting impression of just how unusual Randall is: He is such a strange dog that people gather around to stare at him.

Bold Your Concluding Sentence
Bold your concluding sentence, and then read it by itself. Does it sum up or leave a lasting impression of your topic?

WRITING ACTIVITY 6: Draft a Concluding Sentence

Write a sentence that sums up what you have described or leaves your readers with a lasting impression of your person, place, animal, or object.

Herminia's Discovery Draft

Herminia wrote the following discovery draft describing the statue of an iron horse on her college campus. (Herminia's draft still includes a couple of errors. She will correct these when she edits.)

The Iron Horse

The iron horse sculpture stands by itself in the middle of a small patch of green lawn. The legs support a boxy torso. Like mighty hands, the shoulders hold and brace the body and balance the neck and head; together they extend full-length down to the nourishing grass. The shoulders of this sculpture, broad and jagged, come together to a single point and reach for the sky. The sky is

```
threatening rain. The pose is serene, the appearance
of this grazing iron horse evokes an image of life
and strength.
```

WRITING ACTIVITY 7: Complete Your Discovery Draft

Using your topic sentence, descriptive support, and concluding sentence, write a discovery draft. Concentrate on how best to describe the person, animal, place, or object you have chosen. You'll have time to improve your draft later.

STEP 3: REVISE YOUR PARAGRAPH

To revise a paragraph that describes, you clarify and arrange what you have said so that your fellow students will imagine the person, place, animal, or object you have described well enough to recognize it if they stumble across it.

Strengthening Your Focus

It's important that each sentence in your descriptive paragraph supports and develops your topic sentence. Although you can include information about where you found your subject, as the Sterns did, your paragraph should focus on the thing you're describing. You may have noticed that one sentence in Herminia's draft did not specifically focus on the iron horse itself:

The importance of building support is explained on pp. 38–39.

```
The sky is threatening rain.
```

When Herminia revised her paragraph, she improved her focus by deleting this sentence.

Building Your Support with Descriptive Details

A key part of revising a paragraph that describes is to be sure that you have included enough details to let your readers imagine what you are describing. Descriptive details include adjectives and adverbs — such as colors, shapes, positions, and textures — that help your reader imagine your subject. For instance, "the girl in the car" is general. In contrast, "the red-haired, freckled girl asleep in the backseat of the Jeep" uses descriptive detail.

Student writer Herminia added new details to her revised paragraph to help her readers better "see" the iron horse sculpture. For example, she described exactly where the horse was located. She also added descriptive details to some of her other sentences:

DRAFT The legs support a boxy torso.

REVISED The legs support a boxy torso, rusty brown, pitted, and hollow.

DRAFT His shoulders hold and brace the body and balance the neck and head.

REVISED His shoulders hold and brace the body and balance the thick rectangular neck and head.

HOW TO Build Support for a Paragraph That Describes

- Check that you provide enough description to help your reader imagine what you are describing. Add new descriptions to complete your image.
- Add descriptive details to help your reader see, hear, feel, smell, and taste what you are describing.
- Be sure that each descriptive detail adds interest and helps your reader understand your main point.

Using Directional Order to Organize Your Points

To learn more about ordering your points, see pp. 39–42.

A descriptive paragraph usually uses *directional* order to describe a person or an object from one direction to another — such as left to right, top to bottom, or near to far. This helps your readers develop a complete image of what you are describing.

When using directional order, try to include transitional words and phrases, such as *next to* or *above,* that tell your readers how the different details connect to each other.

HOW TO Connect Ideas in a Paragraph That Describes

You can find more information about using transitions on p. 42.

Here are some words and phrases that can help readers follow a description that uses directional order:

- next to
- behind

- in front of
- above
- underneath
- close by
- farther away
- to the left (or right)
- at the same time

When Herminia revised her paragraph on the iron horse sculpture, she reordered her points to describe the horse from its legs to its head (bottom-to-top order). She also added transitions to help her readers visually follow her description.

Cut and Paste
Use the cut and paste features of your word-processing program to move sentences around as you reorder them.

Herminia's Revised Draft

Herminia revised her draft to be better focused, use more descriptive details, follow directional organization, and include transitions. Her revised draft still contains a few errors, but she will correct them when she edits.

The Iron Horse

The iron horse Sculpture stands by itself in the middle of a small patch of green lawn in front of the campus library. The long, thin legs of the horse support a boxy torso, rusty brown, pitted and hollow. Like mighty hands, the shoulders hold and brace the body and balance the thick rectangular neck and head together they extend full-length down to the nourishing grass. The open mouth nibbles the top of the small, green blades of grass the shoulders of this sculpture, broad and jagged, come together to a single point that reach for the sky. If this horse could move, the movements would be slow and deliberite and the walk strong and steady.

```
Although the pose is serene, the appearance of
this grazing iron horse evokes an image of life
and strength.
```

GROUP ACTIVITY: Analyze Herminia's Revised Draft

Use the following questions to discuss with your classmates how Herminia has improved her draft.

1. Compare Herminia's topic sentence in her discovery draft with the one in her revised draft. Is the topic sentence in the revised draft better? Why or why not?

   ____

   ____

2. What descriptive details did Herminia add to her draft to make it more interesting and informative?

   ____

3. In the revised draft, Herminia added transitional words. How do these words help her readers follow her train of thought?

   ____

   ____

   ____

   ____

4. What more could Herminia do to make her draft better?

   ____

   ____

   ____

WRITING ACTIVITY 8 (Group): Peer Review

Form a group with two or three classmates and exchange copies of your drafts. Read your drafts aloud while your classmates follow along. Take notes on your classmates' answers to the following questions about your draft.

1. What do you like best about my paragraph?
2. How clear is my topic sentence? Do you have any suggestions for improving it?
3. Where could I add more descriptive details to help you better imagine this person, place, animal, or object? Do I need to add or delete details to help you imagine what I'm describing?
4. Have I described my topic using directional order? Do you have any suggestions for a better way to order these details?
5. How well do I describe this person, place, animal, or object to my audience, college students?

WRITING ACTIVITY 9: Revise Your Draft

Using Herminia's drafts as a model, revise your own draft. With your classmates' peer review comments in mind, strengthen your focus, build your support with descriptive details, and organize your points using directional order.

STEP 4: EDIT YOUR PARAGRAPH

The fewer errors you make in your paragraph, the better your readers will be able to imagine the person, animal, place, or object you've worked so hard to describe. In this chapter, you will focus on eliminating run-on sentences.

What Is a Run-on Sentence?

A *run-on sentence* occurs when two complete sentences, or independent clauses, are written together without any punctuation between them, as if they were one sentence. Here are some examples of run-on sentences:

RUN-ON For my paragraph I wrote about my favorite instructor I really enjoy her laugh.

RUN-ON I decided to walk right up to the fountain so that I could describe it I got drenched.

RUN-ON Most of my friends like the new Web page I designed now they are using the ideas for their own pages.

See pp. 554–56 to learn more about run-on sentences.

Correcting Run-on Sentences

How do you correct a run-on?

1. *Use a period.*

   CORRECT For my paragraph I wrote about my favorite instructor. I really enjoy her laugh.

2. *Use a semicolon.* You may follow the semicolon with a conjunctive adverb (such as *however, in addition, also, therefore, furthermore*) and a comma if you like:

   CORRECT I decided to walk right up to the fountain so that I could describe it; I got drenched.

   CORRECT I decided to walk right up to the fountain so that I could describe it; as a result, I got drenched.

3. *Use a comma and a conjunction.*

   CORRECT Most of my friends like the new Web page I designed, so now they are using the ideas for their own pages.

HOW TO Correct Run-on Sentences

A run-on sentence consists of two sentences punctuated as one. To correct:

- Separate it into two sentences.

  OR

- Separate the independent clauses with a semicolon.

  OR

- Separate the independent clauses with a comma and a conjunction.

EDITING PRACTICE: Correcting Run-on Sentences

Selecting the method that works the best, correct the run-on sentences in the following items. Some of the sentences are correct.

EXAMPLE

RUN-ON The boy rode his bicycle he didn't know how to ride very well.

CORRECT The boy rode his bicycle, but he didn't know how to ride very well.

1. My favorite teacher is so interesting she knows how to make us laugh.

 ____

 ____

2. I interviewed the museum curator for this paragraph he wasn't anything like I expected.

 ____

 ____

3. The student who slouches into lab each day is interesting I think I'll describe him.

 ____

 ____

4. Every time I pass the poster in the Science Building, it seems to be looking at me now that is really unusual.

 ____

 ____

5. That contraption they have in the gym is strange it looks like a torture device.

 ____

 ____

6. The art studio contains several unique objects the one I like best, though, is the crane.

 ____

 ____

7. You write about the swimming pool I'll write about something else.

 ____

8. The strangest thing around here is that ugly sign in front of the Administration Building nothing could look worse.

 ____

 ____

9. I'll write about that strange lab specimen you asked for it.

___

10. He moved carefully even though he was old he was still a good-looking man.

___

___

Exercise Central
The *Discoveries* Web site includes additional practice exercises in correcting run-on sentences. Go to **bedfordstmartins.com/discoveries**, click on "Exercise Central," and select "Run-on Sentences."

Herminia's Edited Paragraph

Herminia's revised draft had some errors. She corrected these in her edited paragraph. (The underlining indicates where she corrected errors.)

The Iron Horse

The iron horse sculpture stands by itself in the middle of a small patch of green lawn in front of the campus library. The long, thin legs of the horse support a boxy torso, rusty brown, pitted and hollow. Like mighty hands, the shoulders hold and brace the body and balance the thick rectangular neck and head; together they extend full-length down to the nourishing grass. As the open mouth nibbles the top of the small, green blades of grass, the shoulders of this sculpture, broad and jagged, come together to a single point that reaches for the sky. If this horse could move, the movements would be slow and deliberate and the walk strong and steady. Although the pose is serene, the appearance of this grazing iron horse evokes an image of life and strength.

WRITING ACTIVITY 10: Edit Your Paragraph

Using a dictionary and the Handbook in Part Four of this book, edit your draft. Add your corrections to your editing log so you don't make the same errors in the future.

For a review of how to create an editing log, see pp. 45–46.

STEP 5: SHARE YOUR PARAGRAPH

Herminia and her classmates gave their descriptions to the campus newspaper for an ongoing feature on campus life. The newspaper editor printed ten of the best paragraphs without their titles as a quiz, inviting readers to identify or locate the people, places, animals, and objects described in the students' paragraphs. Every contestant found Herminia's horse sculpture easily.

ADDITIONAL WRITING ASSIGNMENTS

1. Write a paragraph for your fellow classmates describing your favorite person. Try to show this person's good qualities through description.
2. Write a paragraph to your instructor describing your study location. Select details that support how well-prepared you are to complete your assignments for this class.
3. Write a paragraph to your campus newspaper describing an area of campus that needs to be renovated or cleaned up. Use the five senses to ensure that you provide a complete description of what needs to be done.
4. Write a paragraph to your local newspaper describing a local performance that you attended. Use details in such a way that your readers will be able to tell whether you enjoyed this performance.

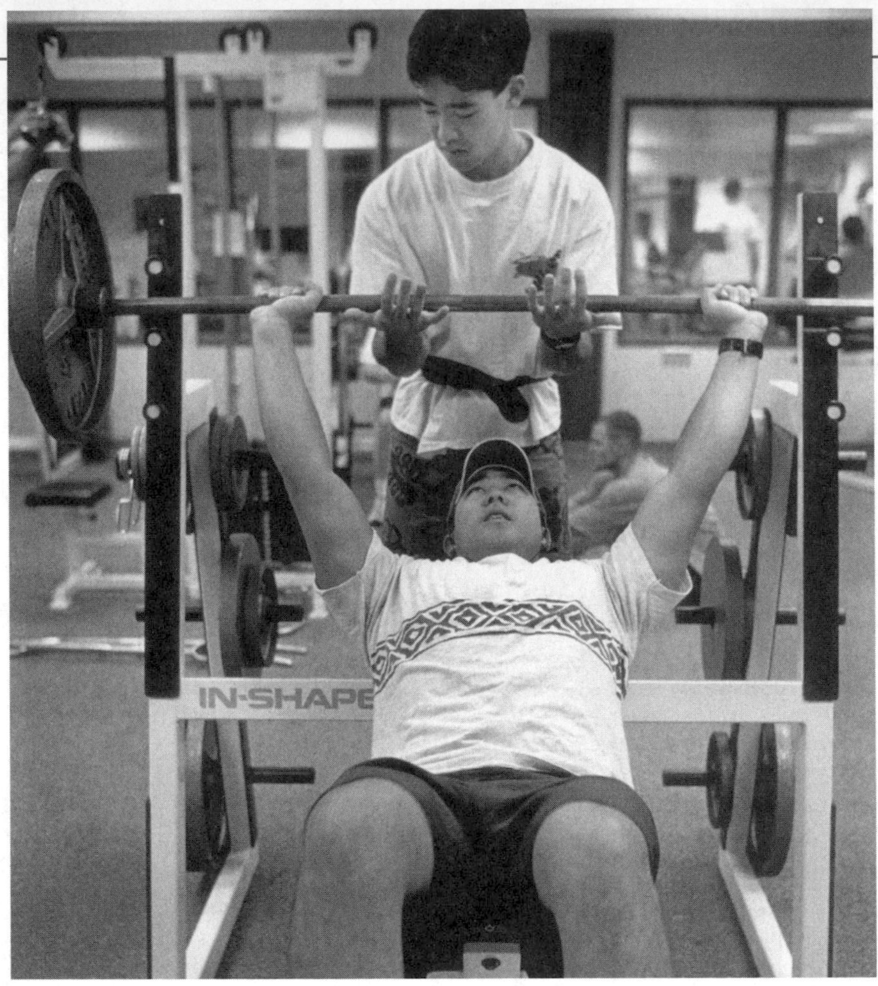

To bench press safely, you should follow a process: first, you should ask a friend to "spot" you, as the young man in this photograph did; next, you should choose an appropriate amount of weight to lift, based on your strength and your goals; finally, you should lift the weight with your arms perpendicular to the floor and your lower back flat. In this chapter, you will describe a process in order to teach your readers how to do something or to explain how something happens or works.

CHAPTER

6

Writing a Paragraph That Explains a Process

In this chapter, you will

- discover how process explanation works.
- outline to gather ideas.
- write about something you do or know.
- use sequential order to organize your points.
- edit for subject-verb agreement.
- create a booklet with your classmates.

UNDERSTANDING PROCESS EXPLANATION

Do you remember when you first learned to drive? Somebody probably taught you how to use the brake and the accelerator, how to shift gears, how to back up, how to merge into traffic, and how to parallel park. That person explained the *process* of driving.

Writers use process explanation to teach other people how to do something or to show how something happens. A recipe, which tells how to cook something, is an example of process writing. A magazine article that outlines how traders buy and sell stock on Wall Street is another example. Process explanation answers questions like these:

- How do you do that?
- How can I do that?
- How does that happen?
- How does that work?

When writing a process paragraph, you use a step-by-step structure to give your readers all of the information they need to do or to understand what you're explaining.

READING PARAGRAPHS THAT EXPLAIN A PROCESS

Process explanation can tell readers how to do something themselves, or it can show how something happens. The following two paragraphs offer examples of each kind of process writing.

How to Do Something

Almost everyone wants to stay cool in the summer. In many areas, people use air conditioning. In some areas with low humidity, swamp coolers — which use water to cool the air — are also popular. In "How to Service Your Swamp Cooler," Robert Rowley explains how to prepare these devices for another year of use.

ROBERT ROWLEY

"How to Service Your Swamp Cooler"

The evaporative cooler — or "swamp cooler" as it is frequently called in the desert Southwest — is a device that uses water evaporation to cool a home. A swamp cooler needs to be serviced every spring before it's turned on for the summer.

All it takes to service the cooler is a few simple steps. First, climb onto your roof and remove the side panels from the cooler. Next, using a whisk broom and dust pan, sweep up the debris from the floor of the cooler. Then, inspect the float (which looks like a plump rubber tube). If it's rusty, you'll have to buy a new float at a hardware store. After finishing with the float, the next step is to test the tightness of the fan belt by gently pulling on the rubber; the belt should give just a bit. Go to the other side of the cooler and plug the water pump into the electrical outlet. Finally, turn on the water by flipping the switch next to the copper pipe. Then, go into your house and flip on the switch that turns on the cooler. You have now successfully serviced your cooler so that it will cool your house for another year.

READING ACTIVITY 1: Build Your Vocabulary

Try to determine the meanings of the following words from "How to Service Your Swamp Cooler." Then, check their meanings by looking the words up in a dictionary.

service ______________________

device ______________________

evaporation ______________________

whisk broom ______________________

debris ______________________

READING ACTIVITY 2: Read to Improve Your Writing

Read and answer the following questions about "How to Service Your Swamp Cooler."

1. What is the topic sentence of the paragraph?

   ____

2. What description and information does Rowley give to make the process clear to his readers?

   ____

   ____

   ____

3. Why does Rowley explain what a swamp cooler is?

____

____

4. What could you teach readers to do?

____

How Something Happens

Smallpox is a deadly disease that medical scientists thought was gone but that seems to be coming back in some parts of the world. In the following paragraph from a book warning that smallpox could be used as a biological weapon, journalist Richard Preston explains what happens to a person who becomes infected with the smallpox virus.

RICHARD PRESTON

from "The Demon in the Freezer"

Smallpox is explosively contagious, and it travels through the air. Virus particles in the mouth become airborne when the host talks. If you inhale a single particle of smallpox, you can come down with the disease. After you've been infected, there is a typical incubation period of ten days. During that time, you feel normal. Then the illness hits with a spike of fever, a backache, and vomiting, and a bit later tiny red spots appear all over the body. The spots turn into blisters, called pustules, and the pustules enlarge, filling with pressurized opalescent pus. The eruption of pustules is sometimes called the splitting of the dermis. The skin doesn't break, but splits horizontally, tearing away from its underlayers. The pustules become hard, bloated sacs the size of peas, encasing the body with pus, and the skin resembles a cobblestone street.

READING ACTIVITY 3: Build Your Vocabulary

Try to determine the meanings of the following words from Richard Preston's paragraph. Then, check their meanings by looking the words up in a dictionary.

incubation _______________________________________

spike _______________________________________

opalescent _______________________________________

dermis ______________________________

sacs ______________________________

READING ACTIVITY 4: Read to Improve Your Writing

Read and answer the following questions about the paragraph from "The Demon in the Freezer."

1. What is the topic sentence of this paragraph?

____

____

2. What examples and descriptions does Richard Preston use to explain the process of becoming sick with smallpox?

____

____

____

3. Why does Preston state that the smallpox virus travels through the air before explaining what happens when a person catches the disease?

____

____

____

____

____

4. What processes do you understand that you could explain to readers?

____

Writing Assignment

Suppose you are participating in a leadership seminar, which has been limited to twenty college students from a variety of majors. The purpose of the program is to encourage students to be leaders in some aspect of their lives. As part of the program, you are asked to share your expert knowledge of something with the other participants.

- Write a paragraph in which you teach your readers how to do something you can do, such as train for a marathon, overcome stage fright, or tune a guitar.

  OR

- Write a paragraph in which you explain how something you're familiar with happens or works, such as a search engine, a local election, or compound interest.

STEP 1: DISCOVER IDEAS FOR WRITING

When writing a paragraph that explains a process, you will find it's best to focus on something that you yourself have done or have worked with. You wouldn't want to teach someone how to install a cable modem, for example, if you haven't installed one yourself. You should also think about who is going to read your paragraph: Will they be interested in what you're explaining?

Choosing a Topic

For more advice on how to choose a topic, refer to p. 19.

The sample paragraphs you read both focus on something the authors know from firsthand experience. Robert Rowley can explain how to service a swamp cooler because he has done it himself; Richard Preston knows how smallpox affects people because he spent years researching the disease and interviewing experts about it.

You can discover your topic by asking yourself questions about what you do. What skills do you have? What are your hobbies? Have you accomplished any goals that you set for yourself? Any of these things might make for a good "how-to" paragraph.

You can also ask yourself what you know because of what you do. If you volunteer with an ambulance crew or a rescue squad, for example, you could describe how the emergency room staff decides which patients to treat first.

Explore Re: Writing Links Libraries
To help you brainstorm topic ideas, go to the Re: Writing Web site at **bedfordstmartins.com/rewriting** and click on "Links Libraries."

Considering Your Audience and Purpose

For this chapter's assignment, your readers are college students who want to learn leadership skills. Because they have decided on a variety of majors, their interests and backgrounds will probably be different from yours. Your paragraph will need to give them new information that they can understand easily. At the same time, you will need to keep your readers' interest by explaining why understanding your topic will benefit them.

Read more about audience and purpose on pp. 20–22.

Consider, also, your purpose for writing. Process explanation is usually informative. Robert Rowley, for example, wrote his paragraph to teach people how to service a swamp cooler. Richard Preston wrote his paragraph about smallpox to let his readers know how it affects people.

Class Web Site

If your instructor has created a class Web site, use the bulletin board to post possible topics. Ask your fellow students which processes interest them the most. Tally their responses to help you choose a topic for your paragraph.

WRITING ACTIVITY 1: Identify Your Audience and Purpose

For this assignment, your readers will be college students with a variety of interests and backgrounds who are in a leadership seminar. Keep this in mind as you answer the following questions.

1. What things can you do or explain well?

____

____

____

2. Of these, what would your readers be most interested to learn?

____

____

____

3. What would make them want to read your paragraph?

____

____

____

4. What will your purpose be in writing this paragraph?

____

____

____

Outlining to Gather Ideas

To learn more about outlining to gather ideas, turn to pp. 26–27.

Now that you have selected a topic, you need to identify the steps involved in your process. You can do this by brainstorming, freewriting, or clustering, but probably the best way to gather ideas for a process paragraph is to make an informal outline.

Informal outlining is a form of brainstorming that organizes your ideas as you write them down. It allows you to make sense of a process before you write a single sentence. Outlining also helps you see where you'll need to include examples or description to make the process clear for your readers.

HOW TO Outline a Paragraph That Explains a Process

- Write your topic at the top of a page.
- Brainstorm all of the steps involved in the process.
- Put the steps in chronological order.
- Identify any steps that you will need to explain in more detail.
- List ideas (such as sub-steps, descriptions, and examples) for each of these steps.

For his paragraph, student writer Bud wanted to explain how to stop procrastinating. He thought of five things people can do to reach this goal, and wrote them down. Then, he added ideas about how each step works. Notice that he outlined more ideas than he could use so that he could select the best ones for his draft.

How to Stop Procrastinating

Figure out why you're procrastinating
- intimidated
- not interested
- too many other things to do

Schedule specific times to work on your project
- same time period every day

early in day to get it over with
make a habit of it
"Chunk" the task into smaller pieces
break up what you need to do
easier to get started
you won't get blocked
Work with a friend
friend must be motivated
don't goof off
share ideas
help each other
time will pass more quickly
Reward yourself when you're done
call a friend
eating, listening to music, playing a game
other rewards?
getting a good grade, I hope

Outline on the Computer
Use the bullets and numbering features of your word-processing program to format your outline. Creating your outline on the computer makes it easy to move ideas around until they make sense.

WRITING ACTIVITY 2: Create an Informal Outline

Outline the process you want to explain. Write down all of the steps involved, and identify the ones you'll need to explain. List sub-steps, descriptions, and examples where you can think of them.

Narrowing Your Topic

For more ideas about narrowing your topic, see pp. 27–29.

Your topic should be narrow enough to be explained in a single paragraph. You don't have to cover every single step of a process, just the important ones.

Suppose you are writing about how to take a good photograph with a digital camera. In your informal outline, you identified a lot of steps: choosing a camera, learning its features, selecting the right resolution, understanding optical and digital zoom, composing the shot, eliminating red-eye, uploading the image to a computer, printing on special paper, and e-mailing the photograph to friends and family. Any one of these steps would take a lot of time to explain, and you can't possibly cover them all in one paragraph. To narrow your topic, you might focus on just one of these steps, such as how to compose an interesting shot.

HOW TO Use Outlining to Narrow a Topic

- Outline the steps and sub-steps of the process you are explaining.
- Notice how many steps and sub-steps you have listed.
- If there are more than three or four steps, eliminate some of the less important steps.
- If one of the steps includes a lot of sub-steps, narrow your topic to focus on only that step.

When Bud gathered ideas about how to stop procrastinating, he came up with five steps. Since covering all of these steps would be too lengthy for a paragraph, he decided to write about only three of them.

WRITING ACTIVITY 3: Narrow Your Topic

Look at the outline you have created for your topic. If there are too many steps for a single paragraph, narrow the topic by explaining only part of the process or deleting any unnecessary steps.

STEP 2: WRITE YOUR DISCOVERY DRAFT

Now that you have selected your topic and identified the steps in the process you will explain, you're ready to begin drafting your paragraph. For a paragraph that explains a process, it's important that you provide enough detail so that a reader can perform the process or clearly imagine how it happens.

Drafting a Topic Sentence

More information about topic sentences can be found on pp. 30–31.

In a paragraph that explains how to do something or how something works, the topic sentence tells what process will be explained. It can also say why it is important to learn the process, or it can preview the major steps.

The following topic sentence identifies the topic and says why that topic is important:

> Preparing to run a marathon is hard but rewarding.

This topic sentence previews the steps in the process:

> To get ready to run a marathon, you need to run at regular intervals eat more carbohydrates, and properly treat your aching muscles.

Either type of topic sentence will work in a process paragraph.

HOW TO Write a Topic Sentence for a Paragraph That Explains a Process

- Identify the process you'll describe.
- Say why the process is important to learn or understand.

  OR
- Consider briefly listing the steps in the process.

WRITING ACTIVITY 4: Draft a Topic Sentence

Look again at your narrowed topic. Write a topic sentence that identifies the process you'll describe. Consider explaining the importance of the topic or the steps in the process.

Adding Support with Description and Examples

Look again at the steps in your informal outline. Are they understandable for somebody who isn't already familiar with your topic? Often, you can make a process easier to follow by providing examples and description that clarify your points.

Learn more about these ways to add support on pp. 31–34.

For his paragraph on overcoming procrastination, Bud chose three steps to explain. Then he brainstormed examples and descriptions for them:

STEP	Break up what you have to do into small pieces.
EXAMPLE	If you need to read twenty pages, start by reading only five.

DESCRIPTION	You don't get intimidated thinking of all that reading you have to do.
STEP	Do the studying with a friend who is a good student.
DESCRIPTION	It makes the time pass faster, and two heads are better than one.
STEP	Reward yourself when you're finished.
EXAMPLE	Listen to music or call a friend.

WRITING ACTIVITY 5: Develop Support

For each of the steps in your process, brainstorm description and examples to help make them easier to understand.

Drafting a Concluding Sentence

To learn more about concluding sentences, see pp. 34–35.

In your concluding sentence, you can briefly sum up the steps in the process. You can also show why the topic is important, or you can remind your readers what they have learned from your paragraph.

Bud came up with three possible concluding sentences for his paragraph:

> Because procrastination can keep you from achieving your goals, be sure to conquer it.
>
> Following these steps will help you conquer the bad habit of procrastination.
>
> When you stop procrastinating, you'll get better grades and be better prepared for the real world.

When he wrote his discovery draft, Bud chose the second option because he wanted to remind his readers what they had learned.

WRITING ACTIVITY 6: Draft a Concluding Sentence

Write several possible concluding sentences for your paragraph. Select the best one for your discovery draft, keeping in mind that you can always improve it as you revise your paragraph.

Bud's Discovery Draft

Bud used some of the ideas he had gathered by outlining steps and brainstorming descriptions and examples, but he also added new ideas as they came to him. Bud's draft contains errors typical of a discovery draft; he'll correct them later.

> Procrastination can keep you from getting good grades or doing well on your job. When you wait until the last minute to do something you usually don't do it well. Here is some ways to stop procrastinating. Break up what you have to do into small pieces. If you need to read 20 pages read only 5. This is called "chunking," and it makes studying seem easier. You don't get intimidated thinking of all that reading you have to do. Do the studying with a friend who is a good student. It makes the time pass faster, and two heads are better than one. But this won't work if you goof off. In the past I've goofed off a lot when I studied with my friends. Reward yourself when you're finished. Listen to music or call a friend. Following these steps will help you conquer the bad habit of procrastination.

WRITING ACTIVITY 7: Complete Your Discovery Draft

Beginning with the material you have already written for your topic sentence, supporting details, and concluding sentence, write a discovery draft on your topic. Pay more attention to getting your ideas down in paragraph form than to details such as grammar, punctuation, or spelling.

STEP 3: REVISE YOUR PARAGRAPH

To revise a paragraph that explains a process, look at your draft through the eyes of your readers. What might they find confusing or unclear? Where might they want more information? Make your paragraph easier to follow by strengthening your focus, building your support, and organizing your points.

Strengthening Your Focus

Every sentence in your paragraph — including examples and descriptions — must support the topic sentence directly. You might have noticed that the following sentence in Bud's draft supported a step but did not specifically relate to his topic.

```
In the past I goofed off a lot when I studied with my friends.
```

Bud deleted this sentence when he revised his paragraph.

Building Your Support with Appropriate Details

Have you ever followed a recipe that assumed you already knew how to do something unfamiliar, like blanching almonds? Or did the recipe include details you didn't need, such as a warning not to get eggshells in the batter?

When you revise your paragraph, make sure that your details are appropriate to your audience and your purpose. They should be specific enough for your readers to understand, but not so detailed that your readers will be frustrated or overwhelmed.

HOW TO Add Details to a Paragraph That Explains a Process

- Look at the steps from your readers' point of view. Does the process make sense for somebody not already familiar with it?
- Add any steps or sub-steps that will make the process clearer for your readers.
- Add description or examples to steps that your readers might not understand.
- Delete any details that your readers don't need.

Consider the sample paragraphs you read earlier. Robert Rowley knew that readers who don't live in the Southwest might not know about swamp coolers, so he explained what they are and described what they look like. Richard Preston, on the other hand, wanted his readers to understand the *symptoms* of smallpox, rather than the biology of how a person becomes infected with it, so he left out complicated details like cellular division and DNA replication.

Using Sequential Order to Organize Your Points

In a process paragraph, the order of your information is important because your readers will be trying to follow or understand the steps you describe.

Many times the most logical order to use is *sequential* order, which explains a process from start to finish. In his paragraph about servicing a swamp cooler, for example, Robert Rowley explained the steps in the order in which a reader would do them. In the paragraph on smallpox, Richard Preston outlined the steps as they happen.

Readers need to understand when one step ends and another begins, so be sure to include transitions to make your process easy to follow.

HOW TO Connect Ideas in a Paragraph That Explains a Process

In a process paragraph, you're likely to use some of the following transitions:

- Words and phrases that show time or sequence: *first, second, third, next, then, before, later, after, finally*
- Words and phrases that show additional information: *also, as well, additionally, in addition, and, moreover, another*

Read more about using sequential order on p. 40.

Use Color
To make it easier to spot your transitions, highlight them in color. Add new transitions where needed.

Bud's Revised Draft

When Bud revised his draft, he changed his mind about what steps he wanted to discuss. He also strengthened his focus and built up his support. His revised draft still contains errors, but he'll correct them when he edits his paragraph.

Get Rid of the Procrastination Curse

Do you always put off doing things you don't like until the last minute? The curse of procrastination can keep you from reaching goals such as getting a promotion or raising your grade-point average. Here is three ways to stop procrastinating. Start off by analyzing why you don't like to do the task. For example, you might not like preparing for an oral presentation because almost everyone who have to talk in front of people gets nervous. Second, divide the task up into small pieces. For example, if you have to read 20 pages just read 5 pages at a time. This is called "chunking," and it makes the assignment seem less intimidating. Most important, remember that time will pass quickly. This is especially true if you have something to look forward too. When you finish, reward yourself with something you like, such as calling a friend or buying a new CD. Your greatest reward will be high grades, a promotion, or a successful presentation. These are three good ways to get rid of the curse of procrastination.

GROUP ACTIVITY: Analyze Bud's Revised Draft

Use the following questions to discuss Bud's revision with your classmates.

1. Compare Bud's opening sentence in his discovery draft with his opening sentence in his revised draft. Is the revised opening better? Why or why not?

   ____

   ____

   ____

2. How has Bud strengthened the focus of his paragraph?

   ____

   ____

3. Bud changed his mind about which steps he would discuss. Are the new steps better or worse than the ones he used in his discovery draft? Why?

   ____

4. What examples and description does Bud include to support his main point?

   ____

5. What can Bud do to make his draft better?

WRITING ACTIVITY 8 (Group): Peer Review

Form a group with two or three classmates and exchange copies of your drafts. Read your draft aloud while your classmates follow along. Take notes on your classmates' answers to the following questions.

1. What do you like best about my paragraph?
2. How clear is my topic sentence? Do you have any suggestions for revision?
3. Evaluate the focus of my paragraph. Do all of the sentences relate directly to the process I'm describing?
4. Are my description and examples appropriate? Where can I improve my details?
5. How well have I organized my points?
6. Do you think you could do this process yourself? How could I make the process easier to follow?

Use the Comment Feature When Peer Reviewing
Ask several classmates for electronic copies of their drafts (on disk or by e-mail). Then use the comment feature of your word-processing program to insert suggestions for revision into your classmates' drafts.

WRITING ACTIVITY 9: Revise Your Draft

Using Bud's revised draft as a model, revise your own paragraph. As you revise, refer to your classmates' responses to the peer review questions. Work on strengthening your focus, building your support, organizing your points, and connecting your ideas.

STEP 4: EDIT YOUR PARAGRAPH

You've been focusing on expressing your ideas and making them clear for your readers. Before you share your final draft, be sure to fix any mistakes in spelling, punctuation, or grammar. In this chapter, you'll focus on correcting subject-verb agreement.

What Is Subject-Verb Agreement?

You know that subjects can be singular or plural. For example, *student* is singular and *students* is plural. You may not have realized, however, that verbs have singular and plural forms, too: A student *studies,* but students *study.*

For more help with subject-verb agreement, see pp. 490–98.

The subject and the verb in a sentence must "agree" in number. In other words, a *singular* subject must have a *singular* verb, and a *plural* subject must have a *plural* verb.

In the sentence below, the singular subject, *Joe,* agrees with the singular verb, *takes:*

subject verb
Joe takes the bus to work every day.

In this sentence, the subject and the verb are both plural:

subject verb
His parents take the train.

Correcting Errors in Subject-Verb Agreement

To make sure that your subjects and verbs agree in number, you need to identify correctly the subject of your sentence and know whether it is singular or plural. Problems in subject-verb agreement often happen when it's not obvious what are the subject and the verb of the sentence.

Recognize Prepositional Phrases

Sometimes, in addition to the subject, a sentence includes a *prepositional phrase,* a word group that begins with a preposition (such as *above, before, into, from, of,* or *on*). Do not mistake a noun within a prepositional phrase for the subject of the sentence.

INCORRECT The books on the table *is* mine.

CORRECT The books on the table *are* mine.

INCORRECT The mist over the mountains *are* beautiful.

CORRECT The mist over the mountains *is* beautiful.

Recognize Indefinite Pronouns

Indefinite pronouns are words that refer to a subject that is not specific. Here are some of the most common indefinite pronouns:

anybody	nothing	everything
no one	everybody	something
anyone	somebody	nobody
none	everyone	
anything	someone	

Although some of them look plural, all of these pronouns are singular. Therefore, they take singular verb forms.

INCORRECT Everything I did to get ready for the exam *were* useless.

CORRECT Everything I did to get ready for the exam *was* useless.

INCORRECT Everybody *know* she's a liar.

CORRECT Everybody *knows* she's a liar.

HOW TO Correct Errors in Subject-Verb Agreement

- Correctly identify the subject of your sentence, being careful to recognize prepositional phrases and indefinite pronouns.
- Decide whether the subject is singular or plural.
- Use singular verbs for singular subjects.
- Use plural verbs for plural subjects.

EDITING PRACTICE: Correcting Subject-Verb Agreement

Underline the correct verb form in each sentence.

1. Dr. Loya (ask, asks) his patients to lower their blood pressure.
2. My friend from the Adirondacks (doesn't, don't) attend college.
3. The people in my neighborhood (drive, drives) too fast.
4. Here (is, are) the forms you requested.
5. Who among the students (is, are) prepared for class?
6. Somebody (has, have) to fix this problem.
7. Everything about you (please, pleases) me.

8. No one in the room (knows, know) the answer.
9. The clothes on the floor (needs, need) to be washed.
10. The people in the back (doesn't, don't) have the right handouts.

Exercise Central
The *Discoveries* Web site includes additional practice exercises on correcting subject-verb agreement. Go to **bedfordstmartins.com/discoveries**, click on "Exercise Central," and select "Subject-Verb Agreement."

Bud's Edited Paragraph

Bud's revised draft had some errors, which he corrected in his edited paragraph. (The underlining shows where he corrected errors.)

Get Rid of the Procrastination Curse

Do you always put off doing things you don't like until the last minute? The curse of procrastination can keep you from reaching goals such as getting a promotion or raising your grade-point average. Here are three ways to stop procrastinating. Start off by analyzing why you don't like to do the task. For example, you might not like preparing for an oral presentation because almost everyone who has to talk in front of people gets nervous. Second, divide the task up into small pieces. For example, if you have to read twenty pages, just read five pages at a time. This is called "chunking," and it makes the assignment seem less intimidating. Most important, remember that time will pass quickly. This is especially true if you have something to look forward to. When you finish, reward yourself with something you like, such as calling a friend or buying a new CD. Your greatest reward will be high grades, a promotion, or a successful presentation. These are three good ways to get rid of the curse of procrastination.

For more information about how to use numbers in your writing, see p. 633.

To improve your spelling, study the spelling rules on pp. 584–88.

WRITING ACTIVITY 10: Edit Your Paragraph

Using a dictionary and the Handbook in Part Four, edit your paragraph for errors in grammar, punctuation, and spelling. In particular, look for errors in subject-verb agreement. Create an editing log so you won't make the same mistakes in the future.

For a review of how to create an editing log, see pp. 45–46.

STEP 5: SHARE YOUR PARAGRAPH

The participants in Bud's leadership seminar agreed that Bud's suggestions for eliminating procrastination were helpful and asked for copies to take with them. Even though you might not be attending a leadership conference, your paragraph can be useful for the other students in your class. With your instructor's help, collect all of your classmates' paragraphs, scan or photocopy them, and staple them together as a how-to booklet that everybody can refer to at home.

Document Design
Gather your classmates' paragraphs on disk and use a desktop publishing program to make your class's collected paragraphs into a professional-looking booklet.

ADDITIONAL WRITING ASSIGNMENTS

1. Write a paragraph for your classmates explaining how to cook your favorite food. Be sure to include all ingredients and to explain clearly the steps in the food preparation.
2. Write a paragraph for your supervisor at your job explaining how to solve a problem in your workplace. First, describe the problem, and then, give several steps for solving it.
3. Write a paragraph for your instructor and classmates in which you describe how to travel from one end of campus to the other in the shortest amount of time. Be sure to describe clearly the route you recommend.

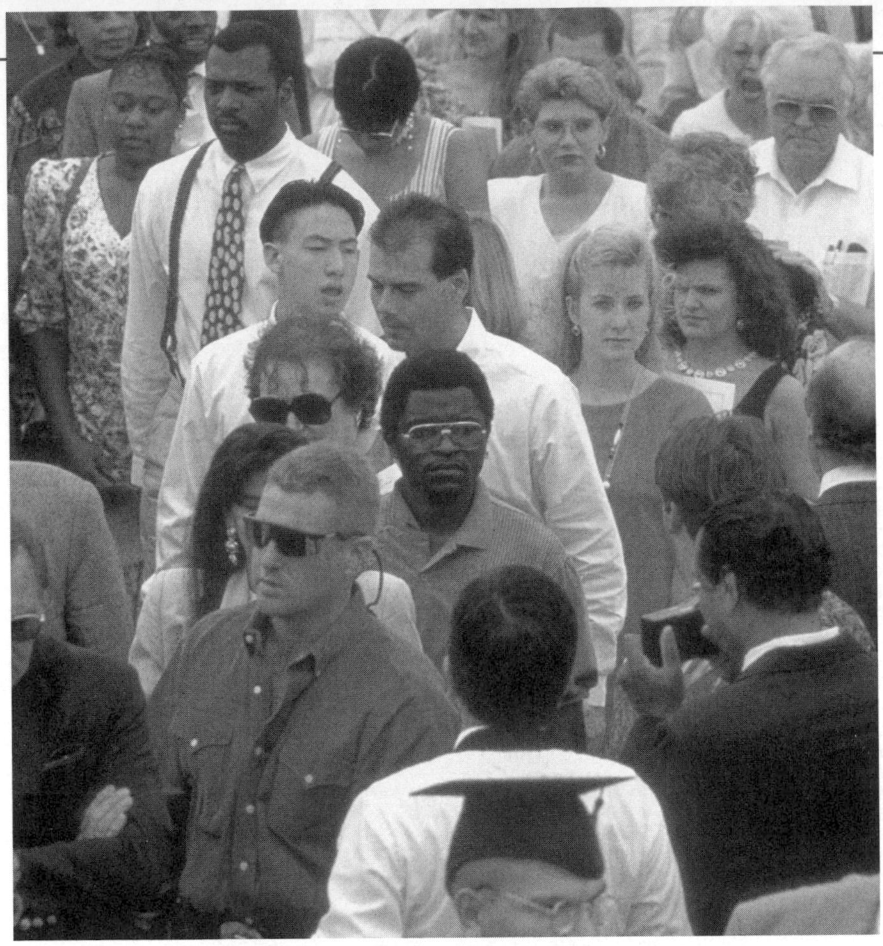

A student who has been to several college graduations noticed that there are two kinds of graduation guests — those who stand, clap noisily, and shout for the graduate they have come to support, and those who applaud their graduate without drawing attention to themselves. Can you think of another interesting way to classify the people who attend a college graduation? In this chapter, you will find a meaningful or memorable way to classify people or services.

CHAPTER 7

Writing a Paragraph That Classifies

In this chapter, you will

- discover how classification works.
- interview to gather ideas.
- write about your college or university.
- use general-to-specific order to organize your points.
- edit for passive voice.
- post your paragraph to a Web site.

UNDERSTANDING CLASSIFICATION

If you've ever been to a professional baseball game, you may have noticed that the people in the stadium seem to fit into categories. There are the people dressed in designer clothes who sit quietly, wearing headphones to hear the game on the radio as they watch from the stands. There are the diehard fans in team colors with painted faces and chests who jump up and down as they watch the game. And there are the preteens, wearing shorts and T-shirts, who seem less interested in the game than in wandering around the stadium to find their friends.

When you group people or things into categories, you are classifying them. For example, people might be classified as nonsmokers, smokers, and ex-smokers. Television programs might be grouped into comedies, dramas, news, and reality shows. The categories you choose tell your readers what you consider important to know about your topic. Classification answers questions like these:

- Can you break that down for me?
- Can you sort that out to help me understand?
- Can you explain what that is a part of?

By classifying things into groups, you provide useful categories and examples to make sense of a topic.

READING PARAGRAPHS THAT CLASSIFY

Read the following paragraphs to see how other writers have used classification to organize their thoughts.

Classifying People

People can be classified in any number of ways. E. B. White, for example, puts New Yorkers into three categories. For people considering a move to the city, his paragraph provides an idea of what to expect from their new home.

E. B. WHITE

"The Three New Yorks"

There are roughly three New Yorks. There is, first, the New York of the man or woman who was born here, who takes the city for granted and accepts its size and its turbulence as natural and inevitable. Second, there is the New York of the commuter — the

city that is devoured by locusts each day and spat out each night. Third, there is the New York of the person who was born somewhere else and came to New York in quest of something. Of these three trembling cities the greatest is the last — the city that accounts for New York's high-strung disposition, its poetical deportment, its dedication to the arts, and its incomparable achievements. Commuters give the city its tidal restlessness; natives give it solidity and continuity; but the settlers give it passion. And whether it is a farmer arriving from Italy to set up a small grocery store in a slum, or a young girl arriving from a small town in Mississippi to escape the indignity of being observed by her neighbors, or a boy arriving from the Corn Belt with a manuscript in his suitcase and a pain in his heart, it makes no difference; each embraces New York with the intense excitement of first love, each absorbs New York with the fresh eyes of an adventurer, each generates heat and light to dwarf the Consolidated Edison Company.

READING ACTIVITY 1: Build Your Vocabulary

Try to determine the meanings of the following words from E. B. White's paragraph. Then, check their meanings by looking the words up in a dictionary.

For advice on how to use a dictionary, turn to pp. 594–95.

turbulence ____________________

inevitable ____________________

disposition ____________________

deportment ____________________

incomparable ____________________

continuity ____________________

indignity ____________________

READING ACTIVITY 2: Read to Improve Your Writing

Read and answer the following questions about "The Three New Yorks."

1. What about New York is E. B. White classifying?

   ____

2. What categories does he use to describe New Yorkers?

   ____

3. White compares commuters to locusts. What does he mean by this comparison?

____

____

____

4. How could you classify the students on your campus?

____

____

____

____

____

____

Classifying Services

In this paragraph from an article on why historically black colleges and universities (HBCUs) are successful, the author classifies the ways in which different members of the college community contribute to student development.

URSULA WAGENER

from "It Takes a Community to Educate Students"

The entire academic community unites to educate a student. Administrative leaders understand the importance of graduating students, not just to enhance the image of the college or to generate additional tuition revenues, but to fulfill the institutional mission. HBCU faculty foster a critical variable in improving academic achievement and graduation rates: strong student/faculty relationships, within and outside the classroom. Many HBCU students take responsibility for their peers, playing the roles of tutor, counselor, and peer dean. All three groups, administrators, faculty, and students, play an important role in "the careful cultivation of history" — the generation of a historically centered belief that they are special people in a special place — reasserting the alumni achievements.

READING ACTIVITY 3: Build Your Vocabulary

Try to determine the meanings of the following words from Ursula Wagener's paragraph. Then, check their meanings by looking the words up in a dictionary.

enhance ____

revenues ____

foster ____

variable ____

cultivation ____

generation ____

reasserting ____

READING ACTIVITY 4: Read to Improve Your Writing

Read and answer the following questions about Ursula Wagener's paragraph.

1. Why does the author choose these three categories of people to demonstrate the success of HBCUs?

____

____

2. What other categories might Wagener have used?

____

____

____

3. How does the classification help readers understand what makes a student successful?

____

____

____

4. What campus services could you classify to help visitors get to know your school?

____

____

____

Explore the Web
Visit your college's Web site to see how your college classifies the people, places, and services on campus.

Writing Assignment

Imagine that you are enrolled in a course that helps new students adjust to college life. For the final project, you and your classmates will create a Web site for future students who wish to learn more about your school.

- Write a paragraph that classifies a group of people on your campus, such as nontraditional students, peer tutors, musicians, dorm residents, or commuters.

  OR

- Write a paragraph that classifies services available to the students at your school, such as financial aid, public parks, volunteer opportunities, discount programs, or student-run clubs.

STEP 1: DISCOVER IDEAS FOR WRITING

When picking something to classify, it's important to have a reason for grouping things into categories. You could, for example, classify people on your campus as students, faculty, and staff, but unless you have a point, the classification would be meaningless. As you look for ideas for your paragraph, then, think about what you like (or don't like) about your school. What should future students know before they enroll?

Choosing a Topic

For this chapter's assignment, you can classify either people or services. Which option you choose depends on what your interests are. If you're fascinated by differences in personality or behavior, for example, you'll more likely want to classify people. Or maybe you're concerned with how students can get the most out of college. In that case, classifying services might be a more interesting exercise for you.

For more advice on how to choose a topic, refer to p. 19.

Consider the paragraphs you read earlier in the chapter. E. B. White classified New Yorkers because people make the city special for him. Ursula Wagener, on the other hand, was more interested in explaining why students at historically black colleges succeed. Her focus was not on the people themselves, but on what they do.

Explore Re: Writing Links Libraries
To help you brainstorm topic ideas, go to the Re: Writing Web site at **bedfordstmartins.com/rewriting** and click on "Links Libraries."

Considering Your Audience and Purpose

For this paragraph, your audience consists of students considering whether to attend your college. Because they will read your paragraph on a Web site, you know that your readers have access to a computer and the Internet. But they may know little or nothing about your community, college, or campus life.

To learn more about analyzing your audience and purpose, see pp. 20–22.

You will do a better job of writing this paragraph if you also analyze your purpose. Most often, writers use classification to inform their readers how people or things are related; this is Ursula Wagener's purpose in "It Takes a Community to Educate Students." Classification can also help writers express their feelings: E. B. White, for instance, classifies New Yorkers to show why he loves the city. For this assignment, you might want not only to inform people about your school, but also to persuade them to enroll (or not). Be sure you know what you want to accomplish before you begin writing.

WRITING ACTIVITY 1: Analyze Your Audience and Purpose

Answer the following questions to help you think about your readers and your purpose.

1. What things will your prospective students already know about the people at your college? What might they not know?

____

____

____

2. What things will your audience likely already know about your campus? What might they not know?

____

____

____

3. How interested will your audience be in your community, your campus, its services, or its extracurricular activities? Which topic do you think will be of most interest to off-campus readers?

____

____

____

4. What is your primary purpose for writing this paragraph?

____

____

____

Interviewing to Gather Ideas

For additional help with interviewing skills, see p. 26.

Finding an expert who knows your topic well may provide you with valuable information to include in your paragraph. For example, if you are classifying activities available near your campus, you might interview someone at the local Chamber of Commerce. If you are writing about students who use the campus fitness center, you could talk to the person who works at the check-in desk.

HOW TO Conduct an Interview

- Choose a knowledgeable person and contact him or her in advance to set up an appointment.
- Prepare interview questions.
- Keep the conversation focused on the questions. Be considerate of your interviewee's time.
- Take notes. Put quotation marks around the person's actual words. You may also use a tape recorder, but ask permission first.
- Ask the person to explain anything you do not understand.
- Send a thank-you note immediately after the interview.

Student writer Cesar wanted to write about nightclubs and restaurants in Juárez, a Mexican town across the border from his Texas campus. Since he had visited these places but knew little about them, he made appointments to interview their managers and prepared the following questions:

- When did your club or restaurant open?
- What are the hours of operation?
- What is the theme of your club or restaurant?
- What makes your club or restaurant unique?
- Why would college students want to come to your club or restaurant?

WRITING ACTIVITY 2: Interviewing

Select a general topic and prepare interview questions to help you learn more about it. Interview an expert to gather information for your paragraph.

Narrowing Your Topic

For a classification paragraph to be effective, your topic must be focused enough that you can make meaningful and logical connections. When selecting items to put into categories, be sure that you have a single principle, or theme, that links them together as a group.

The most effective way to narrow your topic is to narrow your principle of classification. Suppose you want to write about places to visit near your campus. If you interviewed a local expert, you may now have a lengthy list: bookstores, restaurants, coffeehouses, libraries, museums, galleries, bars, concert halls, parks, health clubs, convenience stores, nightclubs, and shopping plazas, for example. To narrow your topic, select a single principle, such as cultural institutions or recreational facilities. Another principle might be inexpensive places or places where local bands perform. To be even more focused, you might classify the places within a single category, such as types of coffeehouses.

HOW TO Narrow a Topic for a Paragraph That Classifies

- Select a general topic.
- Interview an expert for information and ideas.
- Review your interview responses and decide what information interests you most.
- Choose a principle of classification that will provide a limited number of categories for your topic.
- Check that you have enough examples and details to support each category.

WRITING ACTIVITY 3: Narrow Your Topic

Reread the responses to your interview questions. Highlight the three or four most interesting categories for your classification and choose a principle that links them together.

STEP 2: WRITE YOUR DISCOVERY DRAFT

For a paragraph that classifies, a little planning will make the writing easier. As you prepare your draft, you may find that you need to rethink or fine-tune your categories. That's okay: The whole point of drafting is figuring out what you want to say.

Drafting a Topic Sentence

For more help with drafting topic sentences, see pp. 30–31.

The topic sentence of a classification paragraph announces what you are going to classify. If you wish, you may also preview the categories you will include.

The following are topic sentences written by student writers. The first two examples announce what the writer will classify and explain why it is important.

Our campus has three types of arcades that students visit to help them unwind.

First-year students often gain weight because they go to the many fast-food restaurants nearby.

This topic sentence announces what the writer will classify and provides the categories to be included.

Students can improve their grades by taking advantage of services offered by the Tutoring and Learning Center, the Writing Skills Center, and the Academic Development Center.

Whichever approach you choose for your topic sentence, be sure that you have a clear reason for grouping things into categories. Few readers will be interested in a classification that has no purpose.

HOW TO Write a Topic Sentence for a Paragraph That Classifies

- Identify the people or services you will classify.
- Explain what your purpose is for classifying them.
- If you wish, preview the categories you will describe.

WRITING ACTIVITY 4: Draft a Topic Sentence

Referring to your responses to Writing Activities 1, 2, and 3, draft a topic sentence for your paragraph. Use the sample student topic sentences as models.

Brainstorming to Add Support

Now that you know what you are planning to classify and what categories you will use, you need to develop examples and details for each category. Draw on what you already know about your topic, the experience and knowledge of the person you interviewed, and any other information that you have gathered.

To review brainstorming, see p. 24.

Because you're still in the drafting stage, try to write down as many examples and details for each category as you can think of. When you revise, you can always eliminate details or decide to add new ones.

Cesar brainstormed the following examples and details for his classification of places to go in Juárez.

Clubs

- La Serrata
  - Italian theme
  - dressy
  - good music
  - party atmosphere
- Vertigo
  - unusual décor — dragons
  - new music
  - excellent sound system
  - U.S. disc jockeys
- Amazonas
  - jungle atmosphere

Restaurants

- Viva Mexicano!
  - tourist hangout
  - Mexican village décor
  - good food
  - friendly service
- Central Market
  - souvenirs

Search the Web
For additional information on your topic, search the World Wide Web. To practice a keyword search, go to **bedfordstmartins.com/english_research** and click on "Interactive Tutorials."

WRITING ACTIVITY 5: Develop Details

Brainstorm to develop support for your ideas. List each of the categories of people or services that you are classifying and then brainstorm examples and details about each.

Drafting a Concluding Sentence

For more help writing concluding sentences, turn to pp. 34–35.

For a paragraph that classifies, the concluding sentence should fit the different categories back into a coherent whole. You can do this by restating your topic sentence or summing up your main point; you can also indicate why your main point is important or suggest that your readers get to know the people or try the services that you have classified.

Ursula Wagener, for example, concludes by summarizing the impact that an HBCU community has on student success.

> All three groups, administrators, faculty, and students, play an important role in "the careful cultivation of history"--the generation of a historically centered belief that they are special people in a special place--reasserting the alumni achievements.

Wagener's conclusion is effective because it explains how all three groups work together to achieve the same goal.

WRITING ACTIVITY 6: Draft a Concluding Sentence

Draft three possible concluding sentences: one that repeats the main point of your paragraph, one that summarizes the paragraph, and one that encourages readers to get to know the people, visit the places, or try the services you classified. Select the best one, remembering that you can always change your mind.

Cesar's Discovery Draft

After he brainstormed examples and descriptions for his categories, Cesar turned them into full sentences. Notice how he uses the classifying principle of unusual themes to organize his description of Juárez nightclubs and restaurants. Cesar's draft contains errors typical at this stage of writing; he'll correct them later.

> Saturday Night in Juárez
>
> It's Saturday night and you are looking for a good time, but you don't know where to go. Juárez has a variety of restaurants and nightclubs from which to choose. If you would like to learn about Mexican traditions and folklore, you can visit Viva Mexicano! If you decide to visit a nightclub, there are several

to choose from. La Serrata is for people who like to dress up. The best dance music and the best party environment are offered by this club, which every weekend is full of beautiful people. You will be impressed by the beautiful marble decorations from Italy. Vertigo is famous for it's robotic smoke-breathing, laser-shooting dragons and sophisticated sound system, exclusive new music, and disc jockeys who come from all over the U.S. Another place to visit is Central Market where you can purchase souvenirs to take home. If your feeling wild, check out Amazonas. This 3 million dollar club makes you feel like you're in the Amazon jungle. Keep in mind, though, that all of these clubs and restaurants are affiliated with a program called "Designated Driver." Which consists of picking one volunteer in a group of friends to agree to not drink alcohol and to drive his or her friends safely home.

WRITING ACTIVITY 7: Complete Your Discovery Draft

Take the examples and details that you brainstormed for your categories and turn them into sentences. Then, using what you have already written for your topic sentence and concluding sentence, write a discovery draft. For now, concentrate on getting your ideas into paragraph form. Don't worry about focus and organization until you revise.

STEP 3: REVISE YOUR PARAGRAPH

You have now drafted a paragraph that classifies people or services into groups. Set your writing aside for a day or two and then reread it. When you revise, you'll concentrate on strengthening your focus, building your support, and ordering your points.

Strengthening Your Focus

To improve the focus of your paragraph, make sure that all of your categories adhere to a single principle of classification and that each category is similar to the others.

To review the importance of strengthening your focus, see pp. 37–38.

When Cesar reviewed his discovery draft, he noticed that although he meant to use unusual décor as his principle of classification, he included one place that wasn't decorated, the Central Market. He also realized that because he discussed both nightclubs and restaurants, his categories weren't consistent. When he revised, he decided to delete the market and the restaurant and to focus on the three nightclubs. He then rewrote his topic sentence to reflect his new focus.

Building Your Support with Description

Just as the categories in a classification paragraph should be similar to each other in type, they should each contain a similar level of detail. If you go on at length about three categories but merely mention a fourth, readers will wonder why you included the fourth category at all.

Cesar reviewed his draft and noticed that he described the decorations and the music for two of the Juárez nightclubs, but he didn't include the same kind of information for the third. He therefore added this description to help his audience better imagine Amazonas:

```
Twenty-foot palm trees sway over the dance floor
while live bands fill the air with reggae and
tropical music.
```

HOW TO Build Stronger Classification

- Provide enough categories to help your reader understand your main point.
- Check that all of your categories belong to the same principle of classification.
- Check that the categories include the same level of detail.
- Add description where needed to help your reader imagine each category.

Comment on Your Draft
Use the comment function of your word-processing program to note your ideas for revision. The "comments" will appear as highlighted words next to your draft, similar to your instructor's or classmates' handwritten suggestions.

Using General-to-Specific Order to Organize Your Points

For a paragraph that classifies things into groups, use *general-to-specific order* to organize your points. In general-to-specific order, start with the most general idea, what is to be classified, in the topic sentence. The more specific ideas, or classification categories, follow to support and explain the topic sentence. The most specific ideas, the details, are provided as part of each category.

A classification paragraph can be improved by using transitional words to help your readers understand where one category ends and another begins. E. B. White, for example, used *first, second,* and *third* to signal the categories of his classification of New Yorkers.

For more information on using transitions, see p. 42.

HOW TO Connect Ideas in a Paragraph That Classifies

- To show similarities: *in the same way, similarly, in comparison, likewise*
- To show differences: *in contrast, but, on the other hand, however*
- To distinguish categories: *first, second, third; next; another*

Cesar's Revised Draft

Cesar revised his draft by clarifying his principle of classification, rethinking his categories, and adjusting the level of details he included. His revised paragraph still contains some errors in grammar, spelling, and punctuation; he will correct these when he edits.

Saturday Night in Juárez

It's Saturday night and you are looking for a good time, but you don't know where to go. If you like to dance, Juárez has three excellent clubs that offer an exciting time for college students. La Serrata is for people who like to dress up. The best dance music and the best party environment are offered by this club, which every weekend is full of beautiful people. You will be impressed by the beautiful marble decorations from Italy. Vertigo is famous for it's robotic smoke-breathing, laser-shooting dragons and sophisticated sound system, exclusive new music, and disc jockeys who come from all over the U. S. If your feeling wild, check out Amazonas. This 3 million dollar nightclub makes you feel like you're in the Amazon jungle. Twenty-foot palm trees sway over the dance floor while live bands fill the air with reggae and tropical music. Keep in mind, though, that all of these clubs are affiliated with a program called "Designated Driver." Which consists of picking one volunteer in a group of friends to agree to not drink alcohol and to drive his or her friends safely home.

GROUP ACTIVITY: Analyze Cesar's Revised Draft

For tips on how to review a draft effectively, see *pp. 43–45.*

Use the following questions to discuss with your classmates how Cesar improved his draft.

1. Compare Cesar's topic sentence in his discovery draft with the one in his revised draft. How did he improve his topic sentence?

   ____

   ____

2. What is Cesar's classifying principle? How does his classification help readers understand his topic?

   ____

   ____

   ____

   ____

3. In his revision, Cesar deleted two categories: restaurants and the market. How does this improve his draft?

____

____

____

____

4. What can Cesar do to further improve his draft?

____

____

____

WRITING ACTIVITY 8 (Group): Peer Review

Form a group with two or three classmates and exchange copies of your drafts. Read your draft aloud while your classmates follow along. Take notes on your classmates' answers to the following questions.

1. What do you like best about my paragraph?
2. How clear is my topic sentence? How can I improve it to explain better what I am classifying?
3. Evaluate my classification categories. Are they consistent with my topic sentence and with each other? Do any of them need to be removed or changed?
4. Evaluate my description within each category. What can I add to help you understand my thoughts?
5. Are my points in the best possible order? Which categories or sentences would you suggest I move or take out?
6. Does my concluding sentence restate my topic sentence or sum up my main points?

Peer Review Online
If your class has a Web site, you may be able to do peer review online. Access the peer review questions and send your responses to the writer's e-mail address.

WRITING ACTIVITY 9: Revise Your Draft

Review Cesar's drafts and your analysis of how he improved his paragraph. Then, revise your own draft, using your classmates' suggestions as a guide. Improve your topic sentence, strengthen your focus, revise your classification categories, and improve your organization where needed.

STEP 4: EDIT YOUR PARAGRAPH

Now that you have revised your classification paragraph, you're ready to edit it. Get out your dictionary and turn to the Handbook in Part Four of this book to help you eliminate mistakes and weak spots. In this chapter, you will focus on changing sentences from passive to active voice.

What Is Passive Voice?

A sentence in the *passive voice* has a subject that receives an action rather than doing the action. Passive voice is not technically an error, but it tends to weaken your writing by making it wordy and dull.

For more information on active vs. passive voice, see pp. 572–73.

PASSIVE The diner near campus is visited by many students.

PASSIVE The class schedule posted on the office door was examined by students looking for interesting courses.

Using Active Voice

A sentence in the *active voice* has a subject that performs an action. Most readers prefer active voice in most sentences because they like to know immediately who or what is performing the action. Active voice is clearer and more direct than passive voice.

ACTIVE Many students visit the diner near campus.

ACTIVE Students looking for interesting classes examined the class schedule posted on the office door.

HOW TO Write in Active Voice

- Identify the subject and the verb.
- Decide whether the subject is performing the action or receiving the action.
- If the subject is receiving the action, revise the sentence so that it has a new subject that is performing the action.

EDITING PRACTICE: Using Active Voice

Rewrite the following sentences to use active voice.

EXAMPLE

PASSIVE Delicious manicotti was made by Robert.

ACTIVE Robert made delicious manicotti.

1. Professor Humez is liked by all of the students.

   ____

2. Daisy's books were borrowed by her classmate.

   ____

3. The championship was won by our basketball team.

   ____

4. The team was led by Sue.

   ____

5. The administration building was picketed by the students last week.

   ____

6. The salad was prepared by the chef.

   ____

7. The application was received by Francie's mother.

   ____

8. My favorite computer lab was donated by Dell.

    ____

9. The club was founded by Josie, but the dedication was done by Jackie.

    ____

10. A concert will be performed by the rap club on Friday.

    ____

Grammar Practice for Multilingual Writers
The *Discoveries* Web site includes practice exercises for students whose first language is not English. Go to **bedfordstmartins.com/discoveries**, click on "Exercise Central," and select "Passive Voice Sentences."

Cesar's Edited Paragraph

As you may have noticed, Cesar's revised draft had a few errors in grammar, spelling, and punctuation. He edited his paragraph to eliminate these. (The underlining indicates where he corrected errors.)

Saturday Night in Juárez

It's Saturday night and you are looking for a good time, but you don't know where to go. If you like to dance, Juárez has three excellent clubs that offer an exciting time for college students. La Serrata is for people who like to dress up. This club, which every weekend is full of beautiful people, offers the best dance music and the best party environment. You will be impressed by the beautiful marble decorations from Italy. Vertigo is famous for its robotic smoke-breathing, laser-shooting dragons and sophisticated sound system, exclusive new music, and disc jockeys who come from all over the United States. If you're feeling wild, check out Amazonas. This 3 million dollar nightclub makes you feel like you're in the Amazon jungle. Twenty-foot palm trees sway over the dance floor while live bands fill the air with reggae and tropical music. Keep in mind, though, that all of these clubs belong to a program called "Designated Driver," which consists of picking one volunteer in a group of friends to agree to not drink alcohol and to drive his or her friends safely home.

Exercise Central
The *Discoveries* Web site includes additional practice exercises for active vs. passive voice. Go to **bedfordstmartins.com /discoveries**, click on "Exercise Central," and select "Active vs. Passive Voice."

WRITING ACTIVITY 10: Edit Your Paragraph

Using a dictionary and the Handbook in Part Four of this book, edit your draft. In particular, change passive to active voice. Add corrections to your editing log so you won't make the same mistakes in the future.

For a review of how to create an editing log, see pp. 45–46.

STEP 5: SHARE YOUR PARAGRAPH

Cesar and his fellow students visited a campus computer lab to learn how to post their paragraphs to a Web site for people who were considering attending the college. They were delighted to get an e-mail from somebody who found the site and thanked them for providing useful information about their school. Cesar then e-mailed all of his friends to give them the URL so that they could read his paragraph.

ADDITIONAL WRITING ASSIGNMENTS

1. Write a paragraph for your fellow classmates in which you classify the way students behave in college classes.
2. Write a paragraph to your college's board of directors in which you classify campus sports to argue that some of them deserve more funding. You

might focus on sports that include athletes on scholarships or intramural sports that are open to all students.

3. Write a paragraph for your local newspaper in which you classify the types of free entertainment available in your community.
4. Write a paragraph to your state legislator classifying the problems in your community that you would like to see addressed in the next legislature. You might select categories such as deteriorating roads, missed educational opportunities, and high taxes.

One of your friends, a recent college graduate, explained how his graduation from high school was different from his graduation from college. Graduating with friends from his small high school had been fun, but being just one among thousands of graduates at his large college was exhilarating. In this chapter, you also will use comparison and contrast. You will explain how your expectations of college match up with what it's really like, or show the similarities or differences in the advice you've been given on choosing a major or a career.

CHAPTER

8

Writing a Paragraph That Compares and Contrasts

In this chapter, you will

- discover how comparison and contrast works.
- freewrite to gather ideas.
- write about your expectations of the future.
- use subject-by-subject or point-by-point order to organize your points.
- edit for unnecessary repetition and wordiness.
- write a letter to someone at home.

UNDERSTANDING COMPARISON AND CONTRAST

Whether you consciously think about it or not, you use comparison and contrast every day. For example, when you woke up this morning, you may have considered the advantages of having a bowl of cereal versus those of scrambling some eggs. You may have decided whether your brown or blue shirt would go better with your pants, or you may have debated taking one route to campus instead of another.

In college classes, instructors will often ask you to compare and contrast for an assignment or an essay exam. Your history professor might ask you to compare and contrast one president's actions to another's, or your psychology professor might ask you to compare and contrast left and right brain functions.

When you *compare* two or more items, you look for similarities; when you *contrast* them, you look for differences. Comparison and contrast answers questions like these:

- How are these things alike?
- How are these things different?
- Why are the similarities and differences important?

Writers use comparison and contrast to point out the connections among people, places, things, or ideas.

READING PARAGRAPHS THAT COMPARE AND CONTRAST

What we expect often turns out to be quite different from what actually happens. On the other hand, we can be surprised to discover that two things are more alike than we thought. Notice how the authors of the following paragraphs use comparison and contrast to think about similarities or differences that have surprised them.

College

In this paragraph from a memoir, the author contrasts his college classes to what he had thought they would be like.

FRANK MCCOURT

from 'Tis

I never thought college would be all numbers and letters and grades and averages and people putting me on probation. I thought this would be a place where kindly learned men and women would teach me in a warm way and if I didn't understand they'd pause and explain. I didn't know I'd go from course to course with dozens of students, sometimes over a hundred, with professors lecturing and not even looking at you. Some professors look out the window or up at the ceiling and some stick their noses in notebooks and read from paper that is yellow and crumbling with age. If students ask questions they're waved away. In English novels students at Oxford and Cambridge were always meeting in professors' rooms and sipping sherry while discussing Sophocles. I'd like to discuss Sophocles, too, but I'd have to read him first and there's no time after my nights at Merchants Refrigerating.

READING ACTIVITY 1: Build Your Vocabulary

For advice on how to use a dictionary, turn to *pp. 594–95.*

Try to determine the meanings of the following words from Frank McCourt's paragraph. Then, check their meanings by looking the words up in a dictionary.

probation ______________________________

____

learned ______________________________

Sophocles ______________________________

READING ACTIVITY 2: Read to Improve Your Writing

Read and answer the following questions about Frank McCourt's paragraph.

1. List three points of contrast McCourt makes between what college is and what he expected it to be.

____

____

____

____

2. McCourt uses contrast both to explain his views and to state his opinion. From his paragraph, what do you think his opinion of college is?

____

____

3. How does McCourt's opinion compare with your own experiences in college?

____

____

____

____

Career Advice

Leo Buscaglia's respect for education led to his decision to become a teacher. In this paragraph, Buscaglia compares what professional educators and his father taught him about the value of learning.

LEO BUSCAGLIA

from Papa's Ritual

I decided upon a career in teaching fairly early in my college years. During my training, I studied with some of the most renowned educators in the country. When I finally emerged from academia, having been generously endowed with theory and jargon and technique, I discovered, to my great amusement, that the professional educators were imparting what Papa had known all along. He knew that there was no greater wonder than the human capacity to learn, that no particle of knowledge was too insignificant not to have the power to change us for the better. "How long we live is limited," Papa said, "but how much we learn is not. What we learn is what we are. No one should miss out on an education."

READING ACTIVITY 3: Build Your Vocabulary

Try to determine the meanings of the following words from Leo Buscaglia's paragraph. Then, check their meanings by looking the words up in a dictionary.

renowned ____

academia ____

endowed ____________________________

jargon ____________________________

capacity ____________________________

READING ACTIVITY 4: Read to Improve Your Writing

Read and answer the following questions about Leo Buscaglia's paragraph.

1. Buscaglia reveals what he will compare in the third sentence of the paragraph. Is this his topic sentence? Why or why not?

2. List three points of comparison that Buscaglia makes between what he learned from professional educators and what he learned from his father.

3. How does Buscaglia's use of comparison help readers understand why he chose to become a teacher?

4. What is your career choice? How have different friends and family reacted to your choice?

Writing Assignment

You probably have friends or siblings who are thinking about what they will do in the future. Now that you're in college and possibly preparing for a specific career, you can answer some of their questions. Write a letter to someone at home sharing your experiences.

- Write a paragraph in which you compare and contrast your expectations of college with what it's really like.

  OR

- Write a paragraph in which you compare and contrast different advice you have received on your major or choice of careers.

STEP 1: DISCOVER IDEAS FOR WRITING

Writing a paragraph that compares and contrasts is easier if you plan ahead. Before you begin to write, think about what you want to say and how you're going to say it. The next few pages will help you do that.

Choosing a Topic

For additional help with choosing and narrowing your topic, see pp. 19–29.

For this chapter's assignment, you can write about an experience you have already had or about what people have told you to expect from the future.

As you consider these options, keep in mind that it's best to write about something that means a lot to you. If college is what you thought it would be, for example, a paragraph that compares your expectations with your experience won't be interesting for you or your reader. On the other hand, if you're having difficulty choosing a major, comparing and contrasting your options will not only result in an interesting paragraph, it may also help you make up your mind.

Explore Re: Writing Links Libraries
To help you brainstorm topic ideas, go to the Re: Writing Web site at **bedfordstmartins.com/rewriting** and click on "Links Libraries."

Considering Your Audience and Purpose

Since you will send your paragraph to a friend or a family member, you know your audience well. What questions or concerns does this person have about going to college or choosing a career? What do you now know that he or she doesn't?

Consider, also, why you are writing this paragraph. Do you want to share your feelings, give your reader information, or persuade him or her to think a certain way about your subject? Understanding your purpose will help you write an effective paragraph.

To learn more about analyzing your audience and purpose, see pp. 20–22.

To review the purposes for writing, see pp. 21–22.

E-mail Your Reader
Ask your friend or family member what he or she wants to know about college or choosing a career. Your reader's questions will help you decide how to approach your topic.

WRITING ACTIVITY 1: Analyze Your Audience and Purpose

Answer the following questions to help you think about your audience and purpose. Answers will vary.

1. Who will you write to?

____

____

____

2. What will this person probably already know about your career choice or college experiences? What will he or she not know?

____

____

____

3. Of these things, what will interest your reader most?

____

____

____

4. What is your primary purpose for writing this paragraph?

____

____

____

Freewriting to Gather Ideas

You can learn more about freewriting on p. 25.

You can come up with points for your letter by freewriting, or writing for a specific period of time without trying to get things right. Think about what you want to compare and contrast for a minute or two, then start writing about how they're similar or how they're different. When you look back at what you've written, you'll find that you have some good ideas worth exploring in more depth.

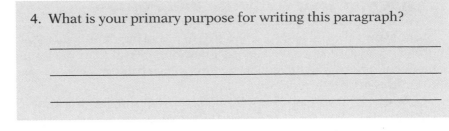

HOW TO Freewrite for a Paragraph That Compares and Contrasts

- Write your topic idea at the top of the page.
- Write about that topic without pausing for at least ten minutes.
- Don't stop, go back, or correct your writing.
- Follow your ideas. Don't worry whether they're good or bad.
- Don't worry about organization, grammar, spelling, or punctuation.

Student writer Monica wanted to tell her younger sister how college is different from high school, but she wasn't sure what she wanted to say. Here is what she came up with when she wrote without stopping for fifteen minutes.

> Remember how we thought that college is the time when you have fun and party? That may be true, but it's also the time when you must study. If you come to college with the perseption that it's party time you will be out in a year. You will meet lots of new people and make lots of friends but there is a line where you have to know how much fun you are going to have and how much work you're going to do. Once you're in college you realize it's nothing like high school. High school for you may be very easy, it was for me. College is different. My high school was very easy. I would rarely do the homework and didn't prepare for tests. I would go to my classes half

of the time and through all of this I was still doing good. As my senior year came I knew that I would be getting ready for college and I knew that the relaxing time was over. From everything I had heard about college I knew that it would be a bit harder than high school. I was right! College classes are not extremely hard, but in order to pass and understand you have to attend class and you have to study. It is a lot of reading and work.

WRITING ACTIVITY 2: Freewrite

First, decide whether you are going to write about your college experience or about career advice you have received. Then freewrite for fifteen minutes on how the things you are comparing and contrasting are similar to and different from each other.

Narrowing Your Topic

To narrow your topic to something you can cover in a paragraph, make sure that you have a single basis for your comparison. For example, if you want to compare and contrast high school and college, you might focus on sports, on classes, or on social activities, but trying to compare all three aspects in a single paragraph would be too complicated.

You must also select just a few points to compare and contrast. If you freewrote on the topic of how people have reacted to your choice of careers, for example, you may have included your parents, your best friend, your high school career counselor, your calculus teacher, and your cousin, but you wouldn't be able to describe all of their advice in one paragraph. To narrow your topic, you might focus on the two or three people whose suggestions have had the biggest impact on your career choice, or on a single piece of advice that many people had in common.

HOW TO Narrow a Topic for a Paragraph That Compares and Contrasts

- Select two or three things to compare and contrast.
- Freewrite on the similarities and differences between your subjects.
- Read over your freewriting and identify two to four points that would make the most interesting and informative paragraph.
- Find a basis of comparison that ties your points together.
- Check that you have enough detail to support each point.

When Monica reviewed her freewriting, she realized that she had too many ideas to discuss in one paragraph. She decided that three of her points were more important than the others: going to classes, doing homework, and studying. She noticed, too, that she had a good basis for comparison: the amount of effort required to succeed.

WRITING ACTIVITY 3: Narrow Your Topic

Reread your freewriting. Highlight two or three points that you think would be of most interest to your audience and identify a basis for your comparison and contrast.

STEP 2: WRITE YOUR DISCOVERY DRAFT

Now it's time to move to the drafting stage of the writing process. You can use your freewriting as a starting point.

Drafting a Topic Sentence

For more help with drafting topic sentences, see pp. 30–31.

A good comparison and contrast paragraph does more than list similarities and differences between two or more things; it lists them for a reason. Your topic sentence, then, should explain why your topic is important. It should also make your basis for comparison and contrast clear.

Here are some examples of topic sentences written by student writers for this assignment.

> Helping my father recover from a stroke made me decide that nursing is a better major than biology.

> My math teacher thinks I should be an accountant, and my cousin thinks I should start my own catering company; surprisingly, their advice has a lot in common.

> My college English class is very much like my Senior English class in high school because they both helped me improve my writing.

HOW TO Write a Topic Sentence for a Paragraph That Compares or Contrasts

- Identify what you will compare and contrast.
- Make it clear whether you will focus on similarities or differences.
- Include the basis of your comparison and contrast.
- State why it is important to understand the similarities and/or differences between your subjects.

When she reviewed her freewriting, Monica realized that she had already written a promising topic sentence:

College is difficult and a big difference from high school.

Monica decided she could use that idea as the main point of her discovery draft.

WRITING ACTIVITY 4: Draft a Topic Sentence

Review your freewriting to determine what your main point will be, then draft a topic sentence for your paragraph. Use the student examples as models.

Adding Support with Details

Now that you know what you are going to write about, you need to develop points of comparison and contrast supported by convincing details.

To review adding support, see pp. 31–34.

Review your freewriting and decide what points of comparison and contrast you will keep. For each point, you will need to provide details to make the connection between your subjects clear. Put all of your points on a sheet of paper and then note down at least one similarity or difference for each.

Create a Table
Use your word-processing program to create a table with three columns. Put the points to be compared in the first column. Then list similarities and differences in the other two columns.

Monica created these columns:

	High School	*College*
Classes	skipped all the time lectures	have to show up talk in class attendance part of the grade
Homework	rarely did it busywork	have to do it a lot of reading
Tests	didn't study multiple choice	study a lot often essays

WRITING ACTIVITY 5: Develop Details

Create columns for the things that you are going to compare and contrast, and list your points of comparison. Brainstorm at least one detail to support each point.

Drafting a Concluding Sentence

For more help writing concluding sentences, turn to pp. 34–35.

Your concluding sentence can remind readers why your comparison and contrast is important, or it can leave them with a memorable point that sums up your main idea.

Leo Buscaglia's concluding sentence, for example, quotes his father's advice and restates the importance of learning:

> **"No one should miss out on an education."**

Frank McCourt's concluding sentence provides one last point to contrast his dream of what college classes would be like with the disappointing reality:

> **I'd like to discuss Sophocles, too, but I'd have to read him first and there's no time after my nights at Merchants Refrigerating.**

WRITING ACTIVITY 6: Draft a Concluding Sentence

Draft a concluding sentence that repeats the main point of your paragraph, sums up your ideas, or emphasizes the importance of your comparison and contrast.

Monica's Discovery Draft

Monica was able to use some of her freewriting for her discovery draft, but she had to throw out a lot of her original ideas and add details to support her points. Her draft contains the kinds of errors that often appear in a discovery draft; she'll correct them later.

It's Not High School

College is the step after high school. Some people in our family choose to go that next step while others go another way. I'm going to tell you what college is really like. College is difficult and a big difference from high school. In order to be successful, you have to put in lots of effort. As you know, high school was easy for me. I rarely did the homework, it was mostly busywork. I would rather spend my time hanging out with friends. Studying for tests was easy: I only had to memorize some facts. I skipped my classes half the time because the teachers just lectured from the textbooks. The textbooks weren't very interesting either. Through all of this I was still doing good. From everything I had heard about college I knew that it would be a bit harder than high school. I was right! College classes are not extremely hard, but you have to show up because attendance is part of your grade. Professors expect you to talk in class. If you don't do the homework, you won't be able to keep up with the discussion. It is a lot of reading and work. And I will be honest, sometimes you feel yourself asking, "Why am I doing this?" But when you look at what it will do for you in the future it's worth it.

WRITING ACTIVITY 7: Write a Discovery Draft

Using what you have already written as a starting point, write a discovery draft. For now, focus on the similarities and differences between your points. You can sort out your organization and clean up the details later.

STEP 3: REVISE YOUR PARAGRAPH

When you revise a paragraph that compares and contrasts, pay special attention to organization and balance so that readers can follow your ideas.

Strengthening Your Focus

To review the importance of strengthening your focus, see pp. 37–38.

To strengthen the focus of a paragraph that compares and contrasts, make sure that each point of similarity or difference sticks to the same basis of comparison. If, for example, you're contrasting your high school cafeteria with your college dining hall, your basis of comparison might be the food. In that case, you could discuss variety, nutrition, taste, and cost, but a description of who eats together would be off-topic.

Also check that each detail supports your topic sentence. Monica included a few sentences that didn't support her point that college requires more effort than high school:

```
I would rather spend my time hanging out with friends.

The textbooks weren't very interesting either.
```

Monica removed these sentences when she revised.

Building Your Support

In a paragraph that compares and contrasts, the items being discussed should get equal treatment. If you have three things to say about one of your subjects, make sure that you have three comparable things to say about the other.

As you revise your paragraph, examine your points closely. Try outlining your discovery draft to check that you have the same level of detail for each point. If any of your categories are less detailed than the others, add information so that your paragraph is complete and easy to follow.

HOW TO Build Stronger Comparison and Contrast

- Provide enough points to help your reader understand the similarities and differences between your subjects.
- Outline your discovery draft to check that you have the same amount of detail for each point.
- Add or delete descriptions and examples where necessary.
- Be sure that the descriptive details add interest and help your reader understand each point.

Student writer Monica wasn't sure if she had developed her points evenly, so she put together the following outline of her discovery draft:

For a review of outlining, see pp. 26–27.

High School

- Homework
  - didn't do it
  - busywork
- Tests
  - memorized facts
- Classes
  - skipped a lot
  - teachers lectured from the books

College

- Classes
  - attendance is part of the grade
  - have to talk in class
- Homework
  - have to do the reading

Monica noticed that although she discussed homework, tests, and classes in high school, she left out college tests. She also said more about high school homework than she did about college homework. When she revised her draft, she added information about college tests and said a little more about the amount of reading necessary to prepare for class.

Using Subject-by-Subject or Point-by-Point Order to Organize Your Paragraph

For a comparison and contrast paragraph, most writers use one of two methods to organize the points they make about their subjects (the things they are comparing or contrasting). Sometimes they use the *subject-by-subject* method — writing everything about one subject first and then writing everything about the other, comparing and contrasting it to the first. Or they use the *point-by-point* method — going back and forth between the subjects, comparing and contrasting them one detail at a time.

For more information on ordering your points, see pp. 39–42.

Reread Leo Buscaglia's and Frank McCourt's paragraphs. Buscaglia uses the subject-by-subject method to write first about what he learned from his formal education and then about his father's advice. McCourt uses point-by-point organization: He writes about what college is really like along with what he had expected it would be, alternating between specific points of the two subjects.

The outline you created to check your paragraph's focus can also help you improve its organization. If you are using point-by-point order, check that you discuss each of your subjects for every point you make. Similarly, if you use subject-by-subject order, make sure that you cover the same points in the same order for each subject.

Order Points Online
If you have a class listserv or Internet discussion group, post your topic and comparison and contrast points and ask students to suggest other possible points of comparison or contrast.

Whichever order you choose, remember to use transitions to help readers understand how your points are organized.

HOW TO Add Transitions to a Paragraph That Compares and Contrasts

The following words and phrases can help readers follow your points:

Comparison	*Contrast*
similar, similarly	different, differently
like	unlike
the same	opposite
as	although, though
compared to	by contrast, in contrast

Monica's Revised Draft

Before you read Monica's revised draft, reread her discovery draft. Then, as you read her revised draft, pay attention to the ways she improved her focus, balanced her details, and rearranged her points. Monica's revised draft has a few errors typical of this stage of the writing process; she'll fix them later.

It's Not High School

College is different from high school because you have to put in a lot of effort in order to succeed. As you know, high school was very easy for me. I skipped my classes half the time because the teachers just lectured from the textbooks. I rarely did the homework, it was mostly busywork. Tests were multiple choice, so studying was easy: I only had to memorize some facts for a test. Through all of this I still did good. College, though, is different. Classes are not extremely hard, but you have to show up because professors expect you to talk in class and you have to participate. If you don't do the homework, you won't be able to keep up with the discussion. Tests are harder too: You have to write essays to show that you understand the material. I found that I probably did more studying in one semester of college than in my whole four years of high school! I will be honest, sometimes you feel yourself asking, "Why am I doing this?" But when you look at what all of the work will do for you in the future, it's worth it.

GROUP ACTIVITY: Analyze Monica's Revised Draft

Use the following questions to discuss with your classmates how Monica improved her draft.

1. How did Monica improve her topic sentence?

   ____

   ____

   ____

   ____

2. How does Monica's comparison and contrast help her readers understand her topic?

   ____

   ____

   ____

   ____

3. In her revised draft, Monica reorganized her points and added details. How does this improve her paragraph?

   ____

   ____

4. What can Monica do to further improve her draft?

For more tips on how to review a draft effectively, see pp. 43–45.

WRITING ACTIVITY 8 (Group): Peer Review

Form a group with two or three classmates and exchange copies of your drafts. Read your draft aloud while your classmates follow along. Take notes on your classmates' answers to the following questions.

1. What do you like best about my paragraph?
2. How can I improve my topic sentence to better describe what I am comparing and contrasting? How can I better explain why my topic is important?
3. Evaluate my comparison and contrast points. Are there points that need to be removed?
4. Evaluate my details within each comparison and contrast point. Do I need to add any descriptions or examples to help you understand my thoughts?
5. Are my points in the most effective order? Should I try a different organizational strategy? Which sentences would you suggest I move?
6. Does my concluding sentence restate my topic sentence or explain why the comparison and contrast is important?

WRITING ACTIVITY 9: Revise Your Paragraph

Using Monica's revision as a model and your classmates' suggestions as a guide, revise your draft. Pay particular attention to balancing your comparison and contrast points and to organizing your ideas.

STEP 4: EDIT YOUR PARAGRAPH

When you wrote your discovery draft, you probably made some mistakes in grammar, spelling, and punctuation. Now you have a chance to fix them. In this chapter, you'll focus on eliminating unnecessary repetition and wordiness.

What Are Unnecessary Repetition and Wordiness?

Repetition — saying the same thing twice — might seem like a good way to emphasize your points, but unnecessary repetition can cause readers to lose interest in what you are saying. If you use different words to express the same idea, you might not even realize that you're repeating yourself. Consider the following example:

You can find additional advice on avoiding unnecessary repetition on p. 581.

REPETITION Before now the groups haven't tried yet to combine their activities together.

REVISED Before now the groups haven't tried to combine their activities.

Yet means "before now," and *combine* means "put together." So *yet* and *together* don't add anything to the meaning of the sentence but are just unnecessary repetition.

In addition to repeating ideas, you may sometimes add phrases to your sentences that don't add any meaning but just fill space. Consider the following example:

WORDY As you might know, my favorite class is history.

REVISED My favorite class is history.

If your readers already know that history is your favorite class, there's no need to tell them again. And if they don't know this about you, pointing out their lack of knowledge is unnecessary because you're giving them the information now.

Here are some more examples of unnecessary repetition and wordy phrases:

REPETITION We wanted to go to the study group because the study group always helps us understand new ideas.

REVISED We wanted to go to the study group because it always helps us understand new ideas.

WORDY As a matter of fact, the study sheets illustrated everything we needed to know.

REVISED The study sheets illustrated everything we needed to know.

Use Color

Highlight in color any words that repeat things you have already said. Omit unnecessary words when you revise.

Eliminating Unnecessary Repetition

Phrases like the ones that follow are unnecessarily repetitious and should be avoided:

past history
at this point in time
end result
yellow color
in my opinion
continue to remain
consensus of opinion
connect together
true fact
8 p.m. at night
truly believe

Be on the lookout, also, for filler phrases that make your writing wordy:

due to the fact that
obviously
like I said
in this day and age
in order to
I think that
as you know
in my opinion
I have found that
to tell the truth

ESL Links

The *Discoveries* Web site includes links to useful ESL sites. Go to **bedfordstmartins.com/discoveries** and click on "ESL Links."

EDITING PRACTICE: Eliminating Unnecessary Repetition

Revise each of the following sentences to eliminate unnecessary repetition or wordy phrases.

1. I believe that it is important to listen carefully.

____

2. Due to the fact that I like to take tests, I studied for weeks.

____

3. Each and every one of my friends is in college.

____

4. The positive benefits of this course are obvious and apparent.

____

5. This last list is the final one we will make.

____

6. You should cooperate and work as a team.

____

7. Like I said, study hard and you'll do well.

____

8. At this point in time, I'm not ready for that exam.

____

9. After a frank and honest exchange, the professor and I came to an agreement and resolution about my grade.

____

____

10. We laughed at the humorous comedy when we all went to the wrong room.

____

Exercise Central
The *Discoveries* Web site includes additional practice exercises in eliminating repetition. Go to **bedfordstmartins .com/discoveries**, click on "Exercise Central," and select "Unnecessary Repetition."

Monica's Edited Paragraph

Monica's revised draft had a few errors in grammar, spelling, and punctuation. She edited her paragraph to eliminate these. (The underlining indicates where she corrected errors.)

College Isn't High School

College is different from high school because you have to put in a lot of effort to succeed. High school was very easy for me. I skipped my classes half the time because the teachers just lectured from the textbooks. I rarely did the homework because it was mostly busywork. Tests were multiple choice, so studying was easy: I only had to memorize some facts. Through all of this I still did well. College, though, is different. Classes are not extremely hard, but you have to show up because professors expect you to talk. If you don't do the homework, you won't be able to keep up with the discussion. Tests are harder too: You have to write essays to show that you understand the material. I probably did more studying in one semester of college than in my whole four years of high school! I will be honest: sometimes you feel yourself asking, "Why am I doing this?" But when you look at what all of the work will do for you in the future, it's worth it.

Switch Computers to Edit
If your class has access to computers, switch terminals with another student and read his or her paragraph. Use bold, underlining, or color to mark any errors you find.

WRITING ACTIVITY 10: Edit Your Paragraph

Using a dictionary and the Handbook in Part Four of this book, edit your paragraph. Look especially for unnecessary repetition.

STEP 5: SHARE YOUR PARAGRAPH

Monica e-mailed her paragraph to her sister Regina, a high school junior who was planning to apply to Monica's college. Regina was surprised to learn that she would have to work so much harder than she was used to, and she promised Monica that she would take her studies more seriously.

ADDITIONAL WRITING ASSIGNMENTS

1. Write a paragraph for your classmates in which you compare and contrast students who are always prepared for class with those who are not. What are the similarities and the differences between these two groups of students?
2. Write a paragraph for an animal shelter Web site comparing and contrasting the advantages of adopting a kitten or puppy with those of adopting an older cat or dog.
3. Write a paragraph to your state representative comparing and contrasting your local roads with those of another city. Which are in better condition? How can the poorer roads be improved?
4. Write a paragraph for a national magazine such as *Newsweek* in which you compare and contrast the advantages and disadvantages of living in your community. What does your community offer to people and companies who might want to move there?

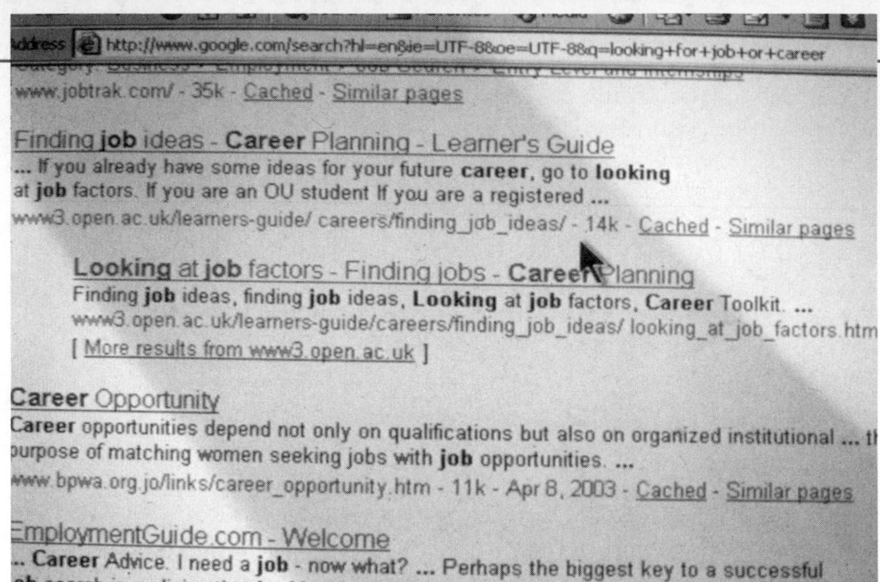

What jobs match your personality and personal values? To find out, you might visit the career center at your college or do online research. In this chapter, you will define a word that reflects your personal values or a term related to a career you want to pursue.

CHAPTER

9

Writing a Paragraph That Defines

In this chapter, you will

- discover how definition works.
- brainstorm to gather ideas.
- write about your values or career goals.
- use progressive order to organize your points.
- edit for pronoun-antecedent agreement.
- share your paragraph with a career counselor.

UNDERSTANDING DEFINITION

When Valentine's Day approaches, many of us shop for greeting cards. For the person we feel romantic about, we buy a card that has a quotation from one of Shakespeare's love sonnets. For family members, we buy cards that express our gratitude for their care. For a friend who just got married, we purchase a card with a joke about what happens when the honeymoon is over.

These Valentine's Day cards express different definitions of love: romantic, familial, friendly. It's amazing how such a common word — *love* — can have so many different meanings.

Writers use *definition* to make an idea clear. Sometimes they define a word their readers might not know. For instance, if you're writing about the importance of exercise for a community newsletter, you would define *aerobic*. Writers also use definition to show that they're using a term in a particular way. For a paper about how to be a good teacher, for example, you should explain your definition of what a good teacher is. Definition answers questions like these:

- What do you mean?
- Can you explain that to me?
- What is it?
- What is it not?

READING PARAGRAPHS THAT DEFINE

A thoughtful definition can often show what is important to us. Read the following two paragraphs to see how other writers have used definition to make their points.

Identity

The American-born daughter of Korean immigrants, Vickie Nam visited South Korea as a teenager. She was surprised to discover that native Koreans immediately recognized her as an outsider.

VICKIE NAM

from "Orientation: Finding the Way Home"

I was a gyo-po, a foreigner. Viewing the city streets from above, stringy black dots bobbed up and down and darted from side to side. On ground level, I noticed that it didn't matter that I looked like everybody else; I was still singled out for being

different. The pictures that were taken on my first day in Seoul tell an interesting story. Now, all I can see is that my Western stance, my Kodak camera, and my Doc Martens were dead giveaways; I might as well have draped myself in an American flag. The thing is, and all of the other American-born kids agreed with this conjecture, even if we weren't wearing Western clothes, the natives still would have pegged us Americans. We joked constantly about our unique gyo-po status; this erased the sting of rejection by the Korean community. To the locals, we smelled funny, we talked funny, and we just didn't belong.

READING ACTIVITY 1: Build Your Vocabulary

Try to determine the meanings of the following words from Vickie Nam's paragraph. Then, check their meanings by looking the words up in a dictionary.

stance ________________________________

conjecture ________________________________

pegged ________________________________

READING ACTIVITY 2: Read to Improve Your Writing

Answer the following questions about Vickie Nam's paragraph.

1. In your own words, define *gyo-po* in a sentence.

   ____

2. Nam writes that "Viewing the city streets from above, stringy black dots bobbed up and down and darted from side to side." What do you think she means by this?

   ____

   ____

   ____

3. What characteristics or qualities made Vickie Nam recognizable as American?

   ____

   ____

   ____

____

____

4. What are some words that other people might use to define you?

____

____

A Career Term

Professionals in many fields — social work, public policy, politics, and economics, to name a few — often grapple with the problems caused by poverty. But many people disagree about who should be considered poor. David K. Shipler offers his own definition of poverty for a book that explores the dilemmas faced by low-wage earners.

DAVID K. SHIPLER

from The Working Poor: Invisible in America

By global or historical standards, much of what Americans consider poverty is luxury. A rural Russian is not considered poor if he cannot afford a car and his home has no central heating; a rural American is. A Vietnamese farmer is not seen as poor because he plows with water buffalo, irrigates by hand, and lives in a thatched house; a North Carolina farmworker is, because he picks cucumbers by hand, gets paid a dollar a box, and lives in a run-down trailer. Most impoverished people in the world would be dazzled by the apartments, telephones, television sets, running water, clothing, and other amenities that surround the poor in America. But that does not mean that the poor are not poor, or that those on the edge of poverty are not truly on the edge of a cliff.

READING ACTIVITY 3: Build Your Vocabulary

Try to determine the meanings of the following words from David K. Shipler's paragraph. Then check their definitions by looking the words up in a dictionary.

irrigates _______________

thatched _______________

amenities _______________

READING ACTIVITY 4: Read to Improve Your Writing

Read and answer the following questions about *The Working Poor.*

1. In your own words, define your idea of "poverty" in a complete sentence.

   ____

   ____

2. According to Shipler, what are some characteristics of poverty in America?

   ____

   ____

3. What is Shipler's main point in this paragraph?

   ____

   ____

   ____

4. What are some terms used in your chosen career that you might define differently than others do?

   ____

   ____

   ____

Writing Assignment

Most colleges and universities have a career center that helps students identify promising occupations and search for jobs. Imagine that you are attending a career planning seminar that aims to match your personality with a potential career. The career counselors have asked you what is important to you.

- Write a paragraph defining a word that reflects your identity or one of your personal values. Some examples might be *creativity, spirituality,* or *nonconformity.*

  OR

- Write a paragraph that defines a term related to a career you want to pursue. For example, hotel managers discover that *hospitality* is an important concept, some stock traders are interested in *junk bonds,* and most chiropractors are dedicated to *holistic medicine.*

STEP 1: DISCOVER IDEAS FOR WRITING

As you think about what you might want to define, be sure to look for a topic that is interesting, important, or controversial enough to explore in depth.

Choosing a Topic

For additional help with choosing your topic, see p. 19.

For this chapter's assignment, you'll be defining something to help explain who you are or what you want to be. Try to choose a word that readers may not know or one that you can present in a new way. Also, remember to choose a topic that is important to you and interesting to your readers.

Consider the paragraphs you read earlier. Vickie Nam defined a word that she knew most of her readers would not know, *gyo-po.* It was also a word that helped her describe how it felt to be different, an important topic for her. David K. Shipler defined a familiar word, *poverty,* in his own way, because his readers are unlikely to agree about what makes a person poor.

Think back to some conversations you've had with friends recently. Were there times when you had to explain what you meant, or when you and a friend didn't agree on the meaning of a word or phrase? Any idea that caused a misunderstanding or a disagreement could be a topic for your paragraph.

Explore Re: Writing Links Libraries

To help you brainstorm topic ideas, go to the Re: Writing Web site at **bedfordstmartins.com/rewriting** and click on "Links Libraries."

Considering Your Audience and Purpose

The audience for your definition consists of the career counselors who are helping you identify potential careers. While they might be familiar with college students in general, they won't know you personally.

Read more about audience and purpose on pp. 20–22.

Because you are using definition to explain to others about the meaning of a word or to try to convince them to think about it in a new way, your main purpose is informative.

WRITING ACTIVITY 1: Identify Your Audience and Purpose

Answer the following questions about your audience and purpose.

1. What will the career counselors already know about you before they read your paragraph? What won't they know about you?

   ____

   ____

   ____

2. Why will they be reading your paragraph?

   ____

   ____

   ____

3. On what basis will they judge your paragraph? List several characteristics they'll want to see.

   ____

   ____

   ____

4. What is your primary purpose for writing this paragraph?

   ____

   ____

   ____

Brainstorming to Gather Ideas

More information about brainstorming can be found on p. 24.

Will you write about a word that explains your values, or will you write about a term related to the profession you plan to enter? Brainstorming can help you decide.

To find a topic for your paragraph, write down all of your ideas without judging which ones are better than others. Express as many ideas as possible so that you can go back and use the ones that are helpful.

HOW TO Brainstorm for a Paragraph That Defines

- Write a general topic idea at the top of a page.
- List any ideas that come to mind as quickly as possible.
- Don't think about whether your ideas are good or not.
- Don't worry about spelling, grammar, or punctuation.
- Review what you've written, looking for words that you could define in a paragraph.

Student writer Sam knew he wanted to write about his career goals, but he didn't know where to start. He brainstormed to find a term he could define.

Career Goals

Do I have one?

I do believe in getting involved.

I wish more people were honest.

Why do politicians lie so much?

I used to work on political campaigns.

My sister still works on them.

She always calls herself an activist.

What exactly is that?

Am I an activist?

Use Color

As you review the ideas you brainstormed, use different colors to highlight words you might choose as your topic.

WRITING ACTIVITY 2: Brainstorm to Choose a Topic

Write "What I Value" at the top of a page and brainstorm ideas for this topic. Then, write "Career Goals" at the top of another page and brainstorm again. Review your brainstorming and choose a word or concept that you can define in a paragraph.

Narrowing Your Topic

Although you're defining only one word or phrase, you still might need to narrow your topic. Suppose you want to define *rock music* because you'd like to work in the recording industry. There are too many kinds of rock music (alternative, heavy metal, classic, acid, modern, and so on) to explain in a single paragraph. Instead of defining *rock music,* try defining just one element of it, such as protest songs.

For more help narrowing your topic, see pp. 27–29.

Some terms have several definitions based on different ways a word is used or has been used in the past. When there are many different ways to define a term, it's best to focus on just one of those meanings. For his definition of poverty, for example, David K. Shipler could have explained the statistical and political meanings of the word, or the differences between kinds of poverty, such as financial and emotional. But if he had done so, he would have taken the focus away from his main point. He also would have had trouble fitting so much into such a short space.

HOW TO Narrow a Topic for a Paragraph That Defines

- Select a word or phrase to define.
- Determine whether this word or phrase can be broken down into types.
- Determine whether this word or phrase has different possible meanings.
- Choose one type or one meaning to define in your paragraph.

WRITING ACTIVITY 3: Narrow Your Topic

Write down the word you plan on defining, then brainstorm for ideas. If the word can be broken down into types, or if there are several ways to define it, narrow your definition so that it can be well supported in just one paragraph.

Use a CD-ROM Dictionary or Encyclopedia
To learn more about your topic, look it up in a CD-ROM dictionary or encyclopedia. If you decide to use information from one of these sources, be sure to identify these sources in your paragraph.

STEP 2: WRITE YOUR DISCOVERY DRAFT

To define a word or term, you first identify what class, or general group, it belongs to. Then you give the qualities or characteristics that set it apart from other things in that class. For instance, a *good teacher* might be defined in the following way:

class / defining qualities

a teacher with knowledge, compassion, and dedication

Throughout a paragraph that defines, you will include examples to illustrate your ideas.

Drafting a Topic Sentence

For more information about topic sentences, go to pp. 30–31.

For a definition paragraph, the topic sentence says what you will define. It can also summarize the meaning of the word. In her topic sentence, Vicki Nam summarizes what she means by *gyo-po:*

I was a gyo-po, a foreigner.

A topic sentence can also define a word in a way that differs from what people expect. David K. Shipler does this in the first sentence of his paragraph on poverty:

By global or historical standards, much of what Americans consider poverty is luxury.

Your topic sentence can also preview the points that you will make in the rest of the paragraph:

Integrative medicine has three major characteristics: it sees a close connection between mind and body, borrows medicine from the Far East, and focuses intensively on the patient's history and personality.

HOW TO Write a Topic Sentence for a Paragraph That Defines

- Identify the word, phrase, or idea that you will define.
- Summarize your definition.
- If your definition is different from what readers expect, briefly explain how.
- Consider previewing the points you'll make in the paragraph.

WRITING ACTIVITY 4: Draft a Topic Sentence

Referring to your brainstorming, draft a topic sentence for your paragraph. You can use the sample topic sentences as models.

Asking Questions to Add Support

You can collect information for your discovery draft by asking the six journalists' questions: *Who? What? Where? When? Why? How?*

Another example of using the journalists' questions can be found on pp. 25–26.

Student writer Sam wanted to define the term *activist* because his sister had started referring to herself as an activist, and he wasn't sure what that really meant. Here is how Sam answered three of the journalists' questions.

Who is an activist?

Someone who wants to change the world.

You can be conservative or liberal.

My sister is very liberal; my son is more conservative.

What does an activist do?

Gets involved in political movements and campaigns.

Goes to protests.

Writes letters.

Sometimes people do violent protests, like burning down buildings.

Why do people become activists?

They want to make the world better.

They want to change laws.

They think that just voting for politicians isn't good enough.

WRITING ACTIVITY 5: Ask Questions

Gather ideas for your draft by answering all six of the journalists' questions about your term: *Who? What? Where? When? Why? How?*

Drafting a Concluding Sentence

Your concluding sentence can summarize your definition, explain why the topic is important, or suggest how the definition relates to readers' lives.

After thinking about his definition of what an activist is, Sam drafted these concluding sentences:

> The next time you hear the word *activist*, you'll know what it means.
>
> More people need to become activists in order to make the world a better place.
>
> The next time you see something that needs to be changed, consider becoming an activist.

When Sam wrote his discovery draft, he used the third sentence because it neatly summarized his points and also connected his definition to his readers' lives.

WRITING ACTIVITY 6: Draft a Concluding Sentence

Write several drafts of a concluding sentence for your paragraph. By writing more than one, you'll have more choices when you finish your draft.

Sam's Discovery Draft

In addition to using some of the ideas he gathered in the prewriting stage, Sam included ideas that came to him as he composed. His draft contains the kinds of errors that often appear in a discovery draft; he'll correct them later.

What Is an Activist?

To some people *activist* is a dirty word. They think these people are violent or get in the way. But most activists are people who just get involved--they're

```
active! Maybe they work on political campaigns or
they protest at a meeting by holding up signs. My
sister for example thinks that the government
shouldn't allow logging and drilling in our national
forests. She gets people to sign petitions and she
protests some politician's speeches. My sister has
two children. My son in high school believes the
opposite. I'm proud that he's an activist. He wants
logging and drilling in the national forests if the
people who live nearby want it. He's also written
petitions and done other kinds of protests. I don't
want my children thinking they can't do anything to
change the world. The next time you see something
that needs to be changed, consider becoming an
activist.
```

WRITING ACTIVITY 7: Write a Discovery Draft

Starting with what you've already drafted for your topic sentence, supporting details, and concluding sentence, write a discovery draft. Include new thoughts as they come to you.

STEP 3: REVISE YOUR PARAGRAPH

For this chapter's assignment, you're writing for career counselors who want to help you choose a career. The details and examples you include need to show that you're knowledgeable about your topic. Be sure, also, that your paragraph is focused and your point is clear.

Strengthening Your Focus

To improve your draft, make sure that every sentence contributes to your definition. Check that the topic sentence summarizes your definition, gives a new definition, or previews your points. Then, check that every supporting sentence gives information or examples about *your* definition. Finally, check that your concluding sentence summarizes the topic sentence or restates your main idea.

You might have noticed that a sentence in Sam's draft was off the topic of his paragraph:

```
My sister has two children.
```

His sister's children have nothing to do with activism, so Sam deleted this sentence.

Building Your Support with Patterns of Writing

To make your definition convincing, you must support your points. You can use any of the other patterns of writing you have learned in this book to develop your paragraph.

Suppose you're defining the word *nurse* to explain how the health-care profession has changed. You might *classify* different types of nurses — registered nurses, licensed practical nurses, nurse practitioners, and so on.

Learn more about classification in Chapter 7.

Or perhaps you want to define *individuality* in a way that differs from how other people define it. You could *compare and contrast* the two definitions of the term. Or, like David K. Shipler, you could compare and contrast different versions of your term. In his definition of *poverty,* he contrasts American ideas of poverty with examples from Russia and Vietnam.

For more help with comparison and contrast, go to Chapter 8.

Sometimes the best way to define something is to use *process explanation* to show how it works. To define *addiction,* for example, you might explain how people progress from casual use to dependence.

Read more about process in Chapter 6.

No matter which technique you use, you'll need to include plenty of *examples* to help your readers understand your ideas. For her definition of *gyo-po,* Vickie Nam mentions her posture, her camera, and her shoes to explain how Koreans recognized her as a foreigner. Her examples from everyday life allow her readers to relate what they already know to a new idea.

Chapter 3 explains how to use examples.

HOW TO Build Stronger Definition

- Include *examples* that your readers can understand to support your ideas.
- Use *description* to show how something looks, feels, smells, sounds, or tastes.
- Use *classification* to break the word into different types.
- Use *comparison and contrast* to show similarities or differences between meanings or types.
- Use *process* to explain how something is done.
- Consider *narrating* an episode to explain why the definition is important.

See Chapter 5 for more information about description.

For more help with narration, go to Chapter 4.

Using Progressive Order to Organize Your Points

Progressive order is also explained on p. 40.

How you order the ideas in a paragraph that defines will depend on your topic and method of development. One good way is to use *progressive order,* in which you put your points in order of how important each one is, with the least important one first and the most important one last. Vickie Nam, for example, waits until the end of her paragraph to explain that being called *gyo-po* made her feel rejected and hurt. This placement indicates the importance Nam places on this idea.

No matter what method of development you use, the ideas in a definition paragraph need to be connected with transitions to prevent your readers from getting lost.

HOW TO Connect Ideas in a Paragraph That Defines

In a definition paragraph, you're likely to use some of the following transitions:

- Words that show likeness or comparison, such as *in comparison* and *similarly.*
- Words that indicate difference, such as *in contrast, on the other hand, while,* and *but.*
- Words that show order, such as *first, next, last,* and *finally.*
- Words that indicate classification, such as *the first type, the second type,* and so on.
- Words that give examples, such as *for example* and *for instance.*

Sam's Revised Draft

Before you read Sam's revised draft, reread his discovery draft. You'll notice that his revision has a stronger focus, better supporting details, improved sentence order, and more effective transitions. This draft still contains errors that Sam will correct when he edits.

What Is an Activist?

An activist is someone who becomes involved in social movements to make the world a better place. Instead of just voting for politicians, they also put pressure on public officials to change policy. Activists are involved in different types of movements. In various parts of the world. Some activists work on political elections. They organize rallies and give away leaflets and pamphlets about their candidates. Other activists try to change policy by protesting. For instance, my sister is a liberal. They want to keep the national parks off-limits to logging for timber and drilling for oil. She has carried signs during politicians' speeches and gone door-to-door to get people to sign petitions. In contrast, my son is conservative. They're in favor of drilling or logging if the people who live nearby approve it. He has written to public officials and published letters in the newspaper. As you can tell from my sister and son, an activist has a variety of beliefs and techniques. The one thing they have in common is the belief that they can make a difference.

GROUP ACTIVITY: Analyze Sam's Revised Draft

With your classmates, use the following questions to discuss how Sam has revised his draft.

1. Compare Sam's original topic sentence to the topic sentence in his revised draft. Is his revised sentence better? Explain.

   ____

   ____

2. What patterns of writing has Sam used in his revised draft? How do they help him express his ideas?

   ____

   ____

   ____

   ____

3. What transitions has Sam added to make his ideas easier to follow?

   ____

4. What can Sam do to make his draft even better?

   ____

Work Online
Group activities can be done online if you have access to a computer. E-mail your classmates with your responses to a particular activity.

WRITING ACTIVITY 8 (Group): Peer Review

Form a group with two or three classmates and exchange copies of your drafts. Read your draft aloud while your classmates follow along. Take notes on your classmates' answers to the following questions.

1. What do you like best about my paragraph?
2. How well does my topic sentence summarize the definition, explain how my definition is different, or preview my supporting points? What suggestions do you have for revision?
3. How focused is my paragraph? Are there any ideas that are off-topic?
4. Evaluate my support. How well do I use patterns of writing to develop my ideas? Do I need more examples?
5. How well did you follow my points? Should any of them be reordered?

WRITING ACTIVITY 9: Revise Your Draft

Keeping your classmates' suggestions in mind, revise your draft for focus, support, and organization. You can use Sam's revised draft as a model.

STEP 4: EDIT YOUR PARAGRAPH

You're writing your paragraph for people who will help you plan your career, so it's important that your final draft have no mistakes. Go over your draft carefully for spelling, punctuation, and grammar. In this chapter, you will focus on correcting pronoun-antecedent agreement.

What Is Pronoun-Antecedent Agreement?

For more help with pronoun-antecedent agreement, see pp. 511–13.

A *pronoun* usually takes the place of a specific noun, called its *antecedent,* in a sentence. The pronoun must agree in number with the noun it refers to: a singular noun takes a singular pronoun, and a plural noun takes a plural pronoun. Consider the following examples:

SINGULAR *Sharon* disagreed with the newspaper editorial, so *she* decided to write a letter to the editor.

PLURAL The *musicians* didn't care if *they* offended people. *They* refused to be censored.

Correcting Errors in Pronoun-Antecedent Agreement

Use a singular pronoun — *I, me, you, she, her, he, him,* or *it* — when you refer to a single thing or person. Use a plural pronoun — *we, us, they,* or *them* — when you refer to more than one thing or person.

In this passage, the pronoun *they* doesn't agree in number with the noun it refers to, *doctor.*

INCORRECT The doctor was late to our appointment. *They* finally showed up after an hour.

To correct this mistake, if there was only one doctor, make the pronoun singular to agree with the noun:

CORRECT The doctor was late to our appointment. *She* finally showed up after an hour.

If there was more than one doctor, make the noun plural, to agree with the pronoun:

CORRECT The doctors were late to our appointment.

They finally showed up after an hour.

When a group of things or people — such as a family, a team, or an audience — is referred to, use a singular pronoun.

INCORRECT Television shows have changed the way the *family* is portrayed. *They* are now shown as being very diverse.

CORRECT Television shows have changed the way the *family* is portrayed. *It* is now shown as being very diverse.

Most indefinite pronouns, which don't refer to a specific person or thing, are singular. Indefinite pronouns include *any, anybody, anyone, each, everybody, everyone, everything, none, no one, someone,* and *something.*

INCORRECT When *someone* is portrayed inaccurately, *they* might be discriminated against.

CORRECT When *someone* is portrayed inaccurately, *he* or *she* might be discriminated against.

CORRECT When *people* are portrayed inaccurately, *they* might be discriminated against.

If you correct a problem in pronoun-antecedent agreement by changing the noun, check that the noun still agrees in number with the verb of the sentence.

HOW TO Correct Errors in Pronoun-Antecedent Agreement

- Check that singular pronouns refer to singular nouns and that plural pronouns refer to plural nouns.
- Use singular pronouns with nouns that name a group, such as *family, audience,* or *band.*
- Use singular pronouns with the indefinite pronouns *any, anybody, anyone, each, everybody, everyone, everything, none, no one, someone,* and *something.*

EDITING PRACTICE: Correcting Errors in Pronoun-Antecedent Agreement

Correct the mistakes in pronoun-antecedent agreement and noun-verb agreement in the following passage.

Press coverage of the last presidential campaign was very biased. In my opinion, the press is usually liberal. Most of the time they don't even bother to hide their bias. For example, anyone who attended the Republican convention were portrayed as being interested only in lowering their taxes. They weren't portrayed as being interested in much else, even education. The Democrats, however, were shown as being involved in a variety of issues. Every Democrat on TV took an interest in not just their taxes, but also their children's education, and other issues as well.

Exercise Central
The *Discoveries* Web site includes additional practice exercises for pronoun-antecedent agreement. Go to **bedfordstmartins.com/discoveries**, click on "Exercise Central," and select "Pronoun-Antecedent Agreement."

Sam's Edited Paragraph

Sam's revised paragraph contained several errors. He corrected these when he edited his paragraph. (Sam's corrections are underlined.)

What Is an Activist?

An activist is someone who becomes involved in social movements to make the world a better place. Instead of just voting for politicians, he or she also puts pressure on public officials to change policy. Activists are involved in different types of movements in various parts of the world. Some activists work on political elections. They organize rallies and give away leaflets and pamphlets about their candidates. Other activists try to change policy by protesting. For instance, my sister is a liberal. She wants to keep the national parks off-limits to logging for timber and drilling for oil. She has carried signs during politicians' speeches and gone door-to-door to get people to sign petitions. In contrast, my son is conservative. He's in favor of drilling or logging if the people who live nearby approve it. He has written to public officials and published letters in the newspaper. As you can tell from my sister and son, activists have a variety of beliefs and techniques. The one thing they have in common is the belief that they can make a difference.

WRITING ACTIVITY 10: Edit Your Paragraph

Edit your paragraph, consulting a dictionary and the Handbook in Part Four of this book. Correct pronoun-antecedent agreement errors, as well as any other errors you may find. Add your corrections to your editing log.

STEP 5: SHARE YOUR PARAGRAPH

After reading Sam's paragraph, his career counselor thought that he might be interested in a career as a lawyer or a government lobbyist and suggested that he apply for an internship with a government agency such as the Environmental Protection Agency. Even if you have not visited your school's career center yet, save your paragraph for any counseling sessions that you might schedule in the future. Naturally, share your paragraph with your classmates and friends — it shows both your writing skills and your personal or career interests.

ADDITIONAL WRITING ASSIGNMENTS

1. Write a paragraph that defines *honesty.* Then exchange your definition with several classmates. Take notes on how each of you defined this word. Present your definitions to the class.
2. Select an idea from another one of your classes and write a definition of it. For instance, for history you might define *reparations,* for computer science you might define *algorithm,* and for art history you might define *modernism.* Teach the definition of this word to the rest of your writing class.
3. Write a paragraph to a high school newspaper in which you define the ideal student. The purpose of the paragraph is to help high school students become better prepared for college.
4. Select a term from current events that people define in various ways, such as *liberal, conservative, family values, affirmative action,* and so on. For your campus newspaper, explain how you define this term, pointing out why you believe other definitions of the word are wrong.

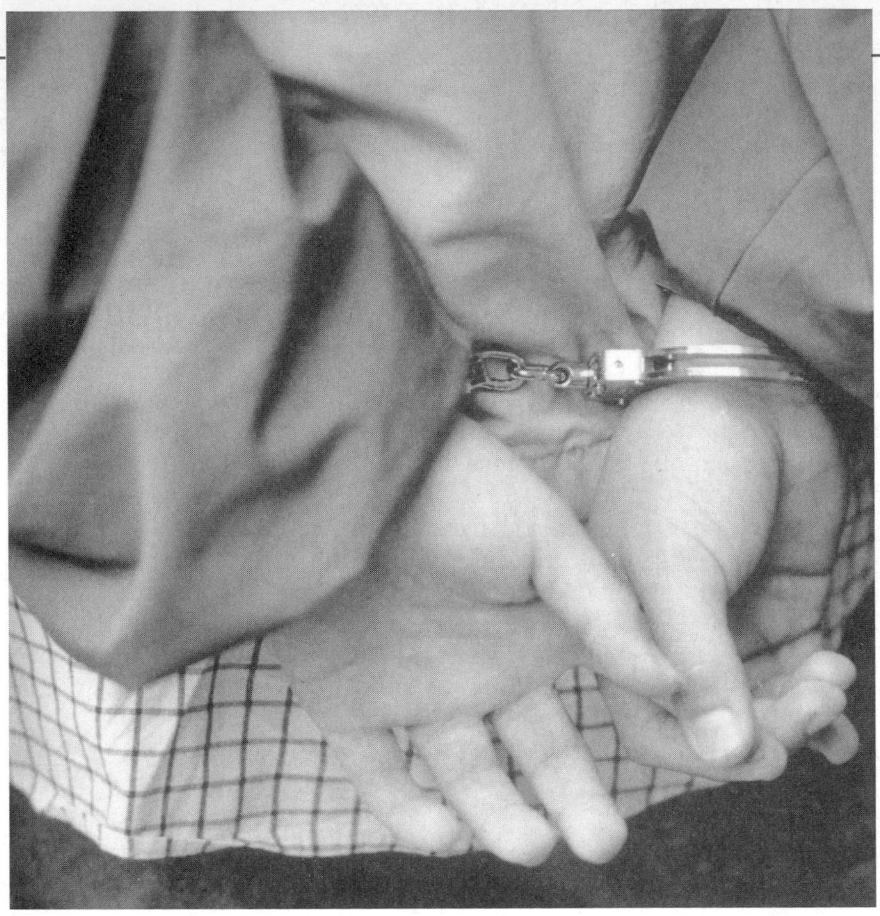

Imagine that this handcuffed teenager was arrested for stealing a pack of cigarettes. The causes of his theft include his addiction to cigarettes and the fact that he is too young to buy cigarettes legally. One of the effects of his theft is that he now must complete twenty hours of community service as part of a highway trash crew. In this chapter, you will write about what causes teenagers to engage in destructive behaviors or about the effects destructive behaviors can have on students' lives.

CHAPTER

10

Writing a Paragraph That Shows Cause and Effect

In this chapter, you will

- discover how cause and effect works.
- cluster to gather ideas.
- write about teenage behavior.
- use progressive order to organize your points.
- edit for dangling and misplaced modifiers.
- send a letter to a high school newspaper editor.

UNDERSTANDING CAUSE AND EFFECT

If you've ever asked yourself *why* or *what if,* you have analyzed cause and effect. *Cause* examines why something happened; *effect* explains the result of it. For example, a low-pressure front causes rain, which in turn makes it possible for flowers to bloom. You work overtime to save money for a vacation, then you go to Las Vegas and win five hundred dollars.

Your college instructors will often ask you to analyze cause and effect for course assignments. In a business class, you might need to explain the causes of a recession. For a course in ecology, you might analyze the effects of acid rain on forests in the northeastern United States. As a final project in your psychology seminar, you might write a paper on both the causes and the effects of bipolar disorder.

Cause-and-effect analysis answers the following kinds of questions:

- Why did that happen?
- What will happen?
- How are these things connected?

Most things that happen have more than one cause, and just about anything that happens will have more than one effect. One job of cause-and-effect analysis is to figure out which causes or effects are most important.

READING PARAGRAPHS THAT SHOW CAUSE AND EFFECT

What makes us do what we do, and how will our actions affect us? The following two paragraphs use cause-and-effect analysis to try to understand human behavior.

The Cause of a Destructive Behavior

One of the most difficult problems facing the United States is substance abuse. Pete Hamill claims that one of the causes of illegal drug use is television.

PETE HAMILL

from "Crack and the Box"

The drug plague also coincides with the unspoken assumption of most television shows: Life should be easy. The most complicated events are summarized on TV news in a minute or less. Cops confront murder, chase the criminals, and bring them to justice (usually violently) within an hour. In commercials, you drink the right beer and you get the girl. Easy! So why should real life be a grind? Why should any American have to spend years mastering a skill or a craft, or work eight hours a day at an unpleasant job, or endure the compromises and crises of a marriage? Nobody works on television (except cops, doctors, and lawyers). Love stories on television are about falling in love or breaking up; the long, steady growth of a marriage — its essential dailiness — is seldom explored, except as comedy. Life on television is almost always simple: good guys and bad, nice girls and whores, smart guys and dumb. And if life in the real world isn't that simple, well, hey, man, have some dope, man, be happy, feel good.

READING ACTIVITY 1: Improve Your Vocabulary

Try to determine the meanings of the following words from Pete Hamill's paragraph. Then, check their meanings by looking the words up in a dictionary.

plague ______________________________

coincides ______________________________

assumption ______________________________

compromises ______________________________

____

essential ______________________________

READING ACTIVITY 2: Read to Improve Your Writing

Read and answer the following questions about "Crack and the Box."

1. Why does Hamill think that watching too much television causes illegal drug use?

____

____

____

2. What examples does Hamill give to illustrate what he thinks about TV?

___

___

___

3. Look at the language that Hamill uses in his last sentence. Who is he imitating? Does this writing style help Hamill convey his point? Why or why not?

___

___

___

4. Why do you think people use illegal drugs?

___

___

___

The Effect of a Destructive Behavior

Alcohol abuse is common on college campuses, especially in the form of "binge drinking," or having four or more drinks at a time. Nutrition expert Jane Brody discusses one of the effects of this behavior.

JANE BRODY

from "The Hangover"

You don't have to be a chronically heavy drinker to suffer the adverse effects of alcohol. One "night on the town" can do it, as millions have discovered the morning after. Hangovers have no respect for race, nationality, or socioeconomic status. Anyone who overdoes it can get one. To a hungover German, it's "Katzenjammer" — the wailing of cats. Italians call it "stonato" — out of tune. To the French it's "la gueule de bois" — woody mouth; in Spain "resaca" — surf of sea; in Norway "jeg har tommermenn" — workmen in my head; and in Sweden it's "hont i haret" — pain in the roots of the hair. But by whatever name, the splitting headache, searing thirst, churning stomach, furry tongue, and shaky jitters of a hangover are an exacting price to pay for an evening's indulgence.

READING ACTIVITY 3: Build Your Vocabulary

Try to determine the meanings of the following words from "The Hangover." Then, check their meanings by looking the words up in a dictionary.

chronically ________________________________

adverse ________________________________

socioeconomic ________________________________

searing ________________________________

exacting ________________________________

READING ACTIVITY 4: Read to Improve Your Writing

Answer the following questions about Jane Brody's paragraph.

1. In your own words, what is Brody's main point?

   ____

2. What are the effects of "a night on the town," according to this paragraph?

   ____

   ____

3. Why does Brody give examples of what hangovers are called in other languages?

   ____

   ____

   ____

4. Name another destructive behavior that young people often engage in. What are the effects of that behavior?

   ____

   ____

Writing Assignment

Concerned by the risks teenagers take, the editor of your former high school newspaper has asked you to write an article to help students better understand their actions.

- Write a paragraph explaining what causes teenagers to engage in destructive behaviors such as smoking, shoplifting, or driving drunk.

  OR

- Write a paragraph that describes the effects a destructive behavior can have on a student's life. Some examples might be skipping classes, taking steroids, or cheating.

STEP 1: DISCOVER IDEAS FOR WRITING

As you think about what you will write, try to find a topic that you already know something about, either from personal experience or from careful study.

Choosing a Topic

For more advice on how to choose a topic, refer to p. 19.

Teenagers often accuse adults of not remembering what it was like to be in high school, but most of us remember it quite well. You might have finished high school last year or two decades ago, but there are probably some things about it that stand out in your mind.

As you look for a topic, turn first to your strongest memories. Did you, or someone close to you, do something that caused problems? Maybe you'd like to understand what happened, or perhaps you want to help someone else avoid pain. Writing about something that matters to you will help you put together an interesting cause-and-effect paragraph.

Explore Re: Writing Links Libraries
To help you brainstorm topic ideas, go to the Re: Writing Web site at **bedfordstmartins.com/rewriting** and click on "Links Libraries."

E-mail Your Topic
E-mail possible topics for your paragraph to several friends or family members. Ask them which topic they think is most interesting and important.

Considering Your Audience and Purpose

Your readers for this chapter's assignment are high school students, many of whom might be engaging in some kind of risky behavior. You'll need to consider the characteristics of these readers — what they already know (or think they know), what they need to know, and how they feel.

Read more about audience and purpose on pp. 20–22.

In addition, understand why you are writing. Cause-and-effect analysis is almost always either informative or persuasive, or a bit of both. Remember that the editor asked you to write because she is worried about the dangerous things students in her school are doing. Therefore, your primary purpose will be to persuade your readers to think differently about their behavior, perhaps even to change it.

WRITING ACTIVITY 1: Identify Your Audience and Purpose

Keeping in mind that your readers are high school students, answer the following questions.

1. What destructive behavior are you thinking of writing about? Why is it important to you?

   ____

   ____

   ____

2. What things will your audience likely already know about the causes and effects of this behavior? What things will they be likely not to know?

   ____

   ____

   ____

3. How interested will high school students be in your topic? How can you write your paragraph to make sure that your audience will stay interested?

____

____

____

4. What will your purpose be in writing this paragraph?

____

____

____

Clustering to Gather Ideas

More information about clustering can be found on p. 25.

Any given behavior might have a number of possible causes and many potential effects. How do you decide how everything is connected and what is most important? To begin figuring that out, try clustering to get a map of your ideas.

HOW TO Cluster for Cause and Effect

- Write "Causes of ________" in the middle of a blank page. Circle the phrase.
- Write down some possible causes for this behavior. Circle each cause and draw a line to the behavior circle.
- List more specific ideas for each of the causes. Circle them and draw lines to the cause circles.
- Follow this same procedure to make an "Effects of _________" cluster on another sheet of paper.
- Review your clusters to find the best ideas to write about.

Student writer Jerome wanted to write about why teenage girls develop eating disorders because his cousin was struggling with bulimia. Here is the cluster he created.

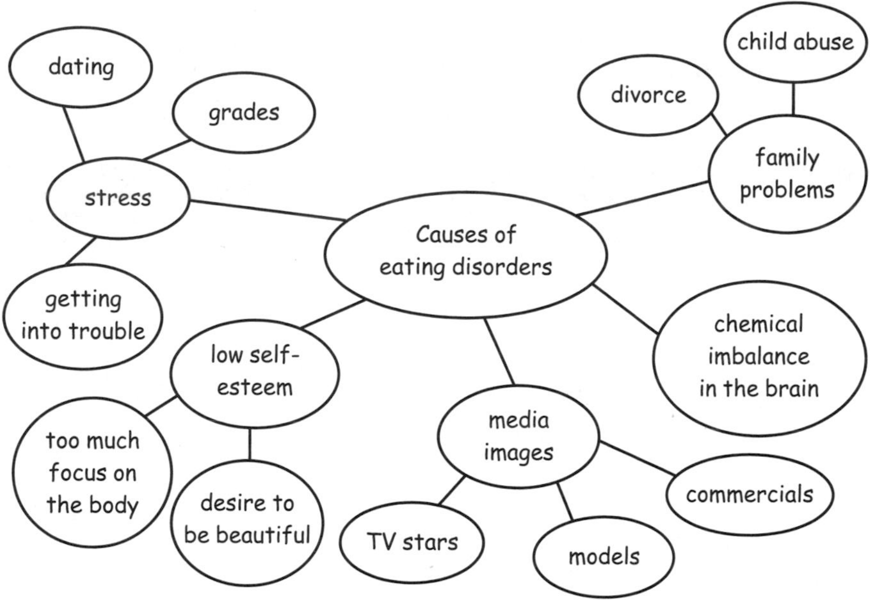

Cluster on the Computer
Use the drawing or picture option of your word-processing program to create your cluster.

WRITING ACTIVITY 2: Cluster to Find Your Topic

Create two clusters: one on the causes of a destructive behavior, and one on its effects. Review your clusters to decide what interests you most and what you have the most information about.

Narrowing Your Topic

Other ways to narrow your topic are explained on pp. 27–29.

You can't address every possible cause or effect of a behavior in a single paragraph. Suppose you are writing about alcohol abuse. Think of all the effects you could discuss: poor grades, health problems, dropping out of school, loss of self-respect, blackouts, car accidents, loss of friends, loss of jobs, getting arrested, and so on. To narrow your topic, you might select just three of the effects you believe are the most important, such as loss of friends, poor grades, and car accidents.

Sometimes, just one cause or one effect can be enough to develop a good paragraph. Look again at Pete Hamill's paragraph. Although his cause-and-effect analysis is very detailed, he is examining one specific cause of illegal drug use: television. Similarly, Jane Brody writes about one effect of drinking too much: a hangover.

HOW TO Narrow a Topic for a Paragraph That Shows Cause and Effect

- Select a topic that interests you and that you know something about.
- Decide whether to focus on causes or effects.
- Cluster on the topic.
- Select one to three of the most important causes or effects from your cluster.
- Check that you'll have enough information to support your points.

When he drew his cluster, Jerome listed five things that cause eating disorders. In order to develop his points with enough details, he decided to focus on three of them — low self-esteem, media images, and stress. He thought these problems were the most likely to cause eating disorders.

WRITING ACTIVITY 3: Narrow Your Topic

Make another cluster for your chosen topic. Use Jerome's cluster as a model. Then, review the cluster on your own or with your classmates. Select the three most important causes or effects to write about.

STEP 2: WRITE YOUR DISCOVERY DRAFT

By now, you should have chosen a behavior to write about and identified three causes or effects that you can examine in your paragraph. Don't worry if you don't know what to say. Simply starting to put your ideas into words will help you discover what your point is.

Drafting a Topic Sentence

Remember that you're analyzing the causes or effects of a destructive behavior because you want high school students to think about the things they do. Your topic sentence, then, should tell your readers what behavior you're examining and why they should know more about it. Your topic sentence can also briefly list the points you will make. Finally, make it clear whether you will focus on causes or effects.

For more information on topic sentences, turn to pp. 30–31.

Here are some examples of topic sentences written for this assignment:

> Understanding the three main causes of teenage suicide might save the life of somebody you love.
>
> Although teenagers often think it's harmless, driving while intoxicated can lead to trouble with the law, serious injury, and even death.

HOW TO Write a Topic Sentence for a Paragraph That Shows Cause and Effect

- Identify your main idea.
- Indicate why your topic is important.
- Indicate whether you will focus on causes or effects.
- Consider briefly listing your points.

Jerome drafted this topic sentence:

> Eating disorders are a result of low self-esteem, stress, and society's emphasis on being thin.

WRITING ACTIVITY 4: Draft a Topic Sentence

Referring to the cluster you made earlier, draft a topic sentence for your paragraph. Use the sample student topic sentences as models. Remember that you can change your sentence if it doesn't work.

Brainstorming to Add Support

Read more about ways of gathering ideas on pp. 24–27.

You have identified three points to support your cause-and-effect analysis. But how will you support your points? Try brainstorming to find examples and details. Because you're still in the drafting stage, generate as many ideas as possible.

Beginning with the three causes he listed in his topic sentence, Jerome brainstormed to develop support:

Low Self-Esteem

Teenagers don't like their bodies.

They don't get enough attention or praise.

They do strange things to make people like them.

Stress

My cousin stressed too much.

She worried about grades and

— about getting a boyfriend.

— about getting into college.

— about her appearance.

Not eating made her feel in control.

Media Images

Models are super thin.

The actresses on *Desperate Housewives* and *Alias* are very thin.

You always hear about dieting tips and food.

Add First, Then Delete

During the drafting stage, focus on adding ideas. Use the cut-and-paste function to omit irrelevant material when you revise. Save the deleted sentences to another file in case you want to retrieve them later.

WRITING ACTIVITY 5: Brainstorm Details

Brainstorm for details to support your ideas. List the points you chose in Writing Activity 3, and then brainstorm for ideas as Jerome did.

Drafting a Concluding Sentence

Remember that you're writing to persuade high school students to change their behavior. The last sentence of a paragraph usually has the most impact, so be sure that your concluding sentence sums up your main point, reminds your audience why that point is important, or suggests a solution to the problem you analyzed.

Turn to pp. 34–35 for more help writing a concluding sentence.

Jerome came up with three possible concluding sentences:

We must work hard to keep young people from developing eating disorders.

To prevent eating disorders, we need to help young people feel better about themselves and learn to handle stress.

These are some of the reasons people get eating disorders.

When he drafted his paragraph, Jerome selected the second sentence because it summed up his major supporting points and suggested a way to solve the problem.

WRITING ACTIVITY 6: Draft a Concluding Sentence

Write several drafts of your own concluding sentence, then select the best one. Be sure to close your paragraph with something that your readers will remember.

Jerome's Discovery Draft

While Jerome used many of the ideas he had already brainstormed, he added ideas as they came to him. His draft contains the kinds of errors typical at this stage of writing; he'll correct them later.

What Causes Eating Disorders?

Eating disorders are a result of low self-esteem, stress, and the media's emphasis on being thin. Many actors and actresses are very thin and well-built, so many teenage girls have low self-esteem. They don't like their bodies. They also get very stressed. My cousin has bulimia. She worries about grades, getting a boyfriend and her looks. Television, magazines, and the movies say you must look thin. Look at the women on *Alias* or *Desperate Housewives*. Not many people are as thin as those actresses. These are two of my cousins favorite shows. One of the biggest things you find in magazines are ads for diet drinks and foods. This makes you want to be thin. To prevent eating disorders, we need to help young people feel better about themselves and learn to handle stress.

WRITING ACTIVITY 7: Complete Your Discovery Draft

Using what you have put together for your topic sentence, support, and concluding sentence, write a discovery draft. Focus on explaining either the causes or effects of your topic.

STEP 3: REVISE YOUR PARAGRAPH

For a cause-and-effect analysis to work, the connections between your points need to be obvious and convincing to your readers. When you revise your draft, concentrate on making sure that your ideas are clearly related to each other.

Strengthening Your Focus

For more help with paragraph focus, turn to pp. 37–38.

Causes and effects often overlap, so make sure that each of your points is distinct from the others. For example, if you were writing about why high school students smoke, you may have identified four causes: peer pressure, advertising aimed at teenagers, a desire to be popular, and easy access to cigarettes. Most students, however, give in to peer pressure because they want to be popular: the two points overlap. You could focus your paragraph by discussing the points as a single idea.

Sometimes your paragraph may appear to be unfocused because you haven't explained how a point relates to the main idea. Suppose that when writing about students dropping out of high school, you state that high schools pay too much attention to athletics. At first this idea might appear to be off-topic. However, if you explain that students who aren't athletic may feel left out and thus stop attending school, then you will have written a focused paragraph.

Building Your Support with Evidence

Pay particular attention to cause-and-effect relationships in your paragraph. There is a difference between cause and coincidence: Simply because one event happened before another, it didn't necessarily make the second event happen. Suppose that your grades declined immediately after you decided never to eat spinach again. Unless you can prove that giving up spinach resulted in an iron deficiency that made you too weak to study, there's probably no connection between your diet and your schoolwork.

Read more about ways of supporting your points on pp. 38–39.

To avoid confusing coincidence with a cause-and-effect relationship, give evidence — in the form of examples, statistics, or facts — to show that events and ideas are connected. Draw on your personal experiences and knowledge and the experiences and knowledge of those you know. You might also want to include expert testimony to support your points.

HOW TO Build Stronger Evidence of Cause and Effect

- Add evidence to clarify the cause-and-effect relationship.
- Add examples to make your ideas more convincing.
- Add description to make your ideas more concrete or vivid.
- Consider including expert testimony to support your points.
- Add definitions if you need to explain words or ideas your readers might not understand.

Jerome found information from the *American Medical Association Family Medical Guide* to support his points that eating disorders are most common in girls and can be caused by low self-esteem and stress. However, he was unable to find statistics or facts to prove that media images cause eating disorders. Because Jerome couldn't find evidence for this idea, he omitted it.

Research Your Topic
Consult a CD-ROM encyclopedia or dictionary in your college library or another reliable reference source for information about your topic.

Using Question-and-Answer Order to Organize Your Points

Other ways of ordering points are explained on pp. 39–42.

To make your paragraph easy to follow, consider using *question-and-answer* order. To do this, start by asking a question about your topic, either in your title or in the first sentence of your paragraph. Then, use the rest of the paragraph to answer it.

As with any piece of writing, the ideas in your cause-and-effect paragraph need to be connected. Use transitional words or phrases that tell your readers when you're moving to a new cause or effect.

See p. 42 for a complete list of transitions.

HOW TO Connect Ideas in a Paragraph That Shows Cause and Effect

- Words and phrases that add ideas include *also, in addition, moreover, another reason.*
- Words and phrases that show result include *as a result, consequently, because, therefore.*

Jerome's Revised Draft

Jerome added evidence to his revised draft to support his ideas better. He also deleted ideas he couldn't prove, reordered his points, and added transitions. Jerome's revised draft still contains errors that he will correct when he edits his paragraph.

What Causes Eating Disorders?

Teenagers get eating disorders because they have low self-esteem and they are too stressed. According to the *American Medical Association Family Medical Guide,* usually anorexics and bulimics are teenage girls with low self-esteem (758). The authors write, "Sometimes an emotionally insecure girl will overhear a casual comment that she is too fat and decide she must lose weight to be popular" (758). A girl can become dangerously thin and still think she is fat with an eating disorder. Other teenagers get eating disorders because they have too much stress. Not eating helps them feel in control. My cousin was pressured to get high grades so she could get into a really good college before developing bulimia. Her doctor says this stress caused her eating disorder. I have learned from my cousins experience that eating disorders are terrible. To prevent eating disorders, we need to help young people feel better about themselves and learn to handle stress.

Works Cited

American Medical Association Family Medical Guide. 3rd ed. New York: Random, 1994.

GROUP ACTIVITY: Analyze Jerome's Revised Draft

Use the following questions to discuss with your classmates how Jerome has improved his draft.

1. Compare Jerome's topic sentence in his discovery draft with the one in his revised draft. How has he improved his topic sentence? How can he make it better?

____

____

____

____

____

2. How has Jerome improved his support?

____

____

____

____

3. In his revised draft, Jerome reordered his points to follow general-to-specific order. Is this an effective change? Explain your answer.

____

____

____

4. What can Jerome do to make his draft even better?

____

____

____

WRITING ACTIVITY 8 (Group): Peer Review

Form a group with two or three classmates and exchange copies of your drafts. Read your draft aloud while your classmates follow along. Take notes on your classmates' answers to the following questions.

1. What do you like best about my paragraph?
2. How clear is my topic sentence? Do you have any suggestions for revision?
3. What, if any, sentences should be deleted because they're off-topic or repetitive?
4. Evaluate my support. How well is the cause-and-effect relationship explained? What evidence, examples, descriptions, or definitions could I add to improve my support?
5. How well do my points follow each other? Do you have any suggestions for a better way to order my points?

Online Peer Review
If you have a class Web site, you may be able to access your classmates' drafts and the peer review questions online and send your responses to your classmates by e-mail.

WRITING ACTIVITY 9: Revise Your Draft

Using your classmates' suggestions, revise your draft. In particular, improve your support by clarifying the cause-and-effect relationship among your points, adding evidence to support your ideas and deleting points that you can't prove.

STEP 4: EDIT YOUR PARAGRAPH

You want your readers to focus on what you have to say, so edit your paragraph carefully before you submit it to your high school newspaper. In particular, concentrate on correcting any misplaced and dangling modifiers.

What Are Misplaced and Dangling Modifiers?

A *modifier* is a word, phrase, or clause that adds information about a sentence's subject, verb, or object. If a modifier is separated from the word or words it modifies, it is misplaced and might confuse readers.

Learn more about correcting misplaced and dangling modifiers on pp. 566–70.

MISPLACED Karen felt satisfied with her new apartment *waiting for the landlord.* [It sounds like the apartment is waiting.]

MISPLACED Anthony *only* jogs in the morning. [Anthony probably does other things in the morning.]

MISPLACED Julia lost her purse at the party *that has gold straps.* [The party does not have gold straps.]

A *dangling modifier* modifies a word that is not in the sentence but only in the writer's mind. It appears to dangle from the sentence because it's not attached clearly to anything.

DANGLING *While trying to eat a taco,* my car went off the road.

DANGLING *Attempting to recover a file on her computer,* anger set in.

DANGLING *Overwhelmed by injuries to key players,* the season was a disaster.

Correcting Misplaced and Dangling Modifiers

To correct a misplaced modifier, put it next to the word or words it modifies.

CORRECT *Waiting for the landlord,* Karen felt satisfied with her new apartment.

CORRECT Anthony jogs *only* in the morning.

CORRECT Julia lost her purse *that has gold straps* at the party.

To correct a dangling modifier, add the word that is being modified to the sentence.

CORRECT *While I was trying to eat a taco,* my car went off the road.

CORRECT *Attempting to recover a file on her computer,* Marie became angry.

CORRECT *Overwhelmed by injuries to key players,* the team had a disastrous season.

HOW TO Correct Misplaced and Dangling Modifiers

- Move misplaced modifiers closer to the word or words they modify.
- Correct dangling modifiers by adding the word that is modified to the sentence.

EDITING PRACTICE: Misplaced and Dangling Modifiers

Underline the misplaced and dangling modifiers in the following sentences, then move, add, or delete words as necessary.

1. Running for the bus, your letter blew away.

 ____

2. I cleaned my refrigerator wearing a bathrobe.

 ____

3. Letty even interviewed with Microsoft after she accepted the job at Dell.

 ____

 ____

4. Written in an hour, Parul submitted her report.

 ____

5. The news report gave details about the scandal on television.

 ____

6. Upset by the cost, the concert was canceled.

____

7. Susan's visa expired while visiting Moscow.

____

8. Protesting the war, the road was packed with people.

____

9. Emily came to the meeting covered with cat hair.

____

10. Cranky after not sleeping well, the noise was too much for him to handle.

____

Exercise Central
The *Discoveries* Web site includes additional practice exercises in correcting misplaced and dangling modifiers. Go to **bedfordstmartins.com/discoveries**, click on "Exercise Central," and select "Misplaced and Dangling Modifiers."

ESL Exercises Online
The *Discoveries* Web site includes links to useful sites for writers whose first language is not English. Go to **bedfordstmartins.com/discoveries** and click on "ESL Links."

Jerome's Edited Paragraph

Jerome's revised paragraph had a few errors in grammar, spelling, and punctuation. He corrected these errors in his edited draft. (The corrected errors are underlined.)

What Causes Eating Disorders?

Teenagers get eating disorders because they have low self-esteem and they are too stressed. According to the *American Medical Association Family Medical Guide*, anorexics and bulimics are usually teenage girls with low self-esteem (758). The authors write, "Sometimes an emotionally insecure girl will overhear a casual comment that she is too fat and decide she must lose weight to be popular" (758). A girl with an eating disorder can become dangerously thin and still think she is fat. Other teenagers get eating disorders because they have too much stress. Not eating helps them feel in control. Before she developed bulimia, my cousin was pressured to get high grades so she could get into a really good college. Her doctor says this stress caused her eating disorder. I have learned from my cousin's experience that eating disorders are terrible. To prevent eating disorders, we need to help young people feel better about themselves and learn to handle stress.

If you'd like to know when to use an apostrophe, read pp. 616–18.

Works Cited

American Medical Association Family Medical Guide. 3rd ed. New York: Random, 1994.

Examine Each Sentence

To produce a list of the sentences in your paragraph, press "enter" after each sentence. Then examine each sentence individually for errors.

For a review of how to create an editing log, see pp. 45–46.

WRITING ACTIVITY 10: Edit Your Paragraph

Using a dictionary and the Handbook in Part Four of this book, edit your draft. Add your corrections to your editing log so you won't make the same errors in the future.

STEP 5: SHARE YOUR PARAGRAPH

After Jerome's paragraph was published in his high school's newspaper, the school nurse decided to start an eating disorder awareness program. The program helps teenage girls improve their self-esteem and teaches stress management. Your paragraph also contains important and useful information, so consider sending a letter to the editor of your own high school newspaper. It just might help someone.

ADDITIONAL WRITING ASSIGNMENTS

1. Write a paragraph for your classmates and instructor about why you decided to go to college. In a class discussion, compare your reasons for going to college with your classmates' reasons.
2. Write a paragraph to an administrator at your college in which you explain why students at your college experience too much stress. At the end of the letter, suggest how the college could help reduce this stress.
3. Write a paragraph to an official in your local government about the effects of a problem in your neighborhood, such as traffic lights that don't work, potholes that are never filled, or weeds that are left untended. Describe in detail the effects of the problem so the official can understand how serious it is.
4. Write a paragraph for your state legislator about the effects that increased tuition rates have on college students. Ask the legislator to help reduce college students' financial pressures.

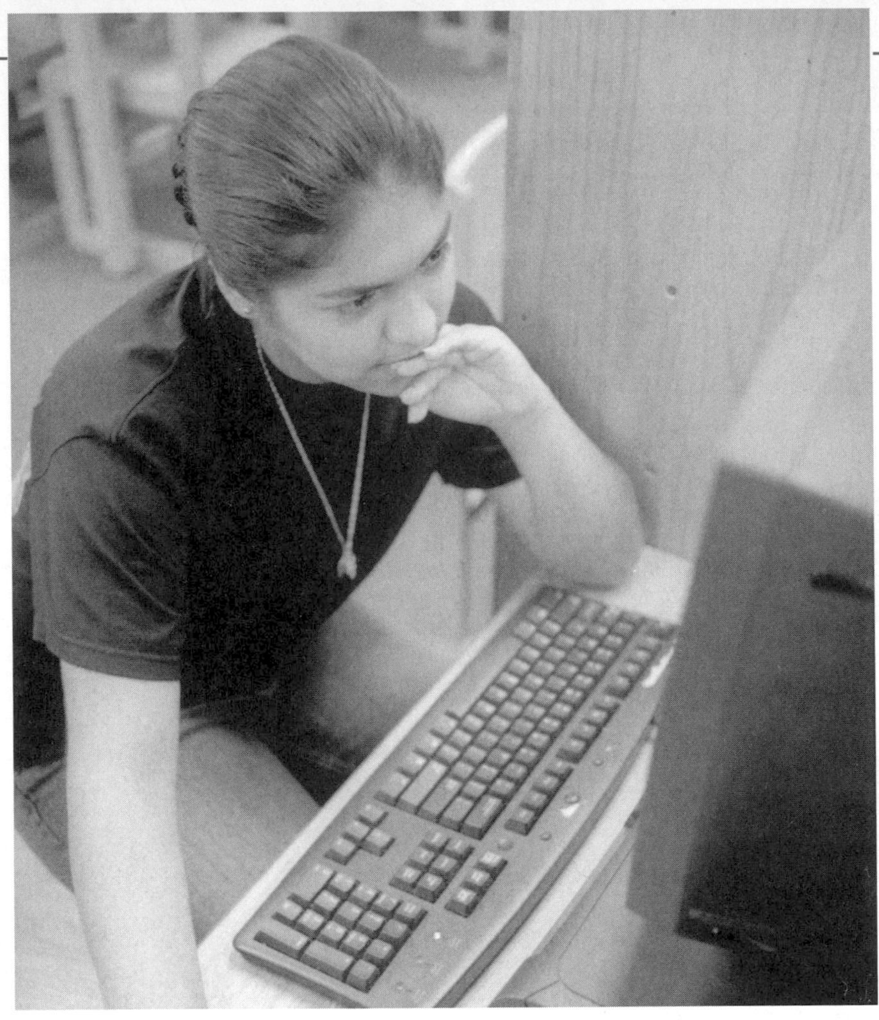

How should your college spend its technology budget? In this chapter, you will argue for or against your school's purchase of a computer application such as wireless networking, a subscription to an online journal for your college library, or virus protection for on-campus computers.

CHAPTER

11

Writing a Paragraph That Makes an Argument

In this chapter, you will

- discover how argumentation works.
- interview to gather ideas.
- write about computers.
- use progressive order to organize your points.
- edit for vague pronoun reference.
- send your paragraph to a school administrator.

UNDERSTANDING ARGUMENTATION

You may not be familiar with the word *argumentation,* but you already know what an argument is. Disagreement is a part of life. Think back to some arguments you may have had recently. Perhaps you expressed anger at a friend who was late meeting you for dinner. You may have disagreed with your boss when he wanted you to work on the day you had a paper due, or you may have snapped at someone who cut in front of you in line.

But an argument doesn't have to be disagreeable. It can be a friendly debate in which two or more people defend different positions on a question. You may have debated with your spouse over where to live or with some classmates over who should lead a group project. Argumentative writing is like a debate: It gives you the opportunity to persuade someone to think as you do on an issue. Argumentation answers questions such as:

- What is your opinion?
- Why do you think that way?
- Why should I agree with you?

Argumentation can be one of the most interesting and rewarding types of writing because it gives you the chance to defend something you believe in.

READING PARAGRAPHS THAT MAKE AN ARGUMENT

Almost everybody uses technology, but people disagree about its benefits and drawbacks. Read the following paragraphs to see how different writers use argumentation to express their opinions about personal computers.

Problems with Personal Computers

Sam Smith argues that he shouldn't be forced to upgrade his computer accessories each time he buys a new computer. The term *Luddite* in the title refers to someone who resists technical advances. (Ned Ludd, a weaver in the early 1800s, smashed weaving machines in an effort to preserve jobs for weavers.)

SAM SMITH

from "The Luddites at Microsoft: Making Machines That Smash Themselves"

I have a new machine. I have moved from Windows 2000 to Windows XP, which means that my old printer doesn't work with it, the old printer cable doesn't work with it, and I no longer can sneak on an old *Excel* program whose serial number I lost but worked fine except for a series of error messages. These are not revelations that arrived simultaneously, but were spaced with annoying distance across the past three days. And they all cost money. My wife tells me I am far too stingy about all this, but I can't get over the feeling that one of the world's richest men ought to be able to manufacture an operating system that lasts at least as long as my Plymouth minivan, which not only is happily in its seventh year but has outlasted its own brand name. Instead, I am forced by the reverse Luddites of Microsoft to upgrade when all I want to do is just to keep on trucking. I don't believe it is really Bill Gates' business to decide when I should improve my lot in life, and it is certainly not his privilege to do so in a totally unannounced fashion.

READING ACTIVITY 1: Build Your Vocabulary

Try to determine the meanings of the following words from Sam Smith's paragraph. Then, check their meanings by looking the words up in a dictionary.

revelations ______________________________

simultaneously ______________________________

reverse Luddites ______________________________

READING ACTIVITY 2: Read to Improve Your Writing

Read and answer the following questions about "The Luddites at Microsoft: Making Machines That Smash Themselves."

1. What is the author's main point in this paragraph?

____

____

____

2. What examples does Smith use to illustrate his main point?

____

____

3. In what way does Smith try to persuade his readers to believe as he does? Do you agree with him?

____

____

____

____

4. What problems have you had with computers?

____

____

____

Benefits of Personal Computers

In this paragraph, the authors of a computer science textbook argue that computers make writing easier.

DAVID PATTERSON, DENISE KISER, AND NEIL SMITH

from Computing Unbound

Writing is an example of an everyday task that computers can simplify. Writing well is an art, difficult to teach or to learn, but best developed by constant practice. Ten or fifteen years ago no one would have suggested that computers could help people write more effectively, but today writing is the predominant use of personal computers, and most professional writers use them. When people could write only with quill and ink, the physical act of writing was slow and making corrections was painful. The invention of the typewriter in the 19th century made it possible to put words on paper much more quickly; electric typewriters and "self-correcting" typewriters simplified the process still further, but editing each successive draft of a composition still required completely retyping the whole manuscript. With a computer, it is possible to edit a composition quickly and easily on the computer screen, and then print it when you have a draft you are pleased with.

READING ACTIVITY 3: Build Your Vocabulary

Try to determine the meanings of the following words from *Computing Unbound.* Then, check their meanings by looking the words up in a dictionary.

predominant ____________________

quill ____________________

successive ____________________

READING ACTIVITY 4: Read to Improve Your Writing

Read and answer the following questions about the paragraph from *Computing Unbound.*

1. What is the main point of this paragraph?

   ____

2. List three details the authors use to argue that technical advances simplify writing.

   ____

   ____

   ____

   ____

3. Do the authors persuade you that computers simplify writing? Why or why not?

   ____

4. What do you like best about computers?

   ____

   ____

   ____

Writing Assignment

Colleges and universities spend a lot of money on technology. Computer systems need regular updating, but budgets are limited. Imagine that your school is trying to decide what new equipment and capabilities to purchase for student use, and that the administration has invited students to make suggestions.

- Write a paragraph arguing that a computer application is essential for student success. Examples might be online courses, a new database for the library, or desktop publishing software for the computer lab.

  OR

- Write a paragraph explaining why a computer application — such as wireless networking, instant-messaging, or Web filtering — is overrated or harmful to students.

STEP 1: DISCOVER IDEAS FOR WRITING

There are probably a lot of things that you like and dislike about computers. Remember that you're trying to do more than simply express your opinion: You're sharing your thoughts in order to convince somebody to take a certain action.

Choosing a Topic

For more help choosing your topic, see p. 19.

You might know right away what you want to argue for or against, but maybe you're not sure. One way to decide is to ask yourself questions. What do you like about using a computer? Are there applications that you use all the time, or is there a technology that you wish you had access to? What frustrates you? Do other people you know feel the same way as you do? Why or why not? Anything you have strong feelings about is a promising topic for your paragraph.

When you choose a topic, be sure that you take a position people might disagree with. There's little point, for example, in arguing that students use the Internet. Nobody would question that. But arguing that students shouldn't do their research on the Web is something that can be debated.

Explore Re: Writing Links Libraries
To help you brainstorm topic ideas, go to the Re: Writing Web site at **bedfordstmartins.com/rewriting** and click on "Links Libraries."

Considering Your Audience and Purpose

To review audience and purpose, see pp. 20–22.

To write an effective argument, first consider your readers, who in this case are the people who decide what technology to purchase for your school. Undoubtedly they already know about the latest computer technology, and it's their job to know something about how students use it. Since they have asked for input, however, you can guess that they don't know everything about how students use computers, or what's most important to undergraduates.

By definition, argumentation is persuasive writing. Because you're trying to convince the administration to act on your suggestions, you'll want to appear well-informed, respectful, and fairly formal. You'll also need to consider how they might disagree with you, and what information might convince them to change their minds.

WRITING ACTIVITY 1: Analyze Your Audience and Purpose

Keeping in mind that your readers will be campus administrators who want your input before they make a purchasing decision, answer the following questions.

1. What will your readers already know about how students use computers? What might they not know?

   ____

   ____

   ____

2. What is your purpose for writing this paragraph?

   ____

   ____

   ____

3. Is your audience likely to agree or disagree with your position? Why?

   ____

   ____

   ____

4. Can you gather enough evidence to convince others to believe as you do?

____

____

____

Interviewing to Gather Ideas

For more information on how to conduct an interview, see p. 26.

Talking to other people will give you valuable support for your argument. Statements made by people with knowledge about your topic are considered *expert testimony.* An argument backed up by expert testimony makes your paragraph more convincing.

For example, if you think that dorm rooms should have high-speed Internet access, you could interview a librarian to find out how often the public terminals have a wait list. If you think students should be able to view their financial-aid records online, you might get the bursar's opinion about whether this would make it harder to keep the records confidential. Providing expert testimony shows your readers that you're arguing from facts, not just personal opinion.

Student writer Omar wanted to argue that computers make students' lives too complicated. To find out whether other students had problems with computers, he set up an interview with the manager of his school's computer lab. He prepared the following questions:

- How many students use the lab?
- When is the lab open?
- Are the computers compatible with other computers students might have access to?
- Do students ever lose their work?
- What other kinds of problems do you see students having with computers?

Generate Questions Online
If you have a class listserv or message board, post your topic and have other students suggest whom you could interview and what kinds of questions you might ask.

WRITING ACTIVITY 2: Interviewing

Select a general topic and prepare questions to help you learn more about it. Interview an expert to gather information for your paragraph.

Narrowing Your Topic

For your argument to be effective, you must have a strong opinion that others might not agree with. Because you're drafting only one paragraph, your topic should also be narrow enough that you can support it with a few well-chosen pieces of evidence. Suppose you want to argue that high-speed Internet access distracts students from their work. You could provide examples of everything they do online, but such a list would be too long to discuss in any detail. Instead, you might choose one or two aspects of the Web that students spend too much time on, such as instant-messaging, playing games, or reading blogs.

For help narrowing your topic, see pp. 27–29.

HOW TO Narrow a Topic for a Paragraph That Makes an Argument

- Select a controversial topic and interview an expert about it.
- Review your interview responses and decide what information is most persuasive.
- Be sure that you can state a strong position.
- Check that you have the right amount of evidence to support your position in a single paragraph.

When student writer Omar first started thinking about his topic, he wanted to argue that computers are more trouble than they're worth. As he started to gather information, though, he realized his topic was too broad. He narrowed his focus to argue that students shouldn't have to use word-processing programs if they don't want to — something much more easily handled in a paragraph.

WRITING ACTIVITY 3: Narrow Your Topic

Reread the responses to your interview questions and highlight the information that is most persuasive. Choose one main point that you have a strong opinion about and that you can support with evidence.

STEP 2: WRITE YOUR DISCOVERY DRAFT

To argue well, you must first select a topic on which people disagree and on which you have a strong opinion. You will state your position, give your reasons for believing the way you do, and provide evidence to support them.

Drafting a Topic Sentence

To review how to write a topic sentence, see pp. 30–31.

The topic sentence of an argumentative paragraph states your position on a controversial subject. It can also identify what you're arguing against, or suggest the reasons for your opinion. Often, a topic sentence will include words like *should* or *should not*. Here are some examples of topic sentences written by students for this chapter's assignment:

> Every college student should be required to own a laptop.

> Although a lot of students want wireless Internet access on campus, it's a luxury we cannot afford.

> Because this is a commuter school, the library needs to provide remote access to its electronic journals.

Usually, you'll want to start with your topic sentence so that your readers know what your point is right away. For example, the authors of the paragraph from *Computing Unbound* place their topic sentence first:

> **Writing is an example of an everyday task that computers can simplify.**

Each sentence that follows this topic sentence provides evidence for the position that computers make writing easier.

If you're arguing an unpopular point, consider presenting your evidence ahead of your topic sentence. This will let you make your case before readers have a chance to reject your opinion.

HOW TO Write a Topic Sentence for a Paragraph That Makes an Argument

- State your position on a controversial topic.
- Consider identifying the opinion that you're arguing against.
- If you wish, briefly state the reasons for your position.

WRITING ACTIVITY 4: Draft a Topic Sentence

Draft three possible topic sentences for your paragraph: one that states your position, one that identifies the opinion you're arguing against, and one that briefly states the reasons for your opinion. You can use the sample student topic sentences as models.

Adding Support with Evidence

To change your readers' minds, you must provide strong evidence to support your opinions. Convincing evidence includes examples that clarify and explain your reasons for thinking the way you do, expert testimony that supports your position, and facts such as names, dates, numbers, statistics, or other information that you can prove is true.

Turn to pp. 31–32 to review the types of details you can add to develop your paragraph.

Student writer Omar went through his notes and listed his reasons for his position on computers. For each reason, he brainstormed examples, expert testimony, or facts to support his argument.

OPINION	Programs are incompatible.
EXAMPLE	I have been working on a word-processing file at home, but when I try to open it in the lab on campus, the computer won't open the disk.
OPINION	Computers are unreliable.
TESTIMONY	The manager of the computer lab says there are always at least two printers that don't work.
OPINION	Technology quickly becomes obsolete.
EXAMPLE	My one-year-old computer is already too slow to run new programs.
OPINION	Computers are expensive to own.
FACT	Common software, such as word processing, can cost more than $300.

WRITING ACTIVITY 5: Develop Evidence

List your reasons for thinking the way you do about your topic. Then, provide at least one example, expert testimony, or fact to support each one.

Drafting a Concluding Sentence

For types of concluding sentences, see pp. 34–35.

Your concluding sentence is your last chance to make an impression on your readers, possibly convincing them to believe as you do or to do something you recommend. Be sure to summarize what is important for your readers to remember about your topic. You might also want to propose something that your readers should do.

Look again at the concluding sentences of one of the paragraphs you read earlier. Smith concludes with the following:

> I don't believe it is really Bill Gates' business to decide when I should improve my lot in life, and it is certainly not his privilege to do so in a totally unannounced fashion.

This is a powerful sentence that persuasively states Smith's position on Microsoft's intrusion into his life.

WRITING ACTIVITY 6: Draft a Concluding Sentence

Write a sentence that restates your position on your topic. Compare it with your topic sentence to be sure that your position is clear in both sentences.

Omar's Discovery Draft

Omar wrote the following discovery draft arguing his position on personal computers. Notice that although he used some of the ideas he gathered in prewriting, he added new ones as they came to him. Like most discovery drafts, Omar's paragraph includes some errors. He will correct these later.

The Complicated Life

As a college student I have many problems as it is and computers just add to the complications. Computers might be useful in running cities and large companies, but they just create complications in my life. How many times has this happened to you? You have been working for weeks on a paper and when you decide to print, the computer won't open the disk. According to the computer lab manager at our school, this is a common senario for college students. It usually leads to having to start all over on your report. Even when you do get your file open, the printer refuses to work. I suggest that professors should accept work from a typewriter as well as neatly handwritten work. Not only professors but society as a whole. Everywhere you turn from résumés to memos and letters must be typed on computers. This is my major problem with computers. Technology is making life easy, but it also creates problems for those of us who want to have an uncomplicated life.

Debate on Computer

If your class has access to instant-messaging, hold a debate on screen. Post your position online and ask others to debate your reasons and evidence.

WRITING ACTIVITY 7: Complete Your Discovery Draft

Using the ideas you have already gathered, write a discovery draft for your paragraph. Concentrate on convincing your readers of your position. You'll have time to improve your paragraph later.

STEP 3: REVISE YOUR PARAGRAPH

To revise a paragraph that makes an argument, look at it from your readers' point of view. Would somebody with a different opinion find your argument convincing? You'll need to express your point clearly and provide solid evidence to get your readers to agree with you.

Strengthening Your Focus

First, check that your topic sentence states a strong opinion on a narrowed topic. Then, examine the reasons and evidence that you used to support your point. You may have included every reason you could think of when you drafted your argument. When you revise, select the best evidence and discard any less important information. Be sure, too, that every sentence in your paragraph relates directly to your topic sentence. If you have a lot of examples that aren't closely related to your point, you may need to narrow your topic further.

When he reviewed his discovery draft, Omar realized it wasn't clear that he was arguing against word-processing requirements at his school, not computers in general. He decided to rewrite his topic sentence to clarify his position. He also deleted sentences that didn't support his main idea:

```
   Computers might be useful in running cities and
large companies, but they just create complications
in my life.

   Not only for professors but society as a whole.
Everywhere you turn from résumés to memos and letters
must be typed on computers.
```

Building Your Support with Reliable Information

Remember that your readers may not agree with your argument. Not only must you include enough evidence to convince your audience, but you must also be sure that your information is reliable. Every claim you make must be something that your readers will agree is reasonable and true.

HOW TO Build Stronger Arguments

- Include enough information to persuade your readers of your position.
- Make sure that all of your information is reliable.
- Provide opposing viewpoints and debate them.
- End with your position on the topic.

Omar reviewed his paragraph and noticed that he couldn't prove one of his claims:

```
   It usually leads to having to start all over on the
report.
```

Because this information was unreliable (there are better ways to solve the problem of a file that won't open), Omar deleted this sentence.

One of the best ways to show that you are being reasonable is to mention or acknowledge points of view that don't agree with yours. In his argument against computer upgrades, for example, Sam Smith admits that not everybody shares his opinion:

> **My wife tells me I am far too stingy about all this, but I can't get over the feeling that one of the world's richest men ought to be**

> **able to manufacture an operating system that lasts at least as long as my Plymouth minivan, which not only is happily in its seventh year but has outlasted its own brand name.**

Notice that after he acknowledges the opposing view, Smith responds to it with his own view. By doing this, he shows that he knows what other people think and explains why he thinks differently.

Use a Newsgroup
Consider joining a newsgroup, or Internet bulletin board, that focuses on issues related to your topic. For a list of newsgroups on various topics, go to the *Discoveries* Web site at **bedfordstmartins.com/discoveries** and click on "Annotated Web Links." Then click on "Newsgroups."

Using Progressive Order to Organize Your Points

In an argumentative paragraph, order your ideas so that you begin with your weakest and end with your strongest point. Sam Smith, for example, started his paragraph with the annoyances of having to upgrade computer equipment. He saves his strongest point, that Microsoft's constant upgrades are unnecessary, for his conclusion.

Other ways of ordering your points are explained on pp. 39–42.

A paragraph that makes an argument can be improved by using transitional words to help your readers follow your logic. In his revised draft, Omar uses *although, for example, also, since,* and *now* to help his readers follow the sequence of events when he uses a computer to write his papers.

Omar's Revised Draft

Before you read Omar's revision, reread his discovery draft. Notice the changes he has made to his paragraph. This draft still contains errors, but Omar will correct them when he edits.

For more information on using transitions, see p. 42.

```
               The Complicated Life
  Now that computers are available to most students,
they require everything to be word-processed.
Although it does make revision easier, it adds to
the complications of being a college student. For
example, computers are quickly outdated. Since my
campus always purchases the latest version of
```

software packages. My one-year-old computer is already incompatible with the computers on campus. Even if I could afford to buy a new computer, which I can't, it would be outdated almost as soon as I purchased it. They are also unreliable. How many times has this happened to you? You have been working for weeks on a paper and when you decide to print, the computer won't open the disk. Even when you do get your file to open, the printer refuses to work. According to the computer lab manager at our school, this is a common senario for college students. We should not be required to use word processing if we don't want to. I suggest that they should accept work from a typewriter as well as neatly handwritten work.

GROUP ACTIVITY: Analyze Omar's Revised Draft

Use the following questions to discuss with your classmates how Omar improved his draft.

1. Compare Omar's topic sentence in his discovery draft with the one in his revised draft. How did he improve his topic sentence?

____

____

____

____

2. How does Omar's evidence help convince his readers of his opinion?

____

____

____

3. In Omar's revised draft, he added additional evidence. How does this improve his draft?

____

____

____

4. In his revised draft, Omar reorganized his evidence. How does this improve his draft?

5. What can Omar do to improve his draft further?

WRITING ACTIVITY 8 (Group): Peer Review

Form a group with two or three classmates and exchange copies of your drafts. Read your draft aloud while your classmates follow along. Take notes on your classmates' answers to the following questions.

1. What do you like best about my paragraph?
2. How clear is my topic sentence? How can I improve it to state my position better?
3. Examine my evidence. Does it seem reliable and true to you? Are there sentences that need to be removed because they are not focused on my topic?
4. Are you convinced by my argument? What information should I add to help convince you?
5. Are my points effectively ordered? Which sentences would you suggest I move?
6. Does my concluding sentence restate my position?

Online Peer Review

If your class has a Web site that posts these peer review questions, you may be able to respond to your classmates' drafts electronically.

WRITING ACTIVITY 9: Revise Your Draft

Using your classmates' suggestions as a starting point and Omar's revision as a model, revise your discovery draft. In particular, tighten your focus, strengthen your evidence, and consider acknowledging opposing points of view.

STEP 4: EDIT YOUR PARAGRAPH

No matter how strong your evidence is, mistakes in grammar, spelling, and punctuation may cause your readers to dismiss your argument. To make sure that they focus on what you have to say, edit your paragraph carefully. In this chapter, you will learn how to correct vague pronoun reference.

Online Writing Centers
A number of college writing centers have online tutoring. Tutors will answer your editing questions electronically. For a list of such centers, go to the *Discoveries* Web site at **bedfordstmartins.com/discoveries** and click on "Annotated Web Links." Then click on "Online Writing Centers (OWLs)."

What Is Vague Pronoun Reference?

You can find more information about vague pronoun reference on pp. 509–10.

A *pronoun* such as *you, he, she, they,* or *it* takes the place of a noun. When you use a pronoun, the noun that the pronoun replaces should be obvious. If a reader can't tell immediately what noun is being referred to, you have a vague pronoun reference that must be made clear.

VAGUE In my hometown, they're very friendly.

VAGUE In the article, it said students really should buy a PDA instead of a laptop.

VAGUE Joe told Jerry that he would have to buy the computer.

Correcting Vague Pronoun Reference

When you use a pronoun to refer to a noun, make sure the reference is clear. To correct vague pronoun reference, follow these guidelines:

1. Replace the pronoun with the noun it refers to.

   CLEAR In my hometown, the store owners are very friendly.

   CLEAR In the article, Bill Gates said that students really should buy a PDA instead of a laptop.

2. Or rewrite the sentence so the pronoun is no longer needed.

   CLEAR Joe said, "Jerry, I'll have to buy the computer."

HOW TO Identify and Correct Vague Pronoun Reference

- Identify any pronouns in your sentence.
- Check that each pronoun clearly refers to only one noun.
- Be sure that the noun is stated.
- Be sure that the pronoun is close to the noun.

EDITING PRACTICE: Correcting Vague Pronoun Reference

Correct vague pronoun reference as needed in the following sentences.

1. Because we know it was Tammy or Olivia, she should admit to leaving the dishes in the sink.

   ____

   ____

2. In my class, they are very happy to work together.

   ____

   ____

3. Robert test-drove a Honda Intrepid and a Suzuki Intruder. He liked it better.

   ____

   ____

4. Jessica told Mary that she needed to get home early to study for a test.

   ____

5. Don't even consider leaving the dog and cat alone. She will tear up the house.

   ____

   ____

6. Tomorrow I will do my homework and clean my apartment. I need to get it finished before I go on vacation.

   ____

   ____

7. So how do I know if the defendant is guilty? He says I have to decide.

   ____

   ____

8. Carla wanted to leave immediately, but he said she needed to get the car repaired first.

   ____

   ____

9. They say you have to accept responsibility for your actions if you want to succeed.

   ____

   ____

10. Whenever Maria explains history to Olivia, she has trouble with the vocabulary.

   ____

   ____

Exercise Central
The *Discoveries* Web site includes additional practice exercises in correcting vague pronoun reference. Go to **bedfordstmartins.com/discoveries**, click on "Exercise Central," and select "Vague Pronoun Reference."

Omar's Edited Paragraph

Omar's revised draft had a few errors in grammar and punctuation. He edited his paragraph to eliminate these. (The underlining indicates where he corrected errors.)

The Complicated Life

Now that computers are available to most students, <u>professors</u> require everything to be word-processed. Although <u>word processing</u> does make revision easier, it adds to the complications of being a college student. For example, computers are quickly outdated. <u>Since my campus always purchases the latest version of software packages, my one-year-old computer is already incompatible with the computers on campus.</u> Even if I could afford to buy a new computer, which I can't, it would be outdated almost as soon as I purchased it. <u>Computers</u> are also unreliable. How many times has this happened to you? You have been working for weeks on a paper and when you decide to print, the computer won't open the disk. Even when you do get your file to open, the printer refuses to work. According to the computer lab manager at our school, this is a common <u>scenario</u> for college students. We should not be required to use word processing if we don't want to. I suggest that <u>professors</u> should accept work from a typewriter as well as neatly handwritten work.

WRITING ACTIVITY 10: Edit Your Paragraph

Using a dictionary and the Handbook in Part Four of this book, edit your draft. Add your corrections to your editing log so you won't make the same errors in the future.

STEP 5: SHARE YOUR PARAGRAPH

Omar sent his paragraph to his campus IT administrator to try to get permission for students to write their papers by hand or on typewriters. Although the administration did not agree with his position, Omar got a friendly letter saying that he made some good points about the frustrations of using word processing. Consider finding out who is responsible for computer purchases at your school and sending a letter to him or her. Your paragraph just might change that person's mind about something important to you.

ADDITIONAL WRITING ASSIGNMENTS

1. Write a paragraph to a family member or friend to persuade him or her to give up a bad habit such as smoking, drinking, or driving recklessly. Provide your reasons for wanting this person to change and evidence that the habit is harmful.
2. Select a movie or television show and write a paragraph that uses argumentation to persuade your classmates to view it or not to view it. Provide evidence to support your position.
3. Write a paragraph to someone in a position of authority on your campus asking that a campus problem be solved.
4. Write a paragraph encouraging someone in your community to run for the school board. Explain why you think this person would be a good candidate and provide evidence that he or she can do the job.

PART TWO

Reading and Writing Essays

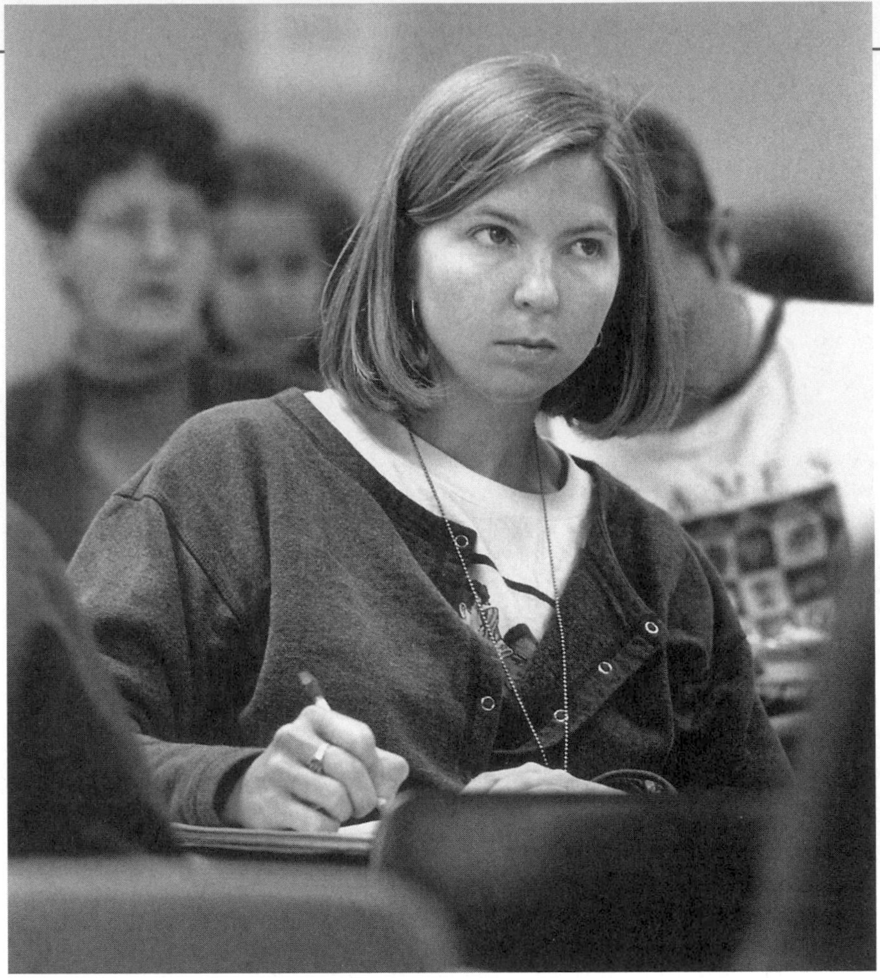

What does it take to succeed in college? In this chapter, you will write an essay that gives other students advice on how to succeed or describes something you are doing or plan to do to ensure your own college success.

CHAPTER 12

Moving from Paragraphs to Essays

In this chapter, you will

- discover how essays work.
- write about success in college.
- learn how to gather ideas.
- learn how to write a discovery draft.
- learn how to revise an essay.
- review how to edit.
- share your essay.

UNDERSTANDING ESSAYS

Have you ever noticed how often people use essays to communicate their ideas with others? You've probably read articles in magazines such as *People* or *Time,* opinion columns or humor columns in your local newspaper, and essays by professional or student writers in your classes. Essays are popular because they allow writers to develop extended discussions on topics that are important to them. They make it possible for writers to gather their best thoughts and put them in order before sharing them.

To review the parts of a paragraph, go to p. 18.

Just as a paragraph is a group of sentences that focus on a single topic, an essay is a group of paragraphs that focus on a single thesis. The parts of an essay are similar to the parts of a paragraph:

Paragraph	*Essay*
topic sentence	thesis statement
support (several sentences)	support (several paragraphs)
concluding sentence	conclusion

The opening paragraph, or *introduction,* of an essay gets the readers' attention and reveals the topic of the essay and the author's purpose for writing. The point or main idea of the essay is given in a *thesis statement,* which usually appears in the introduction. Supporting paragraphs explain particular ideas related to the main idea. The last paragraph, or *conclusion,* summarizes the main idea. The number of paragraphs in an essay will depend on the audience, purpose, and topic: Some essays might contain only three paragraphs, whereas other essays will have many more.

Here is an essay with each of its parts underlined and labeled.

Running Out of Money before Graduation

Charles Smith

introduction

The value of a college education has been documented over the years, not only for the potential earning power that it affords a person, but also for what it teaches people about valuing humanity and service to the community. Since I was old enough to remember, my mother, teachers, and people in my community have talked about the importance of African Americans attending college. Since earning my college degree, I have spent most of my career working in a university with enrollment and retention issues, and assisting college students in persisting to graduation. I have become extremely concerned with the number of students who have enrolled at the university without an educational finance plan.

thesis statement

Throughout the 1970s and the 1980s, aid was plentiful. Students who came from low- or middle-income families who did not receive academic or athletic scholarships could expect to receive some sort of financial aid, whether it was SEOG (supplemental educational opportunity grant), BEOG (basic educational opportunity grant), state aid, guaranteed student loans or some type of grant money. Today, this is not necessarily the case. There was a time when a student's financial aid package was made up of about 60 to 70 percent grant monies. Now more students' packages consist largely of loans.

topic sentence

supporting paragraph

It is important that parents, students and high school counselors realize that the Pell Grant is not the savior for students going to college. We must begin a new and invigorating mission of teaching students and parents to become more realistic and proactive about how much money it takes to go to college today. Two years ago, I began talking with people about developing a financial plan for their children to attend college. Developing financial plans is nothing new, but developing them for college just may be. I am not talking about just depositing money in a state account or federal government program, even though this will help. I am talking about really assisting parents and families in understanding the immediate need to begin planning financially to send their children to college.

topic sentence

supporting paragraph

Often I talk with upperclassmen about how they plan to pay for the rest of their education, and those who do not have scholarships are at a loss. Many are returning graduating seniors and have borrowed all the money they can, owing $20,000 and $30,000 of debt, and yet needing additional dollars to complete their undergraduate degree. At Delaware State University, many students are not able to return to

topic sentence

supporting paragraph

school because they did not plan financially to be in school. They find money for the first year, but have developed no financial plan to assist in completing their education. This situation is occurring at many other universities, according to my colleagues.

conclusion

restatement of thesis

We must begin a self-help program by teaching African Americans and other people of color how to develop a financial plan to not only go to college, but have access to the money needed to complete their education. Academic ability is important, but it is also important for the students to be able to finance the time that will be required to attain their degree. Financial planning sessions can be held on campus, in community centers, churches, malls and wherever possible. If taught properly, even the lowest-income earning person can save and plan. Students must be taught to save the money earned from summer and part-time employment to assist with the cost of their education. We must help families understand that a college education will continue to be one of the great equalizers in our society and will cost much more in the next decade.

The process of writing paragraphs is discussed in detail in Chapter 2.

By writing paragraphs in Part One, you have already practiced much of what you need to know to write an essay. Effective essay writers select a topic, consider their audience and purpose, use a process to bring their thoughts into words, develop and organize these ideas to make a point, and correct any errors before they share their writing with others.

Writing Assignment

People who have never attended college often wonder if they have what it takes to succeed there. Based on your experience, write a brief essay (500 to 750 words) about success in college.

- Write an informative essay that gives new or future students advice on how to succeed in college.

OR

- Write an expressive essay that explains something you have done or are doing to ensure that you succeed as a college student.

STEP 1: DISCOVER IDEAS FOR WRITING

Finding ideas for an essay works the same way as finding ideas for a paragraph. You think about what you might want to write about, consider your audience and purpose, gather ideas, and use those ideas to narrow your topic.

Choosing a Topic

Just as you did when you selected topics for paragraphs, try to find an essay topic that interests you, that you already know something about or are willing to learn more about, and that will interest your readers. The readings in this and other textbooks, your class lectures, discussions with people you know, and any reading you do for pleasure are all good places to start looking for topic ideas.

For more advice on how to choose a topic, refer to p. 19.

Student writer Daniel thought about all of his experiences as a first-year student. He considered his time on the golf team and his run for the student senate, but most of all, he thought about the twenty years he had spent in the military before starting college. Although what Daniel knew the most about was how his military experience prepared him for college, he didn't think that met the requirements of the assignment. He decided, instead, to give other older students advice about going to college.

Considering Your Audience and Purpose

You're writing to communicate something of interest to your readers, so you want to be sure that they understand your main point. The more you know about your audience and what you want to accomplish, the easier it will be for you get your point across to them.

For more information about audience and purpose, see pp. 20–22.

Teaching Tip
To extend the audience beyond the instructor and classmates, encourage students to share their final essays with others who might be interested in their topic.

HOW TO Consider Your Audience

The same questions you used to analyze the audience for your paragraphs can help you analyze the audience for your essay:

- What do my readers already know about my topic? What do they not know about it?
- What opinions might they have about my topic?
- How interested are they in my topic?
- How concerned will they be that I write correctly?

You already know that most writing is done for one of three purposes: to express, to inform, or to persuade. Because essays are longer and more detailed than paragraphs, they'll often have more than one purpose. You might, for example, try to persuade your readers to change their minds about something by giving them new information about it. Similarly, you could share personal experiences to help explain why you're writing an informative essay. When you do have multiple purposes for writing, be sure you know which of those purposes is most important.

HOW TO Identify Your Purpose

- *Expressive.* You share your personal thoughts and feelings about a topic that affects you personally.
- *Informative.* You explain something that you know or have studied to learn more about.
- *Persuasive.* You try to change your readers' minds about a topic.

Because he planned to write an essay for older students who wanted to know how to succeed in college, Daniel knew that his primary purpose was to provide helpful information. His secondary purposes were to share a few of his own experiences and to persuade his readers to follow his advice.

WRITING ACTIVITY 1: Identify Your Audience and Purpose

Keeping in mind that your readers will be people planning or just starting to attend college, answer the following questions. Answers will vary.

1. Who are my readers?

____

____

____

2. What do my readers know about my topic?

____

____

____

3. What do my readers want or need to know?

____

____

____

4. How do my readers feel about my topic?

____

____

____

5. What is my purpose for writing this essay?

____

____

____

Gathering Ideas

In Part One you learned how to brainstorm, freewrite, cluster, ask questions, interview others, and outline to gather ideas for paragraphs. You may continue to use any of these methods to gather ideas for an essay. Because essays require more detail than paragraphs, there are also two other ways of gathering ideas that are especially useful: reading outside sources and keeping a journal.

These methods are explained on pp. 24–27.

Resource Tip
Purves, Alan. "Teaching People Who Don't Write Good." *Journal of Basic Writing* 14.1 (1995): 15–20. This article suggests some of the reasons that basic writers have difficulty gathering ideas for college writing assignments.

Reading Outside Sources

When you gather ideas for an essay, you may discover that you need more information on the topic you have chosen. The library and the Internet can be good sources of information. The more books, articles, and Web pages you read, the more supporting details you'll have for your essay. Regular reading will also help spark your own ideas for writing.

When you use outside reading to gather ideas, keep in mind that some sources are better than others. You want to find information that is reliable. Whenever you look at an article, a book, or a Web page, find out who wrote it and try to figure out the writer's point of view and purpose. Knowing these things will help you decide whether the information is something you should use.

See Chapter 20 for a detailed explanation of how to find and evaluate sources.

HOW TO Evaluate Sources

- Determine who wrote the article, book, or Web site you found.
- Determine the writer's point of view.
- Check that the writer is qualified to provide the information.
- Check that the information is up to date.

Suppose you need information about students' weight for a paper about maintaining healthy eating habits in college. You find a Web site that says most students gain thirty pounds in their first year, but then you notice that the site is hosted by a company that sells diet pills. This is not a source you can trust. A better place to look might be your college's health services Web site or an article by a respected nutritionist.

To learn how to cite your sources, see pp. 458–61.

If you use other writers' ideas in your essay, you must give them credit even if you don't use their exact words. Identify the source of the information in the body of your essay and in a Works Cited page.

Use a Search Engine
To explore your topic on the World Wide Web, use a search engine—a Web site that uses keywords to help you find information on other Web sites. To find a good search engine, go to the *Discoveries* Web site at **bedfordstmartins .com /discoveries** and click on "Annotated Web Links."

Keeping a Journal

For more about keeping a journal, see Chapter 17.

A journal is an informal collection of your thoughts and feelings that you write down in a notebook or a word-processing file. Your journal can serve as a source of ideas for possible paper topics, or it can be a place for jotting down ideas on a topic you have already selected. Keeping a journal helps you become an active thinker and gives you practice putting your ideas into words.

Resource Tip
Gardner, Susan, and Toby Fulwiler, eds. *The Journal Book for Teachers of At-Risk College Writers*. Portsmouth: Boynton/Cook, 1999. These articles describe the importance of having students keep journals.

HOW TO Keep a Journal

- Set aside fifteen to thirty minutes three times a week.
- Record the date and time of each entry.

- Write down whatever comes to mind without worrying about audience or purpose.
- Don't think about spelling, punctuation, or grammar.
- Save everything you write.

Electronic Journals

To keep your journal on computer disk, set up a file called "Journal" and add entries to it just as you would in a notebook. Enter text as quickly as you can, concentrating on your ideas. Resist the urge to delete or correct your writing.

Student writer Daniel wrote this journal entry on the topic of succeeding in college:

> October 18, 2004
> 8:30 p.m.
> A good way to succeed in college is to get involved in campus activities. I was reluctant to do this because I am older than my classmates, but I finally joined the golf team and ran for student senate. The friendships I made have kept me coming to school even when the classes have been really tough.

Because an essay takes more planning than a paragraph does, you may find yourself using a variety of methods to gather ideas. For example, you might begin by brainstorming and then cluster your ideas to help you organize your paragraphs. To provide additional detail, you might interview someone who is an authority on the topic you have chosen and then check out a book she recommended. Use whatever methods work best for you.

Teaching Tip
Encourage students to use the idea-gathering methods that work best for them.

WRITING ACTIVITY 2: Gather Ideas

Use your favorite method to gather ideas for your essay on college success. Read at least one outside source to gather more information. Then write a journal entry about what you know and have learned about your topic.

Narrowing Your Topic

The importance of narrowing a topic is also explained on pp. 27–29.

Just as you did when writing paragraphs, you must narrow your essay topic so that you can stay focused on a main point and develop your ideas in detail. It wouldn't be possible to share everything you know about college success in one essay. Instead, you should focus on one aspect of your advice or experience, such as managing your time, taking good notes, or keeping a positive attitude.

HOW TO Narrow a Topic for an Essay

- Select a topic that interests you.
- Gather as many ideas for that topic as you can.
- Notice whether there are any common themes among your ideas.
- Decide which ideas fit together best.
- Decide which ideas will be most interesting to your readers.
- Be sure that you have a point to make about your topic.

After some thought, Daniel decided that older students beginning college would benefit more from knowing what to expect in college classes than from learning about his experiences on the golf team or his run for the student senate. He therefore narrowed his topic to how to succeed in college classes.

Teaching Tip
Encourage students to share their narrowed topics with their classmates for their reactions.

WRITING ACTIVITY 3: Narrow Your Topic

Review the information you have gathered for your topic. Select the ideas that provide the best information about succeeding in college. Be sure that your topic is narrow enough to explain in just a few pages.

STEP 2: WRITE YOUR DISCOVERY DRAFT

To draft an essay, you'll write a thesis statement, an introduction, supporting paragraphs, and a conclusion. Just as you did when drafting paragraphs, concentrate on writing down your ideas without being too concerned about things such as sentence structure, spelling, punctuation, or grammar. The important thing is to put your thoughts into sentence and paragraph form.

Drafting styles vary widely. Some writers like to draft quickly and then spend a lot of time revising, while others prefer to draft more carefully. Some people start by putting together an outline to guide their writing; others don't think about organization until they've gotten all of their ideas down. The more you practice and experiment with writing, the better you'll know what works for you.

Save and Number Your Drafts
Because you'll be rewriting your essay several times, be sure to number and save each draft as you complete it.

Drafting a Thesis Statement

Just as the topic sentence tells the main point of your paragraph, a thesis statement tells the main point of your essay. Everything you say in the essay should be connected in some way to the thesis statement.

You can review topic sentences on pp. 30–31.

Before you begin drafting your essay, try to express your main point in a sentence or two. Although your thesis statement will most likely change as you discover what you have to say, having one ready before you start writing will help you stay focused on your ideas.

Teaching Tip
Divide students into pairs to write sample thesis statements. Have each pair exchange papers to make suggestions for improvement.

HOW TO Write a Thesis Statement

- State the main point of your essay.
- Express a point of view, not just a fact.
- Show what you think is important about the topic.
- Focus your thesis statement on the main ideas you will cover in your essay.

Share Your Thesis Statement Online
E-mail your thesis statement to your instructor, asking how you could improve it. He or she will be happy to help you.

Where should your thesis statement appear in your essay? Usually, it is part of the introduction. If your readers know your main idea from the start, they have a road map for following the entire essay. On occasion, though, you may wish to save your thesis statement for the conclusion. If your main point will be unpopular with your readers, for example, building up your evidence before stating your thesis can help to bring readers around gradually to your point of view, whereas expressing it directly up front would make them less willing to consider the evidence for it.

WRITING ACTIVITY 4: Draft a Thesis Statement

Write a thesis statement to guide your writing. Be sure that it expresses your point of view. Feel free to change your thesis statement if during the drafting process you discover a better way to express what you have to say.

Teaching Tip
Writing an introduction is often the hardest part of composing an essay. If attempting an introduction intimidates your students or gives them writer's block, encourage them to write the rest of their essays first, saving the introduction for last.

Drafting an Introduction

The introduction to an essay gets your readers' attention and announces your main point. Normally the introduction will consist of one or two paragraphs and conclude with your thesis statement.

Look again at the first paragraph of "Running Out of Money before Graduation." Charles Smith begins with a general statement about the value of a college education, continues with a brief story about his own experience, and concludes with his thesis statement. Using a brief story, or anecdote, is one way to catch your readers' attention, but there are several others that you may use in your introduction. You might provide a surprising fact, for example, ask a question, or describe a vivid image.

HOW TO Write an Introduction

- Get your readers' attention with a brief story or anecdote, a surprising fact, a question, or a vivid image.
- Announce your topic.
- Conclude with a thesis statement.

WRITING ACTIVITY 5: Draft Your Introduction

Write an introduction that attracts your readers' attention, announces your topic, and concludes with your thesis statement. Focus on convincing your readers to continue reading your essay.

Adding Support

Just as you added support to your paragraphs with examples, descriptions, and other details to explain your topic sentence, you will add support to your essay with paragraphs that help your readers understand your thesis statement. A short essay usually includes three to five supporting paragraphs. Each supporting paragraph has a topic sentence that relates to the main point of the essay and includes details to support that topic sentence.

Because an essay is longer than a paragraph, it can be useful to plan your essay by writing a rough outline to identify your main points and show how you will support them. Drafting a rough outline makes it easier to see if you have enough information for your essay.

Here is an example of a rough outline for Charles Smith's essay.

For more information on ways to add support, see pp. 31–34.

Teaching Tip
Encourage students to do some outside reading on their topics. Remind them to include facts rather than rely solely on their opinions.

Outlining is also explained on pp. 26–27.

Thesis Statement

I have become extremely concerned with the number of students who have enrolled at the university without an educational finance plan.

1st Topic Sentence

There was plenty of financial aid in the 1970s and 1980s.
    SEOG, BEOG, state aid, student loans, grants
    financial aid was 60-70 percent grants

2nd Topic Sentence

Students and parents must realize how much money it takes to finance a college education.
    can't rely on a Pell Grant
    savings and grants
    learn to develop a financial plan for college

3rd Topic Sentence

Upperclassmen without scholarships don't know how they will pay for the remainder of their education.
    upperclassmen are $20,000-$30,000 in debt
    not able to finish school

Notice that each of Smith's topic sentences relates to his thesis statement and that each piece of information supports one of the topic sentences.

HOW TO Add Support

- Gather ideas using one or more of the following methods: brainstorming, freewriting, clustering, asking questions, interviewing others, reading outside sources, or writing in a journal.
- Draft a rough outline to organize your support and see where you may need additional information.
- Add support where needed.
- Continue to gather ideas until you have enough support for each paragraph in your essay.

Outline on Computer
Some word-processing programs contain an outline feature that will help you create an outline.

Use Your Computer Wisely
As you develop your support, keep in mind that the best writing tool is not your word processor. It is your mind, which brings ideas and imagination to your writing.

WRITING ACTIVITY 6: Develop a Rough Outline

Develop a rough outline by writing down your thesis statement and the major ideas you have to support it. Then, list supporting details for each major idea. If you discover that you need additional support, use one of the methods of gathering ideas to find more information.

Drafting a Conclusion

When you wrote a paragraph, you drafted a concluding sentence to mark the end of the paragraph. The concluding paragraph of an essay also lets your reader know that you are drawing to a close. When writing a conclusion, don't make the mistake of ending too suddenly or introducing new material. Instead, wrap up what you have already said.

The standard way to end an essay is to restate your thesis in different words. This ensures that your readers remember your main point.

Vary your word choice so that your main point isn't unnecessarily repetitive. The restated thesis can appear at either the beginning or the end of the conclusion.

Consider Charles Smith's essay, "Running Out of Money before Graduation."

Statement of Thesis in Introduction

> **I have become extremely concerned with the number of students who have enrolled at the university without an educational finance plan.**

Restatement of Thesis in Conclusion

> **Academic ability is important, but it is also important for the students to be able to finance the time that will be required to attain their degree.**

Smith's original statement and his restated thesis both make the same point — that college students must plan a way to finance their education. By varying his word choice, Smith emphasizes his main idea in an interesting way.

HOW TO Write a Conclusion

- Sum up what you have said in your essay.
- Restate the thesis to remind readers of the main point.
- Don't end suddenly or introduce new ideas.

WRITING ACTIVITY 7: Draft Your Conclusion

Review your thesis statement and supporting details. Write a conclusion that sums up your ideas and restates your thesis in different words.

Daniel's Discovery Draft

Using the material he developed for his introduction, thesis statement, supporting paragraphs, and conclusion, Daniel wrote the following discovery draft. Note that Daniel's draft includes some errors. He will correct these later.

Advice to Returning Students

I recall sitting in my biology class at ten-thirty in the morning on my first day of college thinking back to my high school experience in the late seventies. I remember that I got away with hardly ever studying for my high school classes. Times had definitely changed, and they will for you, too, if you enter college as a returning student. A great deal of responsibility for being prepared for college classes is left up to you and no one else.

Deciding on a major may be one of the toughest decisions you will have to make when going to college. Of course, you want to choose something that interests you and that promises you a good future. To help you decide on a major and which classes to take, read your college catalogue. This book, available in the campus bookstore, contains a basic four-year plan that gives you a good idea of what you should take. Once you have read the catalogue and decided which classes to take, you must plan your first semesters schedule. Once you know what you want to take, you'll want to ask around to find out which instructors to take and which ones to avoid.

Another key element to doing well is going to class ready to learn. It's best to arrive for class on time and to sit in front of the classroom. When you are not in class, there are many places you can go to study or to get academic help. This college has fine Tutorial Services located on the third floor of the library. They tutor a wide variety of subjects including math, english, science, and foreign languages. The tutors are fellow students who are well trained to help you.

Another way to succeed in college is to get involved in campus activities. I know I was reluctant to do this because I am older than my classmates, but I finally joined the golf team and ran for student senate. The friendships I made have kept me coming to school even when the classes have been really tough.

College is entirely different from your previous life experiences, but it can be even more worthwhile.

HOW TO Format an Essay

- *Center* your title on the first line of the first page.
- *Indent* each paragraph by leaving five blank spaces (or one-half inch) before the first sentence.
- Use one-inch margins on all sides of each page.
- *Double-space* all of the lines.
- Number the pages.
- If you are writing on a computer, choose an easy-to-read font (such as Times New Roman, Garamond, or Courier) and use 10-, 11- or 12-point type.

Teaching Tip
Developing writers often have problems with essay format. Introduce them to a number of writing samples and ask them to analyze the format.

WRITING ACTIVITY 8: Complete Your Discovery Draft

Referring to what you have already developed for your thesis statement, introduction, supporting paragraphs, and conclusion, write a discovery draft. Focus on getting your ideas down on paper.

Teaching Tip
To show students that even advanced writers use the writing process, have them read or listen to your own draft of this assignment. Then ask them for revision suggestions.

STEP 3: REVISE YOUR ESSAY

When you revise, you improve your discovery draft so that your readers will fully understand what you have to say and be interested in reading your essay. You'll use the same steps you used to revise paragraphs: strengthen your focus, build your support, and organize your points. Because an essay is longer than a paragraph, you'll also connect your ideas with keywords and transitions that will help your readers stay focused on your topic.

When you revised paragraphs, you probably tackled focus, support, and organization all at once. Because essays are longer and more complicated, it helps to attend to each of these aspects separately.

To review the process of revising paragraphs, turn to pp. 37–45.

Strengthening Your Focus

When you wrote a paragraph, you considered whether every sentence supported the topic sentence. When writing an essay, you consider whether every paragraph in your essay supports your thesis statement. If you find one that does not, you remove it from your essay or revise it to make clear how it relates to your main point.

You can find more advice on how to strengthen your focus on pp. 37–38.

Check, also, that every sentence within a paragraph supports the topic sentence of that paragraph. If you find sentences that are not related to the topic sentence, remove them.

HOW TO Strengthen Essay Focus

- Check that the thesis statement expresses your point of view on the topic and states why it is important.
- Check that the topic sentence of each paragraph supports your thesis statement.
- Check that each supporting detail within each paragraph supports the topic sentence.
- Delete or revise any paragraphs or supporting details that do not directly support the thesis statement or one of the topic sentences.

When Daniel reread his discovery draft, he decided to remove the paragraph on campus activities because it was not closely related to his main point on how to do better in college classes.

Use Color

Highlight your thesis statement and topic sentences with different colors. For example, you might enter your thesis statement in red and your topic sentences in blue. Making these important sentences stand out from the rest of your essay will help you check that every detail supports them.

WRITING ACTIVITY 9: Strengthen Your Focus

Reread your thesis statement and topic sentences. Does every topic sentence support the thesis statement? Does every sentence in each paragraph support its topic sentence? If not, revise or remove the paragraphs and sentences that do not belong.

Building Your Support

Teaching Tip
Remind students that providing support not only informs their readers but also makes their essays more interesting.

When writing paragraphs, you concentrated on using one method of development at a time. With essays, however, you will want to include paragraphs that use a variety of methods. Each of your paragraphs needs to be developed in enough detail to make your essay informative and interesting.

To build your support, look over your essay to see where you can use any of the methods of development to shape your paragraphs. For example, you may decide that a story about one of your personal experiences can make your essay about college success more interesting, or that you can use description to explain one of your points better. The more methods you are able to use, the more interesting your essay will be to your readers.

HOW TO Build Support

- Use *examples* to make a general idea more concrete (see Chapter 3).
- Use *narration* to tell about events as they happen over time (see Chapter 4).
- Use *description* to show how something looks, sounds, tastes, smells, or feels (see Chapter 5).
- Use *process* to explain how do something or how something works (see Chapter 6).
- Use *classification* to put things into categories (see Chapter 7).
- Use *comparison and contrast* to identify the similarities and/or differences between things (see Chapter 8).
- Use *definition* to tell what something means (see Chapter 9).
- Use *cause and effect* when you want to explain that one event happened as a result of another (see Chapter 10).
- Use *argumentation* to convince readers of your opinion (see Chapter 11).

Student writer Daniel reviewed his discovery draft and realized that he needed to develop his ideas in more detail to help returning students understand how to succeed in college. He decided to tell a story about his personal experience, to add a description of one of his classrooms, to provide examples of campus services, and to use process to explain how to choose classes and plan a schedule.

WRITING ACTIVITY 10 (Group): Build Your Support

With several classmates, discuss the support you used in your discovery draft. Ask your classmates if there are places in your essay where you can use one of the methods of development to improve your support. Do this with each of your classmates' drafts.

Organizing Your Points

To review ways to order points, see pp. 39–42.

Ideally, an essay's organization should move your readers in a smooth, logical way from your introduction through your supporting paragraphs to your conclusion. To check the organization of your discovery draft, create a cluster or an outline of your draft. Do you see a clear organizational pattern? Is each paragraph focused on a single point? By studying the organization of your paragraphs, you will see how you might rearrange your ideas so they make more sense.

HOW TO Organize an Essay

- *Introduction:* Get your readers' attention and state your thesis.
- *Body Paragraphs:* Give the main point of each paragraph in a topic sentence. Use details, facts, and examples to support each topic sentence.
- *Conclusion:* Summarize your main points and refer back to your thesis statement.

Daniel created the following outline of his discovery draft:

Thesis Statement

A great deal of responsibility for being prepared for college classes is left up to you and no one else.

1st Topic Sentence

Deciding on a major may be one of the toughest decisions you will have to make when going to college.

Choose something interesting that will lead to a good career.
Read your college catalogue.
Choose classes.
Plan your schedule.
Find out which instructors are good and which ones to avoid.

2nd Topic Sentence

Another key element to doing well is going to class ready to learn.

Arrive on time and sit in front.
Locate places to study and to get help.
Use the Tutorial Services.

3rd Topic Sentence

Another way to succeed in college is to get involved in campus activities.

golf team and student senate

friendships

Conclusion

College is entirely different from your previous life experiences, but it can be even more worthwhile.

Daniel noticed immediately that many of his supporting points didn't relate directly to his topic sentences. When he revised his essay, he rearranged and expanded his thoughts to ensure that each supporting paragraph was focused on a single topic. (He had already decided to eliminate the paragraph about extracurricular activities.)

WRITING ACTIVITY 11: Organize Your Points

Create an outline or a cluster of the ideas in your discovery draft. Examine the organization carefully to determine whether your sentences and paragraphs are in a logical order. Rearrange your ideas as necessary.

Connecting Your Ideas

When you wrote a paragraph, you used transitions to help your readers follow your organization. Transitional words, phrases, and sentences can also serve as a road map to show readers how the ideas in an essay are connected.

For a list of common transitional words and phrases, see p. 42.

When you write essays, keywords are equally important to help your readers move from paragraph to paragraph. Keywords are important words or phrases that relate to the topic being discussed. By repeating a keyword, you keep your reader focused on your topic. In "Running Out of Money before Graduation," for example, Charles Smith uses the keywords *college, financial plan, financial aid, parents,* and *students* throughout his essay to help his readers remember that each paragraph is on the topic of financial planning for college.

WRITING ACTIVITY 12: Examine Keywords and Transitions

Underline the keywords and circle the transitions in your discovery draft. Mark places where you need to add keywords and transitions to help your reader move from one idea to the next.

Daniel's Revised Draft

Before reading Daniel's revised draft, reread his discovery draft. Notice that in his revised draft he has improved his introduction and conclusion, tightened his focus, added support, and reorganized his paragraphs. This draft still contains some errors that he will correct when he edits his essay.

Just Getting Through

I recall sitting in my biology class at ten-thirty in the morning on my first day of college. It had been twenty years since I graduated from high school, I knew I was in for a big adjustment. The classroom was the size of a football stadium with over two hundred students in it. The instructor looked like a tiny dot or speck at the front of the room. Times had definitely changed, and they will for you, too, if you enter college as a returning student. A great deal of responsibility is left up to you and no one else. Every returning student encounters challenges in college classes, but with a little knowledge in advance, you will be ready for whatever comes your way.

Deciding on a major may be one of the toughest decisions you will have to make. Of course, you want to choose something that interests you and that promises you a good future. If you are having trouble deciding, though, don't panic, you can wait until the end of your second year to declare a major.

To help you decide which classes to take, read your college catalogue, which is available in the campus bookstore. It contains a basic four-year plan that gives you a good idea of what to take. It also contains the number of hours you will have to complete to earn a degree and a lot of other valuable information to help you understand what to expect.

Once you have read the catalogue, you must plan your first semesters schedule. It's best to sign up for the number of classes you feel you can do well in. Most first-year college students take three or four classes (nine to twelve hours) in their first semester. It is most important not to put too much pressure on yourself your first semester is a transitional one, and you want to give yourself time to adjust.

Another key element to doing well is going to class ready to learn. It's best to arrive for class on time and to sit in front. Preparation is vital in college, so you must keep up with your reading and notetaking. But if you discover that you are not doing well, don't be afraid to drop a class and add another one. Use withdrawal only when absolutely necessary, though; too many withdrawals on your transcript could make it seem that you give up too quickly, not a good sign to a future employer.

When you are not in class, there are many places you can go to study or to get academic help, including fine Tutorial Services located on the third floor of the library. The tutors are students who are well trained to help you in a wide variety of subjects, including math, english, science, and foreign languages. Other valuable resources include career services, scholarships, and financial aid. You should also get to know the advisor for your major. This person can answer many of the questions that you may have about college and can help you understand the requirements and regulations.

Don't be afraid to challenge yourself and to ask questions if you need answers. If at any point you stumble, just chalk it up to experience and then do you're very best to improve. College is entirely different from your previous life experiences, but it can be even more rewarding. I hope to see you join the ranks of returning students next year.

GROUP ACTIVITY: Analyze Daniel's Revised Draft

Discuss the following questions with your classmates. Answers will vary. Sample answers given.

1. How did Daniel improve his introduction?
   Daniel improved his introduction by including a personal anecdote to capture his readers' attention.

2. What is Daniel's thesis statement? How is it improved?
   "Every returning student encounters challenges in their college classes, but with a little knowledge in advance, you will be ready for whatever comes your way." Daniel announces his topic and explains why it is important.

3. What support does Daniel provide for his thesis statement? How has he focused this support?
   Daniel's support includes information on selecting a major and creating a class schedule, tips for learning in class, and suggestions on where to seek outside help. He created new paragraphs so that each one has details that relate directly to the topic sentence.

4. How does Daniel conclude his essay? What more could he do to strengthen his conclusion?
   Daniel concludes by encouraging his readers not to be afraid to take a chance on college. He could strengthen his conclusion by reminding prospective students how important a college education is.

5. What else could Daniel do to improve his essay?
   Daniel could include some facts or quotations from outside readings to support what he says.

WRITING ACTIVITY 13 (Group): Peer Review

Form a group with several classmates and exchange copies of your drafts. Read each draft aloud while your classmates follow along. Take notes on your classmates' answers to the following questions about your draft.

1. What do you like best about my essay?
2. Does my introduction attract your attention and announce my topic? How could I make it better?
3. How clear is my thesis statement? Does it give my point of view about the topic?
4. How effective are my topic sentences? Do they focus on my topic?
5. How well did I support my points? Can you suggest areas where I need more support?
6. Does my organization make sense? How could I improve it?
7. Where do I need more keywords and transitions?
8. How strong is my conclusion? Do I restate my thesis and summarize my points?

Teaching Tip
Conduct a mock peer review session by asking a student to read Daniel's discovery draft aloud. Then, have students give Daniel suggestions for revision. Remind students that they need to make their suggestions specific.

WRITING ACTIVITY 14: Revise Your Draft

Taking into account your classmates' suggestions, revise your discovery draft. In particular, strengthen your focus, build your support, organize your points, and connect your ideas. Use Daniel's revision as a model. Answers will vary.

STEP 4: EDIT YOUR ESSAY

You edit an essay the same way you edit paragraphs. Check for errors in spelling, punctuation, and grammar. In each of the next four chapters, you'll also learn how to improve your sentence structure by combining closely related sentences. To edit, you'll need a dictionary and the Handbook in Part Four. You may also use a computer spell-check or ask someone else to look for errors in your writing.

Continue to keep an editing log to record your mistakes and how you corrected them. By reviewing your log regularly, you will learn to avoid making the same errors over and over again.

For more information about editing logs, see pp. 45–46.

Use the Spell-Check and Grammar-Check to Edit
Be careful when you use the spell-check and grammar-check features of your computer's word-processing program. While spell-check helps you spot typos and words that you have misspelled, it won't spot all errors. For instance, it won't notice if you use *their* when you're supposed to use *there*. Grammar-check also has its limitations. For example, it tends to label all long sentences as incorrect, when in fact the length of a sentence has nothing to do with its grammatical correctness.

Daniel's Edited Essay

Daniel edited his essay to eliminate errors in spelling, punctuation, and grammar. (His corrections are underlined here.) His editing log follows the essay.

Just Getting Through

Comma splices are explained on pp. 561–62.

I recall sitting in my biology class at ten-thirty in the morning on my first day of college. It had been twenty years since I graduated from high school; I knew I was in for a big adjustment. The classroom was the size of a football stadium with over two hundred students in it. The instructor looked like a tiny dot or speck at the front of the room. Times had definitely changed, and they will for you, too, if you enter college as a returning student. A great deal of responsibility is left up to you and no one else. Every returning student encounters challenges in college classes, but with a little knowledge in advance, you will be ready for whatever comes your way.

To learn more about pronoun-antecedent agreement, see pp. 511–12.

Deciding on a major may be one of the toughest decisions you will have to make. Of course, you want to choose something that interests you and that promises you a good future. If you are having trouble deciding, though, don't panic, because you can wait until the end of your second year to declare a major.

To help you decide which classes to take, read your college catalogue, which is available in the campus bookstore. It contains a basic four-year plan that gives you a good idea of what to take. It also contains the number of hours you will have to complete to earn a degree and a lot of other valuable information to help you understand what to expect.

Once you have read the catalogue, you must plan your first semester's schedule. It's best to sign up for the number of classes you feel you can do well in. Most first-year college students take three or four classes (nine to twelve hours) in their first semester. It is most important not to put too much pressure on yourself: Your first semester is a transitional one, and you want to give yourself time to adjust.

Learn when to use apostrophes on pp. 616–18.

Another key element to doing well is going to class ready to learn. It's best to arrive for class on time and to sit in front. Preparation is vital in college, so you must keep up with your reading and notetaking. But if you discover that you are not doing well, don't be afraid to drop a class and add another one. Use withdrawal only when absolutely necessary, though; too many withdrawals on your transcript could make it seem that you give up too quickly, not a good sign to a future employer.

When you are not in class, there are many places you can go to study or to get academic help, including fine Tutorial Services located on the third floor of the library. The tutors are students who are well trained to help you in a wide variety of subjects, including math, English, science, and foreign languages. Other valuable resources include career services, scholarships, and financial aid. You should also get to know the advisor for your major. This person can answer many of the questions that you may have about college and can help you understand the requirements and regulations.

If you're not sure what to capitalize, see pp. 626–28.

Don't be afraid to challenge yourself and to ask questions if you need answers. If at any point you stumble, just chalk it up to experience and then do

Review spelling rules on pp. 584–88.

your very best to improve. College is entirely different from your previous life experiences, but it can be even more rewarding. I hope to see you join the ranks of returning students next year.

Teaching Tip
Refer students to the Handbook in Part Four of this book and Exercise Central on the *Discoveries* Web site, where they will find exercises that will help them avoid common errors.

Daniel's Editing Log

DATE September 15

INCORRECT It had been twenty years since I graduated from high school, I knew I was in for a big adjustment.

ERROR comma splice

CORRECT It had been twenty years since I graduated from high school; I knew I was in for a big adjustment.

INCORRECT If you are having trouble deciding, though, don't panic, you can wait until the end of your second year to declare a major.

ERROR comma splice

CORRECT If you are having trouble deciding, though, don't panic, because you can wait until the end of your second year to declare a major.

INCORRECT semesters

ERROR possessive with no apostrophe

CORRECT semester's

INCORRECT It is most important not to put too much pressure on yourself your first semester is a transitional one, and you want to give yourself time to adjust.

ERROR run-on sentence

CORRECT It is most important not to put too much pressure on yourself: Your first semester is a transitional one, and you want to give yourself time to adjust.

INCORRECT english

ERROR capitalization

CORRECT English

INCORRECT you're

ERROR spelling

CORRECT your

WRITING ACTIVITY 15: Edit Your Essay

Using a dictionary and the Handbook in Part Four, edit your essay for errors in spelling, punctuation, and grammar. Record your mistakes and how you corrected them in your editing log so that you won't make the same mistakes in the future.

STEP 5: SHARE YOUR ESSAY

Many student writers just submit their essays to their instructors for a grade. But if you're proud of what you have written, you'll want to share it with your intended audience. You can share your essay in a more public way by reading it aloud in class or sending it to your school or local newspaper. If you have access to the Internet, you might even publish your work by e-mailing it to interested readers or posting it on the World Wide Web.

Daniel found out about a program to help people who have been honorably discharged from the military get ready to attend college. He was eager to share his essay with people like this, so he arranged with the officer in charge of the local program to read his paper out loud during one of the meetings. Daniel was concerned that the people might not relate to his advice, but he discovered that they were pleased to get information from someone who had already accomplished what they were hoping to do.

Teaching Tip
Compliment students who read their essays aloud to the class. Explain what they did especially well.

Teaching Tip
Student responses can help you assess whether students have made the transition from writing paragraphs to writing essays.

ADDITIONAL WRITING ASSIGNMENTS

1. Write an expressive essay for your classmates in which you describe a favorite ritual that you and your family or friends share. For example, you might describe what you do each Fourth of July or on the anniversary of an important date.
2. Write an informative essay for your college newspaper in which you explain one of your pastimes or interests. You might write about music, sports, or a hobby.
3. Write an informative essay for your instructor on the writing process you used to write paragraphs. How will this process change when you write essays?
4. Write a persuasive essay for your campus newspaper in which you take a position on the topic of classroom comfort. For example, you might take a position on uncomfortable desks, difficulty seeing the chalkboard, or the lack of instructional technology.

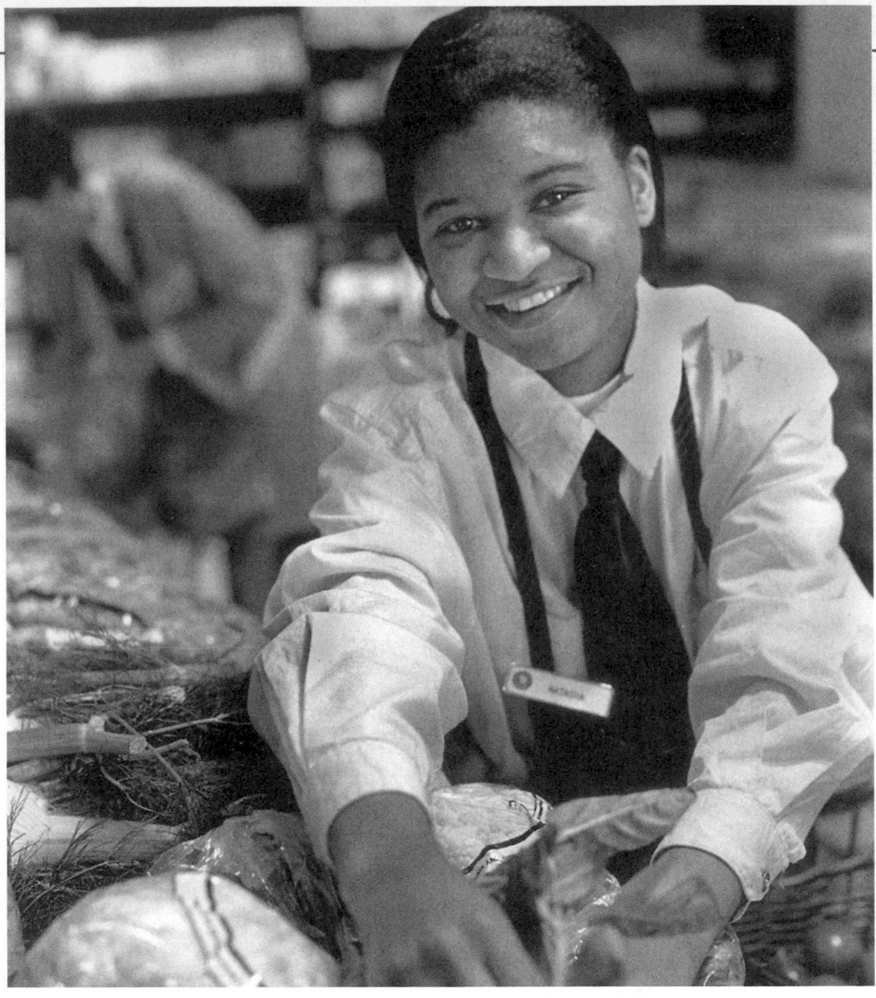

Natasha, who is pictured here, struggled at first with the demands of her new job as the produce manager of a major supermarket. Now she enjoys her responsibilities, which include paying attention to what's new and what's popular in the produce market and ensuring that fruits and vegetables are clean, safe, and high quality. In this chapter, you will describe a major change that you had difficulty getting used to or explain something about your behavior or lifestyle that you decided to improve.

CHAPTER

13

Writing an Essay That Gives Examples

In this chapter, you will:

- review how examples work.
- freewrite to gather ideas.
- write about a change in your life.
- use TIE order to organize your ideas.
- practice sentence coordination.
- submit your essay to a magazine.

UNDERSTANDING EXAMPLES

Teaching Tip
This chapter provides students with the opportunity to write about a change in their lives, developing their ideas by using examples.

Read more about examples in Chapter 3.

Has anybody ever asked you to be more specific? Perhaps you told a friend that you were too busy to see a movie with her, and she asked you why. "Well," you told her, "I have a test on Thursday and two papers due on Friday. I'm supposed to read three chapters for my sociology class by Wednesday. I have to work a double shift tomorrow. I'm not even sure when I'll sleep!" You have used examples to back up your general statement with specific information.

An essay that gives examples provides specifics to make your main point vivid and concrete. The most common type of examples are facts or statements that can be proved to be true. Examples may also be specific cases or events, relevant personal experiences, or other people's opinions.

READING ESSAYS THAT GIVE EXAMPLES

Teaching Tip
Tell your students that they'll be expected to use examples in many of their college assignments. For an art history paper, they might need to give examples of paintings that outraged the public. A business instructor might ask them to identify some benefits that attract good employees. For a sociology exam, they might be asked to discuss examples of deviant behavior.

Teaching Tip
To enhance understanding of using examples, ask students to underline the examples in these essays. Discuss how the authors use the examples to show what they mean.

Life is a series of changes. Sometimes change happens to us; sometimes we decide to do things differently. In the following two essays, the writers use examples to explain a change in their lives.

Adapting to Change

Most people look forward to retirement, but the new lifestyle often comes as a shock. In this essay for *Newsweek*'s "My Turn" column — a space where amateur writers can share their thoughts — Jan Zeh uses examples to explain how her husband's retirement has affected her.

JAN ZEH

The "Golden Years" Are Beginning to Tarnish

My worst nightmare has become reality. My husband retired. As the CEO of his own software company, he used to make important decisions daily. Now he decides when to take a nap and for how long. He does not play golf, tennis or bridge, which means he is at home for what seems like 48 hours a day. That's a lot of togetherness.

Much has changed since he stopped working. My husband now defines "sleeping in" as staying in bed until 6 a.m. He often walks in the morning for exercise but says he can't walk if he gets up late. Late is 5:30. His morning routine is to take out the dog, plug in the coffee and await the morning paper. (And it had better not be late!) When the paper finally arrives, his favorite sec-

tion is the obits. He reads each and every one — often aloud — and becomes angry if the deceased's age is not listed. I'd like to work on my crossword puzzle in peace. When I bring this to his attention, he stops briefly — but he soon finds another article that must be shared.

Some retirement couples enjoy this time of life together. Usually these are couples who are not dependent on their spouse for their happiness and well-being. My husband is not one of these individuals. Many wives I've spoken to identify with my experience and are happy to know that they're not alone. One friend told me that when her husband retired, he grew a strip of Velcro on his side and attached himself to her. They were married 43 years and she hinted they may not make it to 44. Another woman said her husband not only takes her to the beauty shop, but goes in with her and waits! Another said her husband follows her everywhere but to the bathroom . . . and that's only because she locks the bathroom door.

When I leave the house, my husband asks: "Where are you going?" followed by "When will you be back?" Even when I'm at home he needs to know where I am every moment. "Where's Jan?" he asks the dog. This is bad enough, but at least he hasn't Velcroed himself to me — yet.

I often see retired couples shopping together in the grocery store. Usually they are arguing. I hate it when my husband goes shopping with me. He takes charge of the cart and disappears. With my arms full of cans, I have to search the aisles until I locate him and the cart, which is now loaded with strange-smelling cheeses, high-fat snacks and greasy sausages — none of which was on the shopping list.

Putting up with annoying habits is easier when hubby is at work all day and at home only in the evening and on weekends. But little annoying habits become *big* annoying habits when done on a daily basis. Hearing my husband yell and curse at the TV during the evening news was bad enough when he was working, and it was just once a day. Now he has all day to get riled up watching Fox News. Sometimes leaving the house isn't even a satisfying reprieve. When I went out of town for a week and put him in charge of the house and animals, I returned to have my parrot greet me with a mouthful of expletives and deep-bellied belches. It wasn't hard to figure out what had been going on in my absence.

Not that my husband has any problem acting out while I'm around. He recently noticed that our cat had been climbing the palm trees, causing their leaves to bend. His solution? Buy a huge roll of barbed wire and wrap the trunks. After wrapping 10 palms, he looked like he had been in a fight with a tiger and the house took on the appearance of a high-security prison. Neighbors stopped midstride while on their daily walks to stare. I

Resource Tip
Salvatori, Mariolina. "Reading and Writing a Text: Correlations between Reading and Writing Patterns." *A Sourcebook for Basic Writing Teachers*. Ed. Theresa Enos. New York: Random House, 1987: 176–86. This essay stresses the importance of reading in the basic writing class.

Teaching Tip
You may want to emphasize to your students that Zeh is a magazine reader who submitted her own writing, not a professional writer.

stayed out of sight. In the meantime, the cat learned to negotiate the barbed wire and climbed the palms anyway.

It is now another hot, dry summer, and the leaves on our trees are starting to fall. Yesterday my husband decided to take the dog out for some fresh air. They stood in the driveway while he counted the leaves falling from the ash tree. Aloud. Another meaningful retirement activity.

I think my husband enjoys being at home with me. I am the one with the problem. I am a person who needs a lot of "alone time," and I get crazy when someone is following me around or wanting to know my every move. My husband is full of questions and comments when I am on the phone, working on my computer or taking time out to read. It is his way of telling me he wants to be included, wanted and needed. I love that he cares — but he still drives me up the wall.

I receive a lot of catalogs. In one there is a pillow advertised that says grow old with me. The best is yet to be. Another catalog has a different pillow. It reads screw the golden years. Right now it's a tossup as to which pillow will best describe our retirement years together. Just don't ask me while I'm working on my crossword puzzle.

READING ACTIVITY 1: Build Your Vocabulary

Try to determine the meanings of the following words from Jan Zeh's essay. Then, check their meanings by looking the words up in a dictionary.

deceased (2) dead person

reprieve (6) break

expletives (6) swear words

Teaching Tip
Remind students that they improve as writers when they analyze how others write.

READING ACTIVITY 2: Read to Improve Your Writing

Answer the following questions about Jan Zeh's essay. Answers will vary. Sample answers given.

1. In your own words, what is Jan Zeh's main point, or thesis?
   Her main point is that her newly retired husband's behavior is making her crazy.

2. What examples does Zeh provide to explain her point?
   Zeh provides a number of examples to make her complaint specific: Her husband stays home all day; he gets up early; he insists on reading

parts of the paper out loud to her; he needs to know where she is at all times; he goes to the grocery store with her and buys things they don't need; he swears at the television; he makes a fool of himself in public; he interrupts her when she's busy.

3. Why does Zeh include a paragraph that's not about her husband's behavior?

   She gives examples about her friends' retired husbands to show that she's not alone in her frustration. This helps her readers relate to her experience.

4. What major changes have you experienced in your own life recently?

   Starting college would be the biggest one! My parents both retired last year, so I can understand what Zeh is talking about.

Making a Change

In 2000, National Public Radio invited listeners to share their personal experiences for the program *Weekend All Things Considered;* many of the responses to this invitation, which NPR called the National Story Project, were later published in a collection. In her essay for this collection, an anonymous woman uses examples to explain an unusual decision she made.

Resource Tip
More than a hundred essays submitted to the National Story Project were published in Paul Auster, ed., *I Thought My Father Was God: And Other True Tales from NPR's National Story Project* (New York: Picador, 2001).

B.C.

Homeless in Prescott, Arizona

Last spring I made a major life change, and I wasn't suffering from a midlife crisis. At fifty-seven I'm way beyond that. I decided I could not wait eight more years to retire, and I could not be a legal secretary for eight more years. I quit my job, sold my house, furnishings, and car, gave my cat to my neighbor, and moved to Prescott, Arizona, a community of thirty thousand, nestled into the Bradshaw Mountains with a fine library, community college, and a beautiful town square. I invested the proceeds from selling everything and I now receive $315 a month in interest income. That is what I live off of.

I am anonymous. I am not on any government programs. I do not receive any kind of welfare, not even food stamps. I do not eat at the Salvation Army. I do not take handouts. I am not dependent on anyone.

My base is downtown Prescott, where everything I need is within a radius of a mile and a half — easy walking. To go farther afield, I take a bus that makes a circuit of the city each hour and costs three dollars for a day pass. I have a post-office box — cost, forty dollars a year. The library is connected to the Internet, and I have an e-mail address. My storage space costs twenty-seven dollars a month, and I have access to it twenty-four hours a day. I store my clothes, cosmetic and hygiene supplies, a few kitchen items, and paperwork there. I rent a secluded corner of a backyard a block from my storage area for twenty-five dollars a month. This is my bedroom, complete with arctic tent, sleeping bag, mattress, and lantern. I wear a sturdy pack with a water bottle, flashlight, and Walkman, toiletries and rain gear.

Yavapai College has an Olympic-size pool and a women's locker room. I take college classes and have access to these facilities; cost, thirty-five dollars a month. I go there every morning to perform my "toilet" and shower. I go to the Laundromat with a small load of clothes whenever I need to; cost, fifteen dollars a month. Looking presentable is the most important aspect of my new lifestyle. When I go to the library, no one can guess I'm homeless. The library is my living room. I sit in a comfortable chair and read. I listen to beautiful music through the stereo system. I communicate with my daughter via e-mail and type letters on the word processor. I stay dry when it's wet outside. Unfortunately, the library does not have a television, but I've found a student lounge at the college that does. Most of the time I can watch *The News Hour, Masterpiece Theater,* and *Mystery.* To further satisfy my cultural needs, I attend dress rehearsals at the local amateur theater company, free of charge.

Eating inexpensively and nutritiously is my biggest challenge. My budget allows me to spend two hundred dollars a month for food. I have a Coleman burner and an old-fashioned percolator. I go to my storage space every morning and make coffee, pour it into my thermos, load my backpack, go to the park, and find a sunny spot to enjoy my coffee and listen to *Morning Edition* on my Walkman. The park is my backyard. It's a beautiful place to hang out when the weather is clement. I can lie on the grass and read and nap. The mature trees provide welcome shade when it's warm.

My new lifestyle has been comfortable and enjoyable so far because the weather in Prescott during the spring, summer, and fall has been delightful, although it did snow Easter weekend. But I was prepared. I have a parka, boots, and gloves, all warm and waterproof.

Back to eating. The Jack in the Box has four items that cost one dollar — Breakfast Jack, Jumbo Jack, a chicken sandwich, and two beef tacos. After I enjoy my coffee in the park, I have a Breakfast Jack. There's a nutrition program at the adult center where I can eat a hearty lunch for two dollars. For dinner, back to the Jack in the Box. I buy fresh fruit and veggies at Albertson's. Once in a while I go to the Pizza Hut — all you can eat for $4.49. When I return to my storage space in the evening, I make popcorn on my Coleman burner. I only drink water and coffee; other beverages are too expensive.

I've discovered another way to have a different eating experience and to combine it with a cultural evening. There's an art gallery downtown, and the openings of the new shows are announced in the newspaper. Two weeks ago I put on my dress and panty hose, went to the opening, enjoyed eating the snacks, and admired the paintings.

I've let my hair grow long, and I tie it back in a ponytail like I did in grade school. I no longer color it. I like the gray. I do not shave my legs or underarms and do not polish my fingernails, wear mascara, foundation, blush, or lipstick. The natural look costs nothing.

I love going to college. This fall, I'm taking ceramics, chorale, and cultural anthropology — for enrichment, not for credit. I love reading all the books I want to but never had enough time for. I also have time to do absolutely nothing.

Of course there are negatives. I miss my friends from back home. Claudette, who works at the library, befriended me. She was a feature writer for the local newspaper and is adept at getting information from people. Eventually, I told her who I was and how I live. She never pressures me to live differently, and I know she's there for me if I need her.

I also miss my cat Simon. I keep hoping that a cat will come my way, particularly before winter sets in. It would be nice to sleep and snuggle with a furry body.

I hope I can survive the winter. I've been told that Prescott can have lots of snow and long stretches of freezing temperatures. I don't know what I'll do if I get sick. I'm generally an optimist, but I do worry. Pray for me.

READING ACTIVITY 3: Build Your Vocabulary

Try to determine the meanings of the following words from "Homeless in Prescott, Arizona." Then check their meanings by looking the words up in a dictionary.

nestled (1) ______________________________

radius (3) ______________________________

circuit (3) ______________________________

secluded (3) ______________________________

toilet (4) ______________________

percolator (5) ______________________

clement (5) ______________________

adept (11) ______________________

READING ACTIVITY 4: Read to Improve Your Writing

Answer the following questions about B.C.'s essay.

1. In your own words, what is the thesis of "Homeless in Prescott, Arizona"?

____

____

2. What are some examples the author uses to explain how she lives?

____

____

____

3. How does B.C. organize her examples?

____

____

4. What changes have you made recently that you could explain to others in an essay?

____

____

____

Writing Assignment

You are reading your favorite magazine (print or online) and find yourself enjoying an article that was sent in by another reader. You realize that you also have an experience you'd like to share and you decide to submit an article of your own.

- Write an essay in which you use examples to describe a major change that you had difficulty adapting to. For example, you might write about getting married, moving to a new city, or enrolling in college.

  OR

- Write an essay in which you use examples to explain something about your behavior or lifestyle that you decided to improve. Possible topics might include overcoming a fear, taking up a new sport or musical instrument, or being a better listener.

STEP 1: DISCOVER IDEAS FOR WRITING

Before you begin drafting your essay, you'll need to decide what to write about, think about what you are going to say, and find examples that will help you make your point.

Choosing a Topic

Your essay will give examples to describe a change in your life. If you're like most people, you've experienced and made a lot of changes. What, then, will you write about? Start by brainstorming a list of important events in your life, both positive and negative.

Think back to changes that had a big effect on you. Jan Zeh, for example, wrote about a major change that she did not choose but has had to adjust to: her husband's retirement. B.C., on the other hand, wrote about a change that she decided to make in her own life: choosing a lifestyle that most people fear. As you consider possible topics, keep in mind that even a small change can have a big impact.

Explore Re: Writing Links Libraries
To help you brainstorm topic ideas, go to the Re: Writing Web site at **bedfordstmartins.com/rewriting** and click on "Links Libraries."

Considering Your Audience and Purpose

Additional ideas for analyzing audience and purpose are on pp. 20–22.

Your audience for this chapter's assignment consists of other readers of your favorite magazine. You can figure out what will interest them by considering the magazine's general topic. If you're writing for *Snowboarder,* for example, you know that your readers enjoy winter sports and that they are interested in improving their own boarding techniques. They would probably not be interested in your wedding — unless you got married while barreling down a mountain.

You want to connect with your audience, so be sure you know why you're sharing your experiences. If you're writing about a change that you had to adapt to, perhaps you want to express your thoughts and feelings about something you have in common with your readers. If you're writing about something you decided to improve, on the other hand, you may want to inform your readers or to persuade them to do what you did.

WRITING ACTIVITY 1: Identify Your Audience and Purpose

Reflect on your audience and purpose by answering the following questions.

1. What is your favorite magazine? What could you write about that will fit that magazine's general content?

   ____

   ____

   ____

2. How interested will your readers be in your topic? How can you make your essay more interesting for them?

   ____

   ____

   ____

3. What is your purpose for writing this essay?

   ____

   ____

   ____

Freewriting to Gather Ideas

Whether or not you've settled on your topic, freewriting can help you gather ideas for your essay. If you know what you want to write about, freewriting on your topic can help you find examples. If you haven't decided on a topic, try freewriting on a couple of different possibilities to find out which one interests you most.

Learn more about freewriting on p. 25.

HOW TO Freewrite for an Essay That Gives Examples

- Write about a topic without pausing for ten minutes or one page.
- Don't stop, go back, or correct your writing.
- Focus on one example or move to new ones as they pop into your mind.

Student writer Damariz wanted to write an article for her campus magazine. She decided to freewrite about a college course that helped her improve her study skills.

> I have been doing better on exams since I took the university seminar class. I know I have to prepare throughout the whole semester, not just the night before. And I organize my study materials now. I also learn to stay focused on my goals. I learn that just because I fail class I'm not going to drop out of school. I remember my goals and promise to do better next time. Before this class, I wasn't aware of how many resources are available to help you. At the beginning of class we were assigned to a group. I started getting along with different people and being open-minded to ideas. We had a group assignment. At first I was intimidated because I was going to be talking in front of the class, later I realized that I was not the only person who felt that way and that you get better with practice. So now I'm more confident about talking to people.

Invisible Writing

Open a word-processing file, turn down the brightness on your monitor so that you can't see what you are typing, and freewrite on your computer. This "invisible writing" forces you to focus on your thoughts instead of what is on the screen.

WRITING ACTIVITY 2: Freewrite

Freewrite on both possible topics for your essay: (1) a change that you had to adjust to, and (2) something you decided to improve. Review your freewriting to see which topic sparked the most ideas.

Narrowing Your Topic

For more help with narrowing your topic, turn to pp. 27–29.

Now that you have gathered ideas, you're ready to settle on a topic. Start by reviewing your freewriting to see which topic interested you most.

One way to narrow your topic is to group your examples into categories and focus on one of those categories in your essay. Suppose you did the most freewriting on becoming a vegetarian. Instead of plowing through a list of unrelated examples — your weight loss, the difficulty of finding vegetarian meals at restaurants, the impact cows have on the environment, your mother's disapproval, and so on — you might choose instead to focus on ways your new lifestyle has affected your health, on how other people have reacted, or on why you decided to stop eating meat.

HOW TO Narrow a Topic for an Essay That Gives Examples

- Select a general topic.
- Review your freewriting for facts, ideas, and special instances that can serve as examples for this topic.
- If necessary, brainstorm for additional examples.
- Group your examples into categories.
- Select a category that has the right amount of examples to discuss in a short essay.

WRITING ACTIVITY 3: Narrow Your Topic

Review your freewriting and select the topic that interests you most. Brainstorm examples for your topic and group them into categories. Narrow your topic by selecting one category of examples to write about.

STEP 2: WRITE YOUR DISCOVERY DRAFT

Now that you have selected a topic and chosen some examples, you're ready to write your discovery draft. It's okay if your ideas and your writing are rough at this stage. Your goal is simply to put your ideas in writing.

Drafting a Thesis Statement

For an essay that gives examples, the thesis statement states your topic, tells your readers why it is important to you, and makes a general announcement that must be backed up with specifics. For example, the topic of "The 'Golden Years' Are Beginning to Tarnish" is retirement. Jan Zeh's thesis statement expresses her personal feelings on her topic:

Learn more about thesis statements on pp. 265–66.

My worst nightmare has become reality. My husband retired.

This thesis statement prepares readers for an essay that will explain *why* her husband's retirement is a nightmare for Zeh.

HOW TO Write a Thesis Statement for an Essay That Gives Examples

- Announce your topic and explain why it is important to you.
- Express your main point in a general statement.
- Check that you can add specific examples to explain your main point.
- Be prepared to revise your thesis statement as your ideas develop.

Student writer Damariz drafted the following thesis statement to explain why her topic — the University Seminar course — is important:

Few people know how helpful the University Seminar class can be.

Notice that Damariz's thesis statement makes her readers want to know how the class is helpful. It is an excellent lead-in for the examples she will provide.

WRITING ACTIVITY 4: Draft a Thesis Statement

Referring to the examples you are planning to use in your essay, draft a thesis statement that states your topic, tells why it is important, and expresses your point of view. Remember that you can change your thesis statement as many times as you need to.

Drafting an Introduction

Read more about drafting an introduction on p. 266.

Your introduction is the place to interest your readers in your topic and provide your thesis statement. You may also want to include some background information to help your readers understand the examples you will be providing.

In the introduction to "Homeless in Prescott, Arizona," for example, B.C. starts by giving information about how she used to live and explaining why she decided to quit her job and move to Arizona. She then gets her readers' attention with a surprising fact: She lives comfortably on just $315 a month. By starting this way, B.C. makes her readers want to know how she can get by with so little money.

HOW TO Introduce an Essay That Gives Examples

- Catch the readers' attention with a surprising fact or an interesting story.
- Provide information that will help readers understand your topic.
- Consider previewing your examples.
- Conclude with a thesis statement.

WRITING ACTIVITY 5 (Group): Draft an Introduction

Form a group with classmates and tell them what change you are writing about. With your classmates' help, draft an introduction that grabs readers' attention and leads into your thesis statement. Then, help your classmates draft introductions for their essays.

Adding Support with Details

In an essay that gives examples, each example is developed in its own paragraph. Every body paragraph names an example in a topic sentence and supports that topic sentence with details. Make sure that you include enough information to help your readers understand each of your examples.

Suppose you are writing about how adopting a dog changed your priorities, and one of your examples is that you have to walk Shadow every day. It wouldn't be enough to say simply that the dog needs to go out. To develop this example in detail, you might talk about waking up earlier than you used to; getting home by six o'clock every evening; forcing yourself to go outside in bad weather; and arranging for a pet-sitter if you can't walk the dog yourself. If you need more details for your examples, try brainstorming for ideas.

Student writer Damariz needed additional details to explain the examples of her improved study skills. Here is the beginning of her brainstorming:

Example

I read better.

Used to have to reread a lot.

Now I repeat what I'm reading out loud.

Make notes in the margin.

Review regularly.

Example

I am a better listener.

Used to fall asleep.

Take notes.

Participate in class.

WRITING ACTIVITY 6: Develop Examples

List several examples that illustrate your thesis statement, then brainstorm details for each example.

Drafting a Conclusion

Your conclusion wraps up your examples and sums up what you want your readers to remember about your thesis. For example, you might say again how a change affected you or why it was important to improve some aspect of your life.

For more help with drafting a conclusion, see pp. 268–69.

An effective strategy for ending your essay is to refer back to a detail from your introduction. Jan Zeh, for example, concludes by admitting that her annoyance might not be her husband's fault. She ends her essay with this sentence:

Just don't ask me while I'm working on my crossword puzzle.

You might recall that Zeh had included in her second paragraph the sentence, "I'd like to work on my crossword puzzle in peace." By circling back to her introduction, Zeh lets her readers know that her essay is finished.

WRITING ACTIVITY 7: Draft a Conclusion

Write a conclusion that summarizes the main point of your essay; if possible, refer back to a detail from your introduction. Compare your concluding statement to your thesis statement to be sure that your conclusion reinforces your main point.

Damariz's Discovery Draft

Using her thesis statement and the material she drafted for her introduction, supporting paragraphs, and conclusion, Damariz wrote the following discovery draft. Her draft includes some errors, which she will correct later.

University Seminar

During the Spring semester I had the opportunity to take a class called university seminar. Many people take this class just to fulfill a requirement. Few people know how helpful this class can be. Throughout the semester I have improved in several areas thanks to this class. For example, I can read better, I can prepare better for an exam, I have become a good listener in lectures, I have improved my communication skills, and most important of all I have learned how to stay focused to reach my future goals.

Before taking University Seminar, I read and read and most of the times I had to go back and reread everything. I didn't understand. Sometimes I even fell asleep while reading. That doesn't happen to me anymore, because now when I'm reading I repeat what I'm reading and say it out loud. That helps me understand better. I also make notes to the side of the text. When I go back to review, it is easier for me to remember the material.

Since I can read better, I have been doing better on my exams. I know that in order to get a good grade on the exam I must be preparing for it throughout the whole semester, not a week or a day before the test. I have also learned to organize study materials to make it easier for me to study when I need to.

I have become a better listener after taking this class. During lectures I used to fall asleep. If I didn't fall asleep, I would just be doing something else that didn't have to do anything with the class I was in. In University seminar we surveyed our classes and I was able to identify the instructor's teaching style. Once I did that I realized that if I didn't pay attention to the lecture in two of my classes I was not going to be able to pass the classes. I started taking notes and participating in class just like I was told in University Seminar class. I was told that passive learning tends to get boring. I turned my passive way of learning into an active one. Participating and taking notes really helped. I got through the lectures without sleeping.

I have always been a quiet person. I really don't like to talk in front of class. I know that to succeed one must have good communication skills. At the beginning of the class we were assigned to a group. I learned that I had to participate within my group. I started getting along with different people. I learned to be open to different ideas.

I believe that the most important thing I learned in University Seminar was to stay focused on my goals. I tend to get discouraged when things don't turn out the way I planned. I learned that just because I fail a class I'm not going to drop out of school; now I know that it is fine if one fails a class the important thing is to remember the goals that you have and that would make you do better next time. Another thing is that sometimes when I felt really tired, when I was reading, doing homework, or studying and I just wanted to give up, I didn't because I had my goals in my mind and that gave me encouragement to keep going. Now I know that as long as I have a clear view of what I want for the future it's going to be easier for me to get there.

WRITING ACTIVITY 8: Complete Your Discovery Draft

Using the thesis statement, introduction, supporting details, and conclusion that you already have, write a discovery draft. For now, focus on putting your ideas into words. You'll have time to revise and edit later.

STEP 3: REVISE YOUR ESSAY

Now that you have pulled your ideas together for yourself, it's time to make them clearer for your readers. Keep in mind that your audience consists of magazine readers who don't know anything about you. To improve your essay, you'll need to make sure that you have made a point your readers will care about and that you've provided enough detail to help them understand it.

Strengthening Your Focus

Learn more about strengthening your focus on pp. 271–72.

When you drafted your essay, you may have tried to give as many examples as you could think of. Too many examples, however, will overwhelm your readers, making it difficult for them to remember your point. To make your essay effective, you should choose three or four related ideas that you can explain in detail. Check that every example in the essay develops and supports your thesis statement.

Damariz's discovery draft included more ideas than she could explain in detail. To strengthen her focus, she decided to eliminate the paragraph on exams because she had not developed it thoroughly and because the rest of her paragraphs focused on in-class study skills.

WRITING ACTIVITY 9: Strengthen Your Focus

Review your draft and check that every paragraph directly supports your thesis statement. Eliminate any examples that aren't related to your main idea. If you find that you have a lot of examples that don't fit, you may want to revise your thesis statement.

Building Your Support with Process Explanation

Look again at each example you used. Does it support the thesis statement with specific information? Is the explanation detailed enough to be interesting? If not, you'll need to revise your example to provide specific details that support your thesis statement.

To review paragraphs that explain a process, see Chapter 6.

Because your essay explains either a change in your life or a lesson you have learned, at least one of your examples probably involves how you did something. To improve your support, consider developing that example with process explanation. Both of the essays that opened this chapter include a process paragraph. In "The 'Golden Years' Are Beginning to Tarnish," Jan Zeh explains how her husband tried to stop the cat from climbing their palm trees (paragraph 7). And in "Homeless in Prescott, Arizona," B.C. uses process explanation to show how she gets her meals inexpensively (7).

HOW TO Build Support for an Essay That Gives Examples

- Provide enough examples to help your reader understand your main point.
- Add details where needed to develop your examples.
- Consider using process explanation if it's appropriate to develop one of your examples.

Damariz reviewed her discovery draft on how the University Seminar helped her improve her study skills and decided that she had done a good job overall, but could do better at explaining how she prepared to speak in front of the class. When she revised her essay, she used process explanation to develop this example in more detail.

WRITING ACTIVITY 10: Build Your Support

Look closely at each example you included in your discovery draft and check that it is explained in enough detail. Add details where necessary. If one of your examples explains how you did something, rewrite it as a process paragraph.

Using TIE to Organize Your Points

TIE order is also explained on pp. 62–63.

For an essay using examples, you can use *topic-illustration-explanation (TIE)* order to develop your ideas. To use TIE, start each body paragraph with a topic sentence that gives an example related to your thesis statement. Then, illustrate the topic sentence with specific details that explain the example.

B.C., for example, used TIE order to organize some of her examples in "Homeless in Prescott, Arizona." Her essay provides six major examples: (1) her home base, (2) the local community college, (3) inexpensive and nutritious meals, (4) the natural look, (5) the benefits of her lifestyle, and (6) the disadvantages. B.C. illustrates each of these categories with more specific examples that explain her points.

Revise with Color
To help you check the order of your points, use the color feature of your word-processing program. For instance, you might write your major examples in red and your supporting details in green. Highlighting different aspects with color will help you see whether each point is in the best possible order.

WRITING ACTIVITY 11: Organize Your Points

Use *topic-illustration-explanation (TIE)* order to organize your ideas more effectively. Reread your discovery draft and label the sentences in each of your body paragraphs:

- topic sentence (topic)
- supporting examples (illustration)
- details (explanation)

Add examples and explanations where needed.

Connecting Your Ideas

As you revise your essay, make sure that you have included enough keywords and transitions to help your readers follow your ideas.

An essay using examples should include transitional words that let your readers know when you are providing an example.

More transitions are listed on p. 42.

HOW TO Connect Ideas in an Essay That Gives Examples

The following phrases tell your reader that you are providing an example:

- For example,
- For instance,
- To illustrate,
- In particular,
- First, second, third, etc.

Repeating keywords will also make it easier for your readers to stay on track. In "The 'Golden Years' Are Beginning to Tarnish," for example, Jan Zeh repeats the words *husband, retired, house, home,* and *together* to help her readers remember that her point is that her husband's constant presence at home bothers her. B.C. uses *I have, cost, library, college, beautiful, comfortable,* and *warm* several times to help the readers understand that she is still on the topic of living well without a job or a home.

WRITING ACTIVITY 12: Examine Keywords and Transitions

Circle the keywords and underline the transitions you used in your discovery draft. Mark places where you need to add other keywords and transitions.

Damariz's Revised Draft

Before you read Damariz's revised draft, reread her discovery draft. By comparing her drafts, you can see how she tightened her focus, improved her supporting details, and connected her ideas. This draft still contains some errors that she will correct when she edits her essay.

University Seminar: The Key to College Success

During the Spring semester I had the opportunity to take a class called university seminar. Many people take this class to fulfill a requirement. Few people know just how helpful this class can be. Throughout the semester I have improved in several areas thanks to this class. For example, I can read better, I have become a good listener in lectures, I have improved my communication skills, and I have learned how to stay focused to reach my future goals.

Before taking University Seminar, I reread everything. I didn't understand what I was reading. Sometimes I even fell asleep with a book in my hand. That doesn't happen to me anymore, because now I repeat what I'm reading out loud to help me understand better. I also make notes to the side of the text. When I go back to review, it is easier for me to remember the material.

I have become a better listener after taking this class. During lectures I used to fall asleep. If I didn't fall asleep, I would do something else that didn't have anything to do with the class. In University Seminar we surveyed our instructor's teaching styles. I realized that if I didn't pay attention to the lecture in two of my classes, I would not be able to pass them. I started taking notes and participating in class. Our instructor told us that passive learning tends to get boring, so I turned my passive way of learning into an active one. Participating and taking notes really helped. I got through the lectures without sleeping.

I have always been a quiet person. I really don't like to talk in front of class. Now I know that to succeed it is imperative that one has good communication skills. At the beginning of the class we were assigned to a group. I started getting along with different people. I learned to be open to different ideas. We had a group assignment, an oral report on a computer lab on campus. At first I was a little intimidated because I was going to be talking in front of the class. Later I realized that I was not the only person who felt that way. I'm more confident about talking to people now.

I believe that the most important thing I learned in University Seminar was to stay focused on my goals. For example, I tend to get discouraged when things don't turn out the way I planned. I learned that just because I fail a class I'm not going to drop out of school. I'll just remember my goals and do better the next time. Now I know that as long as I have a clear view of what I want for the future, it's going to be easier for me to get there.

GROUP ACTIVITY: Analyze Damariz's Revised Draft

Using the following questions, discuss with your classmates how Damariz improved her draft.

1. How did Damariz improve her introduction?

____

____

2. What examples has Damariz added? How have these details improved her essay?

____

____

____

3. How could Damariz better focus her draft?

____

____

4. What keywords and transitions did Damariz add? Did these help make her ideas easier to follow?

____

____

____

____

5. What more can Damariz do to improve her draft?

____

____

WRITING ACTIVITY 13 (Group): Peer Review

Form a group with several classmates and exchange copies of your drafts. Read your draft aloud while your classmates follow along. Take notes on your classmates' answers to the following questions about your draft.

1. What do you like best about my essay?
2. How well does my introduction attract your attention and announce my topic?
3. How clear is my thesis statement? Does it make you want to hear more details?
4. How effective are my topic sentences? Do they focus the topic of each paragraph?
5. Did I support my points with enough detail? Where do I need more support?
6. How well are my ideas organized? Is there anything I should rearrange?
7. How could I improve my conclusion?

Use E-mail or Online Peer Review
E-mail your draft to several students and ask them to answer the peer review questions in a return e-mail. If you have access to a networked computer lab, you may do peer review online. Send your suggestions for revision to the author's e-mail address.

WRITING ACTIVITY 14: Revise Your Draft

Taking into account your classmates' suggestions, revise your discovery draft. In particular, strengthen your focus, build your support, organize your points, and connect your ideas.

STEP 4: EDIT YOUR ESSAY

When you edit, you improve sentence structure and fix any errors in spelling, punctuation, and grammar. In this chapter you will practice combining closely related sentences.

What Is Sentence Coordination?

Too many short sentences in a row create a choppy effect that can bore your readers. Here are some examples of choppy sentences.

Find out more about combining sentences on pp. 529–40.

CHOPPY My very favorite exercise is rollerblading. My second favorite exercise is skateboarding.

CHOPPY We could go to Washington, D.C., when cherry blossoms are on the trees. We could also visit when snow is on the ground.

CHOPPY I collect as many stamps as I can. I never seem to have enough stamps.

You can make your ideas flow together more smoothly by merging short sentences to form longer, more interesting ones.

Combining Sentences with Coordinating Conjunctions

If two short sentences are closely related and equally important, try combining them with an appropriate coordinating conjunction (*for, and, nor, but, or, yet,* or *so*). Put a comma before the conjunction.

COMBINED My very favorite exercise is rollerblading, and my second favorite is skateboarding.

COMBINED We could go to Washington, D.C., when cherry blossoms are on the trees, or we could visit when snow is on the ground.

COMBINED I collect as many stamps as I can, but I never seem to have enough.

HOW TO Combine Sentences with Coordinating Conjunctions

- Identify sentences that are closely related and equally important.
- Check that each sentence has a subject and a verb.
- Select an appropriate coordinating conjunction (*for, and, nor, but, or, yet, so*).
- Combine the sentences with a comma and a coordinating conjunction.

EDITING PRACTICE: Combining Sentences with Coordinating Conjunctions

Use a comma and an appropriate coordinating conjunction to combine each of the following sets of sentences. Add or delete words when necessary.

EXAMPLE

CHOPPY I like the soup at Souper-Salad. The cornbread is the best.

COMBINED I like the soup at Souper-Salad, but the cornbread is the best.

1. I usually want to go to the movies on Saturdays. I also like to shop on Saturdays.

 ____

 ____

2. I have visited Disneyland twice. I have been to Disney World three times.

 ____

 ____

3. I could work on my research project this weekend. I could also go camping.

 ____

 ____

4. I have always enjoyed reading. I'm going to get a new book today.

 ____

5. My husband and I met on the Appalachian Trail. We don't hike anymore.

 ____

 ____

6. I play chess every chance I get. It's a challenging game.

 ____

7. You know what you like to do in your spare time. Just do it!

____

8. I love the outdoors. When I get a chance, I go to the mountains.

____

9. My hobby is photography. Taking digital pictures is still new to me.

____

10. Joshua doesn't like skiing. He doesn't like snowboarding either.

____

Exercise Central
The *Discoveries* Web site includes additional sentence combination exercises. Go to **bedfordstmartins.com/discoveries**, click on "Exercise Central," and select "Sentence Coordination."

Damariz's Edited Essay

Damariz's revised draft had a lot of choppy sentences that made it difficult to follow her ideas. She edited her draft by combining sentences and fixing other errors. (The underlining indicates where she corrected her draft.)

University Seminar: The Key to College Success

During the spring semester I had the opportunity to take a class called University Seminar. Many people take this class to fulfill a requirement, but few people know just how helpful it can be. Throughout the semester I have improved in several areas thanks to this class. For example, I can read better, I have become a good listener in lectures, I have improved my communication skills, and I have learned how to stay focused to reach my future goals.

To know when to capitalize words, see pp. 626–28.

Before taking University Seminar, I reread everything, but I didn't understand what I was reading. Sometimes I even fell asleep with a book in my hand. That doesn't happen to me anymore, because now I repeat what I'm reading out loud to help me understand better. I also make notes to the side of the text. When I go back to review, it is easier for me to remember the material.

To learn where to put an apostrophe, see p. 616.

I have become a better listener after taking this class. During lectures I used to fall asleep, or I would do something else that didn't have anything to do with the class. In University Seminar we surveyed our instructors' teaching styles. I realized that if I didn't pay attention to the lecture in two of my classes, I would not be able to pass them, so I started taking notes and participating in class. Our instructor told us that passive learning tends to get boring, so I turned my passive way of learning into an active one. Participating and taking notes really helped, and I got through the lectures without sleeping.

I have always been a quiet person, so I really don't like to talk in front of class. Now I know that to succeed I must have good communication skills. At the beginning of the class we were assigned to a group. I started getting along with different people, and I learned to be open to different ideas. We had a group assignment, an oral report on a computer lab on campus. At first I was a little intimidated because I was going to be talking in front of the class, but later I realized that I was not the only person who felt that way. I'm more confident about talking to people now.

I believe that the most important thing I learned in University Seminar was to stay focused on my goals. For example, I tend to get discouraged when things don't turn out the way I planned, but I learned that just because I fail a class I'm not going to drop out of school. I'll just remember my goals and do better the next time. Now I know that as long as I have a clear view of what I want for the future, it's going to be easier for me to get there.

WRITING ACTIVITY 15: Edit Your Essay

Using a dictionary and the Handbook in Part Four, edit your essay. In particular, look for short sentences that you can combine with commas and coordinating conjunctions. Create an editing log so you will learn to avoid your most common errors.

Editing logs are explained on pp. 45–46.

STEP 5: SHARE YOUR ESSAY

Many magazines and online journals publish essays sent in by their readers. Find out if your favorite magazine or Web site publishes readers' essays and, if so, send yours in for consideration.

Damariz submitted her essay to her campus magazine, and the editor decided to publish her work. Friends and fellow students, who were all interested in improving their study skills, agreed that the University Seminar would help them do better in their classes.

ADDITIONAL WRITING ASSIGNMENTS

1. Write an expressive essay for your classmates and instructor in which you use examples to show how you spend your time when you are not at school. Explain your family or work responsibilities or explain a favorite hobby.
2. Write an informative essay for your campus newspaper in which you provide examples of what you and your classmates like best about your campus. For example, you might describe the classes, the faculty, or some of the recreational activities.
3. Write a persuasive essay for your local newspaper providing examples of why you like living in the United States. You might, for example, describe the freedoms Americans enjoy, the standard of living, or the friendliness of the people.

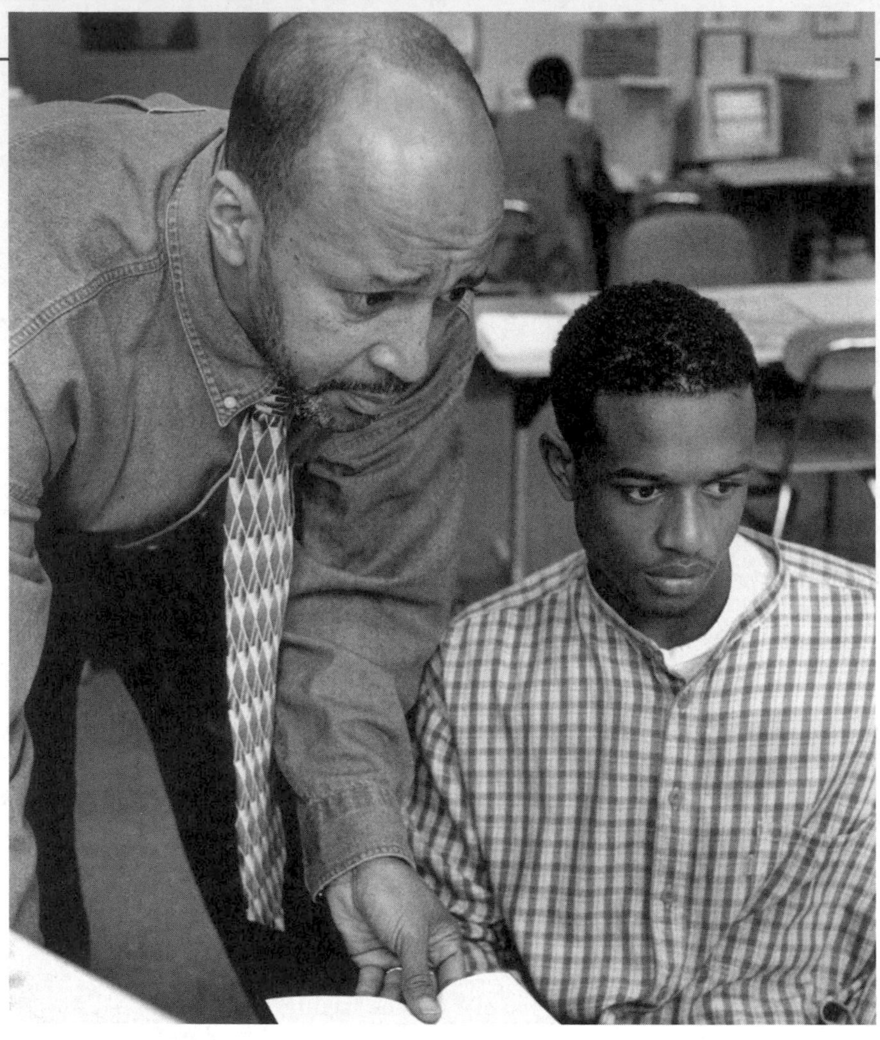

There are many ways to prepare for a profession — from choosing careers that will give you an advantage over competing candidates to doing online research about the field you hope to enter, like the young man pictured here. In this chapter, you will focus on your career goals by writing an essay about an event that interested you in a certain profession or about a job that changed you, perhaps by changing your career direction.

CHAPTER

14

Writing an Essay That Tells a Story

In this chapter, you will

- review how narration works.
- brainstorm to gather ideas.
- write about your career goals.
- try flashbacks to organize your ideas.
- practice sentence coordination.
- use your essay to apply for an internship.

UNDERSTANDING NARRATION

Read more about narration in Chapter 4.

Our lives are filled with stories. Some stories are based on fact, such as biographies and news reports. Other stories are fiction, such as fairy tales, country music songs, and horror novels. You probably tell stories about your own life, such as the time a bear invaded your family's campsite or the morning your tire blew out on the freeway.

An essay that uses narration focuses on an event and generally uses chronological order to tell the story. Narratives contain interesting details that help the reader picture what happened; often they include some dialogue. And of course, a good narrative tells the reader why the event is important.

READING ESSAYS THAT TELL A STORY

Successful people often tell stories about their own lives to explain how they got where they are. The following two essays are good examples of this kind of narrative writing.

Explaining a Career Choice

Gavin de Becker works to help others escape violence. In the following essay, he describes the events in his life that led him to choose this path.

GAVIN DE BECKER

Why I Fight Abuse

I grew up in a violent world. I am not referring to the wars between nations. I am referring to the wars in my family, the ones that left bullets embedded in the walls and floors of our homes, the wars in which police officers were occasional soldiers and my sisters and I were hostages.

I first assumed the role of a parent at 8 years of age, a protector of my younger sister, Melissa. It's clear to me now that predicting and preventing violence was my calling long before it became my profession.

When the U.S. attorney general and the director of the FBI gave me an award for designing MOSAIC, the assessment system now used for screening threats to justices of the U.S. Supreme Court, I am certain neither realized it was actually invented by a 10-year-old boy. But it was. The way I broke down the individual elements of violence as a child became the way

the most sophisticated artificial-intuition systems predict violence today.

My ghosts had become my teachers.

Some years ago, my older sister, Chrysti, said to me, "Isn't it great to know the worst is behind us?" She was referring to our childhood experiences. Our mother was a heroin addict: an intelligent, funny, well-read and beautiful woman — but a heroin addict nonetheless. While she protected us from some harm, she delivered others, and her addiction brought a collection of people into our lives most people would recoil from.

I recall a night I tried to get my mother to stop beating Chrysti. I couldn't, so I sat down on the floor and watched, reasoning that I'd be there if things got too dangerous. Chrysti and I were used to a lot and our pain threshold was high, but that night, after two hours of watching the violence escalate, I intervened to calm my mother. At that moment, Chrysti did something I'd never thought possible: She ran out the front door. I followed her and we ran like free colts down the center of an empty boulevard.

We stopped at an all-night market and decided to make an anonymous call to the police: "There are two kids loitering around here." If we didn't give the cops our names, we concluded, they wouldn't be able to take us back home. And it worked just like that. Our ride from the LAPD showed up within just a few minutes and took us to jail. They could hardly put a 12-year-old boy and a 14-year-old girl in with hardened criminals (though we might have felt at home), so they put us in our own cell.

In the morning, we called our grandfather, who took us home. Two kids found bruised and red-eyed and panting at 3:30 in the morning and nobody asked us a thing. It was as if the police saw these dramas every day, and I know now that they do.

I recall another early morning standing in the UCLA Hospital emergency room, my mother having taken an overdose of sleeping pills in one of several suicide attempts. A nurse had several questions for me, never asking what a barefoot boy was doing there at 4 a.m., the sole family representative. I now know ER nurses have seen far younger children playing adult roles in life's dramas, and they've also seen them brought in beaten, shot, raped.

I recall my mother threatening to kill us by turning on a gas burner while we slept. Chrysti and I modified a screen on our bedroom window so we could get out if we had to. I put a box outside the window and conducted a drill, lifting 4-year-old Melissa down to test that I could get her out quickly. It was my job to be sure the family got through those years alive. We didn't. My mother succeeded in a final suicide attempt when she was 39 and I was 16.

Decades went by before I recognized why I had invested my life in the prediction and prevention of violence — but now I've got the message.

Chrysti died recently, but she was happy I was working to help parents protect children. It's good to know that even the hardest of our childhood experiences have value.

READING ACTIVITY 1: Build Your Vocabulary

Try to determine the meanings of the following words from Gavin de Becker's essay. Then check their meanings by looking the words up in a dictionary.

hostages (1) ______________________________

recoil (5) ______________________________

escalate (6) ______________________________

loitering (7) ______________________________

modified (10) ______________________________

READING ACTIVITY 2: Read to Improve Your Writing

Answer the following questions about "Why I Fight Abuse."

1. In your own words, what is de Becker's thesis, or main point?

____

____

2. What methods of developing ideas (example, narration, description, process, classification, definition, comparison and contrast, and cause and effect) does de Becker use to support his ideas?

____

____

____

3. Adults who were abused as children can grow up to become strong, productive people. What good characteristics does the author appear to have as a result of surviving child abuse?

____

____

4. What experience in your own life has made you interested in a certain career? (The experience doesn't have to be as difficult as de Becker's.)

____

____

____

A Life-Changing Job

Some people have the good fortune to love the careers that satisfy their need for money. Marshall Glickman was not one of these people.

MARSHALL GLICKMAN

Money and Freedom

Making money has always been a passion of mine. At the age of twelve, I was a hustling newspaper boy and baby sitter, squirreling away dollar bills in a small red plastic safe that I hid behind my socks. While my brother was out playing basketball, I was devising plans to build my fortune. I cut lawns, delivered pizza, worked in a warehouse and as a security guard. I even had a scheme in college to capitalize on student birth control and sell condoms by mail order. When I left the brokerage house of Shearson Lehman Brothers last June, I was 24 and earning over $200,000 a year. Today I have no job. I'm not unemployed. I'm retired.

"You'd be a good lawyer," my mother always used to say. My mother is a lawyer and a college professor who routinely puts in a 60-hour week. She loves the law, loves working, and loves the $350,000 suburban home she and my dad live in. My first career plan *was* to become a lawyer, and I entered Northwestern University as a necessary first step. I hoped to impress Stanford Law by majoring in philosophy. Maybe it was the philosophy, maybe the break from home and the exposure to people of different backgrounds, but I began to question my motivations. I read. I spent my summers traveling — out West, through Europe and Kenya. I met people who had little of the respect for the legal profession that had been bred in me. I began thinking of life as a writer, artist, or adventurer.

In my senior year, partly to relieve the anxiety I felt over my future, I began meditating — first for a half-hour, then up to two hours a day. Zen meditation quieted my scheming mind and taught me to focus on the present. I took the test to enter law school, and my scores were good, within 20 points of what I'd predicted. But I knew I was marching toward a life I wasn't interested in. I fantasized about trekking in the Himalayas, bicycling cross-country, meditating in Kyoto, and writing a novel. But while I spoke bravely about freedom and choice, my suburban upbringing rejected a hand-to-mouth existence on the road. I had the heart of a wanderer but the head of an accountant.

So I postponed my adventures until I could afford them. I wouldn't have a career, I said; I would simply make money — fast. Enough money to make me feel I was a success but not so much that I would get sidetracked. My goal was a nest egg of $100,000, but I promised myself I'd work for only three years, even if I fell short of that. Wall Street seemed the most direct route.

The first months at Shearson were a nightmare. "Hello, my name is Marshall Glickman from . . . ." Slam! Busy signal. Wrong number. To reach 60 people, I had to make 200 to 300 calls a day. I took 15-minute lunches, hired three college students to help me call, and purchased names and numbers of prospective clients. Each morning I rose at 5:30, meditated for an hour and ran around Prospect Park. As the sun broke through the darkness, I imagined myself in India, in Oregon. All images of a better life had faded by the time I shuffled home from the office at 9:30 p.m., wolfed my dinner and collapsed on the couch with the same half-read book. My eyes burned from staring at the green glow of my Quotron machine. My neck had a permanent crick from cradling the phone. Three years, I told myself. You just have to hold out for three years. "You're living for tomorrow," said my brother, who is a writer.

Then the market went crazy. Interest rates dropped, and suddenly my phone rang nonstop. The groundwork I had done paid off. I raked in $30,000 to $40,000 a month in gross commissions. By year two, I was the top producer in my office, managing a portfolio of $14 million. Names on my Rolodex included C.E.O.'s, television journalists, professional athletes, actors, and a world-renowned architect, not to mention my grandmother. I was a 10-year-old again, successful beyond my wildest dreams, stuffing money into mutual funds and money markets instead of my little red safe. My meditating dwindled to 20 minutes. I found myself eyeing the price of cars, homes, and exotic vacations. One more good year, I calculated, and I'd double my savings. I'd be a millionaire at 30. Although by now I'd socked away my $100,000, could I walk away while the market was this hot?

I enjoyed the gambling, enjoyed calculating my commissions at the end of each day. I was riding the momentary high, the thrill of the hunt. At the same time, all this unnerved me. I kept reminding myself that Shearson was a means to an end, and I was still committed to that end. Trusting my earlier instincts, I gave notice to my incredulous branch manager two weeks before my third year was up — $135,000 richer. "In another five years you could have been set for life," said my father, who is a businessman.

After I left Shearson, I didn't know what to say when someone asked me what I did. I weighed the value of each day that passed against what I could have earned if I'd still been working.

It was a while before I could pick up a book on a Monday morning without feeling guilty — and poor. Even after I began to travel and those feelings passed, my interest in making money remained. It probably always will. But with $135,000 in the bank and frugal habits, I figure I can continue without working for a long time. I'm going to renovate a house and use the profits to finance a trip to the Orient. I have plans to do some real estate deals, to do some writing, work on a fishing boat in Alaska. It seems possible to do what I want and make some money, too.

Last fall, I pedaled my bike through the Catskill Mountains on the last leg of a trip from Minnesota. At a one-pump station in a town called Big Indian, I called my broker in New York to check on a volatile stock I own. I used to share an office with him. "How's it going, Dave?" I asked. Dave sounded as if he were a soldier reporting bad news from the front. "The market's off 50 points," he moaned. "I'm getting killed." I hung up and chuckled. My worries revolved around saddle sores and flat tires. I climbed back on the bike and felt the sun on my shoulders as the road raced beneath my wheels.

READING ACTIVITY 3: Build Your Vocabulary

Try to determine the meanings of the following words from "Money and Freedom." Then check their meanings by looking the words up in a dictionary.

hustling (1) ______________________

suburban (2) ______________________

meditating (3) ______________________

unnerved (7) ______________________

frugal (8) ______________________

READING ACTIVITY 4: Read to Improve Your Writing

Answer the following questions about Marshall Glickman's essay.

1. What is the thesis, or main point, of "Money and Freedom"? Where in the essay does this thesis appear?

____

____

____

____

2. What three details or examples from Glickman's narrative stand out in your mind?

____

____

3. Explain this sentence from the essay: "I had the heart of a wanderer but the head of an accountant."

____

____

____

4. Have you, or someone you know, experienced the same conflict that Glickman describes? What is your idea of success?

____

____

____

____

____

Writing Assignment

You are applying for an internship offered by the career-services program in your college. This three-month position offers paid employment in a profession you want to enter. To apply, you need to submit school transcripts, two letters of recommendation, and a writing sample. For the writing sample, you have a choice of two topics:

- Write a narrative essay about an event in your life that interested you in a certain profession. For example, helping your parents with their real estate company might have made you decide to start your own business.

  OR

- Write a narrative essay about a job (volunteer or paid) that changed you in a particular way. For instance, a job in a fast-food restaurant might have made you realize the importance of getting an education so you can earn more than the minimum wage.

STEP 1: DISCOVER IDEAS FOR WRITING

What do you want to do after you graduate? Maybe you already have a specific career goal in mind; or perhaps right now you're more focused on simply making it through college. Either way, you probably know why you decided to pursue a degree. Understanding your reasons for going to college will help you discover ideas for an essay about your future plans, whether or not you know what they are.

Choosing a Topic

For this assignment, you can write about an event that led you to decide on a career, or you can write about a job that changed you in some way. How should you decide on a topic?

Some experiences are more significant than others. Try to remember events in your life that had a strong effect on you. If something comes to you right away, it's probably a good start for your topic. What if you haven't ever had a job or aren't sure about which field you want to enter? Just pick a major or a career that interests you for now. You'll have a chance to work out the details when you gather ideas.

FAQs about Topics
The *Discoveries* Web site includes answers to frequently asked questions about topics for each chapter. Go to **bedfordstmartins.com/discoveries** and click on "FAQs."

Considering Your Audience and Purpose

Your essay will be read by the director and assistant director of the internship program at your school's career-services office. Because these people will decide which students get internships, you'll want to tell a story that stands out from the rest. Your narrative should give a good sense of who you are and why the event you're describing was important; it should also make a clear connection between that event and your career goals.

For more information on identifying audience and purpose, see pp. 20–22.

Although you want to persuade the director to select you for an internship, you're writing this essay to help your readers get to know you better. Your primary purpose, then, will be to express your thoughts and feelings.

WRITING ACTIVITY 1: Identify Your Audience and Purpose

Reflect on your audience and purpose by answering the following questions.

1. The position you're applying for is competitive: There are more applications than there are internships. How can you write your essay so that it will stand out from other essays?

   ____

   ____

   ____

2. What might your readers already know about the profession you're considering entering? What won't they know that you need to inform them about?

   ____

   ____

   ____

3. Why are you writing this essay?

   ____

   ____

   ____

4. How concerned will your readers be that you write correctly?

   ____

   ____

   ____

Brainstorming to Gather Ideas

You can probably think of a lot of experiences that influenced your plans for your future, but you may not be able to decide which ones to use for your essay. Brainstorming can help you discover which topic is best.

HOW TO Brainstorm for an Essay That Tells a Story

- Write down "Events That Interested Me in ________" at the top of a blank screen or piece of paper.
- List any ideas that come to mind.
- Don't worry about how good your ideas are. Just get the ideas down in words.
- Follow the same process for "A Job That Changed Me."
- Review the ideas to determine which topic will be most interesting for your readers.

To review how to brainstorm, see p. 24.

Student writer Ofelia brainstormed the following ideas for her essay.

Events That Interested Me in Nursing

My brother broke his arm when he was little
I had my tonsils out in second grade
Throat hurts, hurts
Frightening
Needles and tests
Nurses nice, warm hands
I've never forgotten those nurses
My own daughter has to go sometimes
I'm always watching what the doctors and nurses do
The nurses even make her laugh
Helping sick children

A Job That Changed Me

What jobs have I had?
Fast-food hotdog place
I gained fifteen pounds
Learned that spilled Coke is really messy
Tutored children after school
Learned I don't have a lot of patience
Worked at the call center
At least that job paid better
Actually I liked the job working with kids
Helping them makes me feel good

I always asked them if they'd had a good breakfast
Many didn't so they couldn't concentrate
It worried me
This job taught me I want to help kids

After completing this brainstorming, Ofelia decided to write about how her tonsillectomy made her want to become a pediatric nurse — a nurse who works with children.

WRITING ACTIVITY 2: Brainstorm

Brainstorm about each of the two topics you can select for this assignment. List ideas as they come to you without worrying about grammar or how good they are.

Narrowing Your Topic

You'll find more advice on narrowing your topic on pp. 27–29.

Because you're writing a short essay, you'll need to narrow your topic so that you can tell your story with plenty of details. Suppose you're writing about the time you were a telemarketer at a badly managed workplace. As a result, you decided to get a college degree so you could learn good business practices. You can't write about every unpleasant thing that happened. Instead, select one central event that made you decide to go to college. By focusing on only one event, you can write about it in enough detail to keep your readers' interest.

HOW TO Narrow a Topic for an Essay That Tells a Story

- Review your brainstorming to select one event to write about.
- Brainstorm more about that one event.
- Select the most interesting details about the event.
- Check that you can tell the story in a short essay.
- Check that the story will have a main idea.

WRITING ACTIVITY 3: Narrow Your Topic

Review the brainstorming you completed in Activity 2. Choose the experience that interests you the most and that will be most interesting to your readers. Brainstorm more about that topic to narrow your ideas.

STEP 2: WRITE YOUR DISCOVERY DRAFT

Before you write your discovery draft, you'll draft a working thesis statement and an introduction, add support, and draft a conclusion. Since you're still in the early stages of the writing process, your focus will be on getting your ideas down in words. You'll be able to improve the ideas as you revise and edit.

Drafting a Thesis Statement

The thesis statement in a narrative essay tells your readers the point of the story they're going to read. If you're writing about an event or events that made you decide to enter a profession, your thesis would explain how the events affected your decision. If you're writing about how a job changed you, the thesis would explain what that change was. Having a tentative thesis in mind before you start writing will help you keep your story focused on a point.

Thesis statements are also discussed on pp. 265–66.

HOW TO Write a Thesis Statement for an Essay That Tells a Story

- Tell what event your story is about.
- Express the point of your story.
- Check that your point is focused enough to be developed in a short essay.
- Be prepared to revise your thesis statement as your ideas develop.

Student writer Ofelia drafted the following working thesis statement for her essay:

> Because of the good experiences with nurses I've had all my life, I've decided to become a pediatric nurse.

This thesis statement tells what Ofelia's essay will be about (her experiences with nurses), states that those experiences affected her decision, and explains why (because they were good).

WRITING ACTIVITY 4: Draft a Thesis Statement

Look over your brainstorming and decide what the point of your story is, then draft a thesis statement that expresses your point. If you can't think of a thesis, do some more brainstorming, or use one of the other methods of gathering ideas. Keep in mind that your thesis might change as you develop your ideas.

Drafting an Introduction

Turn to p. 266 for more information on introductions.

Your job in your introduction is to attract readers' attention, give any necessary background information, and indicate the thesis, or main idea, of your narrative.

Examine the introduction to "Why I Fight Abuse":

> "I grew up in a violent world." (This surprising statement captures the reader's attention.)
>
> "I am referring to the wars in my family. . . ." (De Becker gives background information about the type of violence he grew up with.)
>
> "It's clear to me now that predicting and preventing violence was my calling long before it became my profession." (De Becker's thesis explains that even as a child he was working to end violence.)

For additional ways to grab your readers' attention, see pp. 31–32.

HOW TO Introduce an Essay That Tells a Story

- Attract the readers' attention with a surprising fact or a vivid image.
- Give the readers important facts they'll need to know to understand the story.
- Include a thesis statement.

WRITING ACTIVITY 5 (Group): Draft an Introduction

Form a group with several classmates and explain your topic to them. With their help, draft an introduction that leads into your thesis statement. Then help your classmates draft introductions to their essays.

Freewriting to Add Support

Review how to freewrite on p. 25.

The heart of your essay is the story you're telling. Try freewriting on your topic to see what you can remember. Write down your story as though you were telling it to a friend or writing it in a journal. Include everything that comes to mind and don't worry about the organization or the details; just get your story into words. You'll have a chance to polish your ideas later.

After spending a few minutes trying to remember the time she was in the hospital as a child, student writer Ofelia came up with the following freewriting:

> It was a long time ago. My parents and brother went with me but I was scared. After a lot of waiting around it was time for the surgery. I didn't want to go. My parents tried to calm me down, but no good. I never had surgery before. I was scared. All I knew was that they were going to cut something out of my throat. My brother broke his arm once and he told me it hurt real bad. I don't remember the surgery I guess they must have put me under. When I woke up I felt bad. I guess I had a fever. One of the nurses got a doctor. He looked at my chart then he was gone again. He didn't say anything. The nurses were the ones that actually took care of me. They were really nice and told me stories and gave me ice cream. One nurse stayed with me every night and made me feel better.

WRITING ACTIVITY 6: Develop Descriptive Details

Set aside fifteen minutes to a half-hour and write about your topic nonstop. Don't worry if you have the details right or if they're in the right order; just get them down in words. You can turn your freewriting into a discovery draft later.

Drafting a Conclusion

When you finish your story, don't come to a sudden stop. End your essay with a conclusion that restates your main idea and gives your readers a sense of why the experience was important to you.

For additional ways to conclude your essay, see pp. 268–69.

Because you're telling your story to illustrate a point, consider using your conclusion to connect your topic to a larger idea. For instance, you could indicate how the field you want to enter contributes something useful to society, as student writer Ofelia did:

> Based on my observations of pediatric nurses, this is the profession for me. As a pediatric nurse, I would have the knowledge to help children get well. Unlike doctors, I would have the time to work with patients directly. Though the field of nursing can be very stressful, I believe it will be rewarding.

WRITING ACTIVITY 7: Draft a Conclusion

Draft a conclusion to your story that restates your main idea and gives your readers a sense that the story is finished. If it makes sense to do so, connect your topic to a larger idea.

Ofelia's Discovery Draft

Starting with her thesis statement, freewriting, and the first attempts at her introduction and conclusion, Ofelia wrote this discovery draft. Note that Ofelia's draft includes some errors. She will correct these later.

Strong Hands, Soft Medicine

When you're seven years old, being in the hospital is very scary. This is what happened to me when I had my tonsils out when I was a child. My throat burned, I missed my mother, and I didn't know what was happening. A nurse came to my bed, held my hand, and told me everything was going to be fine. Because of the good experiences with nurses I've had all my life, I've decided to become a pediatric nurse.

My Tonsillectomy was a frightening experience. I had to get up really early and go to the hospital. My parents and brother went with me. My brother had been in the hospital before when he broke his arm. After a lot of waiting around, they wheeled me into the operating room. I was so scared my legs were shaking.

Not long after the surgery I began to feel hot, sweaty, and uncomfortable. One of the nurses noticed I had a high fever and didn't look well. She told the doctor right away. The doctor rushed in, spent a few minutes looking at my chart, and told the nurses to give me a different medicine. The nurses took care of me after that.

The worst time at the hospital was when I was alone at night, and I couldn't sleep because I was in pain. The night nurse stayed with me almost the whole time. She held my hand and put a cool cloth on my forehead to make me feel better. Although I was scared because

```
my parents weren't there, she made me feel much
better.
  Based on my observations of pediatric nurses, this
is the profession for me. As a pediatric nurse, I
would have the knowledge to help children get well.
Unlike doctors, I would have the time to work with
patients directly. The field of nursing can be
stressful. I believe it will be rewarding.
```

Gather Ideas during Drafting

If you run out of ideas while drafting, open a new document and use one of your favorite techniques for gathering ideas, such as freewriting or brainstorming. When you think of something you can use, copy and paste it into the draft.

WRITING ACTIVITY 8: Complete Your Discovery Draft

Write a discovery draft, referring to your thesis statement and what you have already written for your introduction, support, and conclusion. Focus on getting your ideas down in essay form; you'll be able to improve these ideas when you revise and edit.

STEP 3: REVISE YOUR ESSAY

The purpose of writing your discovery draft was to put your ideas together for yourself. When you revise, your purpose is to develop and organize these ideas for your readers.

Strengthening Your Focus

When you wrote your discovery draft, you may have tried to include every single thing you could think of to explain your career goals. To strengthen your focus, check that you're describing just one main event. Also, be sure to limit your essay to the most important aspects of that event. This will allow you to give interesting details and to emphasize why the experience was important to you.

Learn more about strengthening your focus on pp. 271–72.

In her discovery draft, Ofelia discussed her brother's experience in the hospital. She deleted this information in her revised draft because it wasn't part of her own hospital stay. As a result, she had room to describe her experience with nurses in more detail.

Use Comment Online
You and your classmates can share drafts by e-mail. Use the comment feature of your word-processing program to write your suggestions on the drafts themselves.

WRITING ACTIVITY 9 (Group): Strengthen Your Focus

Exchange drafts with several classmates and evaluate the focus of each other's essays. Discuss ways to improve each other's focus.

Building Support with Description

Turn to Chapter 5 for a review of writing paragraphs that describe.

While you have experienced the events you're describing in your essay, your readers haven't. Consider adding description to make your story more colorful and interesting. Gather descriptive details by answering the following questions about the event you're narrating:

- How does it smell?
- How does it taste?
- How does it sound?
- What does it feel like?
- What does it look like?

HOW TO Build Support for an Essay That Tells a Story

- Add descriptive details to help readers feel like they were there.
- Use dialogue to show what people actually said.
- Check that the details and dialogue directly support the main point of the essay.

Ofelia used these questions to brainstorm descriptive details about her stay in the hospital:

How does it smell? The hospital smells like medicine. A sharp smell. I smell sweat. The nurse smells like perfume — lavender flowers.

How does it taste?	The nurse gives me vanilla ice cream. It tastes cool and sweet.
How does it sound?	Her voice is calm and soothing. Warm. The hospital seems to buzz with doctors and nurses racing around.
What does it feel like?	My throat burns. I feel hot and uncomfortable. The nurse's hand is soft and cool.
What does it look like?	The hospital room is white. The light glares. The nurse has a big smile. Wrinkles around her eyes.

Use Color to Separate Details
If you answer the questions for gathering details on screen, choose a different color as you enter the answers to each question. For instance, use green to write about smell, red for taste, black for sound, and so on. By using different colors, you'll be able to keep each set of ideas separate from the others.

Although she couldn't use all of them, Ofelia added many of these details to her revised draft to help her readers better understand her feelings about being a seven-year-old in the hospital.

WRITING ACTIVITY 10: Add Descriptive Details

Use the following questions to brainstorm for descriptive details: How does it smell? taste? sound? What does it feel like? look like? Review your answers and decide which details will add interest to your story.

Using a Flashback to Organize Your Points

To review chronological order, see p. 40.

How well you organize your ideas will affect how well you communicate them. For a narrative essay, use chronological order so readers can follow events in the order in which they occurred.

You might also want to consider including a *flashback*. A flashback interrupts the story, jumping back to tell something that happened at an earlier time. Following the flashback, the main story continues. A flashback is useful for contrasting the past with the present and for emphasizing a key idea.

Look again at "Money and Freedom." Although Marshall Glickman tells his story mostly in chronological order, about halfway through (paragraph 6), he flashes back to his childhood:

> **I was a 10-year-old again, successful beyond my wildest dreams, stuffing money into mutual funds and money markets instead of my little red safe.**

By interrupting his tale with a reference to his childhood (which he had described in earlier paragraphs), Glickman emphasizes that his interests remained the same, even if his life had changed drastically.

WRITING ACTIVITY 11: Consider Using a Flashback

Check that your draft is in chronological order. If something is out of order, can you turn it into a flashback that contrasts the present with the past or focuses attention on a key idea? If you haven't used a flashback, where might one be effective?

Connecting Your Ideas

To make sure that the ideas in your draft flow together logically, use transitions to help your readers follow the sequence of events you are describing.

HOW TO Connect Ideas in an Essay That Tells a Story

To show time:	then, since, meanwhile, by then, during, when, soon, after, before, now, sometimes
To show sequence:	first, last, next, finally
To add information:	also, additionally, in addition, too, furthermore

Check also that you include keywords throughout your essay to keep readers on track. In "Money and Freedom," for instance, keywords include *money, work, travel,* and *dreams*. By repeating these words, Marshall Glickman reminds his readers that his central idea is the conflict he experienced between earning a living and living his life.

WRITING ACTIVITY 12 (Group): Examine Keywords and Transitions

With several classmates, circle the keywords and transitions used in "Why I Fight Abuse." Notice how these help de Becker's ideas flow together. Then, analyze your own draft. Where should you add keywords and transitions?

Ofelia's Revised Draft

Reread Ofelia's discovery draft, and then read her revised draft. Pay attention to how she has improved her focus, support, organization, and connections. The draft still contains some errors that Ofelia will correct when she edits.

Soft Hands, Strong Medicine

When you're seven years old, being in the hospital is scary. After my Tonsillectomy, my throat burned, I missed my mother, and I felt confused. Then, a nurse held my hand and said in a soft voice, "Everything's going to be fine." After this, I was releived enough to fall back to sleep. Because of the good experiences I had with nurses when I was in the hospital, I decided to become a Pediatric Nurse.

The third night I was in the hospital, I lay awake remembering the surgery I had gone through. When the nurses had wheeled me into the operating room, I was so scared my legs shook. A doctor gave me a shot. The operating room became blurry. The next thing I knew I was in a hospital bed with a burning feeling where my tonsils used to be. The room smelled of medicine and sweat. People in the hall were talking, laughing, and crying. The nurses were always cheerful.

I had to stay in the hospital for three days because I developed an infection. It made me feel hot, sweaty, and uncomfortable. The nurse told my mother, "I think her fever is too high." The doctor rushed into the room, looked me over, and rushed out. Thanks to the nurse, I got the right medicine. I noticed that the nurses, not the doctors, give the patients personelized care.

I stopped thinking about being in the hospital when the night nurse came into the room. My favorite nurse, she smelled of lavender perfume and had warm hands. She pulled a chair up to my bed, gave me a sip of water, and held my hand. I wanted to tell her thanks. I was too shy. Although I was scared because my parents weren't there, the night nurse made me feel much better.

As I lay in the hospital bed, I decided I wanted to be a nurse. Twenty years later I still haven't changed my mind. As a Pediatric Nurse, I will have the knowledge to help children get well. Unlike doctors, I will have the time to work with patients directly. The field of pediatric nursing can be stressful. I believe it will be rewarding.

GROUP ACTIVITY: Analyze Ofelia's Revised Draft

Using the following questions, discuss with your classmates how Ofelia improved her draft.

1. How has Ofelia improved her introduction?

____

____

____

____

2. How is Ofelia's revised draft better focused than her discovery draft?

____

____

____

3. What supporting details and dialogue has Ofelia added? How do these details and dialogue improve her essay?

____

____

4. How has Ofelia ordered her points more effectively?

5. What keywords and transitions has Ofelia added? How have they helped make her ideas easier to follow?

6. What more can Ofelia do to improve her draft?

WRITING ACTIVITY 13 (Group): Peer Review

Form a group with several classmates and exchange copies of your drafts. Read your draft aloud while your classmates follow along. Take notes on your classmates' answers to the following questions about your draft.

1. What do you like best about my essay?
2. How well does my introduction attract your attention? Does it give enough information for you to understand my story?
3. How clear is my thesis? What do you think is the main point of my story?
4. Evaluate my focus. Which ideas don't help support my main point?
5. Are my points well supported? Where do I need to add descriptive details, facts, examples, or dialogue?
6. How well are my points organized? Is there any place where a flashback can help me tell the story?

Comment Online
Exchange drafts with your classmates through e-mail. Use the comment feature of your word-processing program to write suggestions for revision in the draft.

WRITING ACTIVITY 14: Revise Your Draft

After reviewing your notes from the peer review, revise your discovery draft. Concentrate on strengthening your focus, building your support, organizing your points, and connecting your ideas.

STEP 4: EDIT YOUR ESSAY

Because your essay is part of an application, it's very important that you edit it carefully to eliminate any mistakes in grammar, punctuation, and spelling. Even if your story is interesting and your writing is strong, such errors can give the impression that you're careless or sloppy. Another important part of editing is improving your sentence structure to make your essay read more smoothly and easily. In this chapter, you'll learn to improve readability by combining related sentences.

What Is Sentence Coordination?

Strings of short sentences can make it difficult for readers to understand how your ideas connect to each other. Consider the following sets of sentences:

DISCONNECTED The doctor told me to take the medicine. She told me when I should take it.

DISCONNECTED The curfew doesn't become law until Tuesday. Tonight we can still stay out past midnight.

DISCONNECTED The label says the cookies are low in fat. We should not eat the whole bag.

You can improve the flow of your writing by combining short sentences to show how they are related.

Coordinating Sentences with Conjunctive Adverbs

One way to coordinate closely related sentences is with a semicolon and a conjunctive adverb (also called a *transition*). Here are some of the most common conjunctive adverbs:

For other ways to combine sentences, see Chapter 24 of the Handbook in Part Four.

also	instead
as a result	meanwhile
consequently	moreover
furthermore	nevertheless
however	similarly
in addition	therefore

To combine sentences with a conjunctive adverb, place a semicolon before the adverb and a comma after it. Notice how the ideas in the previous examples read more clearly when they are combined this way.

COMBINED The doctor told me to take the medicine; in addition, she told me when I should take it.

COMBINED The curfew doesn't become law until Tuesday; consequently, tonight we can still stay out past midnight.

The conjunctive adverb can also appear in the middle of the second sentence, as in this example:

COMBINED The label says the cookies are low in fat; we should not, however, eat the whole bag.

As you can see from this example, commas are placed both before and after the conjunctive adverb when it is in the middle of the second sentence.

HOW TO Combine Sentences with Conjunctive Adverbs

- Check that each of the sentences you plan to combine has a subject and a verb and expresses a complete thought.
- Select a conjunctive adverb that shows how the sentences are related.
- Combine the two sentences with a semicolon, the conjunctive adverb, and a comma.
- Put commas before and after a conjunctive adverb that appears in the middle of the second sentence.

EDITING PRACTICE: Combining Sentences with Conjunctive Adverbs

Use conjunctive adverbs to combine each of the following sets of sentences. Add or delete words where necessary.

EXAMPLE

CHOPPY Daniella chose a profession she will enjoy. She is likely to be happy.

COMBINED Daniella chose a profession she will enjoy; as a result, she is likely to be happy.

1. Many parents let their children choose their own profession. My parents always told me to be a doctor.

   ____

   ____

2. I wanted to please my parents. In college I began to study premed.

   ____

   ____

3. I always felt pressure from my parents to make good grades. I studied hard and got on the dean's list.

   ____

   ____

4. I was happy that my parents were proud of me. Something was missing.

   ____

   ____

5. I slowly began to realize I didn't really want to be a doctor. I wanted to be a forest ranger.

   ____

   ____

6. I was scared to tell my parents that I didn't want to be a doctor. I didn't tell them for more than a year.

____

____

7. Finally they noticed that I had changed my major to wildlife management. They asked me to come home for a chat.

____

____

8. They were upset when I told them I wanted to be a forest ranger. They threatened to stop helping me pay my tuition.

____

____

9. They told me that forest rangers don't make much money. I told them that it was more important to me to work outdoors.

____

____

10. Despite their threat, I didn't change my major. My parents have come to respect my decision to become a forest ranger.

____

____

Exercise Central
The *Discoveries* Web site includes additional practice exercises in sentence combining. Go to **bedfordstmartins .com/discoveries**, click on "Exercise Central," and select "Sentence Combining."

ESL Links
The *Discoveries* Web site includes links to useful ESL sites. Go to **bedfordstmartins.com/discoveries** and click on "ESL Links."

Ofelia's Edited Draft

To learn how to improve your spelling, see Chapter 27.

Ofelia's revised essay had some problems with short sentences and errors in spelling and capitalization. Here is her edited draft. (The underlining indicates where she corrected errors.)

To find out when to use capital letters, see pp. 626–28 in the Handbook in Part Four.

Soft Hands, Strong Medicine

When you're seven years old, being in the hospital is scary. After my tonsillectomy, my throat burned, I missed my mother, and I felt confused. Then a nurse held my hand and said in a soft voice, "Everything's going to be fine." After this, I was relieved enough to fall back to sleep. Because of the good experiences with nurses I had when I was in the hospital, I decided to become a pediatric nurse.

The third night I was in the hospital, I lay awake remembering the surgery I had gone through. When the nurses had wheeled me into the operating room, I was so scared my legs shook. A doctor gave me a shot; as a result, the operating room became blurry. The next thing I knew I was in a hospital bed with a burning feeling where my tonsils used to be. The room smelled of medicine and sweat. People in the hall were talking, laughing, and crying; the nurses, however, were always cheerful.

I had to stay in the hospital for three days because I developed an infection. It made me feel hot, sweaty, and uncomfortable. The nurse told my mother, "I think her fever is too high." The doctor rushed into the room, looked me over, and rushed out. Thanks to the nurse, I got the right medicine. I noticed that the nurses, not the doctors, give the patients personalized care.

I stopped thinking about being in the hospital when the night nurse came into the room. My favorite nurse, she smelled of lavender perfume and had warm hands. She pulled a chair up to my bed, gave me a sip of water, and held my hand. I wanted to tell her thanks, but I was too shy. Although I was scared because my parents weren't there, the night nurse made me feel much better.

As I lay in the hospital bed, I decided I wanted to be a nurse. Twenty years later I still haven't changed my mind. As a pediatric nurse, I will have the knowledge to help children get well. Unlike doctors, I will have the time to work with patients directly. The field of pediatric nursing can be stressful; nevertheless, I believe it will be rewarding.

WRITING ACTIVITY 15: Edit Your Essay

Edit your essay for errors in grammar, spelling, and punctuation. Also look for short sentences that you can combine with conjunctive adverbs. Refer to the Handbook in Part Four when necessary. Record your corrections in your editing log.

STEP 5: SHARE YOUR ESSAY

Ofelia and her classmates read their finished essays aloud to each other. She enjoyed listening to her classmates' essays and discussing their career plans. Since Ofelia is planning on applying for a nursing internship in her junior year in college, she put her essay in a safe place so she could use it as part of her application.

ADDITIONAL WRITING ASSIGNMENTS

1. Write an essay for a family member or friend about a special experience you shared. Tell the story of the experience and express what it meant for you. Give the essay to the family member or friend on a special occasion, such as a birthday or an anniversary.
2. Write an essay for your classmates and instructor in which you tell about an important experience in your past. Use description to make your readers feel that they're sharing the experience with you.
3. Write an essay for your local newspaper that explains your idea of a perfect day in your town. The purpose of the essay is to help readers understand what your community has to offer.
4. Write an essay for a national magazine about how increasing tuition rates affect the daily life of a college student. The purpose of the essay is to convince readers that raising college tuition has harmful effects.

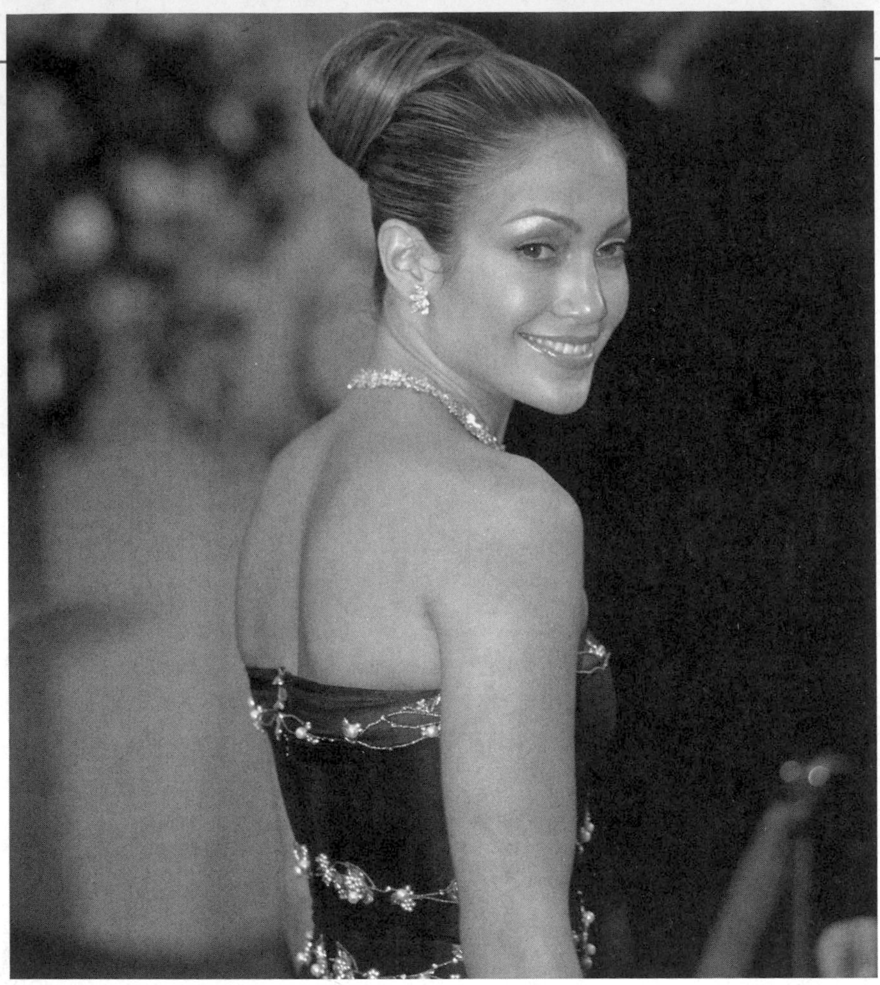

Actress Jennifer Lopez — pictured here at an awards banquet — plays characters who appear on screens around the world. In this chapter, you will consider how American movies, television and radio shows, newspapers, and magazines affect how people around the world think about the United States.

CHAPTER

15

Writing an Essay That Compares and Contrasts

In this chapter, you will:

- review how comparison and contrast works.
- cluster to gather ideas.
- write about the media.
- use subject-by-subject or point-by-point order to organize your ideas.
- practice sentence subordination.
- post your essay to a course Web site.

UNDERSTANDING COMPARISON AND CONTRAST

Whether or not you're aware of it, you use comparison and contrast all the time. Before you enroll your child in daycare, you think about the advantages and disadvantages of the different facilities available in your community. When you hear a new band on the radio, you make a mental note of what other bands it sounds like. When you vote in an election, you consider the differences between the candidates. Comparison and contrast helps us make sense of the world around us.

Read more about comparison and contrast in Chapter 8.

To compare means to look for similarities, while *to contrast* means to look for differences. A comparison-and-contrast essay might emphasize how two or more things are alike or it might emphasize how they are different; it will usually do a little bit of both. Whatever the focus, the comparison and contrast serves a larger purpose: perhaps to make readers aware of something they may not have considered, to argue that one thing is better or worse than another, or to explain a point.

READING ESSAYS THAT COMPARE AND CONTRAST

People living in the United States constantly encounter sounds and images from television, radio, movies, magazines, newspapers, and the Internet. But can we trust what we see and hear? In the following two essays, writers use comparison and contrast to examine the media.

People in the Media

Many people's views of the United States come from newspapers and television newscasts. In "A Case of 'Severe Bias,'" Patricia Raybon argues that media images of black Americans misrepresent them.

PATRICIA RAYBON

A Case of "Severe Bias"

This is who I am not. I am not a crack addict. I am not a welfare mother. I am not illiterate. I am not a prostitute. I have never been in jail. My children are not in gangs. My husband doesn't beat me. My home is not a tenement. None of these things define who I am, nor do they describe the other black people I've known and worked with and loved and befriended over these forty years of life.

Nor does it describe most of black America, period.

Yet in the eyes of the American news media, this is what black America is: poor, criminal, addicted, and dysfunctional. Indeed, media coverage of black America is so one-sided, so imbalanced that the most victimized and hurting segment of the black community — a small segment, at best — is presented not as the exception but as the norm. It is an insidious practice, all the uglier for its blatancy.

In recent months, I have observed a steady offering of media reports on crack babies, gang warfare, violent youth, poverty, and homelessness — and in most cases, the people featured in the photos and stories were black. At the same time, articles that discuss other aspects of American life — from home buying to medicine to technology to nutrition — rarely, if ever, show blacks playing a positive role, or for that matter, any role at all.

Day after day, week after week, this message — that black America is dysfunctional and unwhole — gets transmitted across the American landscape. Sadly, as a result, America never learns the truth about what is actually a wonderful, vibrant, creative community of people.

Most black Americans are *not* poor. Most black teenagers are *not* crack addicts. Most black mothers are *not* on welfare. Indeed, in sheer numbers, more *white* Americans are poor and on welfare than are black. Yet one would never deduce that by watching television or reading American newspapers and magazines.

Why do the American media insist on playing this myopic, inaccurate picture game? In this game, white America is always whole and lovely and healthy while black America is usually sick and pathetic and deficient. Rarely, indeed, is black America ever depicted in the media as functional and self-sufficient. The free press, indeed, as the main interpreter of American culture and American experience, holds the mirror on American reality — so much so that what the media say is *is,* even if it's not that way at all. The media are guilty of a severe bias and the problem screams out for correction. It is worse than simply lazy journalism, which is bad enough; it is inaccurate journalism.

For black Americans like myself, this isn't just an issue of vanity — of wanting to be seen in a good light. Nor is it a matter of closing one's eyes to the very real problems of the urban underclass — which undeniably is disproportionately black. To be sure, problems besetting the black underclass deserve the utmost attention of the media, as well as the understanding and concern of the rest of American society.

But if their problems consistently are presented as the *only* reality for blacks, any other experience known in the black community ceases to have validity, or to be real. In this scenario, millions of blacks are relegated to a sort of twilight zone, where who we are and what we are isn't based on fact but on image and perception. That's what it feels like to be a black American whose lifestyle is outside of the aberrant behavior that the media present as the norm.

For many of us, life is a curious series of encounters with white people who want to know why we are "different" from other blacks — when, in fact, most of us are only "different" from the now common negative images of black life. So pervasive are these images that they aren't just perceived as the norm, they're *accepted* as the norm.

I am reminded, for example, of the controversial Spike Lee film *Do the Right Thing* and the criticism by some movie reviewers that the film's ghetto neighborhood isn't populated by addicts and drug pushers — and thus is not a true depiction.

In fact, millions of black Americans live in neighborhoods where the most common sights are children playing and couples walking their dogs. In my own inner-city neighborhood in Denver — an area that the local press consistently describes as "gang territory" — I have yet to see a recognizable "gang" member or any "gang" activity (drug dealings or drive-by shootings), nor have I been the victim of "gang violence."

Yet to students of American culture — in the case of Spike Lee's film, the movie reviewers — a black, inner-city neighborhood can only be one thing to be real: drug-infested and dysfunctioning. Is this my ego talking? In part, yes. For the millions of black people like myself — ordinary, hard-working, law-abiding, tax-paying Americans — the media's blindness to the fact that we even exist, let alone to our contributions to American society, is a bitter cup to drink. And as self-reliant as most black Americans are — because we've had to be self-reliant — even the strongest of us still crave affirmation.

I want that. I want it for my children. I want it for all the beautiful, healthy, funny, smart black Americans I have known and loved over the years.

And I want it for the rest of America, too.

I want America to know us — all of us — for who we really are. To see us in all of our complexity, our subtleness, our artfulness, our enterprise, our specialness, our loveliness, our American-ness. That is the real portrait of black America — that we're strong people, surviving people, capable people. That may be the best-kept secret in America. If so, it's time to let the truth be known.

READING ACTIVITY 1: Build Your Vocabulary

Try to determine the meanings of the following words from "A Case of 'Severe Bias.'" Then, check their meanings by looking the words up in a dictionary.

tenement (1) ______________________

insidious (3) ______________________

blatancy (3) ______________________

myopic (7) ______________________

aberrant (9) ______________________

affirmation (13) ______________________

READING ACTIVITY 2: Read to Improve Your Writing

Answer the following questions about Patricia Raybon's essay.

1. What is the "severe bias" that Raybon writes about?

____

____

____

2. What evidence — details, examples, and facts — does Raybon use to support her points?

____

____

____

____

____

____

____

3. Raybon often refers to herself in this essay. How effective is this technique?

____

____

____

____

4. Do you believe that other groups of people are portrayed inaccurately by the media? Explain your answer.

____

____

____

Things in the Media

In the following essay from an American history textbook, historian Sarah Stage compares the promises made by early advertisements for electricity with how the new technology actually affected most people.

SARAH STAGE

"Better Living through Electricity"

In the 1920s, after forty years of technological development, prophecies that electricity would be a bearer of leisure and culture seemed about to come true. Thomas Edison, America's greatest inventor of electric marvels, cheerfully predicted that electrified homes would free women from household drudgery. Warming to his subject, Edison suggested that some women might then be able to develop their minds as highly as men. Perpetual light might eliminate the need for sleep. Perhaps, he concluded, someone might even invent electrical means for communicating with the dead.

Edison's hard-driving protégé Samuel Insull led in expanding electricity from commercial to domestic use. Insull's Chicago-based Commonwealth Edison Company, with General Electric and Westinghouse close behind, provided the power to increase the number of homes with electricity from 14 percent in 1920 to 70 percent in 1930. Now the lights that had shone exclusively on the privileged could also shine on average Americans and their aspirations — as long as they lived in the cities.

A barrage of advertising — General Electric alone raised its annual budget from $2 million to $12 million between 1922 and 1930 — fanned Americans' expectations of a better life. Without sooty gaslights, their houses would be easier to maintain, and electric vacuum cleaners would lessen whatever toil was still necessary. Electric refrigerators would keep a wide array of food available for elegant entertaining, electric washers and irons would facilitate high fashion, and radios would bring knowledge and music into comfortable, air-conditioned homes. One General Electric ad cheerily announced that, nowadays, "nobody works but ol' man river." Chiding foolish backwardness, other ads insisted that "any woman who turns the wringer [on a hand-operated clothes washer] . . . who cooks in a hot stuffy kitchen is doing work which electricity will do for a few cents per day." Rather than struggling with wringers and scrub boards, women could relax and listen to the radio "soap operas" sponsored by the makers of the laundry detergents foaming in their automatic washers.

Yet, despite $555 million in utility revenues by 1928, the promise of an idyllic electric future was hard to keep. Because electric companies saw little profit in running lines into sparsely settled rural areas, country folk lacked access. And the urban poor could not afford to buy into the fully wired paradise. Most city homes, for example, stayed with iceboxes until the late 1930s because they were considerably cheaper to buy and use than electric refrigerators. Freezers were so much more expensive that, although the advantages of frozen food were known in the 1920s, their use was limited to hotels and ocean liners until the late 1940s. Television, another invention of the 1920s, remained undeveloped for lack of financial support, and air conditioning was rarely used because the very people in the hottest parts of the country who needed it most were least able to afford it.

To the extent that electric appliances found a place in American homes, they did not bear out utopian dreams of leisure. The gleaming new devices fostered expectations of higher standards of cleanliness that housewives could meet only by operating their appliances early and often. In some affluent homes, the burden was lightened by servants who used the appliances. But the number of domestic servants was declining because the booming 1920s offered better-paying work in offices and factories — including those that manufactured electric appliances. Electricity boosters, however, remained unfazed until the end of the decade.

The gap between technology's promises and real life was magnified by the 1929 stock market crash and ensuing depression, which shattered many consumer dreams. While the means to pay for electricity dwindled, the collapse of Insull's electric empire revealed a tangle of fraud and corruption. Insull was indicted and vilified as the bearer of technology's false hopes. Ironically, in the face of such woes, one of the most popular electric inventions, the radio, provided old-fashioned reassurance. In the 1930s, families that had been lured from their traditional closeness around the hearth by central heating and electric light in every room huddled around technology's electronic hearth — the radio — to hear President Franklin Roosevelt pledge protection of their homes and basic values in his fireside chats. Once prosperity returned, they were assured, the promise of a bright electric future would be renewed.

Hard times eventually eased, and sales of new appliances soared again. But surveys showed that the hours people spent taking care of their households remained essentially the same as before the advent of electricity. Only in the boom years after World War II would electricity begin to deliver on its promise.

READING ACTIVITY 3: Build Your Vocabulary

Try to determine the meanings of the following words from "Better Living through Electricity." Then, check their meanings by looking the words up in a dictionary.

prophecies (1) ______________________________

protégé (2) ______________________________

aspirations (2) ______________________________

barrage (3) ______________________________

idyllic (4) ______________________________

utopian (5) ______________________________

boosters (5) ______________________________

vilified (6) ______________________________

READING ACTIVITY 4: Read to Improve Your Writing

Answer the following questions about Sarah Stage's essay.

1. In your own words, what is the thesis of "Better Living through Electricity"?

____

____

2. What kinds of examples does Stage use to support her point?

____

____

____

3. Why do you think Stage decided to use comparison and contrast to make her point about electricity ads?

____

____

____

____

4. What new products or technologies have you noticed being heavily promoted? Do you think the promises made by advertisers are reasonable? Explain your answers.

____

____

____

Writing Assignment

Imagine that you're taking an online course called "The Media and the World." In the course, which enrolls a lot of international students, you learn about the impact that the media (television, movies, radio, newspapers, and magazines) has on the way that people around the world view the United States. You need to write an essay about how the media portrays American society.

- Compare and contrast how the media depicts a group of people with the way they really are. For instance, you could contrast how college students behave in a recent movie with how they act in real life.

  OR

- Compare and contrast how the media portrays a place or a thing in the United States with how it really is. For example, you could compare how a television show depicts a city with what that city is actually like.

STEP 1: DISCOVER IDEAS FOR WRITING

Before you draft your comparison-and-contrast essay, you'll want to pick a topic that's important to you and be sure that you can provide solid examples to back up your ideas. Remember that readers won't be interested in an essay that uses comparison and contrast for its own sake: Instead, compare and contrast to make a point.

Choosing a Topic

You'll have an easier time writing your essay if you choose a topic that you have had some experience with. If you're interested in how the media portrays a city, for instance, choose a city that you have lived

See pp. 19–29 and pp. 259–64 for more ideas about choosing and narrowing your topic.

in or visited yourself. Similarly, if you are interested in how the media depict a group of people, you'll want to write about a group that you (or a close friend or relative) belong to.

FAQs about Topics
The *Discoveries* Web site includes answers to frequently asked questions about topics for each chapter. Go to **bedfordstmartins.com/discoveries** and click on "FAQs."

Class Web Site
Use your class Web site to post possible topics. Ask your classmates and instructor to tell you which topics they're most interested in. Tally their answers to help you decide on a topic.

Considering Your Audience and Purpose

For more help with audience and purpose, see pp. 20–22.

To write a good essay, you must understand your audience, which in this case consists of your online instructor and classmates, many of whom live outside the United States. These readers might not be familiar with your topic. How will you inform them and keep them interested in what you have to say?

Comparison-and-contrast essays can be expressive, informative, persuasive, or a mix of these purposes. Patricia Raybon, for example, expresses her feelings but is writing to persuade her readers that media portrayals of black Americans are biased. Are you writing to express yourself, to inform others of something you know, or to persuade them to change their minds about an issue?

WRITING ACTIVITY 1: Identify Your Audience and Purpose

Keeping in mind the topic of the essay and your audience of international students, answer the following questions.

1. What aspect of the media and American life are you thinking of writing about? Why is it important?

____

____

____

2. What will your readers probably already know about your topic? What might they not know?

____

____

____

3. How interested will your readers be in your topic? How can you make sure that your audience stays interested?

____

____

____

4. What is your primary purpose in writing this essay?

____

____

____

Clustering to Gather Ideas

Clustering is a technique for gathering ideas in which you organize your thoughts by drawing a kind of picture of them. You write one idea in the middle of a piece of paper and then branch off into more specific ideas.

For more information about clustering, turn to p. 25.

HOW TO Cluster for an Essay That Compares and Contrasts

- Write a topic in the center of a page and draw a circle around it.
- Write other ideas about the topic, circle them, and connect them with a line to the center circle.
- Make your ideas more specific as you continue to cluster.

Student writer Peter was interested in how television portrays people, but he wasn't sure exactly what he wanted to write about. He drew a cluster to find ideas.

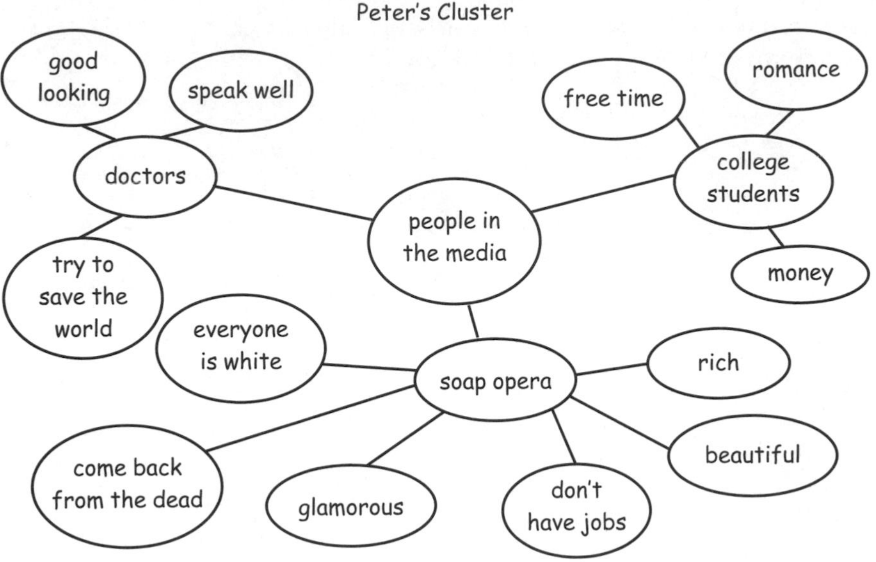

After completing this cluster, Peter realized that he was most interested in soap opera characters. He decided to use soap operas as his essay topic.

Cluster on the Computer
Use the drawing function on your word-processing program to cluster ideas.

WRITING ACTIVITY 2: Cluster Your Ideas

Make a cluster for each of the two possible kinds of topics in the writing assignment. Examine your clusters to decide which one interests you most.

Narrowing Your Topic

Now that you have a topic to work with, decide whether it is narrow enough to explain with just a few points of comparison or contrast. For instance, instead of writing about every aspect of Disneyland in ads and in real life, you might examine the prices, long lines, and access to rides.

Clustering can help you narrow your focus. Starting with one of the clusters you drew earlier, notice which ideas you had the most details for; these could be the major points of your comparison and contrast. Then, draw a new cluster for each of these ideas to make sure that you can provide enough detail to explain it for your readers.

HOW TO Narrow a Topic for an Essay That Compares and Contrasts

- Select a general topic to write about.
- Cluster ideas on how media portrayals of your topic compare and contrast with how it is in real life.
- Select specific points that you can compare and contrast.
- Be sure you can provide enough details about each point to keep your readers interested and informed.

WRITING ACTIVITY 3: Narrow Your Topic

Review the cluster you chose in the previous activity. Choose the points that interest you the most and that you know the most about, then narrow your topic by drawing new clusters for each of those points.

STEP 2: WRITE YOUR DISCOVERY DRAFT

To write your discovery draft, you'll need to prepare a thesis statement and plan an introduction, some supporting paragraphs, and a conclusion. Remember that the point of writing a discovery draft is to gather your thoughts. Whatever you plan can be revised later.

Drafting a Thesis Statement

Go to pp. 265–66 to learn more about thesis statements.

Readers won't be interested in your comparison-and-contrast essay unless it has a thesis, or a point. For instance, the topic of "A Case of 'Severe Bias'" is how black Americans are shown on the news; the thesis is that the depiction is one-sided. Sarah Stage's topic is electricity in the 1920s; her thesis is that the new technology didn't do what advertisers promised. Before you begin to write, try to express your main idea in a working thesis statement that states your topic and says what your main idea is.

Be sure, also, that your thesis expresses a point of view, or opinion, about your topic that you can support. Consider the following two examples:

> **Detroit is not the way it is depicted in Eminem's movie *8 Mile*.**
>
> **Detroit is unfairly depicted in Eminem's movie *8 Mile* as a dirty, dangerous, and boring city.**

The first thesis statement indicates the topic, but it doesn't give readers a reason to read more. The second one is much better because it gives the writer's point of view. It also suggests what the essay's main points of comparison and contrast will be.

HOW TO Write a Thesis Statement for an Essay That Compares and Contrasts

- Identify what you will compare and contrast.
- Express a point of view about your topic.
- Check that your thesis is focused enough for a short essay.
- Consider previewing your major points so that readers know what to expect.
- Plan to revise your thesis statement as your ideas develop.

WRITING ACTIVITY 4: Draft a Thesis Statement

Decide what the thesis of your comparison and contrast will be. Draft a thesis statement that states your main point and expresses your point of view. Don't worry about getting your thesis statement perfect right now: You can revise it later.

Drafting an Introduction

Read more about introductions on p. 266.

In your introduction you attract your readers' attention and give your thesis. You also might need to supply background information, perhaps by defining terms or explaining facts about your topic.

The author of "A Case of 'Severe Bias'" grabs her readers' attention by beginning with the sentence "This is who I am not." She then gives several short sentences to expand on this point: "I am not a crack addict. I am not a welfare mother. . . ." These short sentences make the reader wonder, "What is she really like?" Having gotten readers interested in what she has to say, Raybon presents her thesis that television inaccurately portrays black Americans.

HOW TO Introduce an Essay That Compares and Contrasts

- Attract your readers' attention with a surprising statement, a question, or a brief story.
- Indicate your general topic.
- Give background information if necessary.
- Lead into the thesis statement.

Student writer Peter thought he could capture his readers' attention with an anecdote, or brief story. Because it includes an anecdote, Peter's introduction consists of two paragraphs: the first for the anecdote, the second for his topic and thesis. This is what he drafted:

> Macy Spectra Forrester Forrester Forrester is racing down a mountain in a thunderstorm. She has been married to Thorne Forrester three times. Thorne has just asked her for a divorce because he wants to marry Brooke Forrester. She's a beautiful blonde who has already been married to his father and brother. Suddenly Macy's car runs into a tanker truck, and there's an explosion. But wait! Is the body found in her car really Macy? And will Brooke and Thorne live happily ever after?
>
> This a typical scene from an American soap opera. What's wrong with it? Nothing, unless you live in another country and think the United States is like that. Though entertaining, soap operas give a wrong impression about how people live in the United States.

WRITING ACTIVITY 5 (Group): Draft an Introduction

Form a group with classmates and explain the topic of your essay. With their help, draft an introduction that will capture readers' attention and provide your thesis statement. Help your classmates draft introductions to their essays.

Brainstorming to Add Support

For your essay to be interesting and informative, you will need to find more than just one or two points of comparison and contrast. One way to find these points is by brainstorming. For this comparison-and-contrast essay, organize your brainstorming in two columns: one for the media,

Learn more about brainstorming on p. 24.

and one for real life. By brainstorming, student writer Peter found these points for his essay about how soap operas differ from reality:

Soap Operas	*Reality*
Characters are rich	Most Americans middle class
You never see them work	People work hard
Lots of free time	Busy leading normal lives
Come back from the dead	That's impossible!
Not many African Americans or Latinos	All races and nationalities
All the people are beautiful	Different appearances

Compare and Contrast on Computer

Use your word-processing program to create a table with two columns. Label one column with the name of your topic and label the other column "Reality." Then, brainstorm the similarities or differences between your topic and the reality to find points of comparison and contrast.

WRITING ACTIVITY 6: Develop Support

Brainstorm several points that support your thesis. Use two columns to make sure that you list a similarity or difference for each of your points.

Drafting a Conclusion

Read more about conclusions on pp. 268–69.

In your conclusion you restate your thesis in different words. Sarah Stage, for example, finishes "Better Living through Electricity" with this restatement of her thesis: "But surveys showed that the hours people spent taking care of their households remained essentially the same as before the advent of electricity."

You can also conclude by connecting your main point to a larger idea by suggesting that your readers do something related to your point. Patricia Raybon, for instance, concludes her essay with a call for action: ". . . it's time to let the truth be known."

Student writer Peter drafted this conclusion to connect his points to a larger idea:

Why is it important to know how soap operas distort life in the United States? Because many people in other countries get their main impression of the United States from these shows. They might be so totally turned off that they won't want to have anything to do with us, or they might want to come here because they think life is how it is on soap operas. It's important to know that soap operas are not reality.

WRITING ACTIVITY 7: Draft a Conclusion

Referring to your thesis statement and your brainstorming, draft a conclusion that restates your main idea. If appropriate, connect your ideas to a larger issue or call your readers to action.

Peter's Discovery Draft

Peter wrote the following discovery draft, using his thesis statement and the material he had developed for his introduction, supporting points, and conclusion. Note that Peter's draft includes some errors. He will correct these later.

Soap Operas in the United States:
Don't Believe What You See

Macy Spectra Forrester Forrester Forrester is racing down a mountain in a thunderstorm. She has been married to Thorne Forrester three times. Thorne has just asked her for a divorce because he wants to marry Brooke Forrester. She's a beautiful blonde who has already been married to his father and brother. Suddenly Macy's car runs into a tanker truck, and there's an explosion. But wait! Is the body found in her car really Macy? And will Brooke and Thorne live happily ever after?

This a typical scene from an American soap opera. What's wrong with it? Nothing, unless you live in another country and believe that soap operas show how Americans really are. Though entertaining, soap operas give a wrong impression about how people in the United States live.

In soap operas the characters are usually attractive and rich. Their hair is styled, the makeup is perfect. They're usually thin. They live in big houses with expensive furniture, sometimes on the beach. Even the characters who are supposed to be in college are rich.

Characters in soap opera have all this free time! When do they work? They sit around talking, fighting, and crying. I don't know how they have all that free time.

Characters in soap operas are usually white. There aren't many minorities except sometimes the servants. Occasionally an African American lawyer, doctor, or police officer will appear, but they're not around much.

In the United States, people come in all different shapes and sizes. Most people are middle class, some people are poor, and not very many are rich. People work very hard and don't have time to sit around talking all the time. I know college students don't have much time. People are all races and nationalities. People live normal lives. Strange things don't usually happen to them. People are very different.

Why is it important to know how soap operas distort life in the United States? Because many people in other countries get their main impression of the United States from these shows. They might be so totally turned off that they won't want to have anything to do with us. Or they might want to come here because they think life is how it is on soap operas. It's important to know that soap operas are not reality.

WRITING ACTIVITY 8: Complete Your Discovery Draft

Using your thesis statement as a guide, finish writing your discovery draft. Focus on getting your ideas down in writing. You'll have time to revise and edit later.

STEP 3: REVISE YOUR ESSAY

By writing a discovery draft, you have put your early thoughts into essay form. If you're like most writers, however, you still need to flesh out your ideas and make them clearer for your readers.

Strengthening Your Focus

For more help with focus, turn to pp. 271–72.

To strengthen the focus of your essay, make sure that you have narrowed your topic enough. Student writer Peter, for instance, noticed that the topic of his discovery draft was too broad: Instead of talking about soap operas in general, he decided to narrow his focus to just two of the most popular programs: *The Bold and the Beautiful* and *The Young and the Restless*. That way, he could discuss each of his points in more convincing detail.

Each point of similarity or difference needs to support your thesis statement, and every detail should directly relate to one of your points. Reread your discovery draft with a critical eye and delete any information that is unnecessary. If you find that you have a lot of points or details that don't support your main idea, you may need to discard some of them or revise your thesis statement to include them.

WRITING ACTIVITY 9: Strengthen Your Focus

Check that you have narrowed your topic enough. Reread your discovery draft and delete or revise any information that doesn't directly relate to your thesis statement.

Building Support with Examples

Learn more about building support on pp. 272–73.

For every point of comparison or contrast you make in your essay, you must discuss both of the subjects you are considering in about the same amount of detail. To communicate clearly, support your points with examples. By providing facts and statistics that explain your ideas, you make your essay more informative and believable.

The essays that you read at the beginning of this chapter both contain many examples. Patricia Raybon supports her points with facts about her

HOW TO Build Support for an Essay That Compares and Contrasts

- Provide enough points to help your readers understand your thesis.
- For every point you make, discuss both of your subjects.
- Include examples to support each of your points.
- Be specific. For instance, refer to television or radio shows by name.

life, observations about her neighbors and friends, and references to news reports and movies. These details help her prove that many people have an inaccurate picture of black Americans. Sarah Stage provides plenty of statistics, quotes from advertisements, and facts about electricity usage in the 1920s to support her argument that electricity didn't live up to its early promise. By backing up her assertions with examples, she convinces her readers that she is knowledgeable about her subject.

As Peter reviewed his discovery draft, he realized that he needed more examples to support his points. For instance, his draft refers to "soap operas" but never mentions a specific show. Also, Peter had written that Americans earned a range of incomes and were racially diverse, but he hadn't given specific information. He worked on adding examples when he revised his draft.

Examine Web Pages
If you're referring to a specific television show, movie, newspaper, or magazine, locate its homepage on the Web. You might find information to support your points.

WRITING ACTIVITY 10: Add Examples

Reread your discovery draft and determine how well you have supported your ideas. Did you give examples for each of your points? Mark places in the draft where you need to add supporting details, then find additional examples through observation or research.

Using Subject-by-Subject or Point-by-Point Order to Organize Your Points

For more information about subject-by-subject and point-by-point format, go to pp. 175–76.

Comparison-and-contrast essays are organized either by *subject-by-subject* or *point-by-point* order. In subject-by-subject order, you discuss the two subjects you're comparing separately, first one and then the other, as Sarah Stage does in "Better Living through Electricity." In a sense, your essay is divided into two sections. To use point-by-point order, you organize your essay according to the points you're making in your comparison, as Patricia Raybon does in "A Case of 'Severe Bias.'" In the point-by-point format, you compare and contrast the two items at the same time, going back and forth between the two.

When student writer Peter prepared his discovery draft, he used subject-by-subject order because he thought it would be easier to discuss soap operas and reality separately. However, his classmates thought that his essay didn't hold together that way. They also told him they had a hard time remembering his points about soap operas by the time he began writing about real life. Because of this feedback, Peter decided to use the point-by-point method when he revised. He prepared this outline to reorganize his ideas:

People's appearance and money
  on soap operas
  in real life
Ways people spend their time
  on soap operas
  in real life
People's cultural backgrounds
  on soap operas
  in real life

Peter's revised outline shows that he will spend an equal amount of time comparing people on soap operas and people in real life. As a result, his comparison and contrast will be balanced.

To review how to use outlines, see pp. 26–27.

Use the Outline Function

If you want to create a detailed outline of your draft, use the outline function in your word-processing program.

WRITING ACTIVITY 11: Outline Your Draft

Make a rough outline for your discovery draft, using either subject-by-subject or point-by-point format. Use this outline to identify where you need more supporting details.

Connecting Your Ideas

No matter what type of essay you are writing, you need transitions to make your ideas flow together and to help readers follow your thoughts. This is especially true for a comparison-and-contrast essay because you're shifting back and forth between two subjects.

For more transitions, turn to p. 42.

Including keywords in your essay will help your readers stay on track. In "A Case of 'Severe Bias,'" Patricia Raybon repeats *black Americans, news media,* and *reality.* Some of the keywords in Sarah Stage's "Better Living through Electricity" are *electricity, appliances, expectations,* and *leisure.*

HOW TO Connect Ideas in an Essay That Compares and Contrasts

Include transitions that show both comparison (how two things are alike) and contrast (how two things are different).

Comparison	*Contrast*
similar, similarly	different, differently
like	unlike
likewise	on the other hand, however
as	although, though
compared to	in contrast

WRITING ACTIVITY 12: Examine Keywords and Transitions

Underline the keywords and circle the transitions you used in your discovery draft. Mark places where you need more keywords or transitions to help your ideas flow together better.

Peter's Revised Draft

Before reading Peter's revised draft, reread his discovery draft. Notice that in his revised draft he has improved his focus and support, changed his organization, and added keywords and transitions. This draft still contains some sentence-level errors that Peter will correct later.

Soap Operas in the United States:
Don't Believe What You See!

Macy Spectra Forrester Forrester Forrester is racing down a mountain in a thunderstorm. She has been married to Thorne Forrester three times. Thorne has just asked her for a divorce because he wants to marry Brooke Forrester. She's a beautiful blonde who has already been married to his father and brother suddenly Macy's car runs into a tanker truck, and there's an explosion. But wait! Is the body found in her car really Macy? And will Brooke and Thorne live happily ever after?

This a typical scene from an American soap opera. What's wrong with it? Nothing, unless you live in another country and believe that soap operas show how Americans really are. Though entertaining, soap operas give a wrong impression about how people in the United States live.

In soap operas the characters are usually attractive and rich. For example, in one of the most popular soap operas, *The Bold and the Beautiful,* the main characters belong to the Forrester family. They run a clothing-design company. They live in big houses with expensive furniture, sometimes on the beach. Even the characters who are supposed to be in college are rich. In contrast, most people in the United States are middle class. Their jobs are often dull, their houses comfortable but not fancy, and their cars are usually several years old. In addition, most college students have to work to support themselves.

Characters in soap operas never seem to work. Instead, everyone spends their time talking, fighting, and crying. For instance, on a recent episode of *The Young and the Restless,* the characters had lunch at a fancy restaurant, through a party in someone's living room, and lounged around a pool talking. However, most people in the United States don't have that much free time. Our fairly low unemployment rate shows that most people spend their days at work. When they aren't working, real people raise children, cook meals, go shopping, and clean the house.

Characters in soap operas are usually white. Most minority people are servants. Occasionally an African American lawyer, doctor, or police officer will appear, but not often. In fact, on *The Bold and the Beautiful,* I have seen only one Latina character. She was a maid. I have never seen an Asian American on that show. Of course, in the United States people come from a variety of races and backgrounds. More than a third of Americans are black, Latino, or Asian American. They are doctors, lawyers, and teachers. Not just maids or janitors.

People from other countries need to know that life in the United States isn't like life on soap operas. If people think soap operas are realistic, they might be so totally turned off that they won't want to have anything to do with us they might believe

```
that if they come here they will live like people
on soap operas. We need to find a way to let people know
that American soap operas do not portray American life.
```

GROUP ACTIVITY: Analyze Peter's Revised Draft

Use the following questions to discuss with your classmates how Peter improved his draft.

1. How has Peter strengthened his focus?

___

___

2. What supporting details has Peter added? How have these details improved the draft?

___

___

___

3. How did Peter change his organization? Is this format better than the format he used in his discovery draft? Explain your answer.

___

___

4. What keywords and transitions did Peter add? Did these help make his ideas easier to follow?

___

___

5. What more can Peter do to improve his draft?

___

___

WRITING ACTIVITY 13 (Group): Peer Review

Form a group with several classmates and exchange copies of your drafts. Read your draft aloud while your classmates follow along. Take notes on your classmates' answers to the following questions about your draft.

1. What do you like best about my essay?
2. How well does my introduction attract your attention?
3. How clear is my thesis? Does it give my point of view about the topic?
4. Is my comparison and contrast focused and balanced? Where do I need to add or delete points?
5. Did I support my points with enough examples?
6. Do I use subject-by-subject format or point-by-point format? How well does this format work?
7. How effective is my conclusion? Do you have any suggestions for improving it?

Online Peer Review

If your class has a Web site, you may be able to do your peer review online. Access the peer review questions, answer them, and return them to your classmates on e-mail.

WRITING ACTIVITY 14: Revise Your Draft

Taking into account your classmates' suggestions and using Peter's revision as a model, revise your discovery draft. Strengthen your focus and balance, build your support, organize your points, and connect your ideas with keywords and transitions.

STEP 4: EDIT YOUR ESSAY

Once you have revised your essay for content and organization, you're ready to concentrate on errors in spelling, punctuation, and grammar. Referring to a dictionary and the Handbook in Part Four will help you as you edit. Another part of editing is changing your sentence structure to make your essay read more smoothly. In this chapter, you will practice using sentence subordination to improve the flow of your writing.

What Is Sentence Subordination?

Short sentences can be powerful, but using too many of them in a row can force you to repeat yourself. Here are some examples of repetitive sentences:

REPETITIVE The average newspaper reader doesn't study the paper carefully. The average newspaper reader is very busy.

REPETITIVE The magazine had some bad things to say about Philadelphia. Philadelphia is my hometown.

REPETITIVE The television show was a big hit. The show starred Jennifer Garner.

By using relative clauses to combine sentences, you can eliminate repetition and help your readers determine which of your ideas are most important.

Combining Sentences with Relative Clauses

You'll find more advice on combining sentences by using relative clauses on pp. 526–27.

One way to show the link in meaning between two sentences is to turn the less important one into a relative clause and combine it with the other. A *relative clause* is a group of words that begins with a relative pronoun (*that, who, whom, whose, whatever, which, whoever, whomever,* or *what*). After turning a sentence into a relative clause, you can *subordinate* it to the more important sentence.

COMBINED The average newspaper reader, *who is very busy,* doesn't study the paper carefully.

COMBINED The magazine had some bad things to say about Philadelphia, *which is my hometown.*

COMBINED The television show *that starred Jennifer Garner* was a big hit.

Notice that the relative clause can appear either in the middle or at the end of a combined sentence, and that the revised sentence may or may not include commas. How do you know when to use commas?

1. Use commas when the relative clause provides extra information.

   Las Vegas, *which is in Nevada,* is a famous city.

   This sentence makes sense even if the relative clause is left out: *Las Vegas is a famous city.*

2. Don't use commas when the relative clause provides necessary information.

The Las Vegas *that is in New Mexico* is a pretty town.

Here the relative clause identifies which Las Vegas is being referred to. The sentence would not make sense without it.

HOW TO Combine Sentences with Relative Clauses

- Turn the less important sentence into a relative clause with an appropriate relative pronoun: *that, who, whom, whose, whatever, which, whoever, whomever,* or *what.*
- Combine the two sentences, placing the relative clause in the middle or at the end.
- Use commas around the relative clause when it adds information that readers don't need to understand the sentence.
- Omit commas when the relative clause adds information that readers do need to understand the sentence.
- Don't use commas when the relative clause begins with *that.*

EDITING PRACTICE: Combining Sentences with Relative Clauses

Combine the following pairs of sentences by turning the less important sentence in each pair into a relative clause. Be sure to use commas correctly. Add or delete words as necessary.

EXAMPLE

ORIGINAL Chicago has been the center of Midwestern industry for more than a century. Chicago is known as the Windy City.

REVISED Chicago, which is known as the Windy City, has been the center of Midwestern industry for more than a century.

1. Newspaper editors forget that many people want more news about religion. These people go to church regularly.

____

____

2. Cigarette advertisements try to make smoking look sexy. These advertisements are often aimed at teenagers.

___

___

3. Some advertisements use very thin models. These advertisements can damage girls' self-esteem.

___

___

4. *The Man Show* is often criticized for being sexist. The show started several years ago.

___

___

5. Meryl Streep is one of my favorite actresses. She has won several Academy Awards.

___

___

6. The show portrays doctors in a negative light. It is the show that airs on Saturdays.

___

7. *Cornerstone* magazine portrays professional women as role models. *Cornerstone* is a monthly magazine. It is available in bookstores.

___

___

8. The teams on *Trading Spaces* have to redecorate two rooms in forty-eight hours. The time limit forces them to cut corners.

___

___

9. The article focused on Web companies. It was published in *Forbes* magazine.

___

___

10. National Public Radio broadcasts a variety of informative programs. The programs appeal to all sorts of people.

____

____

Exercise Central
The *Discoveries* Web site includes additional practice exercises in combining sentences. Go to **bedfordstmartins .com/discoveries**, click on "Exercise Central," and select "Sentence Subordination."

Peter's Edited Draft

Peter's revised draft contained several repetitive sentences and some errors in grammar and spelling. His edited draft is below. (The underlining shows where he corrected errors.)

Soap Operas in the United States:
Don't Believe What You See!

Macy Spectra Forrester Forrester Forrester<u>, who has been married to Thorne Forrester three times,</u> is racing down a mountain in a thunderstorm. Thorne has just asked her for a divorce because he wants to marry Brooke Forrester<u>, who is a beautiful blonde who has already been married to his father and brother.</u> Suddenly Macy's car runs into a tanker truck, and there's an explosion. But wait! Is the body found in her car really Macy? And will Brooke and Thorne live happily ever after?

This a typical scene from an American soap opera. What's wrong with it? Nothing, unless you live in another country and believe that soap operas show how Americans really are. Though entertaining, soap operas give a wrong impression about how people in the United States live.

In soap operas the characters are usually attractive and rich. For example, in one of the most popular soap operas, *The Bold and the Beautiful,* the main characters belong to the Forrester family<u>, which runs a clothing-design company</u>. They live in big houses with expensive furniture, sometimes on the beach. Even the characters who are supposed to be in college are rich. In contrast, most people in the United States are middle class. Their jobs are often dull, their houses comfortable but not fancy, and their cars are usually several years old. In addition, most college students have to work to support themselves.

Characters in soap operas never seem to work. Instead, everyone spends their time talking, fighting, and crying. For instance, on a recent episode of *The Young and the Restless*, the characters had lunch at a fancy restaurant, threw a party in someone's living room, and lounged around a pool talking. However, most people in the United States don't have that much free time. Our fairly low unemployment rate shows that most people spend their days at work. When they aren't working, real people raise children, cook meals, go shopping, and clean the house.

Characters in soap operas are usually white. Most minority people are servants. Occasionally an African American lawyer, doctor, or police officer will appear, but not often. In fact, on *The Bold and the Beautiful*, I have seen only one Latina character, who was a maid. I have never seen an Asian American on that show. Of course, in the United States people come from a variety of races and backgrounds. More than a third of Americans are black, Latino, or Asian American. They are doctors, lawyers, and teachers, not just maids or janitors.

To review sentence fragments, see pp. 548–54.

People from other countries need to know that life in the United States isn't like life on soap operas. If people think soap operas are realistic, they might be so totally turned off that they won't want to have anything to do with us, or they might believe that if they come here they will live like the people on soap operas. We need to find a way to let people know that American soap operas do not portray American life.

To review comma splices, see pp. 561–66.

WRITING ACTIVITY 15: Edit Your Essay

Edit your essay for errors in grammar, punctuation, and spelling. Check for short, closely related sentences that you can combine by making one of the sentences a relative clause. Record your changes in your editing log.

STEP 5: SHARE YOUR ESSAY

Peter's instructor posted his edited draft to the course Web site. After reading his essay, several students who lived in Mexico and were taking the class online wrote to tell him about the soap operas, called *novelas,* in their own country.

ADDITIONAL WRITING ASSIGNMENTS

1. Write an essay for your classmates and instructor in which you compare and contrast two kinds of students. Make the essay entertaining by exaggerating your points. Read your finished essay aloud to the class.
2. Write an essay for your local newspaper in which you compare and contrast politicians in the Democratic and Republican parties. What are the differences and similarities between these two types of politicians? Which kind better serves the people in your region?
3. Write an essay for a travel magazine in which you compare and contrast two tourist sites in your area. Your purpose is to convince tourists to visit these sites.

Should young women be required to register for the draft, just as young men are? In this chapter, you will write to persuade readers to share your view on an issue of national importance or suggest a solution to a national problem.

CHAPTER

16

Writing an Essay That Makes an Argument

In this chapter, you will:

- review how argumentation works.
- read outside sources to gather ideas.
- write about a national issue.
- use progressive order to organize your points.
- practice sentence subordination.
- submit your essay to a local newspaper.

UNDERSTANDING ARGUMENTATION

Read more about argumentation in Chapter 11.

Imagine that your political science professor has asked you to attend a public debate on an issue of national importance, one that affects people across the country. The debate is sponsored by the American Civil Liberties Union and is on the topic of gay marriage.

Although nobody yells, each speech that you hear is an argument. Some speakers attempt to persuade you to believe as they do; others try to convince you to do something, such as petition the state legislature. As you listen to the speakers, you are struck by how well they state their opinions, even though you don't agree with everything they say. You notice that the more effective speakers provide examples and expert testimony to back up their arguments, while the speakers who emphasize personal feelings don't seem as convincing.

An essay that makes an argument is similar to one side of a spoken debate. It gives you the opportunity to persuade others to think as you do on an issue or to do something you recommend. Remember that an argument is not necessarily a fight: The most effective persuasive writing uses calm reasoning to explain an opinion.

READING ESSAYS THAT MAKE AN ARGUMENT

Social issues, such as crime or unemployment, often cause serious disagreements. In the following two essays, the writers use argument to explain and support their positions on social issues of national importance.

Arguing a Position

The United States has one of the highest rates of imprisonment in the world. In "Why Prisons Don't Work," inmate Wilbert Rideau argues that sending criminals to jail does not reduce crime.

WILBERT RIDEAU

Why Prisons Don't Work

I was among thirty-one murderers sent to the Louisiana State Penitentiary in 1962 to be executed or imprisoned for life. We weren't much different from those we found here, or those who had preceded us. We were unskilled, impulsive, and uneducated misfits, mostly black, who had done dumb, impulsive things — failures, rejects from the larger society. Now a generation has come of age and gone since I've been here, and every-

thing is much the same as I found it. The faces of prisoners are different, but behind them are the same impulsive, uneducated, unskilled minds that made dumb, impulsive choices that got them into more trouble than they ever thought existed. The vast majority of us are consigned to suffer and die here so politicians can sell the illusion that permanently exiling people to prison will make society safe.

Getting tough has always been a "silver bullet," a quick fix for the crime and violence that society fears. Each year in Louisiana — where excess is a way of life — lawmakers have tried to outdo each other in legislating harsher mandatory penalties and in reducing avenues of release. The only thing to do with criminals, they say, is get tougher. They have. In the process, the purpose of prison began to change. The state boasts one of the highest lockup rates in the country, imposes the most severe penalties in the nation, and vies to execute more criminals per capita than anywhere else. This state is so tough that last year, when prison authorities here wanted to punish an inmate in solitary confinement for an infraction, the most they could inflict on him was to deprive him of his underwear. It was all he had left.

If getting tough resulted in public safety, Louisiana citizens would be the safest in the nation. They're not. Louisiana has the highest murder rate among states. Prison, like the police and the courts, has a minimal impact on crime because it is a response after the fact, a mop-up operation. It doesn't work. The idea of punishing the few to deter the many is counterfeit because potential criminals either think they're not going to get caught or they're so emotionally desperate or psychologically distressed that they don't care about the consequences of their actions. The threatened punishment, regardless of its severity, is never a factor in the equation. But society, like the incorrigible criminal it abhors, is unable to learn from its mistakes.

Prison has a role in public safety, but it is not a cure-all. Its value is limited, and its use should also be limited to what it does best: isolating young criminals long enough to give them a chance to grow up and get a grip on their impulses. It is a traumatic experience, certainly, but it should only be a temporary one, not a way of life. Prisoners kept too long tend to embrace the criminal culture, its distorted values and beliefs; they have little choice — prison is their life. There are some prisoners who cannot be returned to society — serial killers, serial rapists, professional hit men, and the like — but the monsters who need to die in prison are rare exceptions in the criminal landscape.

Crime is a young man's game. Most of the nation's random violence is committed by young urban terrorists. But because of long, mandatory sentences, most prisoners here are much older, having spent fifteen, twenty, thirty, or more years behind bars, long past necessity. Rather than pay for new prisons, society would be well served by releasing some of its older prisoners who pose no threat and using the money to catch young street thugs. Warden John Whitely agrees that many older prisoners here could be freed tomorrow with little or no danger to society. Release, however, is governed by law or by politicians, not by penal professionals. Even murderers, those most feared by society, pose little risk. Historically, for example, the domestic staff at Louisiana's Governor's mansion has been made up of murderers, hand-picked to work among the chief-of-state and his family. Penologists have long known that murder is almost always a once-in-a-lifetime act. The most dangerous criminal is the one who has not yet killed but has a history of escalating offenses. He's the one to watch.

Rehabilitation can work. Everyone changes in time. The trick is to influence the direction that change takes. The problem with prisons is that they don't do more to rehabilitate those confined in them. The convict who enters prison illiterate will probably leave the same way. Most convicts want to be better than they are, but education is not a priority. This prison houses 4,600 men and offers academic training to 240, vocational training to a like number. Perhaps it doesn't matter. About 90 percent of the men here may never leave this prison alive.

The only effective way to curb crime is for society to work to prevent the criminal act in the first place, to come between the perpetrator and crime. Our youngsters must be taught to respect the humanity of others and to handle disputes without violence. It is essential to educate and equip them with the skills to pursue their life ambitions in a meaningful way. As a community, we must address the adverse life circumstances that spawn criminality. These things are not quick, and they're not easy, but they're effective. Politicians think that's too hard a sell. They want to be on record for doing something now, something they can point to at reelection time. So the drumbeat goes on for more police, more prisons, more of the same failed policies.

Ever see a dog chase its tail?

To review methods of building your vocabulary, turn to pp. 578–81.

READING ACTIVITY 1: Build Your Vocabulary

Try to determine the meanings of the following words from "Why Prisons Don't Work." Then, check their meanings by looking the words up in a dictionary.

consigned (1) ________________

legislating (2) ________________

vies (2) ________________

per capita (2) ______________________

infraction (2) ______________________

incorrigible (3) ______________________

abhors (3) ______________________

escalating (5) ______________________

perpetrator (7) ______________________

READING ACTIVITY 2: Read to Improve Your Writing

Read and answer the following questions about "Why Prisons Don't Work."

1. What is the author's thesis or position?

   ____

2. What evidence does Rideau use to support his position?

   ____

   ____

   ____

3. Does Rideau's evidence convince you that prisons don't work? Why or why not?

   ____

   ____

4. What are some national issues of importance to you?

   ____

   ____

Proposing a Solution

In this essay about high school graduates, college funding, and volunteerism, Steven Muller identifies a national problem and suggests a way to solve it.

STEVEN MULLER

Our Youth Should Serve

Too many young men and women now leave school without a well-developed sense of purpose. If they go right to work after high school, many are not properly prepared for careers. But if they enter college instead, many do not really know what to study or what to do afterward. Our society does not seem to be doing much to encourage and use the best instincts and talents of our young.

On the one hand, I see the growing problems of each year's new generation of high-school graduates. After twelve years of schooling — and television — many of them want to participate actively in society; but they face either a job with a limited future or more years in educational institutions. Many are wonderfully idealistic: they have talent and energy to offer, and they seek the meaning in their lives that comes from giving of oneself to the common good. But they feel almost rejected by a society that has too few jobs to offer them and that asks nothing of them except to avoid trouble. They want to be part of a new solution; instead society perceives them as a problem. They seek a cause, but their elders preach only self-advancement. They need experience on which to base choice, yet society seems to put a premium on the earliest possible choice, based inescapably on the least experience.

On the other hand, I see an American society sadly in need of social services that we can afford less and less at prevailing costs of labor. Some tasks are necessary but constitute no career: they should be carried out, but not as anyone's lifetime occupation. Our democracy profoundly needs public spirit, but the economy of our labor system primarily encourages self-interest. The federal government spends billions on opportunity grants for post-secondary education but some of us wonder about money given on the basis only of need. We ask the young to volunteer for national defense, but not for the improvement of our society. As public spirit and public services decline, so does the quality of life. So I ask myself why cannot we put it all together and ask our young people to volunteer in peacetime to serve America?

I recognize that at first mention, universal national youth service may sound too much like compulsory military service or the Hitler Youth or the Komsomol. I do not believe it has to be like that at all. It need not require uniforms or camps, nor a vast new federal bureaucracy, nor vast new public expenditures. And it should certainly not be compulsory.

A voluntary program of universal national youth service does of course require compelling incentives. Two could be provided. Guaranteed job training would be one. Substantial federal assistance toward post-secondary education would be the other. This would mean that today's complex measures of federal aid to students would be ended, and that there would also be no need for tuition tax credits for post-secondary education. Instead, prospective students would earn their assistance for post-secondary education by volunteering for national service, and only those who earned assistance would receive it. Present federal expenditures for the assistance of students in post-secondary education would be converted into a simple grant program, modeled on the post-World War II GI Bill of Rights.

But what, you say, would huge numbers of high-school graduates do as volunteers in national service? They could be interns in public agencies, local, state and national. They could staff day-care programs, neighborhood health centers, centers to counsel and work with children; help to maintain public facilities, including highways, rail beds, waterways and airports; engage in neighborhood renewal projects, both physical and social. Some would elect military service, others the Peace Corps. Except for the latter two alternatives and others like them, they could live anywhere they pleased. They would not wear uniforms. They would be employed and supervised by people already employed locally in public-agency careers.

Volunteers would be paid only a subsistence wage because they would receive the benefits of job training (not necessarily confined to one task) as well as assistance toward post-secondary education if they were so motivated and qualified. If cheap mass housing for some groups of volunteers was needed, supervised participants in the program could rebuild decayed dwellings in metropolitan areas.

All that might work. But perhaps an even more attractive version of universal national youth service might include private industrial and commercial enterprise as well. A private employer would volunteer to select a stated number of volunteers. He would have their labor at the universally applied subsistence wage; in return he would offer guaranteed job training as well as the exact equivalent of what the federal government would have to pay for assistance toward post-secondary education. The inclusion of volunteer private employers would greatly amplify job-training opportunities for the youth volunteers, and would greatly lessen the costs of the program in public funds.

The direct benefits of such a universal national-youth-service program would be significant. Every young man and woman would face a meaningful role in society after high school. Everyone would receive job training, and the right to earn assistance toward post-secondary education. Those going on to post-secondary education would have their education interrupted by a constructive work experience. There is evidence that they would thereby become more highly motivated and successful students, particularly if their work experience related closely to subsequent vocational interests.

Many participants might locate careers by means of their national-service assignments.

No union jobs need be lost because skilled workers would be needed to give job training. Many public services would be performed by cheap labor, but there would be no youth army. And the intangible, indirect benefits would be the greatest of all. Young people could regard themselves as more useful and needed. They could serve this country for a two-year period as volunteers, and *earn* job training and/or assistance toward post-secondary education. There is more self-esteem and motivation in earned than in unearned benefits. Universal national youth service may be no panacea. But in my opinion the idea merits serious and imaginative consideration.

READING ACTIVITY 3: Build Your Vocabulary

Try to determine the meanings of the following words from Steven Muller's essay. Then, check their meanings by looking the words up in a dictionary.

prevailing (3) ____________________

constitute (3) ____________________

profoundly (3) ____________________

post-secondary education (3) ____________________

bureaucracy (4) ____________________

prospective (5) ____________________

subsistence (7) ____________________

intangible (10) ____________________

panacea (10) ____________________

READING ACTIVITY 4: Read to Improve Your Writing

Read and answer the following questions about "Our Youth Should Serve."

1. What are the problems that Muller identifies?

____

____

2. What is the author's proposed solution?

3. What objections and questions does Muller expect his readers to have? How does he respond to these objections and questions?

4. List several ways that you know of to serve your country.

Writing Assignment

Your political science professor has asked you and your classmates to join the discussion of a national issue by writing an essay for the editorial page of your local newspaper. For this assignment:

- Write an argumentative essay to persuade the readers of your local newspaper to agree with your position on an issue of national importance, such as immigration, welfare, or patriotism.

OR

- Write an essay that identifies a national problem and proposes a way to solve it. General topics might include things such as Social Security, divorce, or drug abuse.

STEP 1: DISCOVER IDEAS FOR WRITING

Preparation is the key to effective argumentation. You'll need to choose a topic that you have strong opinions about, gather trustworthy evidence to support your position, and make sure that your topic is narrowed to something that you can reasonably handle in just a few pages.

Choosing a Topic

You'll find more advice on choosing a topic on p. 259.

You may be tempted to write your essay on a topic that people have fought over for many years, such as abortion, gun control, or the death penalty. You'll have more luck, however, if you look for an issue that hasn't received so much attention. You'll be able to offer a fresh perspective on a topic that will interest your readers, and you'll stand a better chance of changing your readers' minds.

To find a workable topic, think about what national issues you have a personal stake in. Wilbert Rideau, for example, is interested in prison reform because he is serving a life sentence in jail. If you're a parent, you might have strong opinions on childcare; similarly, if you're a science major you might be interested in controversies about the use of human test subjects. What matters is to pick something that's important to you and that others may not agree upon. Why argue a position or propose a solution if you don't care about the outcome?

FAQs about Topics
The *Discoveries* Web site includes answers to frequently asked questions about topics for each chapter. Go to **bedfordstmartins.com/discoveries** and click on "FAQs."

Considering Your Audience and Purpose

To write an effective argument, you must give careful thought to your audience. Who reads your local newspaper? To find out, call the newspaper and ask for a reader profile, or search the paper's Web site for demographic information. Once you know who your readers are, consider what they likely know about your topic, how they might already feel about it, and what they would need to know to be convinced to believe as you do.

For more information on analyzing audience and purpose, see pp. 259–61.

Also, consider your purpose for writing this essay. The general purpose of an argumentative essay, of course, is to persuade readers. But are you trying to persuade them to change their minds or to do something?

WRITING ACTIVITY 1: Identify Your Audience and Purpose

Keeping in mind that your audience will be local newspaper readers, as well as the students and instructor in your writing class, answer the following questions.

1. What national issue are you most interested in? What will your audience likely already know about it? What won't they know?

   ____

   ____

   ____

2. How interested will your audience be in this topic? Are they likely to agree or disagree with your position?

   ____

   ____

   ____

3. Can you gather enough evidence to support your position and convince others to believe as you do?

   ____

   ____

   ____

4. What is your purpose for writing this essay?

____

____

____

____

Reading Outside Sources to Gather Ideas

For more help learning to use outside sources, turn to Chapter 20.

One of the best ways to gather ideas for an argumentative essay is to read what others have written about your topic. The more outside sources you read, the more evidence you'll gather to include in your essay and the better you'll understand your own position. Magazines, books, and newspapers in the library or on the World Wide Web can be good sources for information and ideas. Remember, though, that if you use other authors' ideas in your essay, you must give them credit.

As you read your sources, pay attention to the kinds of evidence the writers use and ask yourself how convincing their arguments are. Write down any questions and ideas that occur to you as you read. Doing this will help you discover your position and decide what information will support it.

HOW TO Read Outside Sources to Gather Ideas

- Locate print and electronic sources, such as magazine and newspaper articles, book chapters, and reliable Web sites.
- Evaluate these sources for accuracy and fairness.
- Quote, paraphrase, and summarize information and ideas from your sources.
- Carefully document the sources for a list of works cited.

Student writer Efren was interested in ways to solve the problem of teen pregnancy. After conducting a little research on the Web, he found and printed an interesting report about homeless teenage mothers. Here is a part of the report, along with the notes Efren took on it.

The Catastrophic Cycle

Ultimately, however, it is their children who suffer the most. Due primarily to the effects of single parenthood, low maternal education, and larger family size, children of teenage mothers are at risk of lower intellectual, social and academic achievement. In fact, the daughters of teenage mothers are more likely to become teenage parents.[3] Moreover, if they do follow the route of their mothers they *too* may end up on welfare and in shelters. With over one million teenage women becoming pregnant — and 500,000 giving birth — each year, it has never been more important that we implement aggressive strategies to stem this tide.[4]

Teen pregnancy affects more than the mothers — I hadn't thought about that.

Children of teenage mothers more likely to need welfare — how does that affect taxes?

That many? Wow.

So half of teen pregnancies result in children — what about the other half?

What kinds of strategies will work?

Search the Web

If you have access to the World Wide Web, you can use a search engine to find Web sites on your topic. You may also access newsmagazines on the *Discoveries* Web site. Go to **bedfordstmartins.com/discoveries** and click on "Annotated Web Links."

WRITING ACTIVITY 2: Locate and Read Outside Sources

Search a library or the World Wide Web for information on your topic. Notice how the authors present evidence to support their positions, as well as how you react to their arguments. Take careful notes of any information or ideas that you might want to use in your own essay.

Narrowing Your Topic

Because you're drafting a short essay, you must narrow your topic so that you can provide enough details to convince your readers. For example, Walter Rideau has written a number of books and articles on the topic of prison reform. For the essay "Why Prisons Don't Work," however, he selected only a few of the most convincing reasons for why he believes prisons don't reduce crime.

For more advice on narrowing a topic, see p. 264.

Student writer Efren originally planned to write an essay about teen pregnancy in the United States, but after finding that statistics on teen pregnancy varied by region, he decided to focus his essay on his home state of Texas. From his reading of outside sources, he also discovered that he had strong feelings on the issue of providing birth control in high schools, so he decided to narrow his topic even further to address just that issue.

HOW TO Narrow a Topic for an Essay That Makes an Argument

- Select a debatable national issue or social problem that interests you and will interest your readers.
- Read outside sources to gather evidence (examples, facts, and expert testimony) and ideas.
- Based on the evidence you find most convincing, select one aspect of the issue or problem that you feel strongly about.
- Take a position on the issue or propose a solution to the problem.

WRITING ACTIVITY 3: Narrow Your Topic

Review the reading you have done on a national issue or problem and select an aspect of that issue or problem that you feel strongly about. Then, narrow your topic to a position or proposed solution that can be argued with only a few points of evidence.

STEP 2: WRITE YOUR DISCOVERY DRAFT

Don't worry if you're not sure exactly what you want to say yet. As most writers discover, preparing a draft is one of the best ways to find out what you think about an issue or a problem. Putting your ideas into words will help you figure out where you stand and what evidence works best.

Drafting a Thesis Statement

Read more about thesis statements on pp. 265–66.

For an essay that makes an argument, the thesis statement should state the topic and explain your position on it. For example, here is Rideau's thesis statement in "Why Prisons Don't Work."

> **The vast majority of us are consigned to suffer and die here so politicians can sell the illusion that permanently exiling people to prison will make society safe.**

This thesis statement lets readers know that the essay will be about prisons. It also presents Rideau's position — that prisons do not reduce crime.

Here are some examples of thesis statements written by students for this chapter's assignment:

> Women should be allowed to go into combat because they are physically and mentally capable of doing the job.
>
> Under the freedoms protected by the First Amendment, Americans should have the right to burn the flag without being persecuted.
>
> We can reduce the number of healthy animals that are put to sleep each year by requiring people to get licenses to keep pets.

Most often, the thesis statement is provided in an essay's introduction, as Rideau's is. If readers are likely to disagree with your position, however, you may want to save your thesis statement for the conclusion. That way, you have a chance to present your evidence before readers can reject your argument.

HOW TO Write a Thesis Statement for an Essay That Makes an Argument

- State your position on a debatable topic or propose a solution to a problem you have identified.
- Check that the thesis statement focuses your topic.
- Check that you have convincing evidence to support your position or solution.
- If you wish, preview the evidence that you will present in your essay.

Remember that you're preparing a thesis statement to help guide your ideas. Because your opinion or your focus might change as you get further into your draft, you may find that you need to revise your thesis statement, possibly more than once. That's fine. Just try to have a rough idea of what your point will be before you write.

WRITING ACTIVITY 4: Draft a Thesis Statement

Draft a thesis statement for your essay. Remember that it should state your topic and either provide your position or propose a solution.

Drafting an Introduction

Turn to p. 266 for more information about introductions.

In your introduction, you want to attract your readers' attention and interest them in reading more about your topic. One good way to do this is to present a startling fact or to make a bold statement. If your topic is not well known, you might also need to supply a definition or background information.

In "Why Prisons Don't Work," for example, Walter Rideau grabs his readers' attention by letting them know that he is spending the rest of his life in prison for murdering a bank teller. He provides information on why people end up in prison, then presents his position. Steven Muller, on the other hand, begins "Our Youth Should Serve" by stating that high school graduates are not mature enough for college or the workforce. This statement causes readers to ask, "So what are high school graduates ready to do?" Muller uses the rest of the essay to answer this question.

HOW TO Introduce an Essay That Makes an Argument

- Catch the readers' attention with a startling fact or bold statement about your topic.
- Provide background information to help your readers understand the issue or problem.
- Include a thesis statement. (If you are saving your thesis statement for your conclusion, provide a transition to your first piece of evidence.)

WRITING ACTIVITY 5: Draft an Introduction

Write an introduction that will get readers' attention and make them want to read the rest of your essay. Be sure to provide any background information that your readers will need to understand your point.

Adding Support with Evidence

For additional ways to build support, see pp. 267–68.

Now that you have an idea of what your point will be, you are ready to support it. You'll want to write one paragraph for each of the reasons behind your position. Each of these paragraphs should use strong, convincing evidence, such as examples and expert testimony, to explain and support your position. One of the most common types of evidence is facts — names, dates, numbers, statistics, and other data about your topic that can be proven to be true.

For an essay that makes an argument, it also important to mention any opposing viewpoints and explain why you disagree with them. By doing this, you demonstrate that you know your topic well and have considered other people's views before forming your own opinion. Student writer Efren, for example, identified three viewpoints that oppose his position on birth control in high schools:

> Some argue that allowing birth control in high schools may lead to an increase in sexual activity among teens.
>
> Some people cite religious teachings and moral grounds to claim that providing contraception to teens is wrong.
>
> Others argue that discussions about sex and birth control should be left to the family and kept out of the educational system.

When he wrote his discovery draft, Efren was careful to respond to these opposing viewpoints with evidence that supports his own argument.

WRITING ACTIVITY 6: Gather Evidence

Review your reading notes and select the facts, expert opinions, observations, and examples that best support your position. Be sure you that you identify any opposing viewpoints and can provide evidence to argue against them.

Drafting a Conclusion

Your conclusion is your last chance to make an impression on your readers, possibly swaying them to believe as you do. It should summarize what is important for your readers to remember about your position, or it should propose a solution. If you didn't reveal your thesis statement in your introduction, be sure to include it in your conclusion.

For more help with your conclusion, review pp. 268–69.

Let's look again at the essays you read earlier. In his conclusion, Walter Rideau repeats his argument that prisons are ineffective at preventing crime. He then asks the question "Ever see a dog chase its tail?" to stress his point that the current system doesn't work. Steven Muller, on the other hand, summarizes how students and society would benefit from his proposal and ends with his thesis statement:

Universal national youth service may be no panacea. But in my opinion the idea merits serious and imaginative consideration.

WRITING ACTIVITY 7: Draft a Conclusion

Write a conclusion that restates your position on an issue or proposes a solution. Compare it with your thesis statement to be sure that your position is clear.

Efren's Discovery Draft

Student writer Efren wrote the following discovery draft about why Texas high schools should provide their students with birth control. Note that Efren's discovery draft includes some errors. He will correct these later.

Should Birth Control Be Available in High Schools?

About one million teenage girls in the United States become pregnant every year. The state of Texas has the second-highest teen pregnancy rate in the nation. Texas does not allow birth control in high schools. Distributing contraceptives in Texas high schools will lead to lower teen birthrates.

Boys and girls first become in tune with their sexual urges during the high school years. Portrayals of sex in the media, including television, books, movies, and even video games, make young people want to lose their virginity. It can be very exciting to connect and have new experiences with members of the opposite sex. Most teenagers lack the knowledge they need when they come across an opportunity to do something with their sexual feelings. Some people argue that allowing birth control in high schools may lead to an increase in sexual activity among teens. Considering the consequences teenagers face when deciding to be sexual, however, it is only wise to provide them with contraception. It is crucial for the education system to intervene. These students make life long mistakes.

Teenage pregnancy not only affects the teen mother and her family but the public in general. Teenage pregnancy leads to a tax increase in order to provide services to poor teen families. Poor families are unable to provide birth control to their teens. Allowing contraception in the high schools can help teenage girls avoid dependence on the Welfare System. Providence of birth control in Texas high schools would lead to lower taxes and more money in everyone's pocket.

Allowing birth control in Texas high schools will result in healthier and improved lives among high school students. Every day, high school students engage in unprotected sexual activity. Teenagers are jeopardizing their futures and even their lives. Providing birth control to them would result in lower rates of pregnancy and sexually transmitted diseases. It would also allow sexually active students to finish high school and move onto college, hence improving their standard of living.

Those who oppose providing birth control in high schools cite religious teachings and moral grounds to claim that providing contraception to teens is wrong. It is a mistake to impose someone else's ideas about religion on a problem that affects so many people. Others argue that discussions about sex and birth control should be left to the family and kept out of educational system. What these people fail to see is that schools already act as a parental figure in many ways, such as offering counseling and instilling ideals and values that students often carry into adulthood.

Considering the overwhelming number of teens having unprotected sex and the social consequences of their behavior, it is time to protect our youth against unwanted pregnancies, sexually transmitted diseases, and poverty. We can improve the lives of our youth by providing the tools they need to make better choices in their lives.

WRITING ACTIVITY 8: Complete Your Discovery Draft

Using the thesis statement, introduction, and conclusion that you have already written, write a discovery draft that explains the reasons for your position. Concentrate on convincing your readers with facts. You'll have time to improve your essay later in the writing process.

STEP 3: REVISE YOUR ESSAY

Set your paper aside for a day or two and then reread it. If possible, share it with others to see if they find your argument convincing and to get their opinions of how you might improve it. When you revise, you'll make your argument more effective by strengthening your focus, building your support, organizing your points, and connecting your ideas.

Strengthening Your Focus

More reasons for strengthening your focus are explained on pp. 271–72.

You may want to list many reasons why you believe as you do, thinking that the more reasons you give, the more likely you are to persuade your readers. The problem with this strategy is that you may not have the space to provide enough details to convince your readers of each of your points.

When writing an argumentative essay, you may also be tempted to explain your personal feelings on an issue. Emotional arguments, however, are rarely convincing. Examine your draft and consider each of your points carefully. If you can't back up an opinion with facts, leave it out.

Student writer Efren reviewed his discovery draft and realized that some of his points were opinions that he couldn't prove with the evidence he had collected. Although he could have done more research to back up these points, Efren decided to delete the following sentences:

> Portrayals of sex in the media, including television, books, movies, and even video games, make young people want to lose their virginity.

> Poor families are unable to provide birth control to their teens.

WRITING ACTIVITY 9: Strengthen Your Focus

Check that your thesis statement states a position on a debatable topic, then check that every point in your essay supports that position. Delete any opinions that do not support your thesis or that you cannot back up with factual evidence.

Building Your Support with Cause-and-Effect Analysis

As you revise your essay, you'll want to examine your evidence to be sure that it is convincing. Do you need to add details to support your points? Look at your claims and decide whether you need to add any other facts, expert opinions, or examples to back them up. Remember that you'll need to tell your readers where your information came from.

Chapter 10 explains how to write a paragraph that shows cause and effect.

You might also consider whether using cause-and-effect analysis can help you support your argument. If you're proposing a solution to a problem, you can show what effects your solution will have. Steven Muller, for example, uses cause and effect to show his readers how universal national youth service would benefit the young people who participate in it (paragraph 9). If you're taking a position on an issue, you might use cause-and-effect analysis to prove a point. Wilbert Rideau, for example, explores the results of Louisiana's tough prison policies to argue that getting tough on crime doesn't work (paragraph 3).

HOW TO Build Support for an Essay That Makes an Argument

- Check that you provide factual evidence to support each of your points.
- Where possible, add facts, examples, and expert testimony to convince your readers of your position.
- Consider using cause-and-effect analysis to develop one or more of your points.

Efren reread his discovery draft and decided that his argument would be more persuasive if he added some of the facts and quotations that he had found in his outside sources. He also thought he might be able to use cause-and-effect analysis to make his point that providing birth control in high schools could improve teenagers' lives.

Post Your Draft to the Internet
Share your drafts online either through e-mail, a class listserv, or a Web site. Ask your classmates to respond by suggesting ways to improve your supporting evidence.

WRITING ACTIVITY 10: Build Your Support

Examine your evidence. Ask yourself what facts, examples, and expert testimony you can add to better convince your readers of your opinion. Consider whether cause-and-effect analysis can help you develop any of your points.

Using Progressive Order to Organize Your Points

Learn more about progressive order on p. 40.

If you organize your points in a logical way, your readers are more likely to become convinced of your position as they read through your essay. Creating an outline of your draft will help you see how you have ordered your ideas and will help you find ways to improve your organization. When reviewing your outline, think about which of your points will be more persuasive than others. However you organize them, save the most convincing point for last so that your readers are still thinking of it when they reach your conclusion. You might want to start out with the weakest point and build up to the strongest one. Or you could start out with another strong point and put the weaker ones in the middle.

To review how to create an outline, turn to pp. 26–27.

Opposing points can be tricky to fit into your argument. Where should you put them? If your readers are more familiar with or sympathetic to opposing views than your own argument, you may want to begin with the opposing points. You might even start each paragraph with an opposing viewpoint and then argue against it, as Wilbert Rideau does in "Why Prisons Don't Work." You can also save all of them for near the end of your essay and spend one paragraph arguing against them, as student writer Efren did in his discovery draft.

Use Boldface
Use the bold function to highlight the opposing points in your essay. Check where you have placed these opposing points and be sure that you have argued against each of them.

HOW TO Order Points in an Essay That Makes an Argument

Your Points

- Begin with the least convincing point and end with the most convincing point, or
- Begin with a strong point, put the weaker points in the middle, and end with a strong point.

Opposing Points

- Begin with opposing points and argue against them one by one, or
- Save opposing points for near the end of the essay and argue against them all at once.

WRITING ACTIVITY 11: Order Your Points

Outline your draft and examine how your points are organized. Reorganize your paragraphs as necessary to put your strongest point last. Note that you may also need to reorganize sentences within paragraphs to improve the logic of your argument.

Connecting Your Ideas

Repeating keywords will help link your ideas together. For example, Wilbert Rideau uses *prison, crime, society, criminals, violence,* and *politicians* to remind his readers that he is talking about the value of prisons in our society. Steven Muller repeats the words *young people, volunteer, public, national service, education, job training,* and *society* to remind his readers that he is talking about the benefits of national service for young people and society at large.

In addition to using keywords to link details, you can improve a persuasive essay by using transitional words and phrases that help your readers follow the logic of your argument.

HOW TO Connect Ideas in an Essay That Makes an Argument

The following transitions are especially helpful in argumentative writing:

because	since
as a result	therefore
hence	clearly
of course	although
however	for example
for instance	as
on the one hand/on the other hand	

WRITING ACTIVITY 12: Examine Keywords and Transitions

Underline the keywords and transitions in your discovery draft. If necessary, add keywords and transitions to help your readers follow your train of thought.

Efren's Revised Draft

Before reading Efren's revised draft, reread his discovery draft. Notice that in his revised draft he has added evidence to support his points. He also reorganized some of his paragraphs and made some cuts to improve the logic of his argument. This draft still contains some errors that Efren will correct when he edits his essay.

Should Birth Control Be Available in High Schools?

About one million teenage girls in the United States become pregnant every year. Ninety-five percent of those pregnancies are unintended, and nearly one-third end in abortion or miscarriage. The state of Texas has the second-highest teen pregnancy rate in the nation. Texas does not allow high schools to provide birth control. Distributing contraceptives in Texas high schools will not only lead to lower teen birthrates but will also help students make better choices, improve teenagers lives, and save the public money.

Boys and girls begin to become in tune with their sexual urges during the high school years. It can be very exciting to connect and have new experiences with members of the opposite sex. Most teenagers lack the knowledge they need when they come across an opportunity to do something with their sexual feelings. Some people argue that allowing birth control in high schools may lead to an increase in sexual activity among teens. Considering the consequences teenagers face when deciding to be sexual, however, it is only wise to provide them with contraception. It is crucial for the education system to intervene. These students make life long mistakes.

Every day, high school students engage in unprotected sexual activity. A recent study conducted by Homes for the Homeless revealed that only 39 percent of teenagers who have sex use contraception regularly. As a result, teenagers have the highest rate of sexually transmitted diseases such as gonorrhea, chlamydia, and HIV. Allowing birth control in Texas high schools will result in healthier and improved lives for high school students by preventing sexually transmitted diseases among teenagers. Providing contraceptives will also reduce the teen pregnancy rate. Making it more likely that sexually active students can finish high school, move onto college, and improve their standard of living.

Teenage pregnancy affects not only the teen mother and her family but also the public in general. Teenage pregnancy leads to a tax increase in order to provide services to poor teen families. In one year, the government spent over 25 million dollars providing Aid to Families with Dependent Children (AFDC), the Women, Infants, and Children program (WIC), and other services to families of teen mothers. Worse, 65 percent of teen mothers drop out of high school and end up homeless and on public assistance. Clearly, contraception can help teenage girls avoid dependence on the Welfare System. Providence of birth control in Texas high schools would lead to lower taxes and more money in everyone's pocket.

Those who oppose birth control in high schools cite religious teachings and moral grounds to claim that providing contraception to teens is wrong. It is a mistake to impose someone else's ideas about religion on a problem that affects so many people. Others argue that discussions about sex should be left to the family and kept out of the educational system. What these people fail to see is that schools already act as a parental figure in many ways, such as offering counseling and instilling ideals and values that students often carry into adulthood.

Considering the overwhelming number of teens having unprotected sex and the personal and social consequences of their behavior, it is time to protect our youth against unwanted pregnancies, sexually transmitted diseases, and poverty. We can improve the lives of our youth by providing the tools they need to make better choices in their lives.

GROUP ACTIVITY: Analyze Efren's Revised Draft

Use the following questions to discuss with your classmates how Efren improved his draft.

1. Compare Efren's thesis statement in his discovery draft with the one in his revised draft. How did he improve his thesis statement?

   ____

   ____

   ____

   ____

2. Efren added facts and examples to support his points. How did this improve his draft?

   ____

   ____

   ____

3. How has Efren improved the order of his points?

4. What keywords and transitions does Efren use?

5. What can Efren do to improve his draft further?

WRITING ACTIVITY 13 (Group): Peer Review

Form a group with two or three classmates and exchange copies of your drafts. Read your drafts aloud while your classmates follow along. Take notes on your classmates' answers to the following questions.

1. What do you like best about my essay?
2. How clear is my thesis statement? How can I improve it to state my opinion better?
3. Evaluate my evidence. Is it focused? What evidence would you suggest I add to help convince you of my opinion? What evidence should I remove?
4. Are my points in the most effective order? How can I improve the treatment of the opposing points?
5. Where should I add keywords and transitions?
6. Does my conclusion summarize my main points or propose a possible solution? How could I improve it?

Online Peer Review
If peer review questions are available online, you may wish to conduct peer review electronically.

WRITING ACTIVITY 14: Revise Your Draft

Taking into account your classmates' suggestions and using Efren's revision as a model, revise your discovery draft. Strengthen your focus, build your support, organize your points, and connect your ideas.

STEP 4: EDIT YOUR ESSAY

Before you send your essay to the local newspaper, examine it carefully for mistakes in spelling, punctuation, and grammar. Regardless of how well you have supported your position on an issue or your solution to a problem, errors like these will distract readers and weaken your argument. Take out your dictionary and turn to the Handbook in Part Four to make sure that your essay is error-free.

You'll find more information about subordinating conjunctions on pp. 523–27.

You can also strengthen the impact of your writing by combining closely related sentences. In this chapter, you will practice using subordinating conjunctions to make the relationship between your sentences clear.

What Is Sentence Subordination?

For other ways to combine sentences, see Chapter 24.

If two short sentences in a row are closely related in meaning but unequal in importance, try *subordinating* the less important sentence to the more important one. In Chapter 15, you learned to do this with relative pronouns. You can also combine unequal sentences with subordinating conjunctions.

Let's review the most common subordinating conjunctions:

after	although	because
before	even though	if
since	that	though
unless	until	when
where	whether	while

Adding one of these conjunctions to the beginning of a sentence will make the sentence a *subordinate clause,* or a group of words that contains a subject and a verb but cannot stand alone. Readers understand that the part of a combined sentence that can stand alone is more important than the part that can't.

Combining Sentences with Subordinating Conjunctions

In the following sentence pairs, the less important sentence has been changed to a subordinate clause and combined with the other sentence.

UNEQUAL I started studying every night. I did better on my exams.

COMBINED After I started studying every night, I did better on my exams.

UNEQUAL You'll like that class. The professor posts his notes on the Internet.

COMBINED You'll like that class because the professor posts his notes on the Internet.

UNEQUAL You'll feel healthier if you include fresh vegetables in your diet. Eating right can be time-consuming.

COMBINED Although eating right can be time-consuming, you'll feel healthier if you include fresh vegetables in your diet.

UNEQUAL I would like to use a PDA to organize my time. I hope I can earn enough money to buy one.

COMBINED I would like to use a PDA to organize my time if I can earn enough money to buy one.

Notice that when a subordinate clause starts a sentence, it is followed by a comma. In general, if the subordinate clause comes at the end of the sentence, no comma is needed before it.

HOW TO Combine Sentences with Subordinating Conjunctions

- Identify pairs of short sentences that are related in meaning but unequal in importance.
- Decide which sentence is more important.

- Turn the less important sentence into a subordinate clause by beginning it with a subordinating conjunction.
- Use a comma after a subordinate clause that begins a sentence. In general, do not put a comma before a subordinate clause that ends a sentence.

EDITING PRACTICE: Combining Sentences with Subordinating Conjunctions

Combine the following pairs of sentences by using subordinating conjunctions. You may have to delete or add words, and there may be more than one correct way to combine the sentences.

1. Using the Internet to access class notes really helps. It is less helpful if you have a dial-up connection.

 ____

 ____

2. Meraldo left for the bookstore. He can buy a prepaid phonecard there.

 ____

 ____

3. Most residence hall rooms have an Internet connection. Students require access to the Web to research their papers.

 ____

 ____

4. Almost all of my classmates study at the café. It can get very noisy.

 ____

 ____

5. I don't have a computer. I can borrow my sister's laptop whenever I need it.

 ____

 ____

6. Some of the tutoring labs are open during the holidays. It's convenient for students.

____

____

7. Anthony skiied into the parking lot and fell down. I nearly fell down laughing.

____

____

8. Carlos might get a promotion this week. We will buy a new television to celebrate.

____

____

9. Marianne was my hero. She stopped helping me with algebra.

____

10. Laurinda convinced me to study harder. I began to like college.

____

Exercise Central
The *Discoveries* Web site includes additional practice exercises in combining sentences. Go to **bedfordstmartins .com/discoveries**, click on "Exercise Central," and select "Sentence Subordination."

Efren's Edited Essay

As you may have noticed, Efren's revised draft had a few choppy sentences, as well as errors in spelling, punctuation, and grammar. He edited his essay to eliminate these problems. (The underlining indicates where he made changes.) Efren also added in-text references and a list of works cited.

Should Birth Control Be Available in High Schools?

About one million teenage girls in the United States become pregnant every year. Ninety-five percent of those pregnancies are unintended, and nearly one-third end in abortion or miscarriage (Morris 22). Texas has the second-highest teen pregnancy rate in the nation because the state does not allow high schools to provide birth control (Texas). Distributing contraceptives in Texas high schools will not only lead to lower teen birthrates but will also help students make better choices, improve teenagers' lives, and save the public money.

Boys and girls begin to become in tune with their sexual urges during the high school years. Although it can be very exciting to connect and have new experiences with members of the opposite sex, most teenagers lack the knowledge they need when they come across an opportunity to do something with their sexual feelings. Some people argue that allowing birth control in high schools may lead to an increase in sexual activity among teens. Considering the consequences teenagers face when deciding to be sexual, however, it is only wise to provide them with contraception. It is crucial for the education system to intervene before these students make lifelong mistakes.

Every day, high school students engage in unprotected sexual activity. A recent study conducted by Homes for the Homeless revealed that only 39 percent of teenagers who have sex use contraception regularly. As a result, teenagers have the highest rate of sexually transmitted diseases such as gonorrhea, chlamydia, and HIV (Centers for Disease Control). Allowing birth control in Texas high schools will result in healthier and improved lives for high school students by preventing sexually transmitted diseases among teenagers. Providing contraceptives will also reduce the teen pregnancy rate, making it more likely that sexually active students can finish high school, move on to college, and improve their standard of living.

Review sentence fragments on pp. 548–54.

Teenage pregnancy affects not only the teen mother and her family but also the public in general. Teenage pregnancy leads to a tax increase in order to provide services to poor teen families. In one year, the government spent over 25 million dollars providing Aid to Families with Dependent Children (AFDC), the Women, Infants, and Children program (WIC), and other services to families of teen mothers (Morris 1). Worse, 65 percent of teen mothers drop out of high school and end up homeless and on public assistance (Homes 2). Clearly, contraception can help teenage girls avoid dependence on the welfare system. Providing birth control in Texas high schools would lead to lower taxes and more money in everyone's pocket.

Those who oppose birth control in high schools cite religious teachings and moral grounds to claim that providing contraception to teens is wrong. It is a mistake to impose someone else's ideas about religion on a problem that affects so many people. Others argue that discussions about sex should be left to the family and kept out of the educational system. What these people fail to see is that schools already act as a parental figure in many ways, such as offering counseling and instilling ideals and values that students often carry into adulthood.

Considering the overwhelming number of teens having unprotected sex and the personal and social consequences of their behavior, it is time to protect our youth against unwanted pregnancies, sexually transmitted diseases, and poverty. We can improve the lives of our youth by providing the tools they need to make better choices in their lives.

For more information on how to cite your sources, see pp. 458–61.

Works Cited

Centers for Disease Control and Prevention. "Most Teens Not Provided STD or Pregnancy Prevention Counseling during Checkups." 6 Dec. 2000. Centers for Disease Control and Prevention. 25 Oct. 2004 <http://www.cdc.gov/nchstp/dstd/Press_Releases/Teens2000.htm>.

Homes for the Homeless. The Age of Confusion: Why So Many Teens Are Getting Pregnant, Turning to Welfare and Ending Up Homeless. April 1996. Academic Search Premier. U of Texas at El Paso Lib. 27 Oct. 2004 <http://www.academicsearchpremier.org/search>.

Morris, Leslie, Cheryl A. Ulmer, and Jaya Chimnani. "A Role for Community Health Corps Members in Youth HIV/AIDS Preventive Education." Journal of School Health 73.4 (2003): 22-36. Academic Search Premier. U of Texas at El Paso Lib. 24 Oct. 2004 <http://www.academicsearchpremier.org/search>.

Texas. Department of Health. "Texas Health Fact Sheet." Dec. 2000. Texas Department of State Health Services. 27 Oct. 2004 <http://www.tdh.state.tx.us/dpa/cfs00/texas00.PDF>.

WRITING ACTIVITY 15: Edit Your Essay

Using a dictionary and the Handbook in Part Four of this book, edit your essay. In particular, use subordinating conjunctions to combine closely related short sentences. Reread your corrections in your editing log.

STEP 5: SHARE YOUR ESSAY

Efren sent his essay to the local newspaper, which published it on the editorial page. He received a number of calls from friends and family complimenting him on his work. Now that you have finished your own argumentative essay, be sure to submit it to your local paper so that your intended audience has a chance to read it. You'll likely be pleased by the response.

ADDITIONAL WRITING ASSIGNMENTS

1. Write an argumentative letter to a family member or friend encouraging this person to give up a bad habit such as smoking, drinking, or eating junk food. Be sure to support your position with evidence of the problem from outside sources.
2. Write an argumentative essay to the editor of your local newspaper in which you propose a solution to a local problem. For example, you might argue for improved parks, better roads, or a new theme park to attract tourists.
3. Write an argumentative essay to a member of Congress stating your opinion on an international issue such as space exploration, global warming, or the destruction of rain forests. Read outside sources to make sure that you have enough background information to write intelligently on the topic you have chosen.

PART THREE

Other Kinds of Writing

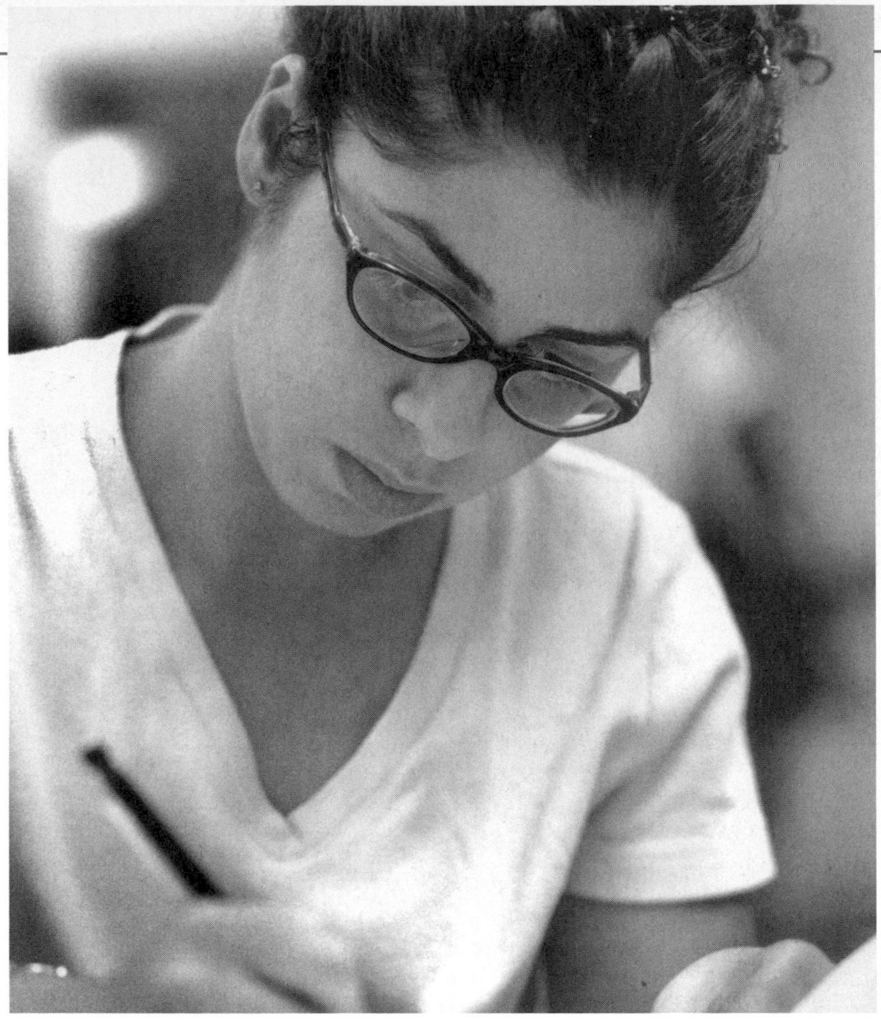

This young woman is writing notes in the margins of a student essay that her class is discussing. After class is over, she plans to write down in her learning log what she heard and thought about during class. A learning log is one of several kinds of journals you will learn about in this chapter.

CHAPTER

17

Keeping a Journal

In this chapter, you will

- learn what a journal is.
- learn how a journal improves your writing.
- practice keeping three types of journals.

UNDERSTANDING WHAT A JOURNAL IS

How many times has someone said to you, "Anything worth doing is worth doing well"? Perhaps you heard these words from your music teacher as you practiced for your first recital or from the coach of your Little League team as you practiced stealing bases. You knew that you were being encouraged to work hard, to practice regularly, and to give your best effort. To be a better writer, you must have this same commitment.

Definition of a Journal

A journal is a notebook where you jot down your thoughts, opinions, feelings, and memories. You can buy a special notebook or keep your journal in one section of a loose-leaf notebook. To keep a journal, you write for ten to fifteen minutes each day about issues and ideas that matter to you.

Writing Assignment

Write for ten to fifteen minutes on the topic of journals. Have you ever kept a journal? If so, what type of journal did you keep? How did keeping a journal help you as a writer? If you have never kept a journal, how will keeping a journal help you become a better writer?

USING JOURNALS TO IMPROVE WRITING

Keeping a journal provides the opportunity to practice what you are learning, experiment with different writing strategies, and find topics for your paragraph and essay assignments. What's more, you do all of this for yourself, without worrying about how this writing will be graded.

Writing Practice

When you write a journal entry, you start by putting down the date and time. You generally use complete sentences and paragraphs. By doing so, you're working on your ability to join words together in a standard way. At the same time, you're putting together groups of sentences that relate to one another to form paragraphs. With journal writing, you give yourself the opportunity to practice the skills needed to write for your college classes and for the workplace.

To review how to keep a journal, turn to pp. 262–63.

HOW TO Use a Journal to Practice Writing

- Record your personal thoughts, opinions, feelings, and memories in a notebook for ten to fifteen minutes each day.
- Write in complete sentences and paragraphs.
- Don't worry about spelling, punctuation, or grammar.
- At the end of the week, reread the entries and write a sentence or two that sums up what you have learned about yourself.

ACTIVITY 1: Practice Writing a Journal Entry

In complete sentences and paragraphs, write for fifteen minutes on what has happened to you today. Reflect on your entry and list three ways that such writing practice will help you improve as a writer.

Experimental Entries

As a student writer, you may be so concerned with your instructor's response to your essays that you find it difficult to try new writing strategies. Journal writing gives you the opportunity to be adventurous and try something new. For example, if you wrote a journal entry about your favorite place, you might write something like this:

> When I look at the desert, I enjoy the flatness of the land and the absence of bright colors. To my eyes, the browns and the grays of the plants and rocks are a nice contrast to the blue of the sky.

One way to experiment with your writing is to change the point of view. You could try writing this journal entry without using the pronoun *I*. Instead, you would use the second-person pronoun *you* or third-person pronouns such as *he, she, it, they,* and *one*. Changing the pronouns completely changes the point of view.

To read more about pronouns, turn to pp. 509–13.

For example, if you wrote the above journal entry in the third person, you might write something like this:

> When visitors look at the desert, they mention the flatness of the land and the absence of bright colors. To their eyes, the browns and the grays of the plants and rocks are a contrast to the blue of the sky, but they don't always find the colors appealing.

Another way to experiment is to use dialogue. Instead of describing something that happened, have people tell the story by putting words in their mouths.

> When my grandmother visited last summer, she said, "The desert is flat and has no color." I replied, "Yes, but the browns and the grays of the plants and rocks are a nice contrast to the blue of the sky."

HOW TO Use a Journal to Experiment

- Use your imagination. Create a story out of an experience that you have had.
- Try telling the story from someone else's point of view.
- Use dialogue to show what people would say to each other in your story.

ACTIVITY 2: Experiment with Your Journal Entry

Using the journal entry you drafted in Activity 1, rewrite it from the point of view of someone who spent time with you today. How would this person describe your day? What did this person say to you that could be included as dialogue?

Topics

To review how to choose topics, see p. 19.

A journal also helps you come up with topics for other pieces of writing. For instance, imagine that you decide to write a journal entry about a party that you went to last Saturday night. You describe the people you saw there, place them into different social groups, and discuss how they interacted.

It might seem that this entry is about nothing more than a party. A more careful reading, however, leads you to a topic for an essay. This one journal entry gives you plenty of evidence for an essay on how people tend to break into social groups and how these groups interact.

HOW TO Use a Journal to Find Topics

- Reread your journal entries, looking for ideas that interest you, that you know something about, and that others might be interested in.
- Place a *T* for "topic" next to those ideas that might be used for essays.
- Choose one of these topics and narrow it.
- Explore your narrowed topic by writing more about it in your journal.

ACTIVITY 3 (Group): Find Topics in Your Journal Entry

Reread your journal entries. Write down one possible essay topic that could come from your journal entry. Share your topic choice with your classmates.

KEEPING DIFFERENT TYPES OF JOURNALS

There are three types of journals that you might be asked to keep in your college classes: personal journals, dialogue journals, and learning logs.

Personal Journals

In a personal journal, you record events that happen to you and your reactions to them. You capture the emotions that you feel as you face new and different experiences. When you're writing a personal journal, you know that others aren't going to read it. Therefore, you don't worry about sentence structure, spelling, punctuation, or grammar.

Here are two entries from student writer Shannon's personal journal:

> September 18
>
> I've missed the last three days of class because I have the flu. I am way behind I know. I'm scared of getting dropped in my UNIV class. I don't know why they have an attendance policy in a college class. It's not like this is high school. I guess I'm feeling better if I can complain this much.

September 21

My mom used to sing a song on days like this. One part went "rainy days and Mondays always get me down." That sounds about right. I think back to when the semester was getting started and I was registering for classes. I wanted to sign up for 18 hours. I was crazy. My mom said I was crazy. Thank goodness my advisor wouldn't let me sign up for 18 hours. There's no way I'm telling my mom that she was right about college taking up more time than high school.

HOW TO Keep a Personal Journal

- Set aside ten to fifteen minutes each day to write in your journal.
- Write about your daily activities.
- Write about songs you hear on the radio, articles you read in the paper, or conversations you hear as you walk across campus.
- Write quickly without worrying about spelling, punctuation, or grammar.
- Once a week, write a few sentences that sum up what you have learned about yourself.

Keep a Personal Journal on Computer
You may prefer to keep your personal journal on a computer disk. Set up a file called "journal" and then add entries to it each day. Enter text as quickly as you can. Resist the urge to backspace, delete, or correct your writing.

ACTIVITY 4: Practice Keeping a Personal Journal

Try keeping a personal journal for two to three days. For ten to fifteen minutes each day, write about what happens to you and how you feel about it. To get started, try responding to some of the following questions:

- What am I most proud of in my life?
- How did I spend my last twenty dollars?
- What do I see myself doing in ten years?

- When my friends describe me, what do I think they say?
- When my enemies describe me, what do I think they say?
- How did I end up where I am right now?

Dialogue Journals

While personal journals are a good way to start writing down your thoughts and feelings, dialogue journals help you practice communicating with a reader, someone who will respond to what you have written. Generally, your topics will continue to be the same as they are in your personal journals, but you'll want to take enough care with your sentence structure, spelling, punctuation, and grammar that your reader can figure out what you're trying to say.

The following is an entry from student writer Aaron's dialogue journal:

> One thing that upsets me is that instructors assign group projects but don't allow class time for us to work on them. Not everyone has time to meet with others and complete a project. It was bad enough in high school when we had group work, but it is really terrible in college because of the varying ages and lifestyles of the group members. I'm in a group now with a single mom, a guy who goes to school full-time and works a 40 a week job, me — who is on call to pick up people and take them to and from the airport — and this fourth guy who comes to class in the morning straight from his job at the 24-hour discount store.

The following is classmate Shannon's response:

> True, but this group project is not an extracurricular activity. If we don't do it, we get an *F* for 20 percent of our grade. Maybe our group can split into smaller groups that CAN meet. Maybe we'll have to use e-mail or telephone calls to keep in touch. I know we'll find a way, Aaron.

HOW TO Keep a Dialogue Journal

- Write for ten to fifteen minutes on a topic that interests you.
- Hand your journal to a reader who will respond to what you have written.
- Continue to exchange your journal with your reader, adding new entries each time.

Keep a Dialogue Journal Online
If you have a class Web site, post your entries to a class bulletin board. You could also send e-mail messages back and forth to a classmate, saving each entry to your computer disk.

ACTIVITY 5: Practice Keeping a Dialogue Journal

Find a writing partner, someone who will read your journal and respond to it. Write about something that interests you and then share it with your partner, asking your partner to respond. Continue to exchange this dialogue journal for two to three days. If you need some ideas for topics, consider the following questions:

- What's the last movie that you saw, and what did you like most about it?
- When was the last time you were really angry? Why?
- What's your biggest regret in life so far?
- What's the last book that you read for fun, and what do you remember most clearly about it?
- What's one thing you can do to make the world a better place? And will you do it?

Learning Logs

A third type of journal is the learning log, which specifically helps you organize the material that you're learning for your classes. In a learning log, you write down the main ideas that you've learned from listening to your instructor or reading your textbook. As you write down these ideas, you develop the details of what you understand and you ask questions about what you don't understand. Your learning log will give you a head start when you get ready to start writing your study guide before an exam because it already includes all the main points of any lecture or reading.

The following is an entry from student writer Alejandro's learning log:

> Tomorrow I'm having a quiz in my English class, and it's going to be about coordination. Coordination allows writers to connect sentences correctly with proper English. There are three methods that one can use to connect sentences.

Method One: independent clause, comma, coordinating conjunction, and independent clause

Method Two: independent clause, semicolon, and independent clause

Method Three: independent clause, semicolon, conjunctive adverb, comma, and independent clause

I know these three methods and will use them on the test.

HOW TO Keep a Learning Log

- Take notes in class as you normally would.
- After class, devote at least ten to fifteen minutes to writing down your response to what you learned.
- Summarize, define words, and write questions that might appear on an exam.
- Ask your instructor to explain any ideas you note in your log because you don't understand them.
- Connect what you have learned to your own experience, thinking about how this information will be useful.

Keep a Learning Log on Computer
You may prefer to keep your class notes and learning log on a laptop computer. Consider using different fonts for summaries, definitions, and questions. Boldface new words.

ACTIVITY 6: Practice Keeping a Learning Log

For two to three days, keep a learning log for your writing class. If you're not sure how to start, try answering the following questions:

- What was the main point that the instructor was trying to get across in class today?
- What parts of today's lecture did I not understand? Why?
- Where are there gaps in my notes? How am I going to get the information that I'm missing?
- What words in my notes do I need to look up?
- What parts of the lecture might I be tested on?
- What parts of the lecture might show up as essay questions on the next exam?

At the end of the week, discuss with your instructor which type of journal you should continue to keep for the remainder of this writing class.

ADDITIONAL WRITING ASSIGNMENTS

1. In your journal, write a summary paragraph describing the three types of journal entries. Which would you prefer to keep and why?
2. In your journal, write a paragraph that explains how a learning log differs from regular class notes. How would a learning log be helpful to you as a student?
3. Choose one idea for a topic from your journal entries. Write a paragraph to your instructor explaining why you would like to write on this topic for one of your assignments.
4. Write a letter to a friend or family member explaining that you are keeping a journal for your writing class. Share one or two journal entries and explain how keeping a journal is helping you become a better writer.

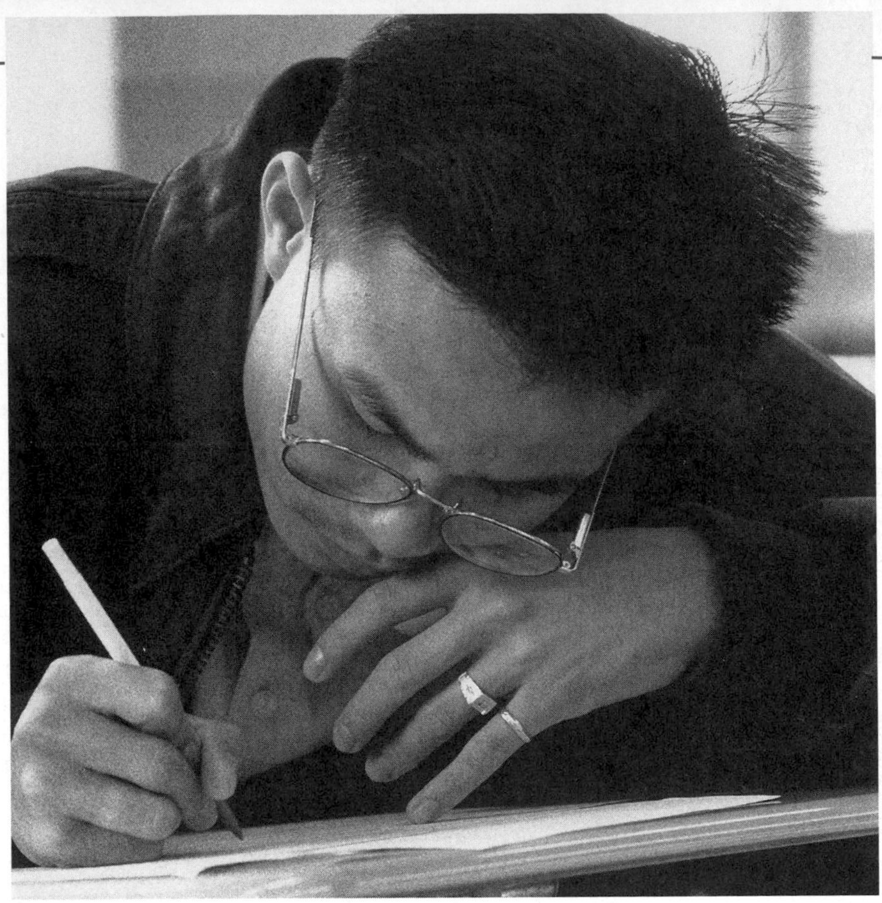

This young man prepared for his essay exam by making predictions about what questions might be asked and by creating a study guide for each possible question. Now, his careful preparation is paying off. In this chapter, you will learn more about how to prepare for and take essay exams.

CHAPTER

18

Taking Essay Exams

In this chapter, you will

- learn what an essay exam is.
- learn how to prepare for an essay exam.
- learn strategies for taking an essay exam.

UNDERSTANDING WHAT AN ESSAY EXAM IS

You may be nervous about taking exams. The idea that exam grades may make the difference in whether you succeed or fail in a course is enough to make anyone anxious, so you'll want to have a plan to prepare for and take exams. Fortunately, you have already practiced many of the skills needed to prepare for one type of test — the essay exam.

Definition of an Essay Exam

An essay exam is made up of one or more questions to which you must respond in complete sentences and paragraphs. You are expected to organize your thoughts and present them clearly to show what you know about a topic. Your response may be shorter than an essay you write outside of class, but it still includes all parts of the essay: an introduction, a thesis statement, support paragraphs, and a conclusion.

To read more about parts of an essay, turn to pp. 256–58.

Sample Essay Exam Question and Answer

The following is an example of an essay exam question and a student response.

Essay exam question

In Chapter 12, you learned that there is a process for writing an essay. Imagine that you have been asked to tutor fellow students to write. Explain the stages of the writing process.

Student response

The Writing Process

Thesis statement

Introduction

The writing process refers to the stages you go through to be sure that you have written an essay that communicates your thoughts to someone else. You don't have to use the writing process to write a quick e-mail to a friend, but you use it when you are writing an essay that will be graded or a memo for your boss.

First support paragraph

The first stage of the writing process is gathering ideas. You can't write what you don't know, so you must take some time to get your ideas together. You determine who your reader is and what that person needs to know about your topic. You think about whether you're writing to share your own thoughts, inform your reader of something you've learned, or persuade your reader to change his or her mind. You decide on a topic and narrow it so that you can cover it in a few pages, and you spend time gathering ideas for what to say.

The second stage is drafting. In this stage, you write down your ideas on paper without worrying too much about whether you're spelling words correctly or getting every comma in place. The idea is to take what is in your head and get it on paper. Some people draft quickly and then take their time revising. Other people draft slowly and so spend less time revising.

Second support paragraph

The third stage is revising. Revising gives you the chance to rewrite your essay so that your ideas are clearer, more interesting, and easier to follow. You first make sure that every sentence in the essay is focused on the thesis statement. You add supporting details where they are needed. Then, you add transitional words and phrases to help your reader follow what you are saying. It's often helpful to have other people read your essay and give you ideas about how to revise it so that you see what a reader needs in order to understand your thinking.

Third support paragraph

The fourth stage is editing. When you edit, you give your essay a "shave and a haircut." You use a dictionary, a handbook, and your computer word-processing software to help you check for errors in spelling, punctuation, and grammar. This is important because if there are too many errors in your essay, your reader may not pay attention to what you're trying to say.

Fourth support paragraph

Once you've edited your essay, you're ready to share it with your reader. You might hand it to the reader, mail it, or read it aloud. You've spent a lot of time writing this essay, so you want to be sure that someone benefits from your hard work.

Fifth support paragraph

If you work through the writing process when writing an essay, you know that you have done your very best to present what you know in an organized and clear way.

Conclusion

Writing Assignment

Write a paragraph for your classmates in which you describe how you prepare for essay exams. What strategies have worked for you? What suggestions do you have for reducing the worry and stress of getting ready for a test?

PREPARING FOR AN ESSAY EXAM

Instructors like to give essay exams because they know that you must understand a topic thoroughly to be able to write an essay response. You'll want to make sure that you have done everything you can to succeed: attend class, take good notes, read your textbook, and review important material regularly. In addition to having good overall study habits, you can use strategies such as questions, predictions, and study guides to do your best on essay exams.

Questions

When your instructor announces that an essay exam is coming up, you'll want to start asking questions right away. Knowing what to expect when you begin an essay exam will help you during the exam. In addition to asking questions, you can usually find out more about the exam by reading your syllabus and talking to former students.

HOW TO Ask Questions About an Essay Exam

- What class material will the exam cover?
- How many essay questions will there be on the exam?
- How much detail should each response include?
- Will students be allowed to use notes or the textbook during the exam?
- How much time will be allotted for the exam?
- How will the exam be graded?
- Are there recommendations for what to review?

Reviewing Past Exams
Some instructors post past exams on their class Web sites. Ask whether you can review past exams as a way to prepare for an upcoming exam.

Predictions

As you start to prepare for an essay exam, you'll want to go through your notes looking for information that might make good essay exam questions. Compare your predictions about exam questions with the information that the instructor gave you about the upcoming exam.

Spend extra time studying those areas that both you and the instructor have indicated are important.

If your instructor suggests areas for review that you have not marked in your class notes, then look for information that relates to that topic. If you need to, go back to your original sources, your lecture notes, your reading notes, and your textbooks to be sure that you have enough information to work with.

Study Guides

Once you know that your class notes have the information you need to answer any possible essay questions, you're ready to create a study guide. Write down each possible essay question. Underneath each question, write down a list of short phrases that include all of the information needed to answer the question. In the time that remains before the exam, review these study guides until you have memorized the information.

Resist the urge to write down a complete essay answer for each possible essay question. When students try to memorize essay answers, they almost always forget the prepared answer. Memorize only the information that you'll need to create the answer once you're taking the exam.

HOW TO Prepare for an Essay Exam

- Ask questions about the exam.
- Reread your lecture notes and create study guides.
- Review textbook material, especially summaries, charts, and diagrams.
- Study review sheets or other handouts.
- Prepare by listing points for possible essay exam questions.
- Consider other ways to prepare such as forming a study group, completing Web site exercises, or creating flash cards.

ACTIVITY 1: Prepare for an Essay Exam

Make a list of the strengths and weaknesses in the way you study and prepare for essay exams. Develop a plan in writing for how you will improve your weaknesses.

TAKING AN ESSAY EXAM

After preparing for an essay exam, your next step is to make sure that you do your very best during the test. As soon as the instructor hands out the exam, you'll want to take the time to read it carefully. Take a deep breath, read the instructions, read the essay questions, and come up with a plan.

Answer Plans

Once you have decided how much time you have to spend on each question, you need to understand clearly what each question is asking. As you read through the first question, underline all of the important pieces of information.

Next, you need to decide how you're being asked to share this information with your instructor. Are you being asked to define, to compare and contrast, to describe, to classify, or to give examples? Circle the keywords that explain how to answer the question.

To review how to brainstorm a list, see p. 24.

If you have space on the exam sheet, jot down a list of points that you can use to respond to the question. This way you won't forget the information later as you become more pressed for time.

Written Responses

To review methods of development, read pp. 264–69.

Once you know what you're going to say, write as quickly and as neatly as you can. Instructors want to be able to read your writing, but they understand that you're under pressure. They don't expect perfect penmanship. Because of time pressure, it's best not to write a rough draft of your answer and then try to polish it. Your instructor would prefer a more detailed answer to a perfect-looking one that provides few details.

Revised and Edited Responses

More information on organizing an essay can be found on pp. 274–75.

Reread both the question and your answer. Does your response answer the question? Did you leave out anything that you really should have put in? If you decide that you left something out, write it in the margin or at the end of the page and draw an arrow to show where it belongs in your essay.

Then, take a few minutes for a quick edit of your essay. Proofread for spelling, punctuation, and grammar errors, making the corrections neatly above the sentences or in the margin. Your instructor will be impressed that you took the time to reread and correct obvious errors.

For a complete list of transitions, see p. 42.

HOW TO Take an Essay Exam

- Look over the whole exam, and think about how much time you have to complete it.
- If some questions are worth more than others, plan to spend the most time on those questions.
- Analyze each question by underlining important information and circling words that tell you how to answer the question.
- Write down a list of the points you want to make.
- Write a response in essay form.
- Allow time to revise and edit your response.

Using a Laptop
Some professors will permit you to bring a laptop computer to the exam. Check to see if you can write your response on computer and then print it nearby.

ACTIVITY 2: Write an Essay Exam Response

Select one of the following essay exam questions. Read and mark the question as you analyze it; then, write a response.

1. Explain the parts of an essay to someone who is just learning what an essay is. How does each part contribute to the reader's understanding?
2. One stage of the writing process requires that you revise the draft of your essay. Write an essay for your instructor, describing the process you use to revise. If you have worked with a peer review group, explain how this group has helped you during the revision stage.

ADDITIONAL WRITING ASSIGNMENTS

1. You have learned that writers should know their audience and purpose when they write. Write an essay for a close friend describing the importance of audience and purpose. Contrast the three purposes so that your reader will understand how they differ from each other.
2. One strategy for eliminating errors in your writing is to keep an editing log. Define the term *editing log* for a fellow student, and explain how keeping one helps you eliminate errors. Give examples from your own writing experience.
3. Your writing instructor would like to know what you have learned that will help you write better essay exam responses in other classes. Describe what you have learned about writing and how you will apply that to help you write better responses.
4. Write an essay for the campus newspaper in which you give advice on how to reduce the worry and stress of preparing for and taking tests. Give suggestions for what to do before, during, and after each exam. Include examples of how these strategies have worked for you.

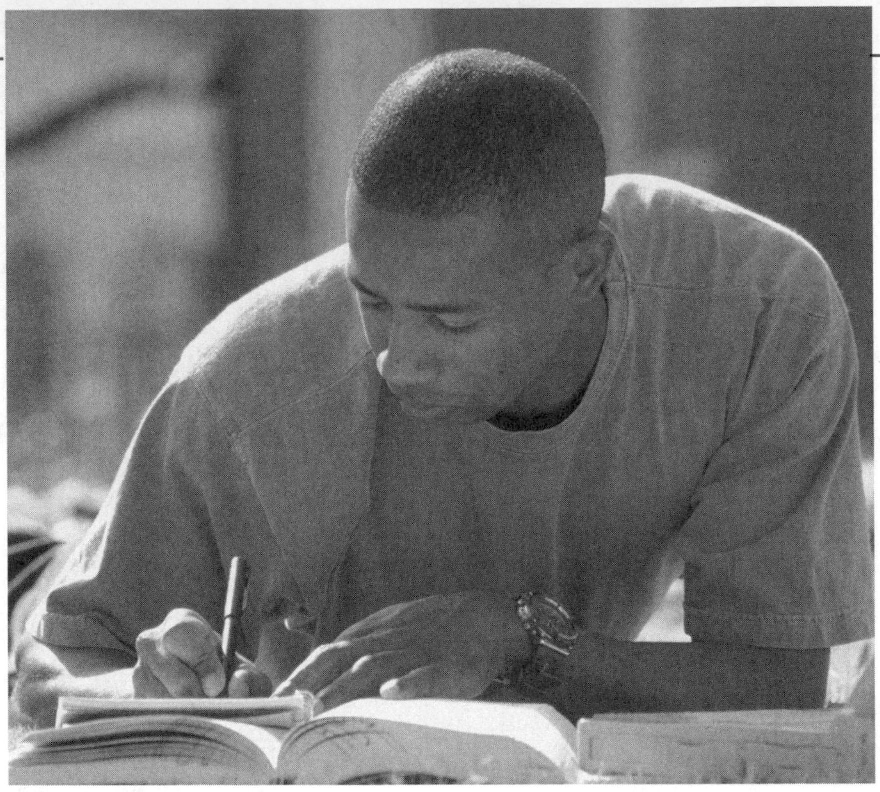

The young man in this picture is writing a summary paragraph for an essay he just finished reading. As you'll learn in this chapter, writing summaries is a good way to make sure that you understand something you have read or heard.

CHAPTER

19

Writing a Summary

In this chapter, you will

- learn what a summary paragraph is.
- learn why we write summary paragraphs.
- practice writing summary paragraphs.

UNDERSTANDING WHAT A SUMMARY PARAGRAPH IS

Imagine that when you returned home from class yesterday, your sister met you at the door and asked, "How was your day?" When you responded, did you give her a minute-by-minute description of everything you did from the moment you left the house? Probably not. Instead, you offered some sort of summary: "It was fine. I got my chemistry midterm back. I passed. I didn't understand everything my math instructor said today, so I spent an hour after class with the tutor. I understand it now."

Definition of a Summary Paragraph

A summary paragraph is a condensed version of a longer piece of writing. It includes the title, the author's name, the main idea, and important supporting points from the original writing. However, a summary paragraph is written in your own words.

HOW TO Recognize a Summary Paragraph

- A topic sentence states the title, the author's name, and the main idea of the original text.
- Important supporting points are included.
- Details are omitted.
- A concluding statement restates the topic sentence or makes an observation about the original text.
- The summary is written in the summary writer's own words.

Writing Assignment

Select your favorite sample essay from this textbook. Write a summary of this essay to read aloud to your classmates. Discuss what important supporting points you included and why.

ACTIVITY 1 (Group): Recognize the Parts of a Summary Paragraph

With several classmates, reread the essay on pages 256–58 and then read the summary paragraph below. Underline the sentence that includes the title, the author's name, and the main point of the summary. Number the supporting points. Underline the concluding statement. Discuss how this summary paragraph condenses the original essay.

Summary Paragraph for "Running Out of Money before Graduation" by Charles Smith

In the essay "Running Out of Money before Graduation," Charles Smith shares his concern that college students and their parents often don't have a plan for how they will finance the student's education. In the 1970s and 1980s, there was plenty of federal and state financial aid money available. But this is no longer the case. Because students can't rely solely on government grants and not all students qualify for scholarships, Smith proposes that college and high school administrators become more proactive in helping students and parents understand what it will take to finance a college education. Even more important, they must help low-income earners come up with a financial plan. The result will be more people of color finishing college and sharing in the benefits of having a college education.

USING SUMMARY PARAGRAPHS

In college classes and in the workplace, you are often asked to write summary paragraphs. An instructor may ask you to summarize a section of a textbook, the results of a lab experiment, or the key points of a lecture. Your boss may ask you to summarize a sales report, customer-service evaluations, or your accomplishments of the last week. You write these summary paragraphs to present information quickly, test your understanding, and include outside sources.

Quick Information

A summary paragraph allows you to share information quickly. This can be important when your reader doesn't have time to read the original text. When you summarize, you take a lot of information and filter out what isn't absolutely necessary for a general understanding of the topic.

Clear Understanding

A summary paragraph helps you and your reader figure out what you know and don't know. For instance, you can't summarize the causes of the War of 1812 unless you know them. A sure way for you and your reader to test whether you know a certain piece of material is to see whether you can summarize it accurately.

Information from Outside Sources

A summary paragraph helps you record information from outside sources. When you read outside sources to find information for a paper you're writing, you can't quote everything you read. Instead, you select the most important points to include in your essay. Learning to summarize helps you streamline the process of reading and recording information from outside sources.

To read more about how to write summaries of outside reading, turn to pp. 457–58.

Summarizing from a Web Site

If you are writing a summary of text from a Web site or other electronic source, cut and paste the original text into your word processor. Delete all but the main idea and important supporting points. Rewrite what remains in your own words. If you use any of the author's exact words, be sure to place them in quotation marks. Provide a citation for your summary so that your reader will be able to find the original.

HOW TO Use a Summary Paragraph

- A summary paragraph eliminates unnecessary information.
- It checks understanding.
- It records information you gathered from reading outside sources.

ACTIVITY 2: Analyze a Summary Paragraph

Read the following paragraphs from the book *A History of Reading* by Alberto Manguel. Then, read the summary paragraph and answer the questions that follow it.

From *A History of Reading* by Alberto Manguel

In all probability, writing was invented for commercial reasons, to remember that a certain number of cattle belonged to a certain family, or were being transported to a certain place. A written sign served as a mnemonic device: a picture of an ox stood for an ox, to remind the reader that the transaction was in oxen, how many oxen, and perhaps the names of a buyer and seller. Memory, in this form, is also a document, the record of such a transaction.

The inventor of the first written tablets may have realized the advantage these pieces of clay had over holding the memory in the brain: first, the amount of information storable on tablets was endless — one could go on producing tablets *ad infinitum*, while the brain's remembering capacity is limited; second, tablets did not require the presence of the memory-holder to retrieve information. Suddenly, something intangible — a number, an item of news, a thought, an order — could be acquired without the physical presence of the message-giver; magically, it could be imagined, noted and passed on across space and beyond time.

Summary Paragraph

In *A History of Reading,* Alberto Manguel argues that the written word probably resulted from the need to document business dealings. The first benefit of writing information down is that the amount of information to be documented is limited only by how much writing material is on hand. The second benefit is that written information can be understood by a reader alone, with no other person needed to remember or deliver it. Writing makes it possible to communicate with those far away in time and space.

1. How does the summary paragraph condense the main point of the original essay?

____

____

____

2. What are the most important supporting points in the original essay? Does the summary paragraph include these points?

____

____

____

____

____

3. How does the summary paragraph conclude? How does this concluding sentence condense the original conclusion?

____

____

____

____

WRITING SUMMARY PARAGRAPHS

Like any other skill, writing summary paragraphs takes practice. A number of strategies will help you consistently write better summary paragraphs.

Material to Be Summarized

As soon as you realize that a piece of writing provides useful information, stop and reread the material. Look up any words that you don't understand. Identify any people who are mentioned, making sure you know who they are, what they do, and why their names appear. If any dates appear in the material, know what they refer to. As you read, underline the important supporting points.

Topic Sentence

To review the parts of a paragraph, read p. 18.

In the first sentence of your summary paragraph, identify the title, the author's name, and the main idea of the original source in your own words. This is the sentence that tells your reader what the original text is about.

Important Supporting Points

Based on your underlining, decide which pieces of information you need to include to get the main idea across quickly. Write these down in your own words. Try to stay true to what the original author intended. For example, if the author writes that you shouldn't mix bleach and ammonia, the summary shouldn't give the impression that it's okay to mix bleach and ammonia.

Concluding Sentence

Write a concluding sentence that restates the topic sentence or makes an observation about the original text. This concluding sentence helps bring the summary paragraph to a close and helps your reader understand what you consider to be important about the original text.

HOW TO Write a Summary Paragraph

- Reread the material to be summarized, underlining the important points.
- Write a topic sentence that includes the title, the author's name, and the main idea.
- Include the important points that you underlined while reading.
- Write a concluding sentence.
- Use your own words.

Using the Computer to Improve Summaries
Use your word-processing program to draft and revise a summary paragraph more quickly. Post your paragraph to a class Web site or e-mail it to your fellow students for suggestions for improvement.

ACTIVITY 3 (Group): Write a Summary

Individually, write a summary paragraph of the following paragraphs by Rebecca Hirschfield. Then, share your summary paragraphs with several classmates. Discuss ways to improve your summary paragraphs.

"The Lullaby Cure" by Rebecca Hirschfield

Hospitalization can stress out anyone, but especially severely premature babies, who are born neurologically immature. Florida State University music therapist Jayne Standley and her colleagues are reducing the trauma and speeding the pace of the infants' progression with a simple tool: a customized pacifier and a round of lullabies.

Babies born before the 34th week have not yet developed the crucial "suck-swallow-breathe" response required in feeding. To help preemies along, Standley and her colleagues invented a pressure-sensitive pacifier wired to a tape player that rewards hearty suckling with a lullaby. Researchers had previously found that playing lullabies noticeably reduces premature infants' hospital stays. Songs helped here too. Babies trained with the musical pacifier suckled 2.4 times as fast as those denied such reinforcement. Some drained an entire bottle of milk after just 15 minutes of condition. "We thought it was our imagination — the response seemed too dramatic," Standley recalls.

Ohmeda Medical in Columbia, Maryland, will begin selling a wireless version of the musical pacifier to neonatal intensive care units later this year.

For additional ways to prepare for upcoming exams, see pp. 428–30.

ADDITIONAL WRITING ASSIGNMENTS

1. Choose a passage from one of your textbooks and summarize it to prepare for an upcoming class discussion or exam.
2. Summarize what you learned about summarizing from reading this chapter.
3. Choose an article from a newspaper or magazine and summarize it for your classmates.
4. Watch a national news program on television and summarize what you learned for your instructor.

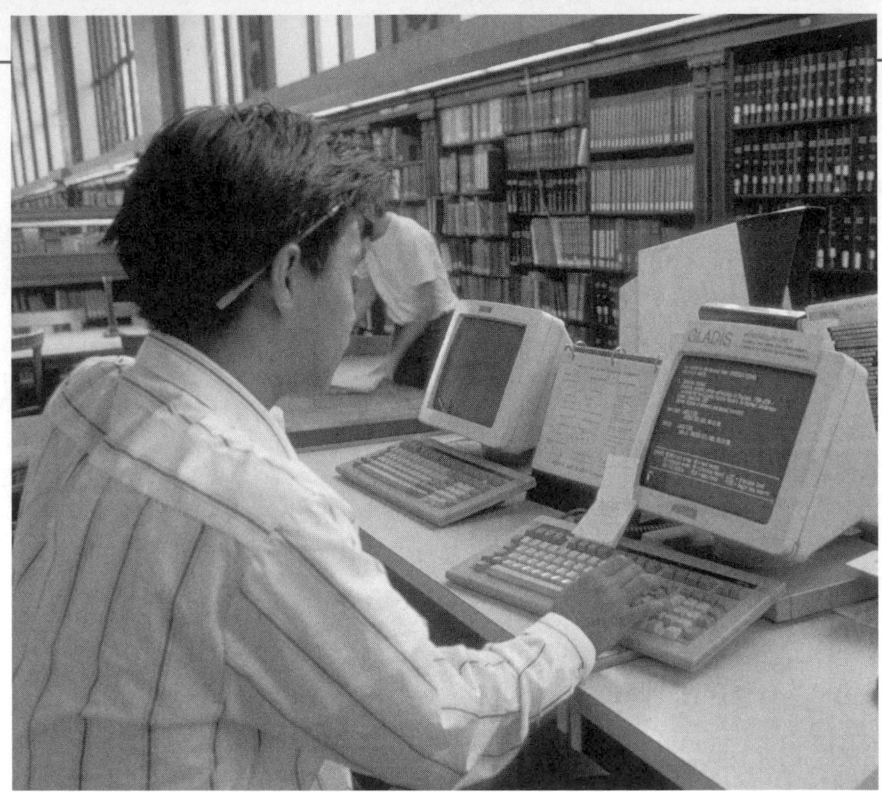

This young man is locating books and articles using a database he can access through his university's computer network. In this chapter, you will learn how to use and document sources in your own writing.

CHAPTER

20

Using Sources in Your Writing

In this chapter, you will

- learn what sources are.
- learn when you should use sources.
- discover how to find sources in the library and on the World Wide Web.
- find out how to evaluate sources.
- learn how to avoid plagiarism.
- learn how to take notes on sources.
- find out how to use and document sources in your writing.

UNDERSTANDING WHAT SOURCES ARE

A student who's writing an essay on vegetarianism for a nutrition class needs information about the benefits of giving up meat. An administrative assistant writing a memo requesting a raise wants statistics about the average wages for the job across the nation. A Girl Scout leader producing a newsletter for parents wants to know the origins of scouting in the United States.

These three examples illustrate how useful it is to know how to find and use information in your writing. Nowadays information is readily available, especially in libraries and on the Internet. As a result, you need to develop research skills so you can locate the information you need. You also need to know how to use this information in your writing. Developing these research and writing skills will make you more effective as a writer.

Definition of a Source

A source consists of a book, magazine, newspaper, or Web site that you access in the library or on the Internet. A source can also be an expert on your topic whom you interview. The idea, fact, or statistic that you gather from this source will support a particular point in your writing.

HOW TO Recognize an Essay That Uses Sources

- Some information is quoted. The author's name and the page number are given in parentheses.
- Some information is given without quotation marks because it's paraphrased, or put into the writer's own words. The source of the information and the page number are given in parentheses.
- A list of "works cited" at the end of the essay gives publishing information about the material that was quoted and paraphrased.

Writing Assignment

When have you used sources from the library or the World Wide Web in your writing? Write a paragraph for your classmates and instructor in which you describe a time when you had to use sources. You could describe a writing task that you did for school, work, or personal use. Explain the types of sources you found and how you used them in your writing.

KNOWING WHEN TO USE SOURCES IN YOUR WRITING

When to use sources depends on the type of writing you're doing. For writing assignments based on your own experience or knowledge, sources won't be necessary. For example, if you're writing a report for your supervisor about the products you have sold in the last three months, you won't need sources because the information you provide will come from your own records.

In contrast, if you're writing a paragraph or an essay on a topic beyond your own experience or knowledge, sources can help you demonstrate your points. The sources will give you information produced by experts on the topic. For instance, if you're writing a letter to your local newspaper about the need to conserve water, you could include information about the amount of water your city currently uses—information you access from the official Web site of the city engineer's office.

Consider your audience when deciding about sources. Read about audience on p. 20.

HOW TO Know When to Use Sources

- Don't use sources when you're writing about your own experience or knowledge.
- Consider using sources when your topic is beyond your own experience and knowledge.
- To be sure, ask your readers if they expect you to use sources in your writing.

FOCUSING YOUR SEARCH FOR SOURCES

Finding sources for your writing can be time-consuming unless you know exactly the information that you need. Therefore, write a draft of your paragraph or essay without sources first. Revise this draft until you know your main points. Then, write notes to yourself in the draft about the information you need.

When student writer Shannon wrote an essay for her University Studies class on the effect of going without sleep (called *sleep deprivation*) on college students, she wrote a discovery draft before she found sources to support her points. Here is a passage from her discovery draft, with notes to herself about the information she needed.

> First of all, what is sleep deprivation? [Find a definition.] The effects of sleep deprivation on college students can be harmful. Students have problems concentrating, which can affect their

grades. They are more likely to get into car accidents. [Find more effects of sleep deprivation.] Because of these negative effects, sleep deprivation is a condition that should be taken seriously.

When Shannon went to the library to find sources for her paper, she saved time because she knew exactly what information she needed.

HOW TO Focus Your Search for Sources

- Write at least one draft of your paper without sources.
- In the draft, write notes to yourself about the information you need.
- Use these notes to focus your research.

Write Notes in Color
To make your notes in your draft easier to spot, use the color function of your word-processing program to type them.

USING KEYWORDS

To find sources on a topic, you'll need to use *keywords,* or words that describe the topic. You'll use keywords to access information in the library or on the Internet. By changing your keywords, you can increase or decrease the number of sources you locate on a particular topic. To increase the number of sources, use keywords that are more general; to decrease the number, use keywords that are more specific.

When she began to research the topic of sleep deprivation, Shannon first used the keyword *sleep.* After typing in this word on the computer, she received the message that the computer program had found 4,900 articles on this topic. She then narrowed her search by typing in *sleep deprivation.* She was given a list of 199 articles. This was still too many articles for her to examine, so she typed in *sleep and college students.* This time she received a list of 15 articles, a number that she could manage.

HOW TO Use Keywords to Find Sources

- Write down a list of words that describe your topic. These are your keywords.
- Increase the number of sources by using keywords that are more general.
- Decrease the number of sources by using keywords that are more specific.
- Use *and* to join keywords if you want sources that contain both keywords.
- Use *not* to join keywords if you don't want sources that contain the second keyword, as in *sleep deprivation not disorders.*
- Keep trying different keywords until you find the sources you need.

English Research Room
To practice using keywords, access the English Research Room at **bedfordstmartins.com/english_research**.

ACTIVITY 1 (Group): Practice Using Keywords

With several classmates, list several writing topics. Brainstorm for keywords on each topic.

FINDING SOURCES IN THE LIBRARY

Generally, the first place to look for sources is in your college or public library. Library sources are valuable because they have been collected, organized, and screened by library professionals.

Books

If you consult a book on your topic, make sure it was recently published, within the last five years if possible. Also, you need to find out if its author is an expert in the field. Information about the author is usually given in the front or back of the book. If the author has an advanced degree in the field, most likely he or she is an expert. Finally, skim the book before you begin reading to see whether it contains the information you need. Examine the chapter titles and subheadings. Since you probably won't have time to read the whole book, you'll know which parts to read.

To locate books on your topic, do a subject (or topic) search in the library catalog, which most likely will be available online. You can search the catalog by title, author, subject, or keyword. Since you won't know the title or author of a book, do your search by typing in the subject heading or a keyword. The catalog will provide you with a brief description of any books the search finds and their call numbers. Each book in the library will have its call number on its spine and will be located on a shelf that is labeled with the call numbers it contains.

Reference Works

Some of the most useful sources you can use are reference works such as dictionaries and encyclopedias. A dictionary can provide you with definitions of important terms, while an encyclopedia entry can give you a broad overview of a topic. Encyclopedias are either *general,* such as *The World Book Encyclopedia,* or *specialized,* which means the book concerns only one subject area. For example, *The Encyclopedia of Psychology* is devoted to topics dealing with psychology.

Some dictionaries and encyclopedias are online. Printed reference books are located in the library's reference section. A librarian or a posted sign will tell you the location of this area. Articles in reference books usually are presented in alphabetical order according to their subjects.

Magazine Articles

To find a magazine article on your topic, consult a *periodical index,* which is a listing of magazine and newspaper articles. Some of the most useful periodical indexes are *InfoTrac, NexisLexis,* and *Readers' Guide to Periodical Literature.* Most libraries have their periodical indexes on computers. After accessing a periodical index, type in your subject or a keyword, and a list of articles will appear.

Student writer Shannon used the keywords *sleep and students* in *The Readers' Guide to Periodical Literature.* Here's one of the entries she received:

> **Teenagers in high school need proper amount of sleep to excel in school, study reveals. Source: Jet v. 91 (Feb. 10 '97) p. 62**

Shannon decided that this article might be useful, so she did a search in the library catalog to make sure that the library subscribed to *Jet.* From the catalog she got the call number for *Jet* and was able to find the magazine on the library shelves.

Many electronic periodical indexes contain the full text of the articles they list, so you won't need to locate the physical copy of the article on the library shelves.

Newspaper Articles

Finding a newspaper article on your topic is similar to finding a magazine article. First, you need to consult a periodical index. Some indexes that list only newspapers are *NewsBank* and *The New York Times Index*. Your local newspaper is probably indexed as well. After accessing the index on the computer, type in your subject or keyword, and a list of articles will appear. As with magazine articles, the full text of some newspaper articles may also appear in the index.

HOW TO Find Sources in the Library

- Find books by searching the library catalog. Be sure the books were recently published and written by experts. Read chapter titles and subheadings to determine whether a book contains the information you need.
- Find reference works (such as encyclopedias) online or in the reference section of your library.
- Find magazine and newspaper articles by searching indexes such as *Infotrac* or *NewsBank*.
- Use keywords to search the library catalog and indexes.

ACTIVITY 2: Locate Books and Articles

Choose a topic you're interested in and locate a book, reference-work entry, magazine article, and newspaper article on that topic. If you're going to write a paragraph or an essay on that topic, keep a record of the publishing information for each source. (See the list on pp. 455–56.)

FINDING SOURCES ON THE WORLD WIDE WEB

The Web contains an amazing amount of information, but this information isn't organized in any particular way. As a result, you need to use search engines and subject directories to find sources for your writing.

Search Tools: Search Engines and Subject Directories

Search tools—Web sites that you can use to look for specific kinds of information on the Web—include Google (www.google.com), Lycos (www.lycos.com), WebCrawler (www.webcrawler.com), and Yahoo! (www.yahoo.com). Search tools are based on two methods of searching: search engines and subject directories. A *search engine* uses keywords to sort through items on the Web. A *subject directory* sorts Web sites into categories and then allows you to search by keywords within categories. Most search tools combine the two methods. If you know exactly what keywords to look for, you may find the information you need faster by starting out with a search engine. On the other hand, starting out by using a subject directory may save you time by narrowing down your search so that you won't have so many search results to look through.

Useful Sites

The following Web sites contain useful information that might help you in your search for sources.

Online Encyclopedias

Britannica Online	www.eb.com
Encyclopedia Smithsonian	www.si.edu/resource/

News Sites

CNN News	www.cnn.com
MSNBC	www.msnbc.com
Newsweek	www.newsweek.com
Time	www.time.com

Mark Useful Web Sites
When you find a Web site that you'll want to return to, use the "bookmark" or "favorites" function of your Internet browser. This function will store the Web site's name and address so you can return to it later.

ACTIVITY 3 (Group): Use Search Engines and Subject Directories

With several classmates, choose a topic you're interested in and list keywords for that topic. Type those keywords into four different search tools, two that use only search engines and two that use subject directories. Compare and contrast your four searches. Explain to the class which search tools your group preferred and why.

EVALUATING SOURCES

As you begin to find sources on your topic, you'll need to make sure they're reliable and relevant.

Reliable Sources

To be reliable, a source needs to be accurate and objective. In other words, the source shouldn't try to twist the facts to make a point. Sources on the Web are often unreliable because people can post whatever they want. Check that your Web sources are produced by sponsors with good reputations, such as a well-known magazine or government organization. If you can't find information about the author or group that created the site, it's not a good source.

Relevant Sources

To be relevant, a source should directly relate to your topic. You might find a source that deals with your general topic but still doesn't give the information you're seeking. For instance, student writer Shannon found several sources on sleep deprivation and elderly people. Because her topic was sleep deprivation and college students, however, she didn't use these sources. To find relevant sources, use keywords that directly relate to your subject. In addition, read the title, headings, and subheadings of sources to make sure they'll give you the information you want.

HOW TO Evaluate Sources on the Web

- Check that Web sources are sponsored by well-respected organizations or companies.
- In general, avoid sources that are trying to sell something. Sources that have addresses with *.edu* (academic institutions) or *.gov* (government agencies) are usually the most reliable.
- Use appropriate keywords to find sources that directly relate to your topic.
- Read the title, headings, and subheadings of sources to make sure they relate to your topic.

Retrace a Web Search
Use the "history" function on your Internet browser to keep track of Web sites you have visited. This function makes it easier for you to remember how you arrived at a particular site.

ACTIVITY 4 (Group): Evaluate Web Sources

With several classmates, choose a topic you're interested in. Locate three sources on the Web on that topic. Evaluate each source to determine its reliability and relevance. As a group, present your evaluations to the class.

AVOIDING PLAGIARISM

Plagiarism occurs when you use someone else's words or ideas in your writing without revealing where those words or ideas came from. Plagiarizing can result in serious penalties, from failing a course to being expelled from college.

HOW TO Avoid Plagiarism

- As you research, keep track of the information you gather. Photocopy sources or save them to disk.
- When you use an author's exact words in your writing, put quotation marks around the words. Give the author and page number in parentheses, and include the source in your list of works cited.
- When you paraphrase (put someone else's words into your own words), give the author and page number in parentheses, and include the source in your list of works cited.

TAKING NOTES

As you're reading your sources, take notes on information that you might use in your writing.

Notecards

You can also keep notes in a learning log. Read about learning logs on pp. 420–21.

One way to take notes is to use three-by-five-inch index cards. On one side, write down the information about your topic and the page where you found it; at the top of this side, give the card a label to identify the information. On the other side of the card, record the information that identifies the source. Here's one of Shannon's notecards.

Daytime Sleepiness

"Recent statistics reveal that 53 percent of people ages 18 to 29 say they suffer from daytime sleepiness." Only 33 percent of people over 30 have daytime sleepiness.

p. 115

William C. Dement and Christopher Vaughn.

The Promise of Sleep: A Pioneer in Sleep Medicine Explores the Vital Connection between Health, Happiness, and a Good Night's Sleep. New York: Delacorte, 1999.

Following Shannon's example, put quotation marks around the author's exact words.

Information about Sources

As you take notes, you'll need to record information about your sources that you'll use when you write your paragraph or essay. This information varies according to the type of source. Here are descriptions of the information you'll need for various types of sources and the order in which you'll present that information.

Book: author, title, city and name of publisher, year of publication, page numbers

Entry in Reference Book: author (if given, it usually appears at the end of the entry), title, name of reference book, year of publication

Magazine Article: author, title, name of magazine, date of publication, page numbers of whole article, page numbers of information you used

Newspaper Article: author, title, name of newspaper, date of publication, name of edition (if given), section and page numbers of whole article, page numbers of information you used

Web Site: author of site and specific document, title of site and specific document, publication information for any print version of the source, name of any institution or organization that sponsors the site, date of online publication or most recent update, most recent date you accessed the site, address (URL) of Web page containing the information you used or (if that URL is very long or not provided) of the site's search page or homepage

HOW TO Take Notes on Your Sources

- Use three-by-five-inch index cards.
- On one side, write the information about your topic, the page number, and a label. Put quotation marks around any exact words you're copying.
- On the other side, write the publishing information (author, title, and so on).
- Double-check that you've written the correct publishing information for each type of source.

Taking Notes

Take notes in your word-processing program in a separate document or file. When you write your paragraph or essay, you can move back and forth between screens as you paste your notes into the text.

ACTIVITY 5: Practice Note-taking

Return to one of the sources you located earlier in this chapter. On an index card, take notes about a main idea in this source.

USING SOURCES TO SUPPORT YOUR MAIN IDEAS

Sources are useful for supporting your main ideas, but don't let the sources take over your writing. Your thoughts and voice should dominate. Generally, no more than 20 percent of your paragraph or essay should be quotations and paraphrases.

Quotations

Quotations contain the author's exact words. Introduce each quotation with a phrase such as *according to* or *as one expert has written.* After the quotation, put the author's last name and the page number of the quotation in parentheses. If you've already mentioned the author's name in your introductory phrase, just use the page number. If the quotation is at the end of a sentence, the period goes after the closing parenthesis.

> *As one sleep expert has written,* "Recent statistics reveal that 53 percent of people ages 18 to 29 say they suffer from daytime sleepiness" (Dement 118).

> *According to sleep expert William Dement,* "Recent statistics reveal that 53 percent of people ages 18 to 29 say they suffer from daytime sleepiness" (118).

Paraphrases

A *paraphrase* consists of someone else's ideas expressed in your own words. The advantage of using paraphrases instead of quotations is that the information is presented in your own style. Here's an example of a paraphrase.

> Sleep expert William Dement points out that more than half of those between the ages of 18 and 29 are often sleepy in the daytime, according to recent surveys (118).

As this example shows, a paraphrase not only uses different words from the original text, but it often also uses a different sentence structure. For example, the information that appears at the end of the sentence in the original source can appear at the beginning of the sentence in the paraphrase.

As with quotations, use an introductory phrase to signal readers that the information is paraphrased. Give the author's name and the page number in parentheses after the paraphrase, or give just the page number if you mention the author's name in the introductory phrase.

Summaries

A *summary* is a short version of a longer piece of writing. It contains only the important points of the piece and omits details and examples. The summary begins with the title of the piece, the author's name, and the main idea of the piece. The rest of the summary contains the supporting points. Quotations and paraphrases from the original piece are sometimes included. If you use a summary of outside

Read more about writing summaries in Chapter 19.

material in your essay, give the page number(s) of the material you are summarizing.

When you find a source related to your topic, consider summarizing it. Writing a summary can help you understand the source, as well as let you practice using quotations and paraphrases.

HOW TO Use Quotations, Paraphrases, and Summaries

- Limit quotations and paraphrases to no more than 20 percent of your paragraph or essay.
- Quote by putting quotation marks around the original words of the source.
- Paraphrase and summarize by putting the source's words into your own words.
- Introduce each quotation, paraphrase, and summary with a phrase such as *According to . . . .*
- After a quotation, a paraphrase, or a summary, put the author's name and the page number in parentheses. If the author has already been mentioned, just use the page number.
- Each quotation, paraphrase, and summary must be included in your list of works cited.
- Write a summary, or short version, of each of your sources to help you understand them.

ACTIVITY 6: Practice Summarizing, Quoting, and Paraphrasing

Choose one of the sources you have previously located and write a summary of it. Use at least one quotation and paraphrase.

DOCUMENTING SOURCES

To document your sources correctly, prepare a list of works cited and format each source correctly.

List of Works Cited

In addition to giving the author and page number of each of your sources in your paragraph or essay, you need to include a list of works cited at the end of the text. In this list you'll include the information that your readers need if they want to look up the sources themselves. Each source will have its own *citation,* or entry, in the list. This chapter follows the format for works cited used by the Modern Language Association (MLA), which is preferred in the field of English.

HOW TO Prepare a List of Works Cited

- Start the list on a new page.
- Put your last name and the page number in the upper-right-hand corner.
- Put *Works Cited* in the center of the first line.
- Double-space the entire page, even within citations.
- Alphabetize all the entries by the author's last name or by the title if no author is given for the source.
- Start each citation at the left-hand margin. If a citation is more than one line, indent the other lines one-half inch or five spaces.
- End each citation with a period.
- Underline or italicize the titles of books, encyclopedias, magazines, newspapers, and Web sites.
- Put in quotation marks the titles of magazine or newspaper articles and specific documents on Web sites.
- Give the publication information for each source, such as place of publication, publisher's name, and year for books, or the name of the magazine, journal, or newspaper and date of publication for articles.
- Include only the sources you actually mention in your paragraph or essay.

Correct Citation Format

The specific format of each citation depends on the type of source. Here are some of the more common types of MLA-style entries.

Book with One Author

Moorcroft, William H. Sleep, Dreaming and Sleep Disorders: An Introduction. Lanham: UP of America, 1993.

Book with More Than One Author

Payne, Wayne A., and Dale B. Hahn. Understanding Your Health. St. Louis: Times Mirror, 1986.

Encyclopedia Article

Radcliffe, Donald V. "Sleep." Compton's Encyclopedia. 1995 ed.

Magazine Article

Onderko, Patty. "Tired Teens: The Health Risk High Schools Ignore." American Health Sept. 1999: 56-57.

Newspaper Article

Brody, Jane E. "New Respect for the Nap, a Pause that Refreshes." New York Times 4 Jan. 2000: F7.

If a magazine or newspaper article appears on more than one page and the page numbers are not consecutive, give the number of the first page with a plus sign after it: "A1+."

Personal Interview

Andrew, Eric. Personal interview. 12 Oct. 2004.

Telephone Interview

McDowell, Laura. Telephone interview. 13 Sept. 2004.

Article from a Library Subscription Service

If your article came from an electronic database service that your library subscribes to, create the same citation that you would for the print version. If the service gives only the first page number, use a hyphen and a space after the number. Then add the name of the database, the name of the service, the name and location of the library, the date you accessed the article, and the Web address (URL) of the service's homepage, if it's available.

Baxter, S. "The Last Word on Gender Differences." Psychology Today Mar. 1994: 50- . Readers' Guide Abstracts. FirstSearch. U of Arizona Lib., Tucson. 13 Feb. 2002 <http://www.firstsearch.oclc.org>.

Document from a Web Site

When your source is a document from a Web site, give the author's name if known, the titles of the document and the site, the date of electronic publication or the most recent update, the name of any institution or organization that sponsors the site, the most recent date you accessed the site, and the address (URL). Put the URL in angle brackets. If the address won't fit on one line, divide it only after a slash, and don't add a hyphen after the slash.

"Adolescent Sleep Needs and Patterns." National Sleep Foundation. 2000. National Sleep Foundation. 24 Oct. 2000 <http://www.sleepfoundation.org/publications/sleep_andteens_report1.pdf>.

Use a Bibliography Program

Some software programs will organize your citation information into the proper formats for a particular documentation style. If you use such a program, be sure to check that all entries are correctly formatted for MLA style.

ACTIVITY 7 (Group): Practice Making a List of Works Cited

With several classmates, prepare a list of works cited that contains several sources that you have previously located.

SAMPLE ESSAY THAT USES SOURCES

Here is student writer Shannon's essay using sources. Note that she has formatted the essay according to the MLA documentation style.

1"

½"

Stein 1

Shannon Stein

Professor Kerns

UNIV 1301

22 March 2003

Five More Minutes?

Introduction catches reader's attention.

For college student Arlene, there aren't enough hours in the day. Her classes start early, she grabs a quick lunch, and her afternoon lab ends late. Work keeps her busy for a couple of hours, but now it's time to study. There's a chapter to be read for history, a rough draft to be written for English, and ten calculus problems to be completed before she can get some sleep. She really wants to talk to friends or see that new Nicole Kidman movie. But who has time? It's two a.m. already, and her day starts all over again in four and a half hours.

1" 1"

Thesis is stated.

Because college students tend to be young and healthy, they think that they can handle not getting enough sleep. In fact, in college, staying up all night to study for tomorrow's psychology exam seems to be a rite of passage. But the frequent or long-term lack of sleep, which is called sleep deprivation, can have serious negative consequences.

Information is paraphrased.

At what point can a person be considered sleep deprived? In the United States, the old saying is that everyone needs eight hours of sleep in order to be healthy. Sleep expert William C. Dement agrees that this average works for most people, but he feels that a better way of looking at sleep need is to figure one hour of sleep for every two hours of being awake (69).

Introductory phrase is used.

Recent research has shown, however, that people in one age group, those thirteen to nineteen years old, require at least ten hours of sleep per night (Holden 39). This group includes most first-year college

Stein 2

students. If classes, on average, start between 8:00 and 9:00 in the morning and students get up at 7:00 a.m. in order to get ready for class, then they would have to go to bed at 9:00 p.m. on average. That's not likely to happen, considering the demands on the time of most college students.

What happens, then, to all these sleepy students? According to the World Book Encyclopedia, people who go for long periods of time without enough sleep "lose energy and become quick tempered" (507). The longer they go without sleep, the harder it becomes for them to concentrate. If people go without sleep long enough, then they can actually have hallucinations or become psychotic (507).

Background information from a reference book is given.

In fact, researchers have found that "sleep deprivation can have some of the same hazardous effects as being drunk" ("Sleep Deprivation" 1). According to one psychologist, sleep loss not only makes it harder for students to learn but causes them to have more car wrecks, become more likely to use drugs, and become more violent (Dement and Vaughn 116).

Quotation is used.

Even if they don't suffer these more drastic consequences, staying awake during early morning classes is a physical challenge for students. Their bodies are crying out to be asleep. The stereotype is that college kids are lazy and party animals. The research suggests that maybe they are trying to do too much in one day.

What should be done? Congress is now offering money to high schools that are willing to start classes later in the day so that students can get more sleep in the morning (Holden 39). Perhaps colleges should consider offering more classes later in the morning. Or maybe college students should not sign up for early morning classes. In addition, people should be

Paraphrased information is used.

Stein 3

a little less judgmental about college students who sleep late on the weekend; they are not necessarily lazy, just sleep deprived.

Introductory phrase is used.

And maybe college students themselves need to consciously try to get to bed earlier. After all, the Journal of the American Medical Association recently published a study that shows that students who go to bed earlier receive higher grades than those students who consistently go to bed at later times. In fact, A and B students average thirty-five more minutes of sleep per night than D and F students ("Teenagers"). So if college students want a higher GPA, then they had better start making sleep as high a priority as they do class time and study time.

So what should college student Arlene do as she struggles through another day of sleepiness? As much as she doesn't want to admit it, Mom was right. Go to bed! Now!

1"

½"

Stein 4

Works Cited

Dement, William C., and Christopher Vaughn. The Promise of Sleep: A Pioneer in Sleep Medicine Explores the Vital Connection between Health, Happiness, and a Good Night's Sleep. New York: Delacorte, 1999.

Book

Hartmann, Ernest. "Sleep." The World Book Encyclopedia. 2000 ed.

Reference book

1" Holden, Constance. "Combating Student Torpor." Science 3 July 1998: 39. 1"

Magazine article

"Sleep Deprivation as Bad as Alcohol Impairment, Study Suggests." CNN.com.health. 20 Sept. 2000. Cable News Network. 15 Mar. 2003 <http://www.cnn.com/2000/HEALTH/09/20/sleepdeprivation>.

Web site

"Teenagers in High School Need Proper Amount of Sleep to Excel in School, Study Reveals." Jet 10 Feb. 1997. Readers' Guide Abstracts. FirstSearch. U of Texas-El Paso Lib. 15 Mar. 2003 <http://www.firstsearch.oclc.org/>.

Magazine article from an electronic database

ADDITIONAL WRITING ASSIGNMENTS

1. With several classmates, type your names into a Web search engine. Explore some of the sources you find. Present your findings to the class.
2. Choose a product you're interested in purchasing, such as a car, DVD, or cell phone. Research this product using library and Internet sources. Considering cost, reliability, and style, which brand would be the best for you to buy? Write a paragraph in which you explain your decision.
3. Who represents you in your local, state, and national government? Use library and Internet sources to compile names and addresses of these representatives. Write a letter to one of them about an issue that concerns you. Be sure to choose the representative who can best address this issue.
4. Choose a controversial issue that's in the news. Locate several library or Internet sources that take different positions on this issue. Summarize these sources. At the end of the summary, state your own position.

PART FOUR

Handbook with Exercises

When we write, we want to communicate our ideas clearly to demonstrate our knowledge of our topic and to ensure that our readers understand what we mean. In this Handbook you'll find opportunities to further practice and improve your writing. For example, you'll learn how to format a paragraph and an essay. You'll learn to improve your sentences and to combine short sentences into longer, more interesting ones. You'll learn how to vary your word choice and to eliminate errors. If you are a multilingual writer, you'll find an entire section devoted to helping you write more effectively.

Plan to use this Handbook in several ways. Use it as a reference guide when you have a question about format, sentence structure, grammar, spelling, or punctuation. Complete certain practice exercises to help you target specific errors that occur in your writing. Consult it during the editing stage to help you complete your editing log. And most important, use it to help eliminate errors from your writing.

HANDBOOK CONTENTS

CHAPTER 21

Formatting Paragraphs and Essays

You know whether you're attending a basketball game or a soccer match by the format of the game and the rules by which each is played. Like different sports, various writing assignments also have different formats. For example, lab reports, research papers, paragraphs, and essays are each developed using a particular format. The format signals readers what to expect from a specific piece of writing. The following are guidelines to help you format the paragraphs and the essays that you are writing for this textbook.

A. DEFINITION OF A PARAGRAPH

A *paragraph* is a group of sentences focused on one topic. A paragraph includes a topic sentence that states the main point that you want to communicate, followed by sentences that provide the ideas and details that support the topic sentence. It ends with a concluding sentence that restates your main point or summarizes your topic. When writing a one-paragraph paper, you also add a title. The title should introduce the topic and catch the reader's attention.

To review the parts of a paragraph, read p. 18.

Paragraph Format

A paragraph may be any length but usually runs about one hundred to two hundred words or about one-half to two-thirds of a double-spaced word-processed page. To prepare a one-paragraph paper, use the following format that includes a heading, a title, and one-inch margins.

[Your Name]
[Your Instructor's Name]
[Course Title and Number]
[Date]

Title

[Indent 5 spaces] Topic sentence: ______________________________

____.

Supporting detail 1: ______________________________________

____

____

____.

Supporting detail 2: ______________________________________

____.

____

____.

Supporting detail 3: ______________________________________

____

____.

____.

Concluding sentence: ______________________________________

To review ways to develop supporting details, see pp. 31–34.

ACTIVITY 1: Develop a Paragraph

On a separate sheet of paper, complete a one-paragraph paper using the following sentence starters. Remember to use the proper paragraph format shown in the sample.

Topic sentence: My favorite college instructor is ____________________.

Supporting detail 1: First, I admire this instructor because __________

____.

____

An example of this is ______________________________________

____.

Supporting detail 2: Another reason I admire this instructor is

____.

For example, ______________________________

____.

Supporting detail 3: The final reason I admire this instructor is

____.

For instance, ______________________________

____.

Concluding sentence: In conclusion, my favorite college instructor

____.

____

____

____

B. DEFINITION OF AN ESSAY

An *essay* is a group of paragraphs focused on one topic. An essay begins with an introductory paragraph that includes a thesis statement that states the main point you want to communicate. Next come paragraphs that provide the ideas and details that support the thesis statement. A short concluding paragraph ends an essay. An essay also includes a short, lively title to introduce the topic.

To review the parts of an essay, turn to p. 256.

Essay Format

An essay usually runs three to five double-spaced word-processed pages. To prepare an essay, use the format on p. 472, which includes a heading, a title, and one-inch margins.

Use Your Word-Processing Program to Format
Many word-processing programs contain templates for different types of writing assignments. Use one of these templates or save the essay template shown in the sample to your computer disk.

[Last Name and Page Number]

[Your Name]
[Your Instructor's Name]
[Course Title and Number]
[Date]

Title

[Indent 5 spaces] ____________________
____
____________________.

Thesis statement: ____________________
____________________.

[Indent 5 spaces] Topic sentence: ____________________
____________________.

Supporting details: ____________________
____
____________________.

[Indent 5 spaces] Topic sentence: ____________________
____________________.

Supporting details: ____________________
____
____________________.

[Indent 5 spaces] Topic sentence: ____________________
____________________.

Supporting details: ____________________
____
____________________.

[Indent 5 spaces] Concluding paragraph: ____________________
____
____
____________________.

ACTIVITY 2: Develop an Essay

On a separate sheet of paper, write an essay using the format shown in the sample and the following sentence starters.

[First paragraph] Introduction: The past year has been interesting because ______________________________

______________________________.

Thesis statement: My greatest accomplishment this past year was ___

______________________________.

[Second paragraph] Topic sentence: First, I ______________________________

______________________________.

Supporting details: For example, ______________________________

______________________________.

[Third paragraph] Topic sentence: Second, I ______________________________

______________________________.

Supporting details: For example, ______________________________

______________________________.

[Fourth paragraph] Topic sentence: Third, I ______________________________

______________________________.

Supporting details: For instance, ______________________________

______________________________.

[Fifth paragraph] Conclusion: In conclusion, I accomplished this because ______________________________

______________________________.

CHAPTER

22 Writing Sentences

Every sentence needs to have a subject and a verb and to express a complete thought.

A. SUBJECTS

The subject tells *who* or *what* is doing something or being something. Usually the subject is a noun — a person, place, or thing. But a subject can also be a pronoun — a word that takes the place of a noun.

Wilbur laughs.

He is in a good mood.

Compound Subjects

Sometimes a sentence has more than one subject. A subject with more than one part is called a *compound subject.*

Abid and Sam cooked the meal.

The monkey and the lion helped the princess.

Tips for Multilingual Writers

Be careful not to leave out the subject in a sentence.

INCORRECT	My sister likes her history course. Is her favorite class.
CORRECT	My sister likes her history course. *It* is her favorite class.
INCORRECT	Calls her daughter every day.
CORRECT	*Eloise* calls her daughter every day.

Remember not to include a pronoun that refers to the subject as part of the subject.

INCORRECT George he cooked the meal.

CORRECT George cooked the meal.

INCORRECT Cinderella she went to the ball.

CORRECT Cinderella went to the ball.

ACTIVITY 1: Add Subjects

Complete each of the following sentences by adding a subject.

EXAMPLE The old __dog__ sleeps all day.

1. My __________ works at the post office.
2. The _______________ complained about the cold weather.
3. ___________ and __________ worked together on the project.
4. Every _________ deserves lots of love.
5. __________ attended the soccer game.
6. The colorful __________ made the room much prettier.
7. This __________ needs your attention immediately.
8. Jamiel's ____________ was due at 10:00 a.m. on Friday.
9. __________ and __________ go rock climbing in New Mexico.
10. The ___________ employs many undergraduate students.

Subject Pretenders

Sometimes the subject of a sentence is hard to identify because of a *subject pretender.* One type of subject pretender is a prepositional phrase, which begins with a preposition.

Prepositions

A preposition is a word that expresses how other words are related in time, space, or another sense.

Common Prepositions

about	despite	on
above	down	out
after	during	over
against	except	past
among	for	since
as	from	to
at	in	toward
before	inside	under
behind	into	until
below	like	up
beneath	near	upon
beside	next to	with
between	of	within
by	off	without

Tips for Multilingual Writers

Prepositions that show time, such as *for, during,* and *since,* may have differences in meaning.

For usually refers to an exact period of time that something lasts, one that has a beginning and an end.

I worked as an accountant *for* two years.

The traffic has been stalled *for* thirty minutes.

I've been a student here *for* one month.

During usually refers to an indefinite period of time in which something happens.

Several times *during* the week I thought of you.

He wants to see his family sometime *during* the holidays.

It got cold *during* the night, but I don't know exactly when.

Since usually refers to a period of time that has passed between an earlier time and the present.

Since getting married, I've been happy.

Mae has lost weight *since* she became a vegetarian.

Eddie has been more outgoing *since* entering the first grade.

ACTIVITY 2: Identify Prepositions

Underline the prepositions in the following paragraph.

EXAMPLE Bridget and Thoren walked <u>to</u> the library.

Bridget and Thoren walked toward the reference desk. They had many questions for the reference librarian because they had a research project due in their sociology class the following week. Bridget left the assignment directions at home, but Thoren carried an extra copy with him between the pages of his sociology textbook. The librarian found several sociology reference books on the shelves behind her desk. She helped Bridget and Thoren find newspaper and magazine articles by using the library databases and looking under the most useful subject headings. They sent copies of the best articles to their e-mail accounts. Then, they photocopied entries from the reference books using the machine under the library stairs.

ACTIVITY 3: Add Prepositions

Complete each of the following sentences by writing a preposition in the space provided.

EXAMPLE I never leave home __without__ my cell phone.

1. The swimmer dove ____ the pool.
2. The novel *Beloved* was written ____ Toni Morrison.
3. Kendra wears several bracelets ____ her left wrist.
4. Evan bought a car ____ the Internet.
5. ______ her last class, Berta eats her lunch.
6. Malcolm goes to sleep every night ____ midnight.
7. Hiding your house key ______ the doormat is a bad idea.
8. Jessica had Dr. Chen ____ her statistics professor.
9. Entering the office, Bruce suspected everyone had been talking ______ him.
10. Every day, the children walked ____ a house that they thought was haunted.

Prepositional Phrases

A prepositional phrase consists of a preposition and its object. The object is a noun or pronoun, together with any words that describe or refer to the object. Here are some examples.

Preposition +	*Object*	= *Prepositional Phrase*
into	the classroom	into the classroom
before	you	before you
on	a bright summer day	on a bright summer day

ACTIVITY 4: Write Prepositional Phrases

Complete each of the following sentences by adding a prepositional phrase.

EXAMPLE The babysitter took the children for a walk.

1. Isaac bought his computer ______________.
2. My humanities study group meets __________.
3. Songs __________ are very popular.
4. The children ate the cookies that they found ___________.
5. When the power failed, I was __________.
6. ______________, James practiced his guitar.
7. ____________, the mechanic repaired the van.
8. Zaini caught the bus _________.
9. The sparrows flew _____________.
10. Everyone walked home ____________.

A prepositional phrase cannot be the subject of a sentence.

The groceries *in the car* need to be brought inside.

In the sentence above, *in the car* is a prepositional phrase. The subject of the sentence is *groceries.*

The doctor *from next door* bandaged my knee.

From next door is a prepositional phrase. The subject of the sentence is *doctor.*

Because you know that the subject of a sentence is never in a prepositional phrase, you can find the subject easily. First, cross out all the prepositional phrases; then, decide which of the other words is doing something or being something.

The girl ~~in the doorway~~ looks ~~like my niece.~~

The subject of the sentence is *girl.*

The bell ~~on the steeple~~ ~~of the church~~ rang three times.

The subject of the sentence is *bell.*

HOW TO Find the Subject of a Sentence

- Cross out all prepositional phrases.
- Decide which of the remaining words is doing something or being something.

ACTIVITY 5: Identify Prepositional Phrases and Sentence Subjects

In each of the following sentences, cross out the prepositional phrases and circle the subject.

EXAMPLE The book ~~on the table~~ was open.

1. The tenants down the hall are seldom home.
2. Darryl bought a used car for three thousand dollars.
3. The flowers in that yard need to be watered.
4. After the midterm, the biology class became more difficult.
5. Inside those boxes, you will find my old textbooks.
6. The guests at the party appreciated the DJ.
7. Without his friends, Rashid felt somewhat shy.
8. The information from that Web site is not very reliable.
9. The questions on the worksheet covered the last seven chapters.
10. Two of Kristina's best friends joined a sorority.

ACTIVITY 6: Identify Subject Pretenders

In the following paragraph, cross out the prepositional phrases and circle the subject of each sentence.

EXAMPLE The (paintings) ~~in the entryway~~ belong to donors.

Everybody who participated in the art show benefited from the experience. One of my classmates from my drawing class won a prize for his entry. Consequently, three of his drawings now are on display at City Hall. Although I did not win anything, I received dozens of compliments on my ceramics. Three people who asked for my telephone number have ordered vases from me. Around the park where the show took place was a temporary fence made of plywood. Graffiti artists painted the fence with their best efforts. This fence was the most popular work of art at the show. It has been moved to an elementary school that needed a new fence along a busy street.

B. VERBS

The *verb* in a sentence expresses action or links the subject to the rest of the sentence.

Action Verbs

In the following sentences, the verb expresses action.

Mary Louise *drives* the truck.

The dog *ate* my homework.

The musician *played* a great set of songs.

Linking Verbs

In these next sentences, the verb links the subject to the rest of the sentence. The most common linking verbs are forms of the verb *to be: am, are, is, was, were, be, been, being.*

I *am* tall.

The children *were* hungry.

Miriam *is* ready to graduate.

Helping Verbs

Helping verbs include *am, are, is, was, were, be, have, has, had, do, does, did, may, might, must, can, could, shall, should, will, would.* A helping verb is used with another verb form, called the main verb, to form a phrase that acts as the verb of the sentence.

Moira *was helping* her brother change the tire.

Cho *had studied* all night.

You *must register* before the end of the month.

Compound Verbs

Sometimes a sentence has more than one verb. A verb with more than one part is called a *compound verb*.

Alfred Hitchcock *frightened* and *thrilled* moviegoers.

The children *sat* and *waited* for their parents to get them.

I *can use* your help and *would be* grateful for it.

ACTIVITY 7: Identify Subjects and Verbs in Sentences

In each of the following sentences, circle the subject and underline the verb.

EXAMPLE (I) enjoy singing in front of people.

1. My friend and I sing every week at a retirement home.
2. Currently, we are the only visitors who sing.
3. We have enjoyed the visits immensely.
4. A doctor arranged our visits last year.
5. We accepted her offer immediately.
6. The residents and employees enjoy our weekly visits.
7. The residents have asked us to come more often.
8. A new piano arrived last month.

9. It has improved our performance.
10. The audience requests different songs for every concert.

ACTIVITY 8: Add Verbs

Complete each of the following sentences by adding a verb.

EXAMPLE A typical student desires many electronic devices, such as a computer, calculator, and personal CD player.

1. A successful businessperson ______ a thousand dollars to the free clinic.
2. Rosario ______ Employee of the Month.
3. A pack of dogs ______ our backyard last summer.
4. The activity leader ______ the children to sign up for free swimming lessons.
5. Armando ______ a dozen roses on the table.
6. Social workers ______ the case of the abandoned children.
7. Frederick ______ overnight at a friend's house before the big test.
8. The track team ______ at the football field.
9. Police officers ______ the hillside for clues.
10. Many champion ice skaters ______ their training at a very young age.

Verb Pretenders

Verb pretenders (also called *verbals*) look like verbs but do not act as verbs in sentences. The most common verb pretenders are verb + *-ing* and *to* + verb combinations.

cooking	to cook
working	to work
studying	to study

Verb + -ing

When an *-ing* verb appears in a sentence without a helping verb, it does not act as the verb of the sentence. Instead, it modifies, or describes, other words in the sentence.

I took a picture of the man *swimming* in the fountain. (*Swimming* describes the man.)

Working hard, we completed the job in a day. (*Working* describes the subject of the sentence, *we.*)

The *barking* dogs kept me awake at night. (*Barking* describes the dogs.)

ACTIVITY 9: Identify -*ing* Verbs

In the space provided, indicate whether the -*ing* verb in each of the following sentence acts as a modifier or as part of a verb.

EXAMPLE The drooping plant needed to be watered. modifier

1. Claudia is driving across the United States. ________
2. Joanne sent her father a singing telegram for his birthday. ________
3. That diving board is too slippery. ________
4. I was diving into the waves when I scraped my knee. ________
5. The biscuit recipe requires a tablespoon of baking powder. ________
6. Stamping on the accelerator, William made his tires screech. ________
7. Susan is leaving on vacation the day after tomorrow. ________
8. Brent went to the mall for a new pair of running shoes. ________
9. Because of her back problems, Kata felt better sleeping on the floor. ________
10. Jumping up and down, the children showed their excitement. ________

ACTIVITY 10: Use Verbs and Verb Pretenders

For each of the following -*ing* verbs, write two sentences. In the first sentence, use the word as a verb. (You'll need a helping verb, too.) In the second sentence, use the word as a modifier to describe another word.

EXAMPLE working

Verb: Jared was working in the dean's office.

Modifier: I cannot find a working computer in the lab.

1. sewing

   Verb: ______

   Modifier: ______

2. running

   Verb: ______

   Modifier: ______

3. whistling

   Verb: ______

   Modifier: ______

4. glowing

   Verb: ______

   Modifier: ______

5. cutting

   Verb: ______

   Modifier: ______

To + *Verb*

The *to* + verb combination also looks like a verb but does not act as a verb in a sentence; instead, it acts as either a noun or a modifier that describes something.

I can't wait to open my gifts. [Because *to* comes in front of *open, open* does not act as a verb. Instead, *to open* modifies *wait.*]

I always open my gifts before my birthday. [Here *open* acts as a verb.]

Susan had a plan to buy apples. [Because *to* comes in front of *buy, buy* does not act as a verb. Instead, *to buy* modifies *plan.*]

Susan buys apples from the farm. [Here *buys* acts as a verb.]

My goal is to study medicine. [Because *to* comes in front of *study, study* does not act as a verb. Instead, *to study* acts as a noun.]

Many Americans study medicine overseas. [Here *study* acts as a verb.]

HOW TO Find the Verb in a Sentence

- Locate the word or words that express the action or link the subject to the rest of the sentence.
- Check that the word is not a verb pretender.
- When a verb + *-ing* combination appears in a sentence without a helping verb, it's a verb pretender.
- When a *to* + verb combination appears, it's a verb pretender.

ACTIVITY 11: Use *to* + verb Combinations

Complete each of the following sentences with a *to* + *verb* combination.

EXAMPLE Mauricio used a hammer to crack the coconut.

1. Rebecca waited ____________________.
2. ____________________ was the children's favorite thing to do.
3. Sunay promises ____________________.
4. Half the apartments in this building do not seem ____________________.
5. Before sitting down to breakfast, Erica's parents needed ____________________.
6. ____________________ is Kyle's only chore this morning.
7. Bryan likes ____________________.
8. After a day of skiing, Richard and Elizabeth want ____________________.
9. Connie's old job was ____________________.
10. ____________________ may be Lon's greatest talent.

ACTIVITY 12: Find Subjects and Verbs

In each of the following sentences, circle the subject and underline the verb. Do not confuse verbs and verb pretenders.

EXAMPLE The smiling (woman) <u>accepted</u> the award.

1. Kim agreed to have the meeting at her house.
2. While taping the playoffs, Hugo watched a documentary.
3. Stepping carefully, Nizar tried to avoid the wet paint.
4. The hikers reached their campground by sunset.
5. Mosquitoes were annoying the sunbathers.
6. Adam washed his hands before kneading the bread dough.
7. The people on the street hoped to glimpse the famous actress.
8. Opening the newspaper, Maya began to read the classified ads.
9. After work, Tim and Linda lack the energy to cook dinner.
10. Slipping the diamond ring on Leticia's finger, Nahum asked her to marry him.

ACTIVITY 13: Identify Subjects and Verbs

In the following paragraph, circle the subjects and underline the verbs.

EXAMPLE (Ivor) decided to major in music.

Ivor needed to interview a local drummer for a term project. Before contacting the musician, he read about her career. Feeling nervous, he wrote her a letter to request an appointment. To his surprise, the drummer invited him to watch a rehearsal. Her band was playing a new song. Ivor took many notes while listening to them. He wanted to describe his first impressions completely. After the rehearsal, the band kept asking him questions about his assignment. Answering the musicians politely, he wondered how to change the subject. Finally, the drummer told the band to let Ivor begin his interview.

Verb Tense

For more help with verb tense, including irregular verbs, see pp. 488–89.

The *tense* of a verb shows the time that the action or condition takes place. The three basic tenses in English are *present, past,* and *future.*

The *present tense* shows an action or condition taking place at the time the writer is writing. The present tense can also show an action that happens more than once.

Bruce *has* a big kitchen.

He *cooks* every evening.

The *past tense* shows something that began and ended in the past. To form the past tense of most verbs, use the *-ed* form of the verb.

Last week, Bruce *cooked* for his friends and family.

The *future* tense shows something that will take place or will probably take place. To form the future tense, use *will* or *be going to* and the present tense of the verb.

I *will learn* the periodic table next week.

These studies *are going to* make a difference in my grade.

As a general rule, stay with the tense you begin with at the start of a paragraph unless the time you are talking about changes. Avoid shifting from one tense to another for no reason, because these shifts may confuse your readers.

ACTIVITY 14: Correct Awkward Shifts in Verb Tense

Edit the following paragraph to correct unnecessary shifts in verb tense. The first sentence in the paragraph is correct.

EXAMPLE My stepdaughter angered me, but I ~~try~~ tried to understand.

For a long time, my stepdaughter, Jeannie, was unhappy to have me as part of her family. I try to get to know her better, but she will complain that I invade her privacy. As a newcomer, I understood that our relationship will require effort from both of us. It was not enough that I was friendly. Jeannie also has to want us to be friends. I am not happy with the two of us being strangers, but I can wait for her to feel more comfortable around me.

ACTIVITY 15: Correct Awkward Shifts in Verb Tense

Edit the following paragraph to correct unnecessary shifts in verb tense. The first sentence in the paragraph is correct.

EXAMPLE Manny finds bottles on old farmland, where he like~~d~~s to explore.

Manny collects antique bottles. He will buy bottles if he liked them, but he prefers to find them in the ground. He will find bottles everywhere. However, he has the best luck at construction sites on old farmland. Often, bottles appeared on the surface after a good rain. He will use special tools for excavating bottles, including a set of brushes. He did not want to break the bottles as he removed them from the ground. After finding a new bottle, Manny will add it to his display case.

Regular Verbs

Regular verbs are verbs whose past tense and past participle end in *-ed*. Past participles are forms of a verb that are used with *has, have,* or *had,* as in the following examples.

I *have* studied Spanish for two years.

My father *had drunk* all of the free champagne.

Common Regular Verbs

Verb	*Past Tense*	*Past Participle*
cook	cooked	cooked
measure	measured	measured
study	studied	studicd
walk	walked	walked

Irregular Verbs

Irregular verbs are verbs whose past tense and past participle do not end in *-ed* but are formed in a variety of other ways. As a result, they are often misused or misspelled. Review the forms of irregular verbs so you won't make errors.

Common Irregular Verbs

Verb	*Past Tense*	*Past Participle*
be	was, were	been
begin	began	begun
catch	caught	caught
choose	chose	chosen
come	came	come
do	did	done
drink	drank	drunk
eat	ate	eaten
feel	felt	felt
fly	flew	flown
get	got	got, gotten
go	went	gone
leave	left	left
ride	rode	ridden
seen	saw	seen

ACTIVITY 16: Identify Regular and Irregular Verbs

In each of the following sentences, underline the verb and identify it as a regular or an irregular verb.

EXAMPLE The letter carrier knocked on the door. Regular

1. Tama placed the lettuce in the bowl. ________
2. Devi knew Henry and Paolo already. ________
3. Somebody stole my wallet! ________
4. Dwayne watched television at night. ________
5. Wei cooked dinner for his family. ________
6. The moths flew around the lamp. ________
7. Alice drank a bottle of water. ________
8. Zafir caught a cold on the airplane. ________
9. The mechanic looked under the hood. ________
10. The telephone rang at midnight. ________

ACTIVITY 17: Use Regular and Irregular Verbs

In each of the following sentences, write the correct form of the verb in the space provided. If necessary, consult your dictionary for the correct form.

EXAMPLE Richard found his sunglasses in his car. *(find)*

1. When he was little, Jaime ______ his money in a shoe box. *(keep)*
2. Isabel has ______ with a rock band for five years. *(sing)*
3. Last semester, Charlie ______ about his grades. *(worry)*
4. Yesterday morning, the actors ______ very convincing in their costumes. *(look)*
5. Patrick and Hugh have ______ music at every school in town. *(teach)*
6. Experts say that the ocean liner *Titanic* ______ because it was badly made. *(sink)*
7. My grandfather ______ that picture when he was twelve years old. *(draw)*
8. Who has ______ my car without my permission? *(drive)*
9. The brothers ______ for hours at the family reunion last August. *(talk)*
10. Sigrid has ______ Naomi for her lab partner. *(choose)*

C. SUBJECT-VERB AGREEMENT

A complete sentence contains a subject and a verb. The subject tells who or what is doing something or being something, and the verb expresses the action or links the subject to the rest of the sentence. To maintain *subject-verb agreement,* a singular subject must have a singular verb form and a plural subject must have a plural verb form.

Singular and Plural Forms

A *singular* subject consists of one thing.

the student

A singular verb form in the present tense usually ends in *-s.*

studies

The student studies for the test.

A plural subject consists of more than one thing.

the students

A plural verb form in the present tense generally does not end in *-s*.

study

The students study for the test.

To check for subject-verb agreement, you must first identify the subject of the sentence. Remember that prepositions and other words sometimes occur between the subject and verb. Once you identify the subject, you can add the correct verb form.

INCORRECT *Elaine go* to the amusement park. [singular subject, plural verb form]

CORRECT *Elaine goes* to the amusement park. [singular subject, singular verb form]

INCORRECT The *cars swerves* to avoid hitting the fence. [plural subject, singular verb form]

CORRECT The *cars swerve* to avoid hitting the fence. [plural subject, plural verb form]

ACTIVITY 18: Identify Subject-Verb Agreement

In each of the following sentences, underline the correct verb form.

EXAMPLE The cat (<u>naps</u>, nap) every afternoon.

1. This book (costs, cost) less at the store across the street.
2. The runners (competes, compete) against one another every year.
3. The door (sticks, stick) in rainy weather.
4. The airlines (offers, offer) advice for children traveling alone.
5. Lester (works, work) as a team mascot.
6. Strawberries (remains, remain) fresh for only a few days.
7. Dr. Darin (sees, see) patients late in the day.
8. Phoebe (drives, drive) a vintage automobile.
9. Kathy and Karen (attends, attend) an accelerated science program.
10. Dancing (is, are) a form of art, a form of exercise, and a form of recreation.

ACTIVITY 19: Add Verbs that Agree

Add a singular or plural verb form to each of the following sentences as needed to maintain subject-verb agreement.

EXAMPLE My mother-in-law __bakes__ the best empanadas.

1. At sunset, the canyon ______ especially beautiful.
2. Your friends ______ your good grades.
3. This radio ______ only three AM stations.
4. Those Web sites ______ the best information on hang gliding.
5. Colleen ______ Japanese and Arabic.
6. Cookies ______ better fresh from the oven.
7. Professor Byer ______ her students to ask questions in class.
8. Leonard ______ at a gym several times a week.
9. Tracy and Lincoln ______ to work together.
10. Stretching ______ an effective way to relax.

Read about subject pretenders on pp. 475–79.

To determine correct subject-verb agreement, be sure that you have correctly identified the subject. Watch out for subject pretenders such as prepositional phrases.

INCORRECT The bowl of cookies *are* on the table. [The prepositional phrase *of cookies* is a subject pretender.]

CORRECT The bowl of cookies *is* on the table. [*The bowl* is the subject of the sentence.]

ACTIVITY 20: Use Correct Verbs

In each of the following sentences, underline the correct verb form.

EXAMPLE The house that is in the photographs (belongs, belong) to my grandmother.

1. To run seven miles (is, are) my goal.
2. The pieces of gum (sticks, stick) to the roof of my mouth.
3. The cat stuck in the bushes (needs, need) to be rescued.
4. The clouds on the horizon (looks, look) threatening.

5. The movies that I like best (is, are) romances and thrillers.
6. One of the children (has, have) a bad cold.
7. To beat my brother in checkers (is, are) my greatest wish in the world.
8. Jennifer Lopez's marriages (is, are) always in the news.
9. Remakes such as *Freaky Friday* often (becomes, become) more successful than the original movie.
10. My pet ferrets, whose names are George and Laura, (eats, eat) more food than I do.

ACTIVITY 21: Maintain Subject-Verb Agreement

Add a singular or plural verb form to each of the following sentences as needed to maintain subject-verb agreement.

EXAMPLE The books on the table belong to Missy.

1. The programs on that television station all _______ reruns.
2. The vase of roses _______ on the coffee table.
3. The hostess who greets the customers _______ a good first impression.
4. Those mushrooms around that tree _______ poisonous.
5. That storeroom, filled with broken computers and printers, _______ to be cleaned out.
6. Professor Wurst, joined by many of his students, _______ for animal rights.
7. The cantaloupes on the kitchen counter _______ ripe.
8. The children at that preschool _______ excellent care.
9. Owen's collection of coins and stamps _______ valuable.
10. A jar full of breadcrumbs _______ in the freezer.

ACTIVITY 22: Insert Correct Verbs

Insert a correct verb form in each of the blanks in the following paragraphs.

EXAMPLE The Dallas Cowboys, which has been called America's team, (needs, need) a new quarterback.

Many people are interested in football, but few people are as obsessed as my husband. Bob, who has been my husband for three years, is in love with the sport. Being married to a football fanatic has its drawbacks. During the football season, each and every Sunday is dedicated to the sport. Bob and his friends gather at our house before noon to begin watching the games. Fortunately, his friend Alex, who is one of the best cooks I've ever met, brings the snacks and drinks. All day I hear cheers and boos coming from the living room. Bob and his friends take the game so seriously they get depressed when their teams lose. Personally, I'd rather have a hobby that is less stressful.

Indefinite Pronouns

Sometimes the subject of a sentence is an *indefinite pronoun.* Here are some singular indefinite pronouns that take singular verb forms.

anybody	everyone	nothing
anyone	everything	somebody
anything	nobody	someone
each	no one	something
everybody		

INCORRECT Each of us *need* to pay five dollars. [*Each* is singular and requires a singular verb form.]

CORRECT Each of us *needs* to pay five dollars.

INCORRECT Anyone *know* the answer. [singular pronoun, plural verb form]

CORRECT Anyone *knows* the answer. [singular pronoun, singular verb form]

INCORRECT Everybody *go* to the movies on Friday night. [singular pronoun, plural verb form]

CORRECT Everybody *goes* to the movies on Friday night. [singular pronoun, singular verb form]

HOW TO Check for Subject-Verb Agreement

- Remember that singular subjects take singular verb forms, and plural subjects take plural verb forms.
- Be sure that you have correctly identified the subject.
- Watch out for subject pretenders, such as prepositional phrases.
- Indefinite pronouns such as *everyone, anyone, something,* and *no one* are singular and take singular verb forms.

ACTIVITY 23: Identify Subject-Verb Agreement

In each of the following sentences, underline the correct verb form.

EXAMPLE Something about that book (makes, make) me uneasy.

1. Nothing about that movie (is, are) worthwhile.
2. Everybody with a special decal (parks, park) in the same lot.
3. Somebody living on my street (plays, play) loud music late at night.
4. No one in that laboratory (has, have) a degree in science.
5. Something inside the car (makes, make) a strange clunking noise.
6. Everyone in Carly's family (speaks, speak) a foreign language.
7. Everything remaining on the floor (does, do) not belong there.
8. Nobody with a new computer (uses, use) the old software.
9. Someone with red lipstick (leaves, leave) smudges on the cloth napkins.
10. Anything on the boat made of wood (requires, require) a waterproof finish.

ACTIVITY 24: Add Singular Verbs

Add a singular verb form to each of the following sentences to maintain subject-verb agreement.

EXAMPLE No one in the room ___needs___ to stand up.

1. Everyone on the Ferris wheel ______ a little queasy.
2. Someone at this company ______ information to a competitor.

3. Anything on this table _______ a dollar or less.
4. Somebody _______ to go to the supermarket.
5. Nobody _______ Sunay to fail.
6. Something in this room _______ like lemons.
7. Nothing _______ wrong with your project.
8. Everything in the garage _______ to Sid and Marnie.
9. No one in our tour group _______ the tour guide.
10. Everybody _______ to return next year.

ACTIVITY 25: Write Sentences with Correct Subject-Verb Agreement

Complete each of the following sentences, making sure that the verb you add agrees with the subject that is provided.

EXAMPLE Everybody goes to Frank's Grill after work on Friday.

1. These young couples _______________________________.
2. This magazine _______________________________.
3. Everyone on this list _______________________________.
4. We _______________________________.
5. I _______________________________.
6. None of the telemarketers _______________________________.
7. The little boy who should have a permission slip _______________ _______________________________.
8. The director of the church choir _______________ _______________________________.
9. The presidents of both classes _______________________________.
10. Nobody _______________________________.

ACTIVITY 26: Select Subjects and Verbs That Agree

In the following paragraph, underline the correct verb forms.

EXAMPLE Shelfu (feel, feels) proud of his Chinese heritage.

Shelfu (belongs, belong) to a troupe of lion dancers. Beginning in October, Shelfu meets once a week with the other lion dancers and (begins, begin) rehearsing for Chinese New Year. After being in the troupe for three years, Shelfu now (dances, dance) as the lion's head. He (shakes, shake) the mane and (pretends, pretend) to roar. Being the lion's head (is, are) a great honor as well as hard work. After Christmas, as Chinese New Year approaches, the troupe members, who all attend the same university, (rehearses, rehearse) every night. Everyone (looks, look) forward to the festivities. In addition to dancing in the New Year's parade, the group of dancers (visits, visit) city schools to teach children something about Chinese culture. The children sitting closest to the lion (screams, scream) when it approaches them. The dancing creature, with his comical but threatening gestures, (delights, delight) and (frightens, frighten) young spectators.

ACTIVITY 27: Correct Subject-Verb Agreement

Revise the following paragraph as needed to correct errors in subject-verb agreement.

EXAMPLE Victoria's job of managing a plumbing supply business satisfies ~~satisfy~~ her.

Victoria manage her father's plumbing supply business. The first thing every morning, with the telephone already ringing, she turns on the computer and take the first orders of the day. The orders early in the morning is usually for emergency jobs and generates repeat business. Victoria's father, who has a good reputation among local plumbers, ask her to give these orders priority. No one, especially someone with clogged pipes, want to wait longer than necessary for repairs. Filling emergency orders are not Victoria's only job duty. She maintains the company budget and decide which bills to pay each day. Surrounded by boxes of hardware, Victoria admit that she had expected to work somewhere more glamorous after receiving her business degree. However, everybody who remembers the company before her improvements admire her work. Her decision to computerize office procedures have made the company more efficient and more profitable.

CHAPTER

23

Expanding Sentences

In addition to containing subjects and verbs, sentences can be expanded to include phrases, clauses, pronouns, adjectives, and adverbs. These expansions give you the opportunity to express yourself effectively for a variety of audiences.

A. PHRASES

If a group of words lacks a subject or a verb or both, it's a *phrase.* A phrase is not a complete sentence. Notice the difference between phrases and sentences in these examples:

See pp. 474–79 and 480–89 for more information about subjects and verbs.

PHRASE To get a good lock for my house.

SENTENCE To get a good lock for my house, I need to talk to a locksmith.

PHRASE To come up with the right answer.

SENTENCE Pam was unable to come up with the right answer.

PHRASE Making her a good dinner.

SENTENCE I want to please my girlfriend by making her a good dinner.

PHRASE Such as a new backpack, a Barbie, a walkie-talkie, a stuffed lizard, and even a computer.

SENTENCE My daughter says she wants a lot of things for her birthday, such as a new backpack, a Barbie, a walkie-talkie, a stuffed lizard, and even a computer.

PHRASE On the shelf.

SENTENCE I can't reach the box on the shelf.

ACTIVITY 1: Identify Phrases and Sentences

For each of the following items, write *S* next to the word groups that are sentences and *P* next to the word groups that are phrases.

EXAMPLE Within the last five years. P

1. To drive down the mountain at night. ___
2. Before paying the bill, she carefully reviewed the statement. ___
3. To find a new job, Felicia updated her computer skills. ___
4. On Tuesday my kindergarten students. ___
5. The anthrax scare turned out to be a hoax. ___
6. For example, a computer, a cell phone, and a DVD player. ___
7. Over there on the table. ___
8. We pushed open the gate. ___
9. To study for Spanish, English, pre-calculus, biology, and economics. ___
10. The fire in the national forest was caused by a careless smoker. ___

ACTIVITY 2: Turn Phrases into Sentences

Expand each of the following phrases into a complete sentence.

EXAMPLE after the rain

After the rain, the air has a fresh smell.

1. talking with their friends

____

____

2. before the start of the semester

____

____

3. finished the group project

4. due to the increase in prices

5. to maintain a good relationship

6. avoiding his old friends from high school

7. a flight of creaky stairs

8. the park in my family's neighborhood

9. an unusual but attractive hairstyle

10. saving her wages from her after-school job

ACTIVITY 3: Connect Phrases to Sentences

Revise the following paragraph to connect the phrases to the sentences that come before or after them.

EXAMPLE Families need to be flexible/In order to deal with hard times.

Ever since my early teen years. My parents have had an untraditional marriage. My mother held a full-time job while my father stayed at home. Taking care of us kids. Until I was thirteen, both my parents worked full-time. Then my dad lost his job. Mom earned enough to support a family as a buyer. For a large department store. She frequently had to travel. The whole family enjoyed her stories about the exciting places she visited. Including Beverly Hills, New York City, Paris, and Milan. It also was comforting having Dad there for us. Caring for us when we were sick and congratulating us when we did well at school. Because of this unconventional arrangement. We kids learned that people sometimes have to be flexible to succeed.

B. CLAUSES

A clause can be a whole sentence or a part of a sentence. There are two kinds of clauses: independent and dependent.

Independent or Main Clauses

An *independent clause,* also called a *main clause,* is a group of words with a subject and a verb that can stand alone as a complete sentence. All sentences contain at least one independent clause, and some contain more than one.

Pat enjoyed his first tennis lesson. [This sentence is an independent clause because it contains a subject and a verb and can stand alone as a sentence.]

He learned to hit a forehand lob, and he learned to serve. [This sentence consists of two independent clauses.]

He decided to sign up for more lessons through the summer. [This sentence consists of one independent clause.]

HOW TO Identify an Independent Clause

- Check that the word group has a subject and a verb.
- Check that the word group can stand alone as a sentence.

ACTIVITY 4: Write Independent Clauses

Expand each of the following word groups into a sentence so that it contains an independent clause.

EXAMPLE After my divorce, I felt determined not to make the same mistake again.

1. The day my divorce became final ________________.
2. Although my wife and I were not getting along, ________________.
3. Because I had sworn to be with her forever, ________________.
4. ________________ even though we tried so hard to stay together.
5. Because we had no children, ________________.
6. When we saw each other for the last time, ________________.
7. ________________ because the bad memories are fading.
8. A year after the divorce, ________________.
9. Although I haven't found someone else to love, ________________.
10. Because I don't want to make the same mistake again, ________________.

Dependent or Subordinate Clauses

Although a *dependent clause* contains a subject and a verb, it cannot stand alone as a sentence. To be part of a complete sentence, it needs to be attached to or part of an independent clause. Dependent clauses are also called *subordinate clauses* because they often begin with one of these words, called *subordinating conjunctions*:

after	if	until
although	since	when
as	that	where
because	though	while
before	unless	

Because my car broke down, I had to reschedule the dentist appointment. [The subordinate clause at the beginning of the sentence contains a subject and a verb, but it cannot stand alone as a sentence.]

Before my uncle retired, he was a welder. [This sentence also starts with a subordinate clause.]

I didn't fly in a plane *until I was seventeen years old.* [This subordinate clause comes at the end of the sentence.]

As these examples show, you use a comma after a subordinate clause that begins a sentence. You generally do not use a comma before a subordinate clause that ends a sentence.

HOW TO Identify a Subordinate Clause

- Check that the word group has a subject and a verb.
- Check that it begins with a word such as *because, until, before, after, although, when,* or *while.*
- Check that it cannot stand alone as a sentence.

ACTIVITY 5: Identify Subordinate Clauses

In each of the following sentences, underline the subordinate clause. One sentence contains two subordinate clauses.

EXAMPLE <u>Though I had a bad cold,</u> I still played in the championship game.

1. When the supervisor entered the office, Dean stopped playing his computer game.
2. On my street, the garbage is always collected before I wake up.

3. We toasted marshmallows and told ghost stories until the fire died.
4. If nobody has any questions, Ms. Skov will distribute the free samples.
5. Antonio wants to become a social worker because a social worker helped him through his long stay in the hospital.
6. While the turkey roasted in the oven, the family played touch football.
7. Unless you pay your parking fines, you will not be allowed to register for classes when the next semester begins.
8. Since Kerry began jogging, she has been having pains in her knees.
9. After he graduates, Conrad wants to tour Mexico.
10. I have hidden your birthday present where you will never find it.

ACTIVITY 6: Identify Subordinate Clauses

In the following paragraph, underline the subordinate clauses.

EXAMPLE Before he moved into his own apartment, Lewis lived with his parents.

This year Lewis moved into his own apartment. After he moved in, he began to clean house regularly. In fact, he enjoys doing housework. If he cleans a little every day, his place always looks presentable. Solutions to his problems pop into his head while he is scrubbing something. When he was cleaning his bathtub, he thought of a better way to budget his paycheck. Although Lewis is not a perfectionist, he takes pride in his apartment because it represents a new stage in his adult life.

Relative Clauses

A subordinate clause may also begin with one of these words, called *relative pronouns*:

that	who
what	whoever
whatever	whom
which	whomever
whichever	whose

A subordinate clause that begins with a relative pronoun is often called a *relative clause.*

Whoever cooked the food should be thanked. [This relative clause is the subject of the sentence.]

Any soldier *who passes the obstacle course* will be allowed to leave. [This relative clause describes the subject and is essential to the meaning of the sentence.]

Private Mejia, *who passed the obstacle course,* was allowed to leave. [Here the relative clause also describes the subject but is not essential to the meaning of the sentence.]

As the last example shows, sometimes commas are used to set off relative clauses from the rest of the sentence. If the relative clause interrupts the flow of the sentence and could be removed without changing the basic meaning of the sentence, use a comma before it, and use another comma after it unless it is at the end of the sentence. Do not use a comma before or after a relative clause that is essential to the meaning of the sentence, as in the first two examples.

HOW TO Identify a Relative Clause

- Check that the word group has a subject and a verb.
- Check that the word group begins with a relative pronoun such as *that, who, what, which, whoever,* or *whichever.*
- Check that the word group cannot stand alone as a sentence.

ACTIVITY 7: Identify Relative Clauses

In each of the following sentences, underline the relative clause.

EXAMPLE I will support <u>whomever you nominate for club president</u>.

1. Janice is the only student who talked to the professor on the first day of class.
2. Ogbert is one of those people who work at night and sleep all day.
3. I worry about students whose extracurricular activities interfere with their studies.
4. Whoever ate Asher's sandwich should fix him another one.
5. I recommend you buy the vehicle that has the least impact on the environment.
6. Jolene is the only student whose research paper received an *A*.
7. Whoever comes home last needs to let the cat out.
8. Frankie is the only boyfriend who ever gave me a bouquet of roses.
9. Miss Sweden is the only contestant who played the accordion in the talent contest.
10. I feel sorry for the people whose jobs were eliminated last year.

ACTIVITY 8: Turn Relative Clauses into Sentences

Add information to each of the following relative clauses to make it a complete sentence.

EXAMPLE Who can sing, dance, and act

The musical requires performers who can sing, dance, and act.

1. That tasted the best

____

2. Who do not smoke

____

3. Whoever sits at the head of the table

____

4. Whom Elena admires

____

5. Who just left for vacation.

____

6. That leaves at 11:15 tonight

____

7. Who does not mind a little hard work

____

8. That does not require batteries

____

9. Whose smile could light up a room

____

10. That the dog ate

____

ACTIVITY 9: Expand Sentences with Subordinate Clauses

Expand each of the following sentences by adding a subordinate clause.

EXAMPLE Because he likes exploring caves, Andrew is studying geology.

1. Carmen wanted a new job ______________________________.
2. The day-care center is having a bake sale ______________________________.
3. ______________________________, Derek rode a bicycle to school.
4. The stores downtown joined in a sidewalk sale ______________________________.
5. ______________________________, the coffee will not taste any better.
6. Cynthia collected old magazines ______________________________.
7. ______________________________, the roads have been undergoing repairs.

8. The Goulds hired the gardener ________________________

____.

9. Monique wanted a laptop computer ____________________

____.

10. ____________________________, you will not improve your physical condition.

C. PRONOUNS

When you expand sentences, you'll be making grammatical choices about how you express your thoughts. One of these choices will concern the use of pronouns. A *pronoun* is a word that grammatically takes the place of a noun or another pronoun. Usually it refers to a specific noun that appears earlier in the sentence or in a previous sentence. The following are common pronouns:

I, me, mine, we, our, ours
you, your, yours
he, him, his, she, her, hers
it, its
they, them, their, theirs
this, these, that, those
who, whom, whose, which, that, what
all, any, another, both, each, either, everyone
few, many, most, nobody, several, some, such
myself, yourself, himself, herself, itself
ourselves, themselves, yourselves

Pronoun Reference

When you use a pronoun that refers to a noun, make sure that it's clear what the noun is. Don't use a pronoun that refers just to a vague idea or that could refer to more than one noun.

For more information about pronoun reference, see pp. 248–49.

VAGUE In my history class, *they* claimed that the Vietnam War protestors were unpatriotic. [Who are *they*?]

CLEAR In my history class, *a group of students* claimed that the Vietnam War protestors were unpatriotic.

UNCLEAR John told Martin *he* needed to study. [Who needed to study?]

CLEAR John told Martin, "I need to study."

CLEAR John told Martin, "You need to study."

CLEAR John needed to study, as he told Martin.

CLEAR John thought Martin needed to study and told him so.

HOW TO Identify and Correct Vague Pronoun Reference

- Check that every pronoun clearly refers back to a noun.
- Replace the pronoun with a noun if the reference isn't clear.
- Or rewrite the sentence to delete the pronoun or change it.

ACTIVITY 10: Correct Vague Pronoun Reference

Rewrite each of the following sentences to correct the vague pronoun reference.

EXAMPLE On that television show, they are always saying the dumbest things.

On that television show, the characters are always saying the dumbest things.

1. At that office, they prefer both male and female employees to wear suits.

____

____

2. The musicians played a waltz and a traditional ballad. It was beautiful.

____

3. Fabiola confessed to Leah that she left her class notes at the restaurant.

____

4. At my health club, they recommend that we warm up before we do aerobics.

5. Seth told Andrew that he needed to drink less on weekends.

6. There are too many scenes of violence and brutality. It should not have won the Academy Award.

7. In the documentary, it claimed that the mayor is corrupt.

8. While on vacation, I learned how to water ski and how to play croquet. It is not as easy as it looks.

9. In San Francisco, they have many landmarks of interest to tourists.

10. If Alicia tries to explain logarithms to Megan, she will become confused.

Pronoun Agreement

A pronoun should agree in number with the noun it refers to. To maintain pronoun agreement, use a singular pronoun to refer to a singular noun and a plural pronoun to refer to a plural noun. Remember that a singular noun also requires a singular verb form and a plural noun requires a plural verb form.

Learn more about pronoun agreement on pp. 202–203.

INCORRECT PRONOUN AGREEMENT — My *friend* is bringing *their* own food to the picnic. [*Friend* is singular, but *their* is plural.]

CORRECT PRONOUN AGREEMENT — My *friend* is bringing *her* own food to the picnic.

CORRECT PRONOUN AGREEMENT — My *friends* are bringing *their* own food to the picnic.

Remember also to use a singular pronoun to refer to a singular indefinite pronoun. Singular indefinite pronouns include *anybody, anyone, anything, everybody, everyone, everything, nobody, somebody, someone,* and *something.*

INCORRECT PRONOUN AGREEMENT — My professor told *everyone* to take *their* laptop off the counter. [*Everyone* is singular, but *their* is plural.]

CORRECT PRONOUN AGREEMENT — My professor told *everyone* to take *his or her* laptop off the counter.

HOW TO Correct Errors in Pronoun-Antecedent Agreement

- Check that singular pronouns such as *I, he, she, his* or *her,* or *it* refer to singular nouns or to singular indefinite pronouns such as *anyone, everyone, everybody, somebody,* and *someone.*
- Check that plural pronouns such as *we, us, them,* and *their* refer to plural nouns.
- Correct errors in pronoun agreement by making pronouns and nouns agree in number.

ACTIVITY 11: Correct Errors in Pronoun Agreement

In each of the following sentences, correct the errors in pronoun agreement as needed.

EXAMPLE ~~A plumber~~ [Plumbers] will have to charge you more if they find cracks in the pipes.

1. A student will find more errors in an essay if they wait a few hours after writing it before proofreading it.
2. I need to talk to someone who has put snow chains on their tires.

3. Everybody brought their donation to the main office.
4. The player shouts "Bingo!" as soon as they have a winning card.
5. A psychiatrist must not betray their patients' confidentiality.
6. A movie star saves their biggest smile for the camera.
7. Nobody admitted that they committed the vandalism.
8. Someone allows their dog to bark all day long.
9. Let me know when everyone has completed their questionnaires.
10. Every parent wants their children to be happy and successful.

ACTIVITY 12: Correct Pronoun Agreement

In the following paragraph, correct the errors in pronoun agreement.

EXAMPLE The proudest day of a parent's life is when ~~their~~ his or her children graduate from college.

The last meeting of my statistics study group was disastrous. We met at the studio apartment of one of the group members, and they did not have enough chairs. Everyone who came was worried about their grade, but not everyone had completed their section of the homework problems. One person had loaned their calculator to a friend and had to share mine. Someone else only wanted us to do their work for them. A third person had to have every little thing explained to them. Finally, somebody left angrily, saying they would save time by doing all the work themselves. This experience taught me something. The success of a study group requires every member to contribute as much as they can. Each person must still understand the basic concepts for themselves. The group then helps the individual refine what they already know.

D. ADJECTIVES

One of the best ways to expand sentences is to use adjectives, which can add interest to your writing.

Adjectives modify nouns or pronouns by describing or adding information about them.

> My *beautiful* mother never goes outside without makeup.
>
> The *green* meadow is always restful on the eyes.

Adjectives may also show comparisons between things. When comparing two things, add *-er* or *more* to the adjective. When comparing three or more things, add *-est* or *most.*

> This car is *larger* than the one I owned before.
>
> This car is the *largest* one I have ever owned.
>
> This car is *more unusual* than my other one.
>
> This car is the *most unusual* one on campus.

ACTIVITY 13: Identify Adjectives

In each of the following sentences, underline the adjectives.

EXAMPLE Senator Johnson is a <u>powerful</u> person.

1. Professor Michaels teaches a worthwhile class.
2. The overdue book is a biography.
3. Andrea likes to eat dark chocolate with a glass of cold milk.
4. Jerome is the tallest person in his family.
5. The blind student folded her collapsible cane and waited for the next train.
6. Rene wears a waterproof jacket in rainy weather.
7. Among the three friends, Didi is the best dancer.
8. Jamie owns a dented blue car.
9. I returned by the fastest route.
10. The defeated team ran off the muddy field.

ACTIVITY 14: Add Adjectives

Complete each of the following sentences by adding an adjective.

EXAMPLE The green coat fits you well.

1. The ________ cat sits in the window.
2. These cherries taste ________.
3. Alfredo took his ________ friend to the party.
4. Soraya has ________ brothers and sisters.
5. On ________ days we wear ________ clothing.
6. I think that the ________ carpet looks pretty with the ________ wallpaper.
7. His family needs to move to a ________ house.
8. That hospital serves ________ meals to its patients.
9. That ________ child never seems to get what he deserves.
10. Arzella is one of the ________ workers but one of the ________ students.

E. ADVERBS

Adverbs are another useful way to expand sentences. *Adverbs* modify verbs, adjectives, or other adverbs by describing or adding information about them. Adverbs usually answer the questions *how, when, where, why,* or *how often.* Many adverbs end in *-ly,* such as *slowly, noisily,* and *loudly.*

My favorite music is *never* played on the radio. [The adverb answers the question *How often is the music played?*]

The children played *joyfully.* [The adverb answers the question *How did the children play?*]

My wife *heartily* ate the dinner I made. [The adverb answers the question *How did the wife eat the dinner?*]

ACTIVITY 15: Identify Adverbs

In each of the following sentences, underline the adverbs.

EXAMPLE Doro forcefully threw the ball at the hitter.

1. The fans waited eagerly for concert tickets.
2. Is it true that crime never pays?
3. Traffic moved slowly on Van Ness Avenue.
4. The bored, complaining student soon dropped the class.
5. The pupils entered school slowly and reluctantly.
6. My aunts and uncles secretly planned a surprise party for my grandfather.
7. The instructor of my Introduction to Ceramics class is very interesting.
8. My study group often remains in the library until it closes.
9. The candidate campaigned well in the urban neighborhoods.
10. Klaus speaks persuasively in front of large groups.

ACTIVITY 16: Add Adverbs

Complete each of the following sentences by adding an adverb.

EXAMPLE Guy practiced the saxophone ___daily___.

1. The customers ___________ drank their iced tea.
2. You have ___________ been to work on time.
3. Melina ___________ eats at fast-food restaurants.
4. The punishment for plagiarism is ___________ severe.
5. Darryl worked ___________ on his English essay.
6. Winnie was talking ___________ before she was interrupted.
7. On Sunday nights, my classmates are ___________ doing their homework.
8. The football team ___________ won the game.
9. Chong is ___________ reliable.
10. Yolanda sneaked up behind her boyfriend and waited ___________ for him to notice her.

CHAPTER

24

Joining Sentences

To express different kinds of ideas, you need to know how to write different kinds of sentences. One way to create different kinds of sentences is to combine them. In this chapter, you'll learn to combine sentences using sentence coordination and sentence subordination.

A. COORDINATION

When you have two or more short, closely related sentences in a row that are equally important, your ideas can seem choppy and unconnected. To avoid this problem, combine the sentences, making them *coordinate,* or equal. To join two equally important sentences, use a coordinating conjunction and a comma or conjunctive adverb and a semicolon.

Coordinating Conjunctions and Commas

One way to combine equally important sentences is to use one of the coordinating conjunctions, which are *for, and, nor, but, or, yet,* and *so.* To remember these conjunctions, imagine the word *FANBOYS.* Each letter in this word is the first letter of one of the coordinating conjunctions.

COORDINATING CONJUNCTIONS

Conjunction	*Definition*
F — for	because
A — and	in addition, also
N — nor	not, neither
B — but	however, unless
O — or	as another possibility
Y — yet	however, unless
S — so	as a result

When you use a coordinating conjunction to combine short, closely related sentences, put a comma before the conjunction. Be sure to select a conjunction that logically connects the sentences.

CHOPPY SENTENCES	The flat tire delayed us. We arrived on time to get our picture taken.
SENTENCES COMBINED WITH *BUT*	The flat tire delayed us, *but* we arrived on time to get our picture taken.
CHOPPY SENTENCES	I combed my son's hair. I tied his shoes.
SENTENCES COMBINED WITH *AND*	I combed my son's hair, *and* I tied his shoes.
CHOPPY SENTENCES	We were ready to pose for the photograph. We smiled and said "Cheese!"
SENTENCES COMBINED WITH *SO*	We were ready to pose for the photograph, *so* we smiled and said "Cheese!"

HOW TO Combine Sentences with Coordinating Conjunctions

- Use one of the FANBOYS conjunctions (*for, and, nor, but, or, yet, so*).
- Put a comma before the conjunction.

ACTIVITY 1: Connect Sentences with Coordinating Conjunctions

Connect each of the following pairs of short sentences with a coordinating conjunction and a comma.

EXAMPLE Chuck went to law school for three years. He never practiced law.

Chuck went to law school for three years, but he never practiced law.

1. Shari was upset when she finished her tax return. She owed more than a thousand dollars.

____

____

2. Lilyrose insisted on painting the room dark green. I would have preferred antique white.

3. I fell asleep on the bus. I missed my stop.

4. Elizabeth carefully read the contract for the house. She still couldn't understand it.

5. I washed my car this morning. I cleaned house this afternoon.

6. Marvin set his alarm clock for 5:30. He had an early plane to catch.

7. Hetty forgot to complete her financial aid forms by the first of February. She didn't receive financial aid for the next school year.

8. Malik spent some time preparing for the interview. He got the job.

9. You can buy the racy red sports car. You can buy the practical brown sedan.

10. Adrianna spent hours looking over travel brochures. She ended up going to the same beach she had visited for the past three years.

Conjunctive Adverbs and Semicolons

Another way to join equally important sentences is to use a *conjunctive adverb* and a *semicolon*. The conjunctive adverb (often called a *transition*) shows how the two sentences fit together. A semicolon is used before the conjunctive adverb, and a comma is used after it.

CONJUNCTIVE ADVERBS

Add an idea: *also, furthermore, in addition, moreover*

Show a different point: *however, instead, nevertheless, otherwise*

Show a similar point: *likewise, similarly*

Stress a key idea: *indeed, undoubtedly, certainly*

Show a consequence or result: *as a result, consequently, therefore, thus*

Point out a sequence: *first, second, next, finally*

CHOPPY SENTENCES	My daughter majored in accounting in college. She really wanted to be an airline pilot.
SENTENCES COMBINED WITH *HOWEVER*	My daughter majored in accounting in college; *however,* she really wanted to be an airline pilot.
CHOPPY SENTENCES	I traveled to Mexico as a child. I want to learn Spanish.
SENTENCES COMBINED WITH *AS A RESULT*	I traveled to Mexico as a child; *as a result,* I want to learn Spanish.
CHOPPY SENTENCES	The neighborhood grocery store is small. It's very expensive.
SENTENCES COMBINED WITH *MOREOVER*	The neighborhood grocery store is small; *moreover,* it's very expensive.

HOW TO Combine Sentences with Conjunctive Adverbs

- Select a conjunctive adverb that shows the logical connection between the sentences.
- Use a semicolon before the conjunctive adverb.
- Use a comma after the conjunctive adverb.

ACTIVITY 2: Connect Sentences with Conjunctive Adverbs and Commas

Read each of the following sentence pairs closely. Next, select an appropriate conjunctive adverb to show how the ideas in the sentences fit together. Then, combine the sentences using the conjunctive adverb and a comma.

EXAMPLE My hours at work have been reduced. I have less money to spend.

My hours at work have been reduced; therefore, I have less money to spend.

1. Akio disliked the political ads during the last election. He decided to register as an Independent.

2. The children gathered roses, violets, and irises from their grandmother's garden. They ironed the flowers in waxed paper and labeled them with black ink.

3. Owners of small specialty stores find it hard to compete with large department stores. They need to advertise their products on television and the Internet.

4. Corinne was hired as a salesclerk. She got a better job the following week and quit.

5. Einstein had a reputation as an absentminded scientist. He could be very forgetful.

____

____

6. Landscape artists are more than just gardeners. They are both scientists and artists.

____

____

7. I stepped out into the foggy morning unable to see a thing. I heard something crunch beneath my feet.

____

____

8. This semester I'm working the graveyard shift at the food mart. I can barely stay awake in my 8:00 a.m. class.

____

____

9. Pacifists often demonstrate against warfare. They have been conscientious objectors during different wars.

____

____

10. Kurt Cobain revealed his personal problems in his songs. He talked about these problems in his journals.

____

____

B. SUBORDINATION

Use *sentence subordination* to combine two sentences that aren't equally important. Subordinating conjunctions and relative pronouns help you express the logical connection between the sentences.

Subordinating Conjunctions

One way to combine two sentences using subordination is to use an appropriate *subordinating conjunction.*

SUBORDINATING CONJUNCTIONS

after	until
although	when
because	whenever
before	where
if	wherever
since	whether
though	while
unless	

The subordinating conjunction begins the part of the combined sentence that's less important to expressing your message.

CHOPPY SENTENCES	People are marrying later in life. The divorce rate hasn't decreased.
SENTENCES COMBINED WITH *ALTHOUGH*	*Although* people are marrying later in life, the divorce rate hasn't decreased.
CHOPPY SENTENCES	Martin made sure to save several thousand dollars. He did this before he quit his job.
SENTENCES COMBINED WITH *BEFORE*	Martin made sure to save several thousand dollars *before* he quit his job.
CHOPPY SENTENCES	You'll never understand the experience of being homeless. The only way to understand it is to live through it.
SENTENCES COMBINED WITH *UNLESS*	You'll never understand the experience of being homeless *unless* you live through it.

Sometimes you can just put the conjunction before the less important sentence of the original two, as in the first example. But often you'll also need to delete part of that sentence or change it in other ways, as in the second and third examples. Sometimes the conjunction you need will already be in the less important sentence, like *before* in the second example.

The word group that begins with a subordinating conjunction is called a *subordinate clause* or a dependent clause. Put a comma after a subordinate clause when it begins a sentence. In general, don't use a comma before a subordinate clause that ends a sentence.

COMMA *After the children sat down,* the family began Thanksgiving dinner.

NO COMMA The family began Thanksgiving dinner *after the children sat down.*

HOW TO Combine Sentences with Subordinating Conjunctions

- Decide which sentence is less important.
- Choose an appropriate subordinating conjunction to express the way the ideas in the two sentences are connected.
- Combine the sentences by putting the subordinating conjunction before the less important part of the new sentence and deleting or changing any other words as necessary.
- Use a comma after the subordinate clause when it begins the combined sentence.
- In general, don't use a comma before the subordinate clause when it ends the sentence.

ACTIVITY 3: Join Sentences with Subordinating Conjunctions

Use a subordinating conjunction to join each of the following pairs of sentences. You might have to delete or change words.

EXAMPLE I aced my chemistry test. I studied three hours last night.

I aced my chemistry test because I studied three hours last night.

1. The number of arrests for illegal drug use has increased. This has happened because there are stricter drug laws.

____

____

2. The newspaper arrived late. I wasn't able to read about the big earthquake in Alaska.

____

____

3. I was lost trying to find your house. Finally, I asked someone for directions.

____

____

4. The friends were in the restaurant. They gossiped about their coworkers.

____

____

5. I have a hard time recycling my garbage. The recycling center is too far from my house.

____

____

6. You have to change your password. Then, you can start playing the game.

____

7. I kept the music low. My grandmother left.

____

8. The politician gave her speech and her followers cheered. I left the rally.

____

____

9. I would have stayed at the test review session longer. The professor did not show up.

____

____

10. I didn't rent the apartment. The building had a leaking roof and a sewer leak.

____

____

Relative Pronouns

Another way to combine choppy sentences is to use a *relative pronoun* to subordinate the information in the less important sentence.

RELATIVE PRONOUNS

that	who
whose	whom
whoever	which
what	whatever
whomever	whichever

As with a subordinating conjunction, the relative pronoun goes before a part of the combined sentence that is less important to the meaning. The word group that begins with a relative pronoun is called a *relative clause.*

CHOPPY SENTENCES	Athletes will stay in shape. They'll stay in shape if they work out regularly.
SENTENCES COMBINED WITH *WHO*	Athletes *who work out regularly* will stay in shape.
CHOPPY SENTENCES	Ryan cooked the enchiladas. They were spicy and delicious.
SENTENCES COMBINED WITH *WHICH*	Ryan cooked the enchiladas, *which were spicy and delicious.*
CHOPPY SENTENCES	One of my favorite songs is "Daydream Believer." I mean the version recorded by the Monkees.
SENTENCES COMBINED WITH *THAT*	One of my favorite songs is the version of "Daydream Believer" *that* was recorded by the Monkees.

Don't use commas before or after a relative clause that is necessary to identify what it refers to, as in the following example:

The essay *that Lucia wrote* was published in the local newspaper.

No commas are used before or after the relative clause because it's a necessary part of the sentence. It tells which essay — the essay that Lucia wrote — was published in the newspaper.

In contrast, use commas when the relative clause gives information that's not essential to the sentence.

The essay, *which is on the topic of terrorism,* is still in my backpack.

Commas are used in this example because the relative clause — *which is on the topic of terrorism* — simply adds information about an essay that's already been mentioned. The meaning of the sentence is still clear without it: *The essay is still in my backpack.*

Don't use commas with relative clauses that begin with *that*:

The essay *that was assigned yesterday* is due in a week.

HOW TO Combine Sentences with Relative Pronouns

- Decide which sentence is less important.
- Choose an appropriate relative pronoun to connect the information in the less important sentence to that in the other sentence.
- Use commas when the relative clause can be deleted and the sentence still includes all necessary information.
- Don't use commas when the relative clause is a necessary part of the sentence.

ACTIVITY 4: Connect Sentences with Relative Pronouns

Use a relative pronoun to combine each of the following pairs of sentences. You may have to add or delete words.

EXAMPLE My dog is my new best friend. She's part border collie and part labrador.

My dog, who's part border collie and part labrador, is my new best friend.

1. Jeans have changed a great deal over the years. Jeans are very popular.

   ____

2. Jeans were invented by Levi Strauss. They were first worn by miners in the 1850s.

   ____

   ____

3. The jeans never tore or fell apart. The jeans were worn by the miners.

____

4. In the 1950s, jeans became popular with teenagers. The teenagers thought that they were cool.

____

____

5. Jeans were a big part of the 1960s. Hippies started wearing them.

____

____

6. One popular style was bell-bottom jeans. This style was often decorated with flowers and peace signs.

____

____

7. I have a picture of my mother wearing jeans. The jeans have frayed hems and many holes.

____

____

8. Now just about everyone wears jeans. These jeans come in many styles.

____

9. One style is cut very low at the waist. This style is popular with young girls.

____

____

10. People wear jeans. These people live all over the world.

____

C. SENTENCE-COMBINING EXERCISES

The following sentence-combining exercises will give you practice using sentence coordination and subordination.

Specific Methods of Combining Sentences

Use the methods identified in the directions for combining sentences in the following activities.

ACTIVITY 5: Combine Sentences Using Coordination

Combine each of the following sets of sentences using either a comma and a coordinating conjunction or a semicolon and a conjunctive adverb. Add or delete words as necessary.

For information on combining sentences with commas and coordinating conjunctions or with semicolons and conjunctive adverbs, see pp. 309 and 339.

EXAMPLE Reality-based TV shows are inexpensive to produce and popular with viewers. Television networks rely on them to increase profits.

Reality-based TV shows are inexpensive to produce and popular with viewers, so television networks rely on them to increase profits.

OR

Reality-based TV shows are inexpensive to produce and popular with viewers; therefore, television networks rely on them to increase profits.

1. In March 2002, *The Osbornes* debuted on MTV. The show received the highest ratings of any MTV show up to that time.

____

____

2. The show was "reality based." Cameras followed the real-life adventures of rocker Ozzy Osborne and his family.

____

____

3. The producers filmed the Osbornes doing ordinary things. The show was anything but ordinary.

____

____

4. The family's Beverly Hills mansion featured Gothic décor. The Osbornes' clothing was equally unusual.

____

____

5. Ozzy had tattoos all over his body. His daughter Kelly's hair kept changing color.

____

____

6. The Osbornes' behavior at first seemed outrageous. They were a loving family.

____

____

7. Ozzy was befuddled and clumsy. He had used hard drugs for many years.

____

____

8. Kelly and Jack squabbled like typical teenagers. Sharon, the wife, held the family together.

____

____

9. Unlike typical teenagers, they weren't forced to go to school. As the show became popular, they began to sing and act professionally.

____

____

10. The show depicted the family dogs messing on the carpet. The family once threw a ham at their loud neighbors.

11. Despite the Osbornes' behavior, many people admired them. They clearly loved each other very much.

ACTIVITY 6: Combine Sentences Using Coordination

Combine each of the following sets of sentences using either a comma and a coordinating conjunction or a semicolon and a conjunctive adverb. Add or delete words as necessary.

For help combining sentences using these methods, see pp. 309 and 339.

EXAMPLE The station wagon used to be one of America's most popular cars. The SUV (Sports Utility Vehicle) has now replaced the station wagon in popularity.

The station wagon used to be one of America's most popular cars, but the SUV (Sports Utility Vehicle) has now replaced the station wagon in popularity.

OR

The station wagon used to be one of America's most popular cars; however, the SUV (Sports Utility Vehicle) has now replaced the station wagon in popularity.

1. In recent years, SUVs have become popular with many American consumers. They have helped automobile companies make bigger profits.

2. At first, they were built for people to drive in extreme conditions and on dirt roads. Now, they are used mostly for city driving.

3. They are bought by parents who like the large size of the cars. They can fit their growing families into SUVs with ease.

4. Some buyers imagine themselves driving off-road in a rugged, beautiful area of the country. They would never actually do that.

5. Energy conservationists have criticized SUVs. SUVs remain very popular.

6. Americans prefer large cars. Europeans buy much smaller cars.

7. Gas in Europe is much more expensive than in the United States. European consumers have good reason to use as little as possible.

8. Japanese-made SUVs are becoming more and more popular with American consumers. The profits of American car companies are expected to decline.

9. In general, Japanese-made cars are still more popular than American cars. Their resale rates are higher.

10. Many Americans love their SUVs. It will be interesting to see how this love affair affects the American economy.

ACTIVITY 7: Combine Sentences Using Subordination

Use subordinating conjunctions to connect each of the following pairs of sentences. Add or delete words as necessary.

See pp. 405–406 for more information about combining sentences with subordinating conjunctions.

EXAMPLE Scientists often use placebos in experiments. They want to test the effectiveness of a new treatment.

Scientists often use placebos in experiments because they want to test the effectiveness of a new treatment.

OR

Because they want to test the effectiveness of a new treatment, scientists often use placebos in experiments.

1. A placebo is a fake treatment for an illness. Sometimes a placebo works as well as real medicine.

2. Scientists use placebos when they test the effectiveness of a new medicine. They do this to make sure the new medicine will really help patients get well.

3. In an experiment, one group of patients will receive the medicine being tested. Another group of patients will receive the placebo.

____

____

____

4. Both the medicine being tested and the placebo can be given in the form of a pill. The placebo pill might be made up entirely of sugar or some other harmless substance.

____

____

____

5. The patients who receive the new medicine are called the experimental group. The patients who receive the placebo are called the control group.

____

____

____

6. The patients don't know which group they're in. This process is called a "blind" experiment.

____

____

7. The new medicine must be very successful in treating the patients in the experimental group. The power of suggestion is so strong.

____

____

8. Sometimes the patients who received placebos improved a great deal. The patients who received the actual medicine improved less.

____

____

____

9. Scientists speculate that placebos work for some people. These people believe strongly that the placebo will make them get better.

10. The placebo effect can be very powerful. Scientists are beginning to study it more seriously.

ACTIVITY 8: Combine Sentences Using Subordination

Use subordinating conjunctions to connect each of the following sets of sentences. Add or delete words as necessary.

Review how to combine sentences with subordinating conjunctions on pp. 405–406.

EXAMPLE People who rush into marriage often end up divorced. They don't know their partner well enough.

People who rush into marriage often end up divorced because they don't know their partner well enough.

OR

Because they don't know their partner well enough, people who rush into marriage often end up divorced.

1. The institution of marriage has changed greatly over the years. Most people still get married.

2. Most experts agree that people should take their time getting to know each other. They should do this before they get married.

3. The couple should know each other well. They have a better chance of not getting divorced.

4. Couples first come to understand the strengths and weaknesses of their potential partners. They do this when they are getting to know each other.

____

____

5. Couples find out if they have similar beliefs and interests. These similar beliefs and interests will help them have a happy marriage.

____

____

6. Couples should discuss each partner's religious beliefs. They need to do this to prevent conflicts in the marriage.

____

____

7. Couples might have problems. This could happen if one partner is a very conservative person and the other is very liberal.

____

____

8. Couples also need to find out how responsible their potential partners are. They need to do this to make sure they can rely on their partners.

____

____

9. Couples need to learn to communicate well. Good communication will help them get through difficult times together.

____

____

10. Marriage is rewarding but often very difficult. It is important for couples to know their partners well. They need to do this before the wedding day.

____

____

ACTIVITY 9: Combine Sentences Using Subordination

Use relative pronouns to connect each of the following pairs of sentences. Add or delete words when necessary.

For more help combining sentences with relative pronouns, turn to pp. 370–71.

EXAMPLE Rocky Mountain National Park is located in one of the most beautiful areas in the country. It contains remote areas where you can find solitude.

Rocky Mountain National Park, which is located in one of the most beautiful areas in the country, contains remote areas where you can find solitude.

OR

Rocky Mountain National Park, which contains remote areas where you can find solitude, is located in one of the most beautiful areas in the country.

1. Rocky Mountain National Park is in Colorado. It is one of America's favorite vacation spots.

2. This park is also one of America's most popular national parks. It is visited by 3 million people a year.

3. Several trails in the park are not well known. These trails are in remote locations.

4. The Tonahutu Creek trail follows the Continental Divide. The trail is 21 miles long.

5. The Never Summer Loop trail is well named. This trail has mountains that are almost 13,000 feet high.

____

____

6. Sometimes the snow never melts on this trail. The snow can be very deep.

____

7. Another trail people don't use very much is the Lost Lake trail. This trail is very steep.

____

____

8. The Lost Lake trail leads to Lost Lake. This lake is surrounded by breathtaking mountain scenery.

____

____

9. These three trails are great for backpacking. Not many people use these trails.

____

____

10. If you go backpacking, you can experience nature without crowds. Backpacking is strenuous and fun.

____

____

ACTIVITY 10: Combine Sentences Using Subordination

For help combining sentences with relative pronouns, see pp. 370–71.

Connect each of the following sentence groups with relative pronouns. Add or delete words when necessary.

EXAMPLE Teenagers are part of the abstinence movement. These teenagers don't have sex until they're married.

Teenagers who are part of the abstinence movement don't have sex until they're married.

1. Abstinence is growing in popularity among young people. Abstinence consists of waiting until marriage to have sex.

2. Abstinence has been called a "sexual revolution." It is a sexual revolution very different from the sexual revolution of the 1960s.

3. The sexual revolution involved not waiting until marriage to have sex. The sexual revolution was the one that happened in the 1960s.

4. The current sexual revolution is a result of several factors. These factors include religion, family pressure, and health issues.

5. One reason for the interest in abstinence is that people are afraid of sexually transmitted diseases (STDs). STDs can cause illness and even death.

6. Other people remain abstinent until marriage because of religious beliefs. These beliefs discourage people from having sex outside of marriage.

7. Although abstinence is becoming more popular, most young people don't wait until marriage to have sex. These young people live in the United States.

8. Some people maintain that sex-education programs should promote only abstinence. These people are usually conservatives.

____

____

9. Other people say that sex-education programs should mention abstinence as only one possibility. These people are usually liberal.

____

____

10. The abstinence movement is an interesting social trend. This social trend might continue to grow in popularity.

____

____

Various Methods of Combining Sentences

Review these methods of combining sentences by reviewing pp. 517–28.

Up to now, you have practiced combining sentences using just one or two methods at a time. Now you will be given more choices about the best method to join particular sentences:

1. a comma and a coordinating conjunction (*for, and, nor, but, or, yet, so*)
2. a semicolon and a conjunctive adverb (*however, in addition, moreover, in contrast, on the other hand, then, finally, indeed, instead, next, therefore, certainly*)
3. a subordinating conjunction (*after, before, although, because, even though, if, once, that, though, unless, until, when, where, while*)
4. a relative pronoun (*who, whom, which, that, what, whoever, whomever, whichever, whatever*)

ACTIVITY 11: Combine Sentences Using Different Methods

Combine each of the following sets of sentences by choosing an appropriate method from the preceding list. Add or delete words as necessary.

EXAMPLE Rap music has always been controversial. Rap music is related to hip-hop.

Rap music, which is related to hip-hop, has always been controversial.

1. Rap music is the subject of much debate. It often contains swear words and insults to women and gay people.

2. At the same time, rap music is popular with many young people. These young people say it has been treated unfairly in the media.

3. In December 2002, Eminem made his acting debut in *8 Mile.* Eminem is a controversial white rapper.

4. *8 Mile* tells the story of a rapper in Detroit. The rapper is very similar to Eminem.

5. The main character is Rabbit. He is a factory worker. He lives in Detroit.

6. Rabbit wants out of his working-class ghetto. He participates in rap contests.

7. He is good at these contests. He beats most of his black competitors.

8. In *8 Mile,* Rabbit is shown as angry. He is also responsible and gentle with his younger sister.

9. *8 Mile* made people more aware of Eminem's talents. He became more popular with people of all ages.

10. Eminem will remain in the spotlight for years to come. Some people may not like it.

ACTIVITY 12: Combine Sentences Using Different Methods

Combine each of the following groups of sentences by choosing an appropriate method from the list on page 540. Add or delete words as necessary.

EXAMPLE Movies about spring break have been popular for years. These movies often show college students partying on a beach.

Movies about spring break, which often show college students partying on a beach, have been popular for years.

1. To many people, spring break is a time when college students go wild. Spring break is a weeklong break in March or April.

2. Spring break is notorious for misbehavior. Some college students drink excessively at this time.

3. Not all college students party over spring break. Many college students don't have time to party.

4. Last spring break I worked overtime to save up money. I needed the money to go to summer school.

5. This spring break I'll probably catch up on my classes. I'm taking six different courses. In three of these courses I have to write research papers.

6. My friend Mike spent spring break taking care of his children. Mike is a single father. He has sole custody of the kids.

7. Some people think college students just goof off. Those people don't know what we go through.

8. Most college students have to work their way through college. They might have children to raise. They might have parents to support.

9. Nationwide, only a small percentage of college students are supported by their parents. Most college students pay their own way.

10. I wish spring break were a real break. It's really just a chance to do more work.

ACTIVITY 13: Combine Sentences Using Different Methods

Combine each of the following groups of sentences by choosing an appropriate method from the list on page 540. Add or delete words as necessary.

EXAMPLE Blindness can lead to lifestyle restrictions. These restrictions will occur unless help is available.

Blindness can lead to lifestyle restrictions unless help is available.

1. Dan Shaw's life was changed. His doctor diagnosed him with retinitis pigmentosa. This is an incurable eye disease. This happened when Dan Shaw was seventeen.

2. Slowly he lost his sight. His life became very limited.

3. He wanted to be more involved with the world. He checked out his options.

4. He didn't want a seeing-eye dog. He had had a dog. The dog had died.

5. He heard about a program run by Janet and Don Burleson. They were training miniature horses as guides for the visually impaired.

6. Dan was interested in having a guide horse. Miniature horses live for thirty to forty years. He would not have to endure the death of the horse.

7. His guide horse leads him everywhere. His guide horse is named Cuddles.

8. Cuddles responds to more than twenty-five voice commands. She is housebroken. She can see in the dark.

9. People are often curious. This happens when they see Dan being guided by Cuddles. They ask Dan questions about Cuddles.

10. Dan is happy to talk to them about Cuddles. He wants others to know about guide horses.

ACTIVITY 14: Combine Sentences Using Different Methods

Combine each of the following sets of sentences by choosing an appropriate method from the list on page 540. Add or delete words as necessary.

EXAMPLE People have a healthy lifestyle. Their chances of getting diabetes will be reduced.

If people have a healthy lifestyle, their chances of getting diabetes will be reduced.

1. About 17 million people in the United States are believed to have diabetes. Nearly 6 million of these people don't know they have diabetes.

2. Diabetes has no cure. It can be controlled.

3. Diabetes can cause heart disease, blindness, kidney failure, and amputations. It is a very serious disease.

4. Most diabetes is Type II. It is associated with obesity. It is also associated with poor lifestyle habits.

5. Children now are fatter. Children exercise less. They eat unhealthy food.

6. Obese children will develop serious health problems. This will happen if they don't lose weight.

7. Children are our future. We need to help children be healthier. We need to help them live long lives.

8. Many schools are teaching children about diabetes. They have many other subjects to teach.

9. Parents should be good role models. They are very busy. Parents should eat well and exercise regularly.

____

____

10. Diabetes is a major health problem. It will continue to get worse. We need to stop the spread of this disease.

____

____

CHAPTER

25 Improving Sentences

To improve sentences, eliminate sentence fragments, run-on sentences, and comma splices. Also, correct misplaced and dangling modifiers, try to use the active voice as much as possible, and use parallel sentence structure for groups of words that are part of a pair or series.

A. SENTENCE FRAGMENTS

To find out more about what parts a sentence needs, turn to p. 65.

A sentence fragment is an incomplete sentence that is presented as if it were a complete sentence. Some sentence fragments are *phrases*—they lack a subject, a verb, or both.

The bank next to the grocery store.

Built a tool shed in the backyard.

At the radio station.

Other sentence fragments are *subordinate clauses*—they have a subject and a verb, but they begin with a subordinating conjunction or a relative pronoun.

SUBORDINATING CONJUNCTIONS

after	until
although	when
because	whenever
before	where
if	wherever
since	whether
though	while
unless	

Learn more about subordinate clauses on pp. 523–24.

Here are three sentence fragments that begin with subordinating conjunctions:

After the wedding is over.

Because it was hot outside.

When I graduate from college.

RELATIVE PRONOUNS

that	who
whose	whom
whoever	which
what	whatever
whomever	whichever

Here are three fragments that begin with relative pronouns:

That they bought at the mall.

Who ran away from home.

Which caused my parents to divorce.

ACTIVITY 1: Identify Sentence Fragments and Complete Sentences

For each of the following pairs, write F after the group of words that is a sentence fragment.

1. The sunbathers left by six o'clock. _______

   The sunbathers before six o'clock. _______

2. Finished by next Friday afternoon. _______

   The report was finished by Friday. _______

3. The last book left on the store shelf. _______

   The last book was left on the store shelf. _______

4. Someone who knows all the answers. _______

   Does someone know all the answers? _______

5. These jars are filled with sand and pebbles. _______

   Many jars filled with sand and pebbles. _______

6. Because Carolina couldn't wait to open her gifts. _______

   Carolina couldn't wait to open her gifts. _______

7. Jack wasn't used to the Nevada heat because he was from New Hampshire. _______

   Jack not used to the Nevada heat because he was from New Hampshire. _______

8. Whenever you're ready. ______

   Give me a call whenever you're ready. ______

9. Leticia didn't drink until she was twenty-one. ______

   Until Leticia was twenty-one. ______

10. While you were singing. ______

    A crowd gathered while you were singing. ______

ACTIVITY 2: Identify Sentence Fragments

In the space provided, indicate whether each of the following groups of words is a sentence fragment or a complete sentence.

EXAMPLE Since it was a cold day. fragment

1. My son plays soccer. ______________
2. In Joshua's old suitcase. ______________
3. Which was the first house constructed of recycled materials. ______________
4. How do you want to pay for your purchases? ______________
5. Because this soup is too salty. ______________
6. The sales associate earned a large commission. ______________
7. Speaking as clearly as he could. ______________
8. A hole in one. ______________
9. This vacuum cleaner is effective on both deep carpets and bare floors. ______________
10. Broke windows throughout the neighborhood. ______________

How do you correct a sentence fragment? One way is to connect it to the sentence that comes before or after it.

FRAGMENT *Although he had to get up early in the morning.* Alex didn't get home until midnight.

SENTENCE Although he had to get up early in the morning, Alex didn't get home until midnight.

FRAGMENT Her favorite gift was the orange teddy bear. *That her grandmother had given her.*

SENTENCE Her favorite gift was the orange teddy bear that her grandmother had given her.

Another way to correct a sentence fragment is to turn it into a complete sentence. If the fragment is a phrase, add any missing subject or verb. If the fragment begins with a subordinating conjunction, delete the conjunction. If the fragment begins with a relative pronoun, change the pronoun to a noun.

FRAGMENT Running down the street.

SENTENCE Matthew was running down the street.

FRAGMENT *Because* the plane was late getting into Chicago.

SENTENCE The plane was late getting into Chicago.

FRAGMENT *Which* violated the drug laws in Turkey.

SENTENCE The prescription violated the drug laws in Turkey.

HOW TO Correct Sentence Fragments

- Connect it to the sentence that comes before or after it.
- Rewrite it as a complete sentence.

ACTIVITY 3: Turn Fragments into Complete Sentences

Eight of the following word groups are sentence fragments. Rewrite each of the sentence fragments to make it a complete sentence. If the word group is a complete sentence, write "complete" in the blank.

EXAMPLE Polluting our beautiful city.

That factory is polluting our beautiful city.

1. After taking a month-long tour of Southeast Asia.

____

____

2. Because the batteries were low.

3. The load of towels still in the dryer.

4. Good attendance is required.

5. Who looked frightened enough to faint.

6. The car arrived with a small scratch.

7. Although french fries are not very healthy.

8. While Victor was learning how to ski.

9. If I knew these people better.

10. Stunned by the unexpected news.

ACTIVITY 4: Correct Sentence Fragments

Each of the following items contains one or more sentence fragments. Make each item into one sentence, either by connecting each fragment to a complete sentence or by rewriting it as a complete sentence.

EXAMPLE Maggy jogged every morning. Because she was preparing to run a marathon.

Maggy jogged every morning because she was preparing to run a marathon.

1. The plane that leaves at 11:15 tonight.

2. Whomever Annabelle picks as her husband. I'm prepared to like him.

3. That gave the children more freedom.

4. Alonzo cares for his sister's children on Wednesday and Thursday nights. Because his sister is taking two evening courses. He's free on these nights.

5. Let's try to go to the concert. If the tickets aren't too expensive and my car is working.

6. I'm jealous of Pete. Whose paper received an A. Even though he didn't spend much time writing it.

7. I could clean my whole house. While the Web page downloads.

8. Her mother didn't like Donna's blue hair. Said it was an embarrassment to the family.

9. I really liked my blind date. Until he lit up a cigarette.

10. Trying to keep my balance while standing on one foot, bending at the waist, and holding my arms in a graceful arc above my head.

____

____

____

ACTIVITY 5: Correct Sentence Fragments in a Paragraph

Rewrite the following paragraph to eliminate the sentence fragments, either by connecting them to other sentences or by rewriting them as complete sentences.

I am studying to become an elementary schoolteacher. Because I want to teach my students to take care of themselves I have a special interest in physical education. During my student teaching I remembered my childhood experiences playing team sports like softball. Alone in left field. My classmates laughing at my mistakes. I should have been taught how to catch a fly ball. Without fear of being hit in the face. I never learned games like soccer and basketball. Which keep every player constantly involved in the game. I want P.E. to be better for my students. All children can learn to enjoy using their bodies. Though not everybody can become a professional athlete. I want my future students to enjoy a lifetime of fitness.

B. RUN-ON SENTENCES

A *run-on sentence* occurs when two sentences (or sometimes more) are incorrectly presented as a single sentence, without any punctuation between them.

RUN-ON	The computer was old it needed to be given away.
CORRECT	The computer was old. It needed to be given away.
RUN-ON	I went to the store I forgot to get the flour.
CORRECT	I went to the store, but I forgot to get the flour.

ACTIVITY 6: Identify Run-on Sentences

In the space provided, indicate whether each of the following word groups is a run-on sentence or a correct sentence.

EXAMPLE Moby Grape was a rock band from the 1960s it was based in San Francisco. ___run-on___

1. Rudy is friendlier than he appears he only frowns to hide his nervousness.__________
2. With her fingers poised over the piano keys, Carmel waited for the conductor's baton to drop. __________
3. That yogurt is too high in carbohydrates for my diabetic diet I need to have the low-fat cottage cheese. __________
4. Hard hats are required in this area the roof is being replaced. __________
5. No one volunteered to supervise the dance until the principal offered to buy the chaperones dinner. __________
6. My wife likes pizza my son likes hamburgers I prefer sushi. __________
7. Ray and Serena put a green decal on their black suitcase so they could recognize it more easily at the airport. __________
8. Delia ran out the door in such a hurry that she left her coat draped over the sofa. __________
9. Kazuko welcomed the visitor into her office she asked her assistant to bring them both coffee.__________
10. Nigel was astonished when he received first prize he never thought that he would win an award. __________

One way to correct a run-on sentence is to turn it into two sentences, adding a period at the end of the first sentence and capitalizing the first word of the second sentence.

RUN-ON The concert was supposed to begin at 8:00 it actually began at 9:30.

CORRECT The concert was supposed to begin at 8:00. It actually began at 9:30.

RUN-ON The digital camera is too expensive it costs more than $300.

CORRECT The digital camera is too expensive. It costs more than $300.

A run-on sentence can also be corrected by putting a comma and a coordinating conjunction (*for, and, nor, but, or, yet, so*) between the two sentences.

See Chapter 24 to find out more about these methods of joining sentences.

RUN-ON The apartment is dirty the kitchen appliances are broken.

CORRECT The apartment is dirty, and the kitchen appliances are broken.

RUN-ON I registered for classes late I still got a good schedule.

CORRECT I registered for classes late, but I still got a good schedule.

A third way to correct a run-on sentence is to put a semicolon between the two sentences. Often you can also use a conjunctive adverb such as *however, therefore, also, instead,* or *as a result* after the semicolon. If you use a conjunctive adverb, put a comma after it.

RUN-ON I've been working out I still haven't lost any weight.

CORRECT I've been working out; however, I still haven't lost any weight.

RUN-ON Computer technology is improving computers are getting cheaper.

CORRECT Computer technology is improving; computers are getting cheaper.

HOW TO Correct Run-on Sentences

- Separate it into two sentences, or
- Add a comma and a coordinating conjunction, or
- Add a semicolon and, if appropriate, a conjunctive adverb.

ACTIVITY 7: Correct Run-on Sentences

Correct each of the following run-on sentences using a period and a capital letter, a comma and a coordinating conjunction, or a semicolon and a conjunctive adverb. One of the run-on sentences includes three sentences; use two different methods to correct it.

EXAMPLE While Fred was watching the news, the electricity went out it was two hours before it came back on again.

While Fred was watching the news, the electricity went out,

and it was two hours before it came back on again.

1. Solange posed for the picture, the feather on her antique hat framing her face she found the waist and collar of the dress a little confining.

2. Before Benjamin applied for a job at Datacorp, he researched the company at the library he wanted to be well prepared for the interview.

3. Waiting for the tour bus, the family shivered on the windy corner they had expected warmer weather on their summer vacation.

4. Leland's motorcycle is his prized possession he had to sell it in order to pay his college tuition.

5. Because Olivia had never been surfing, she took lessons she felt ready to tackle the waves.

6. Paolo has thinning hair, glasses, and stooped shoulders everyone thinks that he is a librarian he actually is a meteorologist at an Antarctic research station.

7. Toni gives her son a generous allowance and does not expect any help around the house from him Toni's brother expects his children to do chores if they want spending money.

8. Dark clouds gather overhead while trees toss in the wind rain does not fall.

9. Eileen wanted to prove her trustworthiness to her parents she made it her responsibility to take her younger brother and sister to school.

10. Using a sharp jerk of his wrist, Simón flipped the pancake in the skillet his uncle taught him this trick when Simón was a child.

ACTIVITY 8: Identify and Correct Run-on Sentences

Seven of the following word groups are run-on sentences. Correct each of the run-on sentences using the following methods: a period and a capital letter, a comma and a coordinating conjunction, or a semicolon and a conjunctive adverb. If the word group is a correct sentence, write "correct" in the blank.

EXAMPLE Janine loved NASCAR races she had the autographs of several famous drivers.

Janine loved NASCAR races, and she had the autographs of several famous drivers.

1. Jasmine's parents made her return the prom dress they insisted that she find one that was less revealing.

2. Aunt Edna poured tea into everyone's cup we sipped politely although we would have preferred coffee.

3. I cannot sleep because the shadows of the tree branches outside my window stretch across my bedroom wall like grasping fingers.

4. Damien put his ear to the door but heard nothing he wished that doors still had keyholes that he could look through.

5. The rain began as soon as Kenneth washed his car it always rained after he washed his car.

6. Hadley smiled at his bookshelf with pride because it was his first one that was not made of boards and cinder blocks.

7. Not a single car at the dealership had been within Bob and Carol's budget they drove their old car home in disappointment.

8. With the trees trimmed back, Malik enjoyed a better view from his living room the lights of the city twinkled below.

9. The professor never found out that I had turned in someone else's essay as my own, probably because the previous one, which I had written myself, received a higher grade.

10. Alyce experimented with one hair color after another starting with burgundy, she then tried orange, blue, and purple none looked natural but all looked pretty.

ACTIVITY 9: Identify and Correct Run-on Sentences in a Paragraph

Revise the following paragraph to correct the run-on sentences.

EXAMPLE Watching the natural world is soothing; in fact, it is as good for the soul as meditating.

The sun burns bright and hot the world is shady and cool under the pine tree. Nestled within a deep hole in the thick needles underfoot, a turtle dozes. I look up a bird feeder is in my hand. The feeder weighs over four pounds I search for a strong, low branch. Two startled doves take flight their wings whistle as if to express their alarm. Three grackles hop from limb to limb, black and almost as big as crows. More grackles join the flock they scream their long, thick beaks gape menacingly. A tiny hummingbird darts between the large, black birds its bright patch of throat feathers flashes red in the flickering light. Several sparrows wait on a nearby telephone wire. Far from the trunk, I find a good branch and attach the feeder with sturdy twine. After I step back, a sparrow flies to the feeder another sparrow joins its companion. The grackles become quiet the doves return. I watch the birds gather on the branches around the feeder it is like a doorway to a world where I do not belong.

C. COMMA SPLICES

A *comma splice* consists of two sentences incorrectly joined with only a comma.

COMMA SPLICE Susan liked the aroma of coffee, she never liked the taste.

CORRECT Susan liked the aroma of coffee, but she never liked the taste.

COMMA SPLICE My son is based in Korea, he'll be home for Thanksgiving.

CORRECT My son is based in Korea. He'll be home for Thanksgiving.

COMMA SPLICE The domestic cat is a great pet, it's a ferocious hunter.

CORRECT The domestic cat is a great pet; furthermore, it's a ferocious hunter.

One way to correct a comma splice is to make the comma splice into two separate sentences by changing the comma to a period and capitalizing the first word of the second sentence.

COMMA SPLICE The Department of Homeland Security was created in 2002, it is responsible for the protection of the United States within its own borders.

CORRECT The Department of Homeland Security was created in 2002. It is responsible for the protection of the United States within its own borders.

Turn to pp. 517–20 for more information about these ways of joining sentences.

Another way to correct a comma splice is to add a coordinating conjunction (*for, and, nor, but, or, yet, so*) after the comma.

COMMA SPLICE Our car trip across country was exhausting, it was also exciting and educational.

CORRECT Our car trip across country was exhausting, but it was also exciting and educational.

A third way to correct a comma splice is to change the comma to a semicolon. You can also add a conjunctive adverb (such as *however, therefore, also, instead,* or *as a result*) after the semicolon. If you use a conjunctive adverb, put a comma after it.

COMMA SPLICE Antibiotics have been widely used, they aren't as effective as they used to be.

CORRECT Antibiotics have been widely used; as a result, they aren't as effective as they used to be.

HOW TO Correct Comma Splices

- Separate it into two sentences, or
- Add a coordinating conjunction after the comma, or
- Change the comma to a semicolon and, if appropriate, add a conjunctive adverb with a comma after it.

ACTIVITY 10: Correct Comma Splices

Correct each of the following comma splices by making the comma splice into two sentences, adding a coordinating conjunction after the comma, or changing the comma to a semicolon and adding a conjunctive adverb.

EXAMPLE Graduating from college in four years is always good, don't worry if you can't do it.

Graduating from college in four years is always good, but don't worry if you can't do it.

1. There were never two people more different than Arnulfo and Hadley, they have been best friends since the second grade.

2. The audience members jumped to their feet and would not stop applauding, I was very proud that I had started the Drama Club.

3. Frank set the tray of ice cream cones on the passenger seat to his right, the children would be delighted with his surprise.

4. Dora gave the old dog a pat on the head, he thumped his tail in greeting without opening his eyes.

5. When we returned home, all the clocks were blinking, the power had gone off and come back on while we were away.

6. Alex balanced her baby brother on her hip, almost three, he was becoming too big for her to carry.

7. Ceci inhaled the rich perfume of the cactus flower, the glowing white blossom would last less than a day.

8. Todd knew that there was a spare key hidden in the rock garden, he could not remember which rock concealed the key.

9. Eddie bought several folk paintings while sailing around the Caribbean islands, his friends appreciated these colorful souvenirs.

____

____

10. Waiting for class to begin, Abigail read her essay one last time, she found a few remaining errors.

____

____

ACTIVITY 11: Edit Comma Splices

Seven of the following sentences contain comma splices. Correct each of the comma splices by making the comma splice into two sentences, adding a coordinating conjunction after the comma, or changing the comma to a semicolon and adding a conjunctive adverb. If the sentence is correct, write "correct" in the blank.

EXAMPLE The number of young peole who vote is declining, the number of elderly people who vote is increasing.

The number of young people who vote is declining; however, the number of elderly people who vote is increasing.

1. Akio immersed the spinach in a basin of water, he separated the leaves from the stems.

____

____

2. After our sixth-grade class collected starfish, sea urchins, and periwinkles on our field trip to the tide pools, we kept the animals alive in a saltwater aquarium.

____

3. When Noel was in high school, his aunt gave him five hundred dollars to invest in the stock market, six months later, he had doubled his money.

____

____

4. After Corinne became a salesclerk, she realized that she had not always been a very nice customer, she resolved to be more patient when she went shopping.

5. The campers shivered happily as Nancy told them the ghost story, her voice alternating between fear and surprise.

6. The war in Iraq disrupted Neil and Joanna's wedding plans, they decided to marry at the courthouse and have a reception after Neil returned home.

7. I heard a sickening crunch as I stepped out into the foggy morning, and I realized I had crushed another snail.

8. Tim appreciated the rich, nutty aroma of fresh coffee, he did not like its taste nearly as much.

9. The firefighters shook their heads in disgust, another pedestrian had tossed a lit cigarette onto a restaurant awning.

10. Reaching the top of the steep, narrow trail, Bronwen admired the view, the beauty of the green river valley made her forget her fear of heights.

ACTIVITY 12: Eliminate Comma Splices from a Paragraph

Eliminate the comma splices from the following paragraph.

EXAMPLE Single people always envy married people, married people always envy single people. [handwritten correction: "and" inserted after "people,"]

After Rachel became engaged, the first person she told was her sister, Bonnie. Rachel was hesitant to tell her parents because they wanted her to wait until after she graduated from college to get married, Bonnie would understand because she had married Kurt when she was Rachel's age. Rachel didn't want her parents to overhear her on the telephone, she went to the couple's apartment to talk. Rachel did not mind helping her sister carry dirty clothes down to the laundry room, she did not mind giving Bonnie change for the machines, ever since she got married, Bonnie never seemed to have any money. Although the laundry room was hot and stuffy, Bonnie said it was a good place for them to talk. Kurt was studying for a midterm, the apartment was so small that Rachel and Bonnie's conversation would have disturbed him. Bonnie admired her sister's new diamond ring, she was even more interested in the ski trip that the engaged couple had planned. Bonnie and Kurt used to take weekend trips together when they each lived with their parents. Folding Kurt's worn jeans, Bonnie said that she envied Rachel, being engaged, according to Bonnie, is much more romantic than being married.

D. MISPLACED MODIFIERS

A *modifier* is a word or group of words that describes or adds information about another word. A modifier should appear as close as possible to the word it modifies.

Jane spent *almost* fifty dollars on her haircut. [The modifier appears next to the word it modifies, *fifty*.]

Spinach contains lutein, a vitamin *that strengthens the eyes*. [The modifier appears next to *vitamin*, which is the word it modifies.]

A modifier is *misplaced* when it appears in the wrong place in the sentence. Either it seems to modify a word other than the one the writer intended, or there's more than one word it could modify and the reader can't tell which one.

MISPLACED The carpentry student nailed the plank to the floor *with red hair*. [Did the floor have red hair?]

CLEAR The carpentry student *with red hair* nailed the plank to the floor.

MISPLACED The restaurant *only* serves lunch on Sundays. [Is lunch the only meal served on Sundays, or are Sundays the only days that lunch is served?]

CLEAR The restaurant serves *only* lunch on Sundays.

CLEAR The restaurant serves lunch on Sundays *only*.

MISPLACED Leo walked outside to smell the flowering rosemary plant *wearing his bathing suit*. [Is the plant wearing his bathing suit?]

CLEAR *Wearing his bathing suit,* Leo walked outside to smell the flowering rosemary plant.

ACTIVITY 13: Identify Misplaced Modifiers

Four of the following sentences contain a misplaced modifier. Underline the misplaced modifier in each of these sentences. Write "correct" after the sentence that does not contain a misplaced modifier.

EXAMPLE My supervisor said I needed to improve my attitude <u>in her office</u>.

1. The beer can almost hit my grandmother thrown out of the car window.
2. The new standards for graduation only required a low-level statistics class.
3. Boris found a pink and squirming nest of baby mice.

4. Leo borrowed a shirt from his brother with long sleeves.

5. My little niece threw her creamed spinach into the air.

To correct a misplaced modifier, place the modifier closer to the word it describes.

MISPLACED The Italian visitors drove a rental car *leaving on vacation.* [It appears the rental car is leaving on vacation.]

CLEAR *Leaving on vacation,* the Italian visitors drove a rental car. [The modifier is placed closer to the word it describes, *visitors.*]

HOW TO Correct Misplaced Modifiers

- Place them as close as possible to the word they modify.

ACTIVITY 14: Correct Misplaced Modifiers

Underline the misplaced modifier in each of the following sentences. Then, rewrite the sentence, moving the modifier closer to the word it modifies and making other changes as necessary.

EXAMPLE Parker told the noisy employees to shape up in his expensive new suit.

Wearing his expensive new suit, Parker told the noisy employees to shape up.

1. My husband and I volunteered at the school antique sale with the best of intentions.

____

____

2. The volunteers put out the hillside fire from the next county.

____

3. The kids I was babysitting from next door played video games for hours.

____

4. Liam greeted the unexpected guests in his old pajamas.

5. My learning group always arranged to meet in the Student Union at my previous college.

6. Rosie almost spent two weeks in Las Vegas and went on to Reno for another week.

7. Dean took the rabbit to the veterinarian that had the sore paw.

8. Taka polished the antique cabinet standing on a stepladder.

9. Annick only told her coach what the doctor had said, but the coach told her parents.

10. My leaky faucet dripped water all day that I need to replace.

E. DANGLING MODIFIERS

A modifier is *dangling* when there's no word in the sentence that it can logically modify. Most dangling modifiers occur at the beginnings of sentences.

DANGLING *Smiling broadly,* the award fulfilled Renee's dreams. [It appears that the award is smiling.]

CLEAR *Smiling broadly,* Renee accepted the award that fulfilled her dreams.

DANGLING *In running for the taxi,* my foot tripped on the crack in the sidewalk. [Is the foot running for the taxi?]

CLEAR *As I was running for the taxi,* my foot tripped on the crack in the sidewalk.

ACTIVITY 15: Identify Dangling Modifiers

Four of the following sentences contain a dangling modifier. Underline the dangling modifier in each of these sentences. Write "correct" after the sentence that does not contain a dangling modifier.

EXAMPLE Deciding to join the team, the coach enthusiastically shook Sara's hand.

1. After finishing all of the basic classes, college became easier.
2. Having admired Elvis since she was a little girl, Caitlin has devoted a whole room to his memorabilia.
3. No one realized the problem with the proposal, pleased by the low cost.
4. To control your anger, a psychologist may be necessary.
5. Tired from the long flight, the crowds in the parking lot were depressing.

To correct a dangling modifier, rewrite the sentence so the reader knows what is being modified. You can add this information either to the modifier or to the rest of the sentence.

DANGLING *Waiting in line,* the wind began to blow. [The reader can't tell who is waiting in line.]

CLEAR *While I was waiting in line,* the wind began to blow.

CLEAR Waiting in line, *I* felt the wind begin to blow.

HOW TO Correct Dangling Modifiers

- Add information about what or whom it is describing.

ACTIVITY 16: Correct Dangling Modifiers

Underline the dangling modifier in each of the following sentences. Then, rewrite the sentence, making it clear what or whom the modifier is describing.

EXAMPLE Gusting to forty-five miles an hour, the tree limb loudly hit the tin roof.

The tree limb loudly hit the tin roof because the winds were gusting to forty-five miles an hour.

1. Shaking the principal's hand, Clarence's goal of a high school diploma became a reality.

2. Fed by hot winds and dry grass, the firefighters faced a difficult challenge.

3. Mom's jigsaw puzzle was complete, snapping the last piece into place.

4. Searching for a new way to treat diabetes, medical advances were made.

5. Seeing her grandson win a prize at the science fair, her heart was overwhelmed with pride.

6. Removing her foot from the accelerator, Diana's car came to a stop.

7. Having saved for years to buy a house, it was exciting that the Kangs' dream was coming true.

8. While window shopping at the mall, a sports watch caught my eye.

9. Deliriously happy, the newlyweds' limousine slowly drove to their hotel.

10. Water leaked into my boat while rowing as fast as possible.

F. ACTIVE AND PASSIVE VOICE

In a sentence written in *active voice,* the subject performs the action; it does something. In a sentence written in *passive voice,* the subject receives the action; something is done to it. Readers prefer the active voice in most sentences because they normally expect the subject to be performing the action, so a sentence where the subject doesn't perform the action takes longer to understand. The active voice is also less wordy than the passive voice.

PASSIVE VOICE The tail of the kite *was caught by* the boy.

ACTIVE VOICE The boy *caught* the kite by the tail.

PASSIVE VOICE The newspaper *is read by* my mother each morning.

ACTIVE VOICE My mother *reads* the newspaper each morning.

HOW TO Use Active Voice

- Decide who or what is performing the action in a sentence.
- Make the performer of the action the subject of the sentence.

ACTIVITY 17: Use the Active Voice

Rewrite each of the following sentences, changing the passive voice to the active voice.

EXAMPLE Tiger Woods was given the green jacket by the tournament's sponsor.

The tournament's sponsor gave Tiger Woods the green jacket.

1. The runners were encouraged by the spectators.

___

2. The memos had been signed by the manager.

___

3. A doctoral degree in physics was earned by Professor Patel.

___

4. An educational play about AIDS was performed by the juniors.

___

5. The baby was taken to the park by his older brother.

___

6. The party was planned by Milo, but all the work was done by his family.

___

7. The assignment was given at the beginning of class by the teaching assistant.

___

8. A swimming pool was installed by the previous owners of the house.

___

9. The movie was made by the Coen brothers, and the hero was played by George Clooney.

____

____

10. Our pets were fed by a neighbor.

____

ACTIVITY 18: Revise for the Active Voice

The following paragraph contains sentences written in the passive voice. Rewrite the paragraph so that all sentences are in the active voice.

EXAMPLE A bus smashed ~~T~~the car that I used to get to school ~~was smashed by a bus.~~

A university education must be paid for. School and work are balanced differently by my friends and me. Monica had both a full-time and a part-time job for two years following high school. Now a job isn't needed during college. She earns high grades because she doesn't have to divide her energies between work and school. A full-time night job was chosen by Willy, and only nine credits are taken by him. He does data entry for the business office of a department store. An administrative position in the same office will be taken by him after graduation. Willy earns enough money by working at night to make payments on a new car. I don't need a car. However, money for college is needed. I chose to take out student loans to pay for my education. My friends and I live very different lives.

G. PARALLELISM

When two or more groups of words in a sentence are parts of a pair or series, these word groups should be *parallel,* or similar in their grammatical structure. The following sentences are written using parallel structure:

> Today, we drove to Philadelphia, visited the Liberty Bell, and ate at our favorite restaurants.

The underlined parts of this sentence are parallel because the group of words in each part follows the same grammatical structure: past tense verb followed by words that modify the verb or complete its meaning.

> My girlfriend is smart in school, friendly to everyone, and fun to be with.

The underlined parts of this sentence are parallel because they follow the same sentence structure: adjective followed by words that modify the adjective.

Here are examples of sentences that do not have parallel structure, each followed by a revised sentence using parallel structure. Notice that the revised sentences are easier to read and understand.

NOT PARALLEL I love going to the movies, reading, and to walk.

PARALLEL I love going to the movies, reading, and walking.

NOT PARALLEL He drove dangerously fast, missed the curve, and wrecks his car.

PARALLEL He drove dangerously fast, missed the curve, and wrecked his car.

NOT PARALLEL I don't like to fill out these financial aid forms that are difficult, long, and have too many words.

PARALLEL I don't like to fill out these financial aid forms that are difficult, long, and wordy.

HOW TO Write Using Parallel Sentence Structure

- Reread each sentence looking for pairs or series of word groups in a sentence.
- Check that each of the groups of words in the pair or series has a similar sentence structure.
- Rewrite any parts of the pair or series that are not parallel in structure.

ACTIVITY 19: Use Parallelism

Rewrite each of the following sentences using parallel structure. If the sentence already uses parallel structure, write "correct."

EXAMPLE My favorite activities include horseback riding, hiking, and to play soccer.

My favorite activities include horseback riding, hiking, and playing soccer.

1. My mother was a hairdresser, taxi driver, and being a secretary.

2. In my University Studies class, I have learned to study more effectively and preparing for an exam.

3. The bookstore has my favorite books: cookbooks, biographies, and novels.

4. I found the concert to be loud, expensive, and was not very entertaining.

5. Going to the dentist is worse than to go to the hospital.

6. The buffet included undercooked shrimp, limp lettuce, and the muffins were stale.

7. Leaving her home to move to a new city, Ceci was filled with fear and anticipation.

8. The squirrel peeked out, stole the nut, and then back to his home.

____

____

9. The Ferris wheel is my favorite carnival ride, but my sister prefers the haunted house and to ride the merry-go-round.

____

____

10. He thinks the world of her, and she thinks he is her world, too.

____

____

ACTIVITY 20: Revise for Parallelism

The following paragraph contains sentences with pairs or series of word groups that are not parallel in structure. Edit the paragraph so that all sentences are parallel.

EXAMPLE We need a visionary leader in each of our groups, but ~~we're knowing~~ ^we know^ this isn't likely.

A visionary leader is someone who is not afraid to lead and of taking the group to a place it would not be otherwise. A visionary leader isn't necessarily the most dynamic person in the group, but who is willing to listen to others. Such a leader constantly works hard to improve conditions for every member of the group, seeks to put the needs of the group members first, and a desire to see the group succeed as a whole. The visionary leader is not always the group member with the most imaginative ideas, but is the member who has the skills and energy to put these ideas into action. We could use more visionary leaders: they touch, inspire, and are changing the world we live in.

CHAPTER

26 Improving Word Choice

Speaking and writing are key ways to communicate your thoughts and feelings to others, and different situations require different word choices. Just as you wouldn't go to a job interview in a wedding dress or to a football game in a bathing suit, you wouldn't write to your boss in the same way that you write to a friend or daughter. You choose the best words for the person and the occasion. But how do you improve your word choice? Following are several strategies for expanding and improving the choice of words you use when you write.

A. VOCABULARY

One way to expand your word choice and to better understand what you read is to develop a broad vocabulary. How can you tell if your vocabulary needs improvement? Do you have difficulty finding the words to express what you want to say or write in class? At a party, do you hesitate to join a conversation because you can't follow what others are saying? Do you find yourself skipping a lot of words in newspapers, magazines, or your college textbooks because you don't know what they mean? If you have answered "yes" to any of these questions, you'll want to work to improve your vocabulary.

HOW TO Improve Your Vocabulary

- Read. The more you read, the more words you'll learn.
- Just ask. If you are with friends or classmates, don't hesitate to ask the meaning of words you don't understand.
- Play word games. Try *Scrabble,* crossword puzzles, a *Word of the Day* calendar, or a Web site that sends you a word each day.
- Keep vocabulary index cards. Write each unfamiliar word on one side of an index card. On the other side, write the definition and use the word in a sentence. Keep these index cards with you for easy study and reference.

ACTIVITY 1: Build Your Vocabulary

Using Chapters 22, 23, and 24 of this Handbook, create vocabulary cards for unfamiliar grammar terms such as *linking verbs*. Write the word on one side of the index card. On the other side, write the definition and a sentence that provides an example.

Meaning from Context

Reading is the most effective way to improve vocabulary. While reading, if you come across a word you don't know, see if you can determine the meaning of the word from the context — that is, from the other words in the sentence. For example, consider this sentence:

> Although Amy is often *morose,* she seems happy today.

What does *morose* mean? Because you know that *although* is a word that shows contrast and Amy seems happy today, then *morose* must be the opposite of *happy.* Amy must often be sad.

ACTIVITY 2: Determine Meaning from Context

Read the following passage from an article about figure skating. Try to determine the meanings of the underlined words from the words around them. Write the meanings next to the words in the spaces provided.

> There are many athletic and artistic elements in figure skating. Initial skills include the all important basic stroking forward, backward, and in both directions. Jumps are so predominant in modern figure skating that we could say that this is the "jump era." There are seven preliminary jumps that can be rotated in the air. Since their inception toward the beginning of the [twentieth] century, these jumps have been doubled and now quite commonly trebled by both men and women.

elements ______________________________

initial ______________________________

predominant ______________________________

preliminary ______________________

rotated ______________________

inception ______________________

trebled ______________________

Learn Roots, Prefixes, and Suffixes

Another way to improve your vocabulary is to memorize the meanings of common word roots, prefixes, and suffixes. A word root is the main part of a word, a prefix is added to the beginning of a word or word root, and a suffix is added to the end of a word or word root. Here are the meanings of some common English word roots, prefixes, and suffixes.

ENGLISH WORD ROOTS

Root	*Meaning*	*Examples*
audi	to hear	audience, audio
bene	to help	benefit, benevolence
geo	earth	geography, geometry
logo	word or thought	logic, biology, geology
manu	hand	manufacture, manual
photo	light	photography, telephoto
tele	far away	telepathy, telegraph
vid, vis	to see	visit, vision, video

ENGLISH PREFIXES

Prefix	*Meaning*	*Examples*
ante-	before	antebellum, antedate
anti-	against	antisocial, antibody
bi-	two	bilateral, bipolar
de-	from	declaw, desensitize
hyper-	over, more	hypersensitive
mal-	bad	malpractice
post-	after	postwar, postscript
trans-	across	transport, transition
uni-	one	uniform, unicycle

ENGLISH SUFFIXES

Suffix	*Meaning*	*Examples*
-acy	state or quality	democracy, privacy
-dom	state of being	kingdom, freedom

-en	cause or become	cheapen, blacken
-ish	having the quality of	clownish
-less	lack of, without	childless, humorless
-ology	the study of	psychology
-ment	condition of	impediment, payment
-sion, -tion	state of being	confusion, transition

ACTIVITY 3: Learn Roots, Prefixes, and Suffixes

Create a vocabulary card for each root, prefix, and suffix in the first column above. Write the root, prefix, or suffix on one side of the index card. Write the meaning and an example on the other side. Review these cards regularly until you have memorized them.

B. UNNECESSARY REPETITION

Although repetition can help you emphasize and connect ideas as you write, too much repetition may lose your reader's attention. Sometimes, you may not even realize that you're repeating words or using words that mean the same thing. Notice the unnecessary words in the following sentences.

REPETITION I wouldn't choose or select that suit.

REVISED I wouldn't choose that suit.

REPETITION We tried to forget the sad events of that day and put them out of our minds.

REVISED We tried to forget the sad events of that day.

REPETITION The positive benefits of this course of action were obvious and apparent.

REVISED The benefits of this action were obvious.

HOW TO Avoid Unnecessary Repetition

Check that each word in a sentence

- adds interest.
- is specific.
- does not restate what you have already said.

ACTIVITY 4: Avoid Unnecessary Repetition

Revise each of the following sentences to avoid unnecessary repetition.

EXAMPLE I will never ever do anything like that again in the future.

I will never do anything like that again.

1. My very favorite song I like the most is "I Can't Make You Love Me."

2. Julia wanted to get caught up and be up-to-date on what was going on in class.

3. Don't confuse me with the facts and data!

4. We never knew or realized how important this event would be.

5. Let's just wait and pass the time until she returns.

C. WORDINESS

Eliminating wordiness is similar to avoiding unnecessary repetition. Repetition results from repeating the same idea in different words, and wordiness results from using too many words to say something or using "filler" phrases that don't contribute to the meaning of a sentence.

Notice the wordiness in the following sentences.

WORDY I would really very much like to go to that game.

REVISED I would like to go to that game.

WORDY I get to make the choice of where I go.

REVISED I get to choose where I go.

WORDY I feel that we have a greater amount of freedom to choose these days.

REVISED We have more freedom to choose today.

ACTIVITY 5: Eliminate Wordiness

Revise the following sentences to eliminate wordiness.

EXAMPLE I believe that you are right.

You are right.

1. I would like to say that I agree with you.

2. I am of the opinion that anyone who writes on this topic as a subject for an essay is not thinking straight.

3. A large number of students in the near future will agree with us.

4. At an earlier point in time, this wouldn't have happened, or it would have been postponed until a later time.

5. I believe that this is true for the reason that students feel differently today than they did at an earlier point in time.

CHAPTER

27 Improving Spelling

As you edit your writing, you'll want to be sure to check your spelling. Misspelled words will cause your reader to focus on your lack of spelling skills rather than on what you have to say. You can often tell if a word is misspelled just by looking at it, or you can use a computer spell-check to catch errors. Because the spell-check can't catch all errors, though, it's useful to improve your spelling.

A. SPELLING RULES

One way to improve your spelling is to learn spelling rules that can help you master the spelling of commonly misspelled words.

Rule 1. Use *i* before *e* except after *c,* or when sounded like *ay* as in *neighbor* and *weigh.*

believe, niece, piece, fierce
receive, ceiling, conceive, deceive
eight, freight, sleigh, weight

Exceptions: either, neither, leisure, height, seize, weird, science, counterfeit

ACTIVITY 1: Use *i* before *e* except after *c*

In the space provided, correct each of the following misspelled words or write "correct" if the word is spelled correctly.

EXAMPLE hieght ___height___

1. conceited ______________
2. recieve ______________
3. neighbor ______________

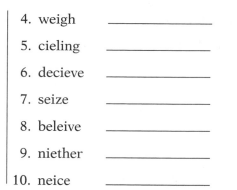

4. weigh ____________
5. cieling ____________
6. decieve ____________
7. seize ____________
8. beleive ____________
9. niether ____________
10. neice ____________

ACTIVITY 2: Correct *i* before *e* except after *c* Errors

Underline each of the misspelled words in the following sentences. Then, write the correct spelling of these words in the space provided. If a sentence has no spelling errors, write "correct."

EXAMPLE Jerry has a neice and nephew. niece

1. Patrice asked Amando for a piece of paper. ________
2. It is important not to carry excess wieght when you are backpacking. ________
3. A good pair of shoes releived Kenia's backaches. ________
4. In his liesure time, Hal likes to go bow hunting. ________
5. Majel concieved of a way to pass the exam without reading the textbook. ________
6. Leonard was so concieted that people tried to avoid him. ________
7. On Christmas, Grandfather treated us to an old-fashioned sleigh ride. ________
8. My favorite beige jacket always looks dirty. ________
9. Tim decieved his teacher by forging his father's signature on his report card. ________
10. When we recieve your order, we will notify you by e-mail. ________

Rule 2. When adding an ending that begins with a vowel (such as *-ed* or *-ing*) to a word that ends with a consonant, double the consonant if it (1) is preceded by a single vowel and (2) ends a one-syllable word or stressed syllable.

bet, betting
stop, stopped
commit, committed
occur, occurrence

Exception: Even if the consonant ends a stressed syllable, do not double it if the syllable is no longer stressed when the ending is added: *refer, reference.*

ACTIVITY 3: Double the Final Consonant

In the space provided, add the correct ending to each of the following words.

EXAMPLE get + *ing* getting

1. travel + *ed* ________
2. dig + *ing* ________
3. omit + *ed* ________
4. control + *ing* ________
5. prefer + *ence* ________
6. scan + *er* ________
7. nag + *ing* ________
8. good + *ness* ________
9. defer + *al* ________
10. hop + *ed* ________

ACTIVITY 4: Correct Final Consonant Errors

Underline each of the misspelled words in the following sentences. Then, write the correct spelling of these words in the space provided. If a sentence has no spelling errors, write "correct."

EXAMPLE The rabbit hoped to the side of the house. hopped

1. Burton stoped kicking the bottom of Bethany's chair only when he fell asleep. ________

2. They never succeeded at ridding their house of ants. ________
3. Felicia felt deep saddness when her friend moved away. ________
4. After tiping over his glass, Lewis apologized and left the room. ________
5. Ron and Leni held hands and planed their future. ________
6. Efren made a referrence to his former girlfriend. ________
7. Delphine repeatted her name three times before the clerk said it correctly. ________
8. The occurence of car theft in the parking lot has doubled in the last year. ________
9. Pegeen believed that Neville was betting on a losing team. ________
10. Stuart laborred over his statistics homework for six hours. ________

Rule 3. Drop a final silent *e* from a word when adding an ending that begins with a vowel. Keep the final *e* if the ending begins with a consonant.

retire, retiring	age, aging	desire, desiring
hate, hateful	state, statement	lone, lonely

Exceptions: ninth, truly, argument, judgment, courageous, manageable

ACTIVITY 5: Drop the Final Silent *e*

In the space provided, add the specified ending to each of the following words.

EXAMPLE perspire + ing ____perspiring____

1. bite + ing ________
2. encourage + ment ________
3. safe + ty ________
4. nine + th ________
5. care + ful ________
6. shine + ing ________

7. true + ly ______________
8. fade + ing ______________
9. use + able ______________
10. state + ment ______________

ACTIVITY 6: Correct Final Silent *e* Errors

Underline each of the misspelled words in the following sentences. Then, write the correct spelling of these words in the space provided. If a sentence has no spelling errors, write "correct."

EXAMPLE He thought that he was ageing too quickly. aging

1. Miria's greatest achievment was hiking the entire Appalachian Trail. ______________
2. This coat has a removeable lining. ______________
3. The lavish meal left us desireing nothing more. ______________
4. Stan remained quiet to avoid an arguement with his friends in public. ______________
5. The shoppers were hopeing to find bargains. ______________
6. The audience made hatful remarks as the senator tried to speak. ______________
7. Clarence did not use the best judgement in choosing a roommate. ______________
8. The surest way to be fired from a job is not to show up. ______________
9. Denise found her courses in managment more interesting than those in marketing. ______________
10. Sheldon spent the rest of the afternoon writeing his résumé. ______________

Rule 4. When adding an ending other than *-ing* to a word that ends in *y,* you sometimes need to change the *y* to *i.* If the *y* is preceded by a consonant, change it to *i;* if you're adding *-s,* also add an *e* after the *i.* If you're adding *-ing* or the *y* is preceded by a vowel, don't change it to *i.*

easy, easiest	duty, dutiful	reply, replies
marry, married	monkey, monkeys	play, played
apply, applying	dry, drying	stay, staying

ACTIVITY 7: Change *y* to *i*

In the space provided, add the specified ending to each of the following words, and write the new word.

EXAMPLE carry + ed ___carried___

1. pay + ing ____________
2. turkey + s ____________
3. say + ing ____________
4. fry + ed ____________
5. pretty + ily ____________
6. plenty + ful ____________
7. hurry + s ____________
8. fly + ing ____________
9. happy + ness ____________
10. play + ful ____________

ACTIVITY 8: Correct *y* to *i* Errors

Underline each of the misspelled words in the following sentences. Then, write the correct spelling of these words in the space provided. If a sentence has no spelling errors, write "correct."

EXAMPLE The couple's happyness left us inspired. ___happiness___

1. To find employment, he read the classified ads. ________
2. We were puzzled by the trickyness of the test question. ________
3. Lester has been studiing all day. ________
4. After several apologys, Wanda finally forgave her brother.

   ____
5. Rainer easyly jumped over the puddle. ________

6. It was difficult to say which sister was most beautyful. ________

7. In warm weather, the clothes dryed very quickly on the line. ________

8. The sounds of the children playing in the street carryed into my sixth-floor apartment. ________

9. The two attornies made an agreement to avoid going to court. ________

10. After staying at campgrounds, I found the motel luxurious. ________

B. COMMONLY MISSPELLED WORDS

The following are one hundred commonly misspelled words. Create spelling lists or cards to practice spelling them correctly.

absence
accommodate
all right
analyze
anoint
anonymous
benefit
boundary
business
category
committee
conscience
conscious
corroborate
counterfeit
dealt
definitely
despair
dilemma
disappoint
ecstasy
eighth
embarrass
exceed

existence
fascinate
February
forty
fulfill
government
grammar
guarantee
guard
height
hoarse
holiday
hygiene
icicles
imagine
indispensable
innocent
irresistible
irritable
jealousy
league
leisure
license
losing

maneuver
marriage
meant
minute
misspelled
necessary
ninth
noticeable
occurrence
often
optimistic
pamphlet
parallel
peculiar
persistent
phenomenon
perseverance
principal
principle
privilege
procedure
pursue
receipt
receive

recommend
repetition
rhythm
ridiculous
roommate
schedule
seize
separate
sergeant
sheriff
sophomore
subtle
succeed
supersede
surgeon
tongue
tragedy
truly
tyranny
undoubtedly
until
vacuum
vengeance
vicious
warrant
weird
wholly
yacht

ACTIVITY 9: Correct Sentences for Spelling

Underline the misspelled words in each of the following sentences. Then, write the correct spelling of these words in the space provided. (There may be more than one error in each sentence.)

EXAMPLE I always recomended vacumming, but I definitly see the benafit of it now. recommended, vacuuming, definitely, benefit

1. When Rafa telephoned, Yoli was studing her chemistry, so he apologyzed for bothering her. ______
2. After beging for three weeks to be given a better work schedule, Alvin stoped asking. ______
3. Gino had been liveing in his apartment for fifteen years when he recieved the eviction notice. ______
4. A counterfiet coin may wiegh less than a genuine one. ______
5. Shelley was carful when she tryed to remove the splinter from the child's finger. ______
6. You can easyly waste your liesure time on activities that you don't really enjoy. ______
7. A student writeing a persuasive essay needs to construct a very strong arguement supporting his or her opinions. ______

8. Krystle prefered ordering from a catalogue to shoping at the mall.

____

9. Unfortunately, Vincent omited his social security number when he applyed for a scholarship. _______________

10. The dutys of the store manager never stoped at five o'clock. ____

____

Exercise Central
The *Discoveries* Web site provides additional practice with these spelling rules. Go to **www.bedfordstmartins.com/discoveries** and click on "Exercise Central." Once you log in, click on any of the exercises under "Spelling."

C. COMMONLY CONFUSED WORDS

Commonly confused words are words that sound similar but have different spellings and meanings.

accept: to agree to	I *accept* your offer.
except: excluding	Everyone *except* Joan was invited.
adapt: to adjust	He had to *adapt* to his new town.
adopt: to take on	He realized that he would have to *adopt* a new attitude.
advice: a suggestion	Please take my *advice*.
advise: to suggest	I *advise* you to slow down.
affect: to influence	Her partying did not *affect* her grades.
effect: a result	The *effect*, though, was that she was under stress.
all ready: prepared	We are *all ready* for the holidays.
already: previously	We have *already* bought all of the food we need.
cite: to refer to	Jerome is always careful to *cite* his sources.
sight: vision	The eye surgery improved her *sight*.

site: a location	This paper was about the *site* of the new museum.
complement: to go well with; something that goes well with something else	This tie does not *complement* your shirt.
compliment: to admire; an expression of admiration	I *compliment* you on your choice of pants.
conscience: moral principles	Josue's *conscience* wouldn't permit him to cheat.
conscious: aware	He was *conscious* of students cheating around him.
farther: a longer physical distance	My aunt lives *farther* away than my family can drive in one day.
further: additional; more	The committee agreed to *further* discussion of the issue.
loose: not tight or secure	Jerry's tooth was *loose.*
lose: to misplace	He didn't want to *lose* it if it fell out.
principal: head of a school; main or leading	The *principal* of my high school was one of the *principal* supporters of the new gym.
principle: a basic truth or belief	He believed in the *principle* of daily exercise.
to: toward	Abigail ran *to* the lake.
too: excessively; also	Her brother, Michael, was *too* slow to keep up and stopped along the way, *too.*
two: the number between one and three	The *two* of them arrived an hour apart.
weather: conditions such as sun, rain, and wind	The *weather* in Washington, D.C., was beautiful.
whether: a word indicating choice or possibility	I had to decide *whether* to leave or stay.

ACTIVITY 10: Correct a Paragraph for Spelling

Correct the misspelled words in the following paragraph by writing the correct spelling above each misspelled word.

EXAMPLE Ahmad loves computers because they ~~effect~~ affect the way he writes.

Ahmad feels the campus computer labs need improveing. Before geting his own computer, he relyed heavily on the labs. Although they were convient, they were to noisey and crowded. Often computers were unavailable because the maintance was so bad. When he found a free computer, he was distractted by the rowdyness of the other students. After recieving a computer from his father, Ahmad lookked foreward to his life being easyer. Unffortunatly, he still had problems when continueing projects that he had begun at home. Once, he used a Macintosh by mistake and accidently reformated his diskete, loosing all his data. Often, he had difficultys printing at the lab, discoverring pages of wierd symbols weather he wanted two or not. The technicians say that his home software isn't compattible with the software at the lab. Now, he's more conscience of mistakes than ever. Ahmad's father tells him that computers have all ready created new problems while solveing other ones.

D. USING A DICTIONARY

A good dictionary can be very helpful to you as a writer. Look at the following entry taken from the *American Heritage Dictionary of the English Language.*

Spelling and syllabication — Pronunciation — Part of speech

Meaning: **yo-yo** (yō´-yō´) *n. pl.* **-yos**. A toy on the shape of a spool, around which a string is wound. The string is attached to the finger, and the yo-yo is spun down and reeled up by moving the hand. [Originally from a trademark.]

Word origin

Spelling and syllabication: The main entry in bold type shows the correct spelling and syllabication of *yo-yo*. If you weren't sure of the spelling or where to divide the word between lines, you could find out by looking it up in the dictionary.

Pronunciation: The second entry shows how to pronounce the word *yo-yo.* If you weren't sure of the pronunciation, you would use this entry as your guide. The accents indicate which syllables to stress. Both syllables are stressed in *yo-yo,* but notice that the first accent is in bold, so you would place extra stress on the first syllable. For other pronunciation marks, look at the bottom of each page of the dictionary.

Part of speech: The third entry, *n,* shows the part of speech. *Yo-yo* is a noun. The dictionary also provides the plural, *pl,* so that you will know that to spell more than one *yo-yo,* you add *-s.*

The most common labels for parts of speech are the following:

n.	noun
v.	verb
adj.	adjective
adv.	adverb
pron.	pronoun
prep.	preposition
conj.	conjunction

Meaning: The next entry shows what the word means and can be helpful if this is a word you don't already know. If a word has more than one meaning, each meaning is numbered.

Word origin: The origin of the word appears in brackets. This dictionary entry shows you that the word *yo-yo* was derived from a trademark or brand name.

HOW TO Improve Your Spelling

- Learn the four common spelling rules.
- Memorize how to spell commonly misspelled words.
- Memorize the correct spelling for commonly confused words.
- Use a dictionary.

ACTIVITY 11: Use a Dictionary

Look up each of the following words in a dictionary and write the spelling and syllabication, pronunciation, part of speech, meaning, and, if provided, the word origin.

EXAMPLE quake

quake (kwak) v. quaked, quaking, quakes. 1. To shake or tremble with instability or shock. 2. To shake or tremble with cold or strong emotion [Middle English quaken].

1. potluck

2. saloon

3. espouse

4. fatten

5. yardmaster

CHAPTER 28

Improving Punctuation

You use punctuation to make it easier for your readers to follow your meaning. Just as your car's taillights communicate that you are planning to stop, turn right, or turn left, punctuation communicates to your readers what to expect next. Readers depend on punctuation to guide them through your text. For example, what does this sentence mean?

Don't let the snake eat Jorge.

Is the snake about to eat Jorge, or is Jorge supposed to prevent the snake from eating? Adding a comma to this sentence makes it clear.

Don't let the snake eat, Jorge.

The reader now understands that Jorge is supposed to prevent the snake from eating its food.

The following punctuation rules will help you make your meaning clear and communicate to your readers more effectively.

A. COMMAS

The *comma* (,) is used to separate parts of a sentence to make the meaning clear.

Rule 1. Use a comma after an introductory word, phrase, or clause.

Actually, snakes like to eat rodents.

After feeding the snake, you can leave for the NASCAR race.

As Jorge explained, snakes eat a variety of foods.

ACTIVITY 1: Use Commas with Introductory Words, Phrases, or Clauses

Add a comma after the introductory word, phrase, or clause in each of the following sentences.

EXAMPLE While I usually like the opera, I didn't like this one.

1. Smelling Janelle's perfume in the apartment Oscar knew that she was ready to go to the party.
2. First Corey fastened his seatbelt and put on his sunglasses.
3. Whether you agree or not I'm taking biology next semester.
4. In Wendy's opinion renting a large apartment is more convenient than owning a house.
5. While the children ate ice cream and cake and played games their parents became better acquainted.

ACTIVITY 2: Write Sentences Using Commas with Introductory Words, Phrases, or Clauses

Rewrite each of the following sentences, adding an introductory word, phrase, or clause followed by a comma.

EXAMPLE Gil and Chet would not stop talking.

During the movie, Gil and Chet would not stop talking.

1. I heard the drone of a small airplane overhead.

   ____

2. She put on more lipstick and mascara.

   ____

   ____

3. Your parents were watching you through the kitchen window.

   ____

   ____

4. We keep reams of paper and extra cartridges for the printer.

   ____

   ____

5. Philip admitted that he was wrong.

____

Rule 2. Use commas to separate three or more words, phrases, or clauses in a series. Do not use a comma before the first item in the series or after the last item.

Jane bought books, games, and CDs at the bookstore.

Before leaving, she talked to her roommate, turned off her computer, and locked her desk.

Jane forgot to feed the dog, she didn't make her bed, and she didn't clean the bathroom as she promised.

ACTIVITY 3: Use Commas in a Series

Add commas as needed to each of the following sentences to separate words, phrases, or clauses used in a series.

EXAMPLE My favorite foods are salmon, fried rice, and chocolate cake.

1. All I had in the refrigerator was a pint of sour milk a block of moldy cheese and a jar of olives.
2. Eileen packed underwear jeans sweaters socks shoes and maps.
3. Vikram walked down the street past the supermarket and around the corner.
4. Jorge filled the sandbox Gunilla set up the swings Noah built the seesaws Calvin welded the slide and Mahela painted the benches.
5. Chewing gum pacing the floor and looking at the clock were the only things to do in the waiting room.

ACTIVITY 4: Write Sentences Using Commas with a Series

For each of the following lists of items, write a complete sentence using these items in a series.

EXAMPLE hills, river beds, dusty trails

For our vacation, we hiked hills, river beds, and dusty trails.

1. pens, pencils, notebooks, folders, erasers

____

____

2. a pad of paper, a pair of scissors, a bottle of glue

____

____

3. on the dashboard, under the front seat, in the trunk

____

____

4. decorating the house, preparing a festive meal, spending time with the family

____

____

5. sang songs, told funny stories, did magic tricks, made balloon animals

____

____

Rule 3. Use a comma to separate two independent clauses joined by a coordinating conjunction.

I wanted to go to the concert, and I wanted to study for my exam.

I knew my test was important, but Shakira is my favorite singer.

I studied all afternoon, so I was able to go to the concert after all.

ACTIVITY 5: Use Commas with Coordinating Conjunctions

Add a comma to each of the following sentences to separate the two independent clauses joined by a coordinating conjunction.

EXAMPLE I wanted to leave early, yet my husband wanted to leave at noon.

1. The wind howled and the snow fell more thickly.
2. Margarita stood on a stepladder but she could not reach the ceiling.
3. Julio drank a second bottle of water yet he still was thirsty.
4. Marcia couldn't sleep for tomorrow she started a new job.
5. I wanted to call you on your birthday but you were out all night.

ACTIVITY 6: Join Sentences with Commas and Coordinating Conjunctions

Use a comma and a coordinating conjunction to join each of the following pairs of sentences into a single sentence.

EXAMPLE My mother loves to travel. She's a little afraid of flying.

My mother loves to travel, but she's a little afraid of flying.

1. Yusef sat in the driver's seat. His brothers pushed the car.

   ____

   ____

2. Aurelia found the strength to run even faster. She saw the banners at the finish line.

   ____

   ____

3. I realized that I had answered the essay question on my history midterm badly. I had only enough time to write a brief concluding paragraph.

   ____

   ____

   ____

4. The doctor gave Samia a pair of crutches. She could walk without further injuring her foot.

   ____

   ____

5. You could come to the dance with me. You could watch reruns on television.

____

____

Rule 4. Use commas before and after a descriptive word, phrase, or clause or an appositive (a noun that renames the noun right before it) if the word, phrase, clause, or appositive interrupts the flow of the sentence or could be removed from the sentence without changing its meaning. If the word, phrase, clause, or appositive is at the end of the sentence, use a comma before it.

My high school reunion, sadly, was missing the person I most wanted to see.

Jessie, who was my high school sweetheart, doesn't live here anymore.

The reunion, held over the Thanksgiving weekend, wasn't nearly as much fun as the last one.

I would really like to see Jessie, my old flame.

ACTIVITY 7: Use Commas with Descriptive Words, Phrases, and Clauses and Appositives

Add commas to each of the following sentences to set off the descriptive word, phrase, or clause or the appositive.

EXAMPLE Johnny, my closest friend, never has to study.

1. Mateo the youngest person in his family is the first to attend a university.
2. The driver of the car in front of us ignoring the stop sign sped through the intersection.
3. Ricky's new saxophone which had cost him his life savings enabled him to join his favorite swing band.
4. My date a massage therapist named Yolanda asked me in to meet her parents.
5. Janine's former roommate surprisingly was happy to see her.

ACTIVITY 8: Add Descriptive Words, Phrases, and Clauses with Commas and Appositives

Rewrite each of the following sentences by inserting the descriptive word, phrase, or clause or appositive provided. Include the required commas.

EXAMPLE Corky flew from his perch to my shoulder. (*my parakeet*)

Corky, my parakeet, flew from his perch to my shoulder.

1. Mr. Gardner ran unsuccessfully for state senator. (*my history teacher in junior high school*)

2. Hector's grandchildren ran into the kitchen. (*smelling the first batch of cookies in the oven*)

3. The library book gathered dust at the back of my closet. (*which I had never read*)

4. Gavin's wife has just published a magazine article about their trip to Bhutan. (*an agricultural advisor*)

5. Sally could not afford a new truck. (*unfortunately*)

Rule 5. Use commas to set off transitional words and phrases from the rest of the sentence.

It wasn't until I visited the museum, however, that I realized how much I liked art.

For example, I discovered I really enjoyed Remington's sculptures.

My friend, on the other hand, preferred Monet's paintings.

ACTIVITY 9: Use Commas to Set Off Transitional Words and Phrases

Add commas as needed to each of the following sentences to set off the transitional words and phrases.

EXAMPLE Surely, my car will be ready soon.

1. Subsequently the rest of the family came down with the flu.
2. Fritz likewise saved copies of his work in his e-mail files.
3. Furthermore the larger company has superior benefits.
4. The two-lane road alongside the freeway nevertheless is very scenic.
5. Only when Belinda heard the applause however did she realize that her speech was convincing.

ACTIVITY 10: Add Transitional Words and Phrases with Commas

Rewrite each of the following sentences by inserting the transitional word or phrase provided. Include the required commas.

EXAMPLE Sandy wants to be given a chance to try. (*nonetheless*)

Sandy, nonetheless, wants to be given a chance to try.

1. Consuelo is allergic to feathers and animal fur. (*however*)

   ____

2. Farak prefers snorkeling to scuba diving. (*on the other hand*)

   ____

3. The people who arrived late waited in the lobby for the first intermission. (*meanwhile*)

   ____

   ____

4. Some members of the city council want to increase the budget for street repairs and expansion of public parks. (*in addition*)

   ____

   ____

5. The tenants are pooling their money to buy the apartment building from the bank. (*as a result*)

____

____

Rule 6. Use a comma to separate the day of the month from the year. If the year is in the middle of a sentence, also use a comma after it.

I will start graduate school on September 4, 2008.

I was born on July 4, 1970, and immediately became the center of my grandmother's attention.

My goal is to have my master's degree by the time I turn forty on July 4, 2010.

ACTIVITY 11: Use Commas in Dates

Add commas as needed to each of the following sentences.

EXAMPLE My birthday is December 8,1977.

1. My father was born September 18 1956.
2. The automobile accident occurred October 30 1999.
3. February 29 2001 is a date that never existed.
4. I first filed an income tax return on April 15 1997.
5. November 8 1990 was the day that my aunt and uncle were married.

ACTIVITY 12: Write Sentences Using Commas in Dates

Complete each of the following sentences, giving the month, day, and year. Use commas as necessary.

EXAMPLE I received my degree on May 5, 1999.

1. Today's date is ______________.
2. ______________ is the date that I was born.
3. The date that I first attended class this semester was ______________.
4. ______________ is the date of the last holiday that I celebrated.
5. Next Saturday's date is ______________.

Rule 7. Use commas in addresses and place names to separate the various parts, such as the street, city, county, state or province, and country. If the address or place name ends in the middle of a sentence, also use a comma after it.

I have lived at 400 Elm Street, Chicago, Illinois, all of my life.

My closest friend now lives at 402 Oak Avenue, Bexar County, Texas.

ACTIVITY 13: Use Commas in Addresses and Place Names

Add commas as needed to each of the following sentences.

EXAMPLE Another friend lives at 632 Pecan Street, Toronto, Canada.

1. His office is located at 4100 Manchester Drive Albany New York.
2. I have some relatives who live in Atlanta Georgia and some who live in Tampa Florida.
3. There is a large medical center in Dane County Wisconsin.
4. Tamara celebrated New Year's Eve in Paris France.
5. I mailed the warranty card to 762 Wallingford Boulevard Fremont Virginia.

ACTIVITY 14: Write Sentences Using Commas in Addresses and Place Names

Complete each of the following sentences, providing the information indicated. Use commas as necessary.

EXAMPLE My favorite relative lives at 1203 Devonshire, Phoenix, Arizona. (*street address • city • state*)

1. I know someone who lives at ____________________________. (*street address • city • state*)
2. I was born in ______________________________________. (*county • state* or *city • country*)
3. A place that I have visited is ____________________________. (*city • state*)
4. My dream vacation would be in __________________________. (*city • country* or *city • state*)
5. My address is ______________________________________. (*street address • city • state*)

Rule 8. Use commas to set off dialogue or a direct quotation from the rest of the sentence. Commas always go *before* quotation marks.

> "Go ahead and start your engines," the announcer said.
>
> According to my brother, "He didn't say it loud enough for all of the racers to hear."
>
> "I said it loud enough," the announcer replied, "for all of the other racers to hear."

ACTIVITY 15: Use Commas with Dialogue and Direct Quotations

Add commas as needed to each of the following sentences.

EXAMPLE My father always says, "Don't judge a book by its cover."

1. "I think Douglas likes you" Charlene whispered to Amber.
2. Brian Wilson sang "I guess I just wasn't made for these times."
3. "Don't kill that spider" Alberto told his son.
4. "You don't need to insure your car" Yasmin joked "if you never drive it."
5. Professor Ambrosini reminds us "Even if it's not on the test, you still need to know it."

ACTIVITY 16: Write Sentences Using Commas with Dialogue and Direct Quotations

Complete each of the following sentences by providing a one-sentence piece of dialogue or quotation. Use commas as necessary.

EXAMPLE I heard a singer on the radio repeat , "Catch a falling star, and put it in your pocket."

1. My friend always tells people ______________________

____

2. I like to say ______________________________

____

3. My favorite movie character says ______________________________

4. ____
according to someone in my family.

5. One memorable teacher often said ___________________________

____

ACTIVITY 17: Use Commas Correctly in Sentences

Using all of the comma rules you have learned in this chapter, add commas as necessary to each of the following sentences.

EXAMPLE Since I had never been to that ski resort, he explained that it was in Jackson Hole, Wyoming.

1. The oldest son Steven surprised his family by bringing home his new wife for they had not known that he had even been dating somebody special.
2. In high school Sofia amazingly decided to take a cooking class to learn how to read package labels how to select and store fresh vegetables and how to prepare quick meals from basic ingredients.
3. Because he knew that I was worried Alexei my oldest friend telephoned to announce "Jackie my new address is 1561 Kendall Avenue Minneapolis Minnesota."
4. Mastering new software therefore involves solving two important problems which are learning what the software can do and figuring out how to get the software to do it.
5. On July 20 1969 when Neil Armstrong stepped onto the surface of the moon he said "One small step for a man; one giant leap for mankind."

ACTIVITY 18: Use Commas Correctly in a Paragraph

Using all of the comma rules you have learned in this chapter, add commas as needed to the following paragraph.

EXAMPLE The day that John F. Kennedy died, November 22, 1963, remains important to older Americans.

One of them remarked "On that day everything changed." Many people began working to end war racism sexism and poverty. Violence increased and two other leaders were shot and killed: Martin Luther King Jr. and Robert Kennedy the president's brother. Finally public figures lost their privacy. In a famous photograph President Kennedy's son salutes the funeral procession. No situation should be more private than a boy saying goodbye to his father. However a child had to share this moment with millions of strangers.

Exercise Central
The *Discoveries* Web site provides additional practice with using commas. Go to **bedfordstmartins.com/discoveries** and click on "Exercise Central." Once you log in, click on "Commas" under the heading "Punctuation."

B. SEMICOLONS

The *semicolon* (;) is used to join independent clauses and to make meaning clear.

Rule 1. Use a semicolon to join two related independent clauses that could each stand alone as a sentence. Semicolons work especially well if the two independent clauses are short and closely related.

I never liked science fiction; it just doesn't make sense to me.

Stephen King is my favorite writer; he knows how to grab his reader's attention.

I can't believe how many books King has written; *Carrie* is still my all-time favorite.

ACTIVITY 19: Write Sentences Using Semicolons to Join Independent Clauses

Add a semicolon and an independent clause to each of the following independent clauses.

EXAMPLE Candace is an accomplished figure skater ; she studied ballet to add grace to her routines.

1. For me, the morning is the most frustrating time of day____

2. My cousin is an excellent athlete ____

3. They have a beautiful view from their window ____

4. Every day I put up with someone with an annoying habit ____

5. Next year, I will have an ideal schedule ____

Rule 2. Use a semicolon to link two clauses that are joined by a transitional word.

> Some people think Stephen King is too gory; nevertheless, they read every one of his books.
>
> I wanted to send a copy of *Misery* to my cousin; however, my father wouldn't let me.
>
> I will buy every book King publishes; for example, I just bought *Dreamcatcher.*

Rule 3. Use a semicolon to separate items in a series that already includes commas.

> My favorite places to visit are Des Moines, Iowa; Orlando, Florida; and Denver, Colorado.

ACTIVITY 20: Use Semicolons Correctly

Use a semicolon to correctly punctuate each of the following sentences.

EXAMPLE I always go to the movies on Friday night; that's the night new movies open.

1. It would be difficult to work full-time while he had five classes however, Noe accepted the job.
2. In the heat of the afternoon, the flowers began to droop a single bee stirred the roses.
3. Next summer, Nadine will see Madrid, Spain Paris, France Rome, Italy and Athens, Greece.
4. Patrick did not have enough time to finish cooking dinner consequently, the stew is very watery.
5. We had to wait two hours to pose for the family photograph by that time, unfortunately, the children were no longer clean and neat.

Exercise Central

The *Discoveries* Web site provides practice additional exercises on using semicolons. Go to **bedfordstmartins.com/discoveries** and click on "Exercise Central." Once you log in, click on "Semicolons" under the heading "Punctuation."

C. COLONS

The *colon* (:) is also useful for making meaning clear.

Use a colon to introduce a list or an explanation. However, use the colon only when the words before it are a complete sentence that could stand alone. Do not use a colon after expressions like *such as* or *for example.*

When you go to the movies, be sure to get the following: popcorn, soda, and a dill pickle.

These is only one way to please Brandon at the movies: buy the foods he loves.

His friends know this about Brandon: the food is more important to him than the film.

ACTIVITY 21: Use Colons Correctly

Add colons as needed in each of the following sentences to introduce a list, clause, or phrase that explains the independent clause. If the sentence is correct without a colon, write "correct."

EXAMPLE I went to the bookstore to buy the following items: a ruler, graph paper, and a calculator.

1. To make your own salsa, you need tomatoes, onions, chiles, cilantro, and salt.
2. I have to do many things to prepare for my guests clean the house, shop for groceries, buy concert tickets, and repair the brakes on my car.
3. Ian can play four different wind instruments flute, clarinet, oboe, and bassoon.
4. This afternoon, two-year-old Ryan was impossible he poured maple syrup on the floor, tore the pages out of a photo album, and flushed a doll down the toilet.
5. Vanessa's mother taught her many old popular dances, such as the twist, pony, swim, jerk, frug, and monkey.

ACTIVITY 22: Write Sentences Using Colons

To each of the following sentences, add a list or a clause or phrase of explanation. Introduce your list, clause, or phrase with a colon.

EXAMPLE Many courses fulfill your science requirement : Crime and Chemistry, Social Issues in Biology, Urban Geography, and Celestial Myths.

1. Vanessa has autographs from her favorite actors ______________

____

2. There are many things we can do next Saturday ______________

____

3. That couple broke up for some very good reasons ______________

____

____

4. I have a lot of homework for tonight ______________

____

____

5. In spite of its reasonable prices, that restaurant has its bad points

____

Exercise Central
The *Discoveries* Web site provides additional practice with using colons. Go to **bedfordstmartins.com/discoveries** and click on "Exercise Central." Once you log in, click on "Colons" under the heading "Punctuation."

D. END PUNCTUATION

The *period* (.), the *question mark* (?), and the *exclamation mark* (!) are the three types of punctuation used to end sentences.

Rule 1. Use a period to end most sentences, including indirect questions and commands. An indirect question reports a question rather than asks one.

He never believed her lies.

He asked her where she had heard such things.

Never lie to me again.

Rule 2. Use a question mark to end a direct question.

Why didn't he realize that she was telling the truth?

How could she make herself any clearer?

Rule 3. Use an exclamation mark to give emphasis or show emotion.

Don't ever doubt my word again!

I will always tell you the truth!

ACTIVITY 23: Add End Punctuation to Sentences

Insert the correct end punctuation mark at the end of each of the following sentences.

EXAMPLE Would you like to go to the store?

1. Now that he is an adult, Rogelio relies on his parents' good advice more than ever
2. When Vera stepped into the cabin that had been in her family for years, she noticed its old, familiar smell
3. Caleb and Genevieve were happy to see that Mr. Siegel had not changed much over the years
4. What did people do with their evenings before the invention of television
5. How dare you behave that way to my friends

ACTIVITY 24: Revise for Correct End Punctuation

Revise each of the following sentences as needed for end punctuation. If the end punctuation does not need to be changed, write "correct."

EXAMPLE Jessie likes me.

1. Ah, this is the life!
2. Does anyone know where the nearest police station is?
3. I wondered what my boss had planned for me?

4. This coat appears to be still in good condition!
5. Olga wanted to know whether a new director had already been chosen.

ACTIVITY 25: Add End Punctuation to a Paragraph

In the following paragraph, insert the correct end punctuation.

EXAMPLE Because of my cousin, Martin, our family just had the best reunion ever.

After leaving the army, Martin decided to go to college Did he study something normal, like history or psychology You don't know Cousin Martin He majored in recreation We all used to ask ourselves if this was a real major It is very real, for our reunion was his senior project He organized everything: transportation, accommodations, catering, and even our matching polo shirts Among the games he invented for us, my favorite was the scavenger hunt The family has become so big that many of us had never met before, so instead of finding objects in our scavenger hunt, Martin made us become acquainted with our more distant relatives For example, I had to find a rocket scientist, and to my surprise, Gwen Cowan, my second cousin, works for NASA Even the newest family members were involved; I met the very young man who had just learned to stand up unassisted Who was that The answer is on the family reunion Web page that Martin constructed as part of his project What grade did he receive The professor gave him an A, of course

Exercise Central
The *Discoveries* Web site provides additional practice with end punctuation. Go to **bedfordstmartins.com/discoveries** and click on "Exercise Central." Once you log in, click on "End Punctuation" under the heading "Punctuation."

E. APOSTROPHES

An *apostrophe* (') is used to show possession and to form contractions.

Rule 1. Use an apostrophe to show that something belongs to someone. If the thing belongs to one person, use *'s* after the noun that refers to the person, even if the noun already ends in *-s.*

> Jessica's nose ring is the topic of conversation in class.
>
> Her friend's ear stud, however, does not generate much interest.
>
> Classmates do not even know about Elvis's belly button ring.

Rule 2. If the thing belongs to more than one person and the noun that refers to these persons ends in *-s,* use only an apostrophe *after* the *-s.*

> All of the students' conversation is about Jessica.
>
> Her friends' body piercings never come up.
>
> The professors' reaction was especially interesting.

If the noun doesn't end in *-s,* use *'s* after it.

> The men's faces were painted with white streaks.
>
> The women's hair was braided with vines and flowers.

Rule 3. Do not use an apostrophe in the plural form of a name unless the word is also showing possession. In that case, use an apostrophe after the *-s* of the plural.

> We always enjoyed seeing the Kennedys.
>
> The Kennedys' house always seemed warm and welcoming.

Rule 4. Do not use an apostrophe in possessive forms of pronouns: *yours, his, hers, its, ours,* or *theirs.*

> The car was missing one of its rear hubcaps.
>
> Because our car was being repaired, our friends let us use theirs.

ACTIVITY 26: Use Apostrophes to Show Possession

In each of the following sentences, underline the words in which apostrophes are missing. Then, write the correct form of the word in the space provided. If the sentence is not missing any apostrophes, write "correct" in the space.

EXAMPLE The Smiths home is located in town. Smiths' ________

1. Donalds clothes were always neatly pressed. ____________
2. The professors worksheets needed to be photocopied. ____________
3. The womens umbrella refused to open, but the rain came down steadily. ____________
4. This carrel is ours. ____________
5. Seth Wilsons motorcycle fell over while he was in the restaurant. ____________
6. Javiers favorite movie is *Open Range*. ____________
7. The Smiths always spend holidays together. ____________
8. The Georges favorite holiday is Labor Day. ____________
9. Jennys wedding will be on Labor Day weekend. ____________
10. The Varelas and Fraires will be at the wedding. ____________

ACTIVITY 27: Write Sentences with Apostrophes That Show Possession

Each of the following words has an apostrophe that shows possession. Use each word correctly in a sentence of your own.

EXAMPLE driver's

The driver's windshield was so dirty that she could not see the road.

1. Doctor Rice's

____

2. children's

____

3. man's

____

4. baseball players'

____

5. Melissa's

____

6. Today's

____

7. girls'

____

8. Brandon's

____

9. Joneses'

____

10. club's

____

Rule 5. Use an apostrophe to form a contraction. A contraction is formed by combining two words into one and omitting one or more letters, with an apostrophe taking the place of the omitted letter or letters. Some college instructors prefer that you not use contractions in college writing.

> It's [it is] always fun to go hunting.
>
> I don't [do not] care if others think that my father and I shouldn't [should not] hunt.
>
> We've [we have] always enjoyed it and wouldn't [would not] stop for anything.

ACTIVITY 28: Use Apostrophes in Contractions

In each of the following sentences, underline the contractions that have missing apostrophes. Then, write the correct form of each contraction in the space provided.

EXAMPLE I <u>cant</u> find my way home. can't

1. Perry doesnt think that its a good idea for his daughter to go swimming while shes getting over a cold. ______
2. When youre tired of shoveling snow, have some of the hot cocoa that I just made. ______
3. Well arrive at Yellowstone Park before sunset. ______
4. The Mitchells arent going to the restaurant tomorrow because they cant get a reservation for that night. ______
5. Because its breezy today, Ive decided to show you how to fly your new kite. ______
6. Dont even get me started on where theyre going. ______
7. Were never going to make it to the top of the hill. ______
8. Weve always wanted to try our hand at racquetball, but I couldnt find anyone who wanted to play. ______
9. She isnt my favorite, but shes my brother's favorite singer. ______
10. Hell never come around to your way of thinking. ______

ACTIVITY 29: Identify Possible Contractions

In each of the following sentences, underline the words that can be made into common contractions. Then, write the contractions in the space provided.

EXAMPLE It <u>does not</u> matter if <u>he is</u> ready to take the test. doesn't, he's

1. Although it is against the rules, we are going to allow you to photograph the science exhibit for your school newspaper. ______
2. Greg and Celine are not sure if the bridge is safe because they cannot see very far ahead through this thick mist. ______

3. The Hendersons hope that they will stay with us. ______________
4. After you are finished with the weight bench, please wipe it down with the towel. ______________
5. Sidra and Darrell do not realize that it is easier to replace the toner in the copy machine before it warms up. ______________
6. There is never enough bread in your house. ______________
7. Who is going to the movies with me? ______________
8. I would rather not have to take the dog's toy away. ______________
9. You should not recommend that restaurant to someone if you would not eat there yourself. ______________
10. It is hard to talk with Dylan because he does not seem to listen to what I say. ______________

ACTIVITY 30: Use Apostrophes Correctly

Each of the following sentences contains apostrophe errors. Add apostrophes where necessary to correct those errors.

EXAMPLE I went with the Joneses to their summer cabin. They're really lucky to have such a place.

1. If I could earn my employers trust, Id be able to do more to improve her business.
2. If hed accept that Jenny isnt interested in him, Isaac would notice the other attractive women in his life.
3. After were finished with the days chores, we can go to the beach.
4. Because Colin still had Raquels car, she wasnt able to join us at the club.
5. Misty couldnt admit to the professor that she hadnt written the research paper herself.

ACTIVITY 31: Use Apostrophes Correctly in a Paragraph

The following paragraph contains several apostrophe errors. Add apostrophes where necessary to correct those errors.

EXAMPLE It isn't always pleasant for my son, Donnie, and me to visit my mom on Sundays.

It isnt always pleasant for my son, Donnie, and me to visit my mom on Sundays. Donnie doesnt like dressing up, and Mom wont let him accompany her to church unless he wears slacks, a long-sleeved shirt, and a tie. Long before the ministers sermon, hes squirming in the pew and pulling at his collar. His grandmothers stern glances certainly dont help the situation. After church, she ignores her grandsons request to go out for hamburgers. My moms idea of a perfect Sunday lunch is a nice plate of liver and onions, which even I cant eat without a lot of ketchup. Mom believes that its childrens duty to obey their elders. As Donnies father, I believe that its an adults responsibility to make obedience fun and easy.

Exercise Central
The *Discoveries* Web site provides practice exercises on using apostrophes. Go to **bedfordstmartins.com/discoveries** and click on "Exercise Central." Once you log in, click on "Apostrophes" under the heading "Punctuation."

F. QUOTATION MARKS

Quotation marks (" ") are used to enclose the exact words of a speaker or writer and the titles of essays, articles, poems, songs, and other short works.

Rule 1. Use quotation marks to set off a speaker's or a writer's exact words.

"I can't believe I said that!" Joshua exclaimed.

"I don't know what you were thinking," I replied, "when you said that."

> According to my textbook author, "We often say things we don't mean when we're stressed."

As these examples show, a period or a comma always goes before closing quotation marks. A question mark or an exclamation mark, on the other hand, sometimes goes before the quotation marks and sometimes after them. It goes before the quotation marks if the quotation itself is a question or an exclamation, as in the first example. It goes after the quotation marks if your sentence is a question or an exclamation but the quotation itself isn't, as in the following example:

> When did people begin to say "Have a nice day"?

Do not use quotation marks around an indirect quotation, one that doesn't use the speaker's or writer's exact words. An indirect quotation is usually introduced with *that*.

> Henry said that he had always wanted to study medicine.

ACTIVITY 32: Use Quotation Marks to Show Exact Words

In the following sentences, place quotation marks around each occurrence of a speaker's or writer's exact words. Some sentences do not require any quotation marks.

EXAMPLE "That was my favorite blouse," she said to her roommate.

1. How was the play? my professor asked the class.
2. The doctor said that I should get more exercise.
3. I'll take popcorn and a soda, I said to the clerk.
4. My aunt always says, A bird in the hand is worth two in the bush.
5. Guess what? she said. I'm pregnant.
6. You should have told me that the dog would bite.
7. Harold shouted, Let's play ball!
8. Even though I didn't want to go, my brother said, Give it a try; you'll have a great time.
9. The officer stated the obvious, Don't drink and drive.
10. How did you respond when he said Forget about it?

Rule 2. Use quotation marks to enclose the titles of articles, essays, book chapters, speeches, poems, short stories, and songs.

I especially enjoy the newspaper column "Our Views."

My last essay was entitled "Dia de los Muertos."

Emily Dickinson wrote the poem "I Dwell in Possibilities."

Sandra Cisneros wrote my favorite short story: "House on Mango Street."

When we go caroling, we always sing "Deck the Halls."

Use italics or underlining, not quotation marks, for the titles of longer works such as books, newspapers, and magazines.

ACTIVITY 33: Use Quotation Marks to Enclose Titles

In the following sentences, place quotation marks around the title of each short work. Some sentences do not require any quotation marks.

EXAMPLE Martin Luther King's "I Have a Dream" speech is often heard in history classes.

1. Her essay, Women in the Military, was a hit with the ROTC cadets.
2. Vivek's favorite column is My Turn.
3. I'm currently reading the novel *Best Friends* by Martha Moody.
4. I bought *People* magazine to read the article Jen and Ben Break Up.
5. Edgar Alan Poe's poem The Raven is usually assigned in American literature courses.
6. In this textbook, Bruce read the chapter entitled Marketing Genius.
7. Shailendra never left home without reading her daily horoscope in *USA Today*.
8. Hugo wrote an essay entitled Get the Most out of College While Jogging.

9. Eminem's Lose Yourself is an extremely popular song.
10. The short story Hills Like White Elephants is written almost entirely in dialogue.

ACTIVITY 34: Use Quotation Marks Correctly

In each of the following sentences, insert quotation marks as necessary.

EXAMPLE My favorite essay this term was "Giving It My All."

1. Dencil said, Ms. Levin will be sorry that she missed you.
2. Yes, Aunt Lydia agreed, the autumn leaves were prettier last year.
3. Why do you always wear purple clothing? asked Josh.
4. Angela recited Walt Whitman's poem A Noiseless Patient Spider at her eighth-grade graduation ceremony.
5. After we read the essay Shooting an Elephant by George Orwell, our class had an interesting discussion.

ACTIVITY 35: Revise for Quotation Marks

In the following paragraph, insert quotation marks as necessary.

EXAMPLE I recited John Gould Fletcher's poem "The Groundswell" for the challenge of mastering the difficult pronunciation.

In my speech class last fall, we began the semester by reciting short creative works in order to practice using our voices well. Choose anything you like, Professor Keroes told us, but make it sound like natural speech. I enjoyed the variety presented by my classmates. Two students performed the husband and wife in the poem The Death of the Hired Man by Robert Frost. Three classmates took turns telling Shirley Jackson's short story The Lottery.

Many students chose songs. Alan did a great job reciting Daysleeper by R.E.M. Professor Keroes seemed pleased. I wish I had a copy of everything to read for fun, he said.

Exercise Central
The *Discoveries* Web site provides practice exercises on using quotation marks. Go to **bedfordstmartins.com/discoveries** and click on "Exercise Central." Once you log in, click on "Quotation Marks" under the heading "Punctuation."

CHAPTER

29 Improving Mechanics

Just as with punctuation, the correct use of the mechanics of writing — elements like capital letters, italics, numbers, and abbreviations — helps your reader understand your meaning. This chapter focuses on the correct use of these elements.

A. CAPITAL LETTERS

Rule 1. Capitalize proper nouns: nouns that refer to a specific person, place, event, or thing. Do not capitalize common nouns: nouns that refer to a general category of persons, places, events, or things.

Proper Noun	*Common Noun*
Ball State University	a university
Costa Rica	a country
Thursday	a day
Dad (used as a name)	my dad
President Bush	a president
Professor Lee	a professor
God	a god
the North	north of the city
The Bill of Rights	amendments
Political Science 102	a political science class

Rule 2. Capitalize the names of organizations, institutions, and trademarks.

My father belongs to the Order of the Elks.

I always vote for the Green Party candidate.

My next computer will be a Dell.

ACTIVITY 1: Correct Errors in Capitalization

Correct the errors in capitalization in each of the following sentences.

EXAMPLE Have you read the book *the four agreements*? [corrected: T F A]

1. Gabriel has wanted to be a green beret since he was a little boy.
2. Pearl dreams of owning a lexus.
3. Rita's family goes to extremes when they decorate their house for halloween.
4. Among the police officers who helped me after my backpack was stolen, officer franklin was the most sympathetic.
5. Avner's Uncle is a jeweler in new york city.
6. At one time, president's day was two separate holidays, lincoln's birthday and washington's birthday.
7. There are better things for you to do than sit around watching soap operas and eating doritos.
8. Alfredo's Mother wants us to join her at the opera.
9. I rode the elevator to the top of the empire state building, but I took the stairs back down.
10. Is Deanna from kansas city, kansas, or kansas city, missouri?

ACTIVITY 2: Use Correct Capitalization in a Paragraph

Correct the errors in capitalization in the following paragraph.

EXAMPLE On T/thursday night after our T/thanksgiving dinner, the family was sitting around.

aunt edna, who teaches geography at middlefield junior high school, proposed a contest. The losers would have to clean up. We divided into teams to see who could name the most states of the united states. My team included my youngest cousins and uncle raymond, who always falls asleep after a meal, so we only had thirty-two states. The best team, which had both grandpa and aunt edna, only named forty-five, and all the teams together couldn't name every one. While little tracy insisted that mexico was a state, everyone forgot delaware. aunt edna said that we were all losers and distributed reese's pieces as a consolation prize. Then we all did the dishes together.

Rule 3. Capitalize all words in titles except articles (*a, an, the*), coordinating conjunctions (*for, and, nor, but, or, yet, so*), and prepositions (*of, on, in, at, with, for*), unless they are the first or last word in the title. Do not capitalize *the* before the names of newspapers.

For Whom the Bell Tolls

Law and Order

The Art of Possibility

the Washington Post

ACTIVITY 3: Capitalize Titles

Correct the errors in capitalization in each of the following sentences.

EXAMPLE Students from westwood community college sold Walnuts and Pecans before Thanksgiving. (corrections marked: westwood → W, community → C, college → C, Walnuts → w, Pecans → p)

1. Because we have pets, my children enjoyed the movie *Cats And Dogs.*
2. Fran was surprised to learn that *Gone With The Wind* was a book before it was a film.
3. Because of the clever robotic toys that she invented, Meredith was interviewed by a reporter from the *Christian science monitor.*
4. At my high school, a history teacher and an English teacher both discussed *a tale of two cities* during the same two weeks.
5. When I was a child, my favorite album was *Peter And The Wolf.*
6. My favorite teacher recommended that I read *the House of the seven Gables* by Nathaniel Hawthorne.
7. Naturally, the only holiday song that my grumpy sister likes is Bob Dorough's "blue Christmas."

8. Harlan dreams of winning a lot of money by appearing on *American idol.*
9. Chrissie always has the latest issue of *reader's digest* on her coffee table.
10. I had to reserve my niece's copy of *Harry Potter and the order of the Phoenix* before it arrived at the bookstore.

ACTIVITY 4: Capitalize Titles in a Paragraph

Correct the errors in capitalization in the following paragraph.

EXAMPLE During ~~s~~S study ~~s~~S skills 101, ~~p~~P professor Weston used the materials we had with us to demonstrate how readers use different techniques.

My instructor compared the *Campus sun* and the *New York times* to show that not even two newspapers should be read the same way. *Portrait Of The Artist As A Young Man* is a difficult book that should be read slowly because the sound of the words helps the meaning. The textbook *physics* also should be read slowly, but because of its vocabulary; the sound of these words has little added meaning. Both *Applications in electrical engineering* and *Western Architecture* have diagrams, but for different reasons. A student is not expected to construct a church from the floor plan in a textbook!

Exercise Central

For additional practice with capitalization, go to **bedfordstmartins.com/discoveries** and click on "Exercise Central." Once you log in, click on "Punctuation" and then "Capitalization."

B. ITALICS

Italicize (or underline in handwritten or typewritten copy) the titles of books, magazines, movies, television shows, newspapers, journals, computer software, and longer musical works, such as compact disks. Do not italicize (or capitalize) *the* before the title of a newspaper.

I read *The Scarlet Letter* in my American literature class.

People magazine is always interesting to read while you're waiting for the doctor.

Matrix Reloaded is exciting to watch.

I'm glad to see *Will and Grace* doing so well in the ratings.

A copy of the *New York Times* is delivered to my door daily.

I have seen copies of the journal *College English* in my instructor's office.

Windows XP works well on Jerry's computer.

Tequila Sunrise by Santana is a departure from his past music.

ACTIVITY 5: Use Italics Correctly

Use underlining to indicate where italics are needed in each of the following sentences.

EXAMPLE How to Lose a Guy in Ten Days was a funny movie.

1. The first novel that I ever read was Treasure Island by Robert Louis Stevenson.
2. When Uriel and Shayna got married, they received a subscription to National Geographic magazine.
3. Every spring the family gathers around the television to watch our favorite movie, The Wizard of Oz.
4. Brendan has every episode of the original Star Trek series on video.
5. Penny reads the Wall Street Journal and the New York Times every day.

ACTIVITY 6: Use Italics Correctly in a Paragraph

In the following paragraph, underline to indicate where italics should be used.

EXAMPLE The reference librarians were happy to receive Professor David's complete Oxford English Dictionary.

When Professor David retired, he donated much of his large personal library to the university. For thirty years, he had subscribed to the Classics Journal. His copies filled a gap in the library's collection. He also donated extra copies of books that were important to his career, including the Iliad and the Odyssey, both translated by Richmond Lattimore. Friends of the professor say that his collection of vinyl jazz records is equally impressive. His copy of the album Kind of Blue autographed by Miles Davis is very valuable.

Exercise Central
For additional practice with using italics, go to **bedfordstmartins.com/discoveries** and click on "Exercise Central." Once you log in, click on "Punctuation" and then "Italics or Underlining."

C. ABBREVIATIONS

An *abbreviation* is a shortened version of a word or phrase.

Rule 1. Use standard abbreviations for titles before or after proper names.

Dr. Charles Elerick

Ms. Nancy Chin

Peggy Sullivan, D.D.S.

William Smith, Jr.

Rule 2. Use abbreviations for the names of organizations, corporations, and societies. The first time you use the name in a piece of writing, spell out the name and give the abbreviation in parentheses after it. Then, if you mention the name again, you may use just the abbreviation.

NBC (National Broadcasting System)

IBM (International Business Machines)

YMCA (Young Men's Christian Association)

Rule 3. Use abbreviations for specialized terms. If the term is unfamiliar to your readers, spell it out the first time you use it.

VCR (videocassette recorder)

RAM (random access memory)

ESP (extrasensory perception)

ACTIVITY 7: Use Common Abbreviations

In each of the following sentences, underline the words that could be written as abbreviations. Write the abbreviation in the space provided.

EXAMPLE My favorite news station is Cable News Network. CNN

1. Doctor Koster is always very busy late in the afternoon. ________
2. The headquarters of the United Nations is in New York City.

   ____
3. The stores sold out of Ricky Martin's latest compact disk before noon. ________
4. Many people observe the birthday of Martin Luther King Junior by going to church. ________
5. Don't forget to program the videocassette recorder before we leave for the game. ________

Exercise Central

For additional practice with abbreviations, go to **bedfordstmartins.com/discoveries** and click on "Exercise Central." Once you log in, click on "Punctuation" and then "Abbreviations."

D. NUMBERS

When to spell out numbers and when to use numerals can be confusing. In general, spell out numbers from one through ninety-nine, numbers expressed in two words (two hundred, three thousand), or numbers that begin a sentence. Use numerals for all other numbers, including decimals, percentages, page numbers, years, and time of day.

Justin borrowed thirty-two diskettes from Casey.

Casey had offered 150 from his personal supply.

One hundred fifty diskettes seemed like a lot to keep on hand.

The diskettes measure 3.25 inches.

Justin needed diskettes for 50 percent of his classes.

His computer science professor asked the students to turn to page 48 in the text.

Justin's class was at 7:00 p.m.

ACTIVITY 8: Use Numbers Correctly

Using the preceding guidelines, underline the correct form in each of the following sentences.

EXAMPLE Page (thirteen/13) contains all of the information you need.

1. (One hundred/100) winners were selected at random.
2. Students who are in the top (10 percent/ten percent) of their graduating class in high school are guaranteed a place at state universities.
3. (3 out of 4/Three out of four) people who take the motivational training say that they notice significant benefits.
4. Becky intends to have (6/six) children.
5. Roger bought a bottle of (50/fifty) aspirin for his desk drawer at work.

ACTIVITY 9: Decide How to Write Numbers

Complete each of the following sentences, spelling out a number or writing a numeral as necessary.

EXAMPLE Bookings of international flights are down ___40___ percent.

1. There are approximately ________ people in my smallest class.
2. When I was a child, ________ people lived with me.
3. I own ________ pairs of shoes.
4. Where I live, the sales tax is ________.
5. I plan to graduate in ________ semesters.

Exercise Central

For additional practice with numbers, go to **bedfordstmartins.com/discoveries** and click on "Exercise Central." Once you log in, click on "Punctuation" and then "Numbers."

CHAPTER

30

Guide for Multilingual Writers

A. ARTICLES

English has three articles: *the, a,* and *an. The* is the *definite article; a* and *an* are *indefinite articles.*

All three of these articles appear before the noun they refer to; if the noun is preceded by one or more adjectives, the article comes before the adjectives.

- *The* is used with nouns that refer to one or more specific things.

  I love *the* beautiful Victorian house.
  (Here *the* is referring to a specific house.)

  I love beautiful Victorian houses.
  (No house in particular is being referred to.)

  The roses bloom in May.
  (Particular roses are indicated.)

  Roses bloom in May.
  (Roses in general bloom in May.)

- In many cases, *the* refers to a noun that has been mentioned before.

  In buying a *car,* Chon focused mainly on appearance. *The car* he purchased looked sleek and sporty.

- *A* and *an* are used with nouns that refer to things not specifically known to the reader, perhaps because they haven't been mentioned before.

  A bird swooped out of the sky.
  (The reader has no prior knowledge of the bird.)

  A factory can create both jobs and pollution.
  (No factory in particular is being mentioned.)

A day in the sun would do me good.
(This article refers to some day in the sun, but not to a specific day.)

- *A* and *an* are used only with singular count nouns. Count nouns name things that can be counted, such as *book* or *cat*. They have plural as well as singular forms: *books, cats*. *The* is used with both singular and plural count nouns and also with noncount nouns. Noncount nouns name things that can't be counted, such as *information, homework,* or *advice*.
- *A* comes before words that begin with consonant sounds (such as *b, c, d, f, g*). Notice that even though the letter *u* is a vowel, *a* is used before some words beginning with *u,* in which the *u* is pronounced with a *y* sound before it.

  a book   a hat   a cat   a movie   a speech

  My husband said he will never wear *a* tie again.

  I plan to buy *a* uniform at the store.

- *An* comes before words that begin with vowel sounds (*a, e, i, o, u*) to make them easier to pronounce. Notice that even though the letter *h* is a consonant, *an* is used before some words beginning with *h,* in which the *h* is silent (not pronounced).

  an effort   an honor   an illness   an opera

  An elephant is an interesting animal to watch.

  An umbrella would have been useful today.

ACTIVITY 1: Add Missing Articles

Revise each of the following sentences to include the missing articles.

EXAMPLE First concert of the season is always held first week in September.

The first concert of the season is always held the first week in September.

1. I found wallet and key chain; wallet was leather and key chain was silver.

____

____

2. On plane flight to Chicago, Ramon met old friend.

3. Only way to succeed as writer is to write and learn from your mistakes.

4. When she tripped over rock, Penny tore jeans that she had bought yesterday.

5. When you finish with stationary bicycle, please let Howard use it.

6. Please come to our party on first Saturday of April.

7. Spices in bottles that are on shelf are too old to use.

8. Campground near beach is best place for us to spend night.

9. After hour, Yesenia decided to leave house and go to movie.

10. Sandor bought T-shirt and decal for his car at only bookstore on campus.

ACTIVITY 2: Add Missing Articles in a Paragraph

Revise the following paragraph to include the missing articles.

EXAMPLE Cynthia completed her homework for ^the^ last day of class.

Beryl is specialist in textiles. She can tell difference between handmade and machine-made lace and knows names of different kinds of lace. Mostly she works with antique rugs, because purchase of rug is big investment. When investor wants to buy rug, he or she consults Beryl. Beryl will tell buyer if rug was made from natural or synthetic fibers. She also can tell whether dyes used in rug were natural or synthetic. These factors determine true value of rug. She has prevented many people from making big mistake.

B. COUNT AND NONCOUNT NOUNS

As mentioned earlier, *count nouns* can be singular or plural: *computer* or *computers*. *Noncount* (or *mass*) nouns usually can only be singular, even though their meaning may be plural. Here are some noncount nouns:

advice	mail	information	homework
equipment	education	knowledge	evidence
furniture	vocabulary	justice	poverty
anger	honesty	courage	employment

- Don't use indefinite articles (*a* and *an*) with noncount nouns.

INCORRECT Her mother gave Molly an advice about her boyfriend.

CORRECT Her mother gave Molly advice about her boyfriend.

- Noncount nouns can't be made plural, so don't add *-s* or *-es* at the end.

INCORRECT I need to buy furnitures for my apartment.

CORRECT I need to buy furniture for my apartment.

- To express a quantity for a noncount noun, use *some, any,* or *more.*

CORRECT Her mother gave Molly some advice about her boyfriend.

CORRECT I need to buy more furniture for my apartment.

ACTIVITY 3: Use Count and Noncount Nouns Correctly

Revise each of the following sentences in which there is an error in the use of count and noncount nouns. If a sentence is correct, write "correct" after it.

EXAMPLE Cynthia completed her homeworks a few minutes before class started.

1. All four of my grandparents experienced poverties when they were young.
2. Too much knowledges can be a dangerous thing.
3. My roommate showed more courage than I did by confronting the burglar in the kitchen.
4. I will buy furnitures after I move into my new apartment.
5. My mails arrived every day by 3:00.
6. I learned some vocabularies by keeping a list of words and their definitions.
7. My professor lets me use an equipment in the lab.
8. You will need more evidence to prove your hypothesis.
9. I gained so much informations just by reading the book about economics.
10. Martin Luther King Jr. fought for civil rights and a justice for African Americans.

C. PREPOSITIONS

Prepositions always begin a prepositional phrase — that is, a phrase that includes a preposition and its object.

Learn more about prepositions on pp. 475–80.

at her dinner   in her office   on his folder

In English, the most common prepositions are *in, on,* and *at.*

- *In* indicates an enclosed area; a geographical area such as a city, state, or country; or a period of time, such as a month, a year, a season, or part of a day.

in a box	in the car	in the fall
in England	in the classroom	in 2002
in June	in the evening	in winter
in Chicago	in Texas	in the 1990s

In New Mexico, you can find Pueblo pottery in Santa Fe.

He wanted to get the book that was in the math lab.

In 2007, I will graduate from college.

I hoped to take a short trip in June.

- *On* indicates the top of something, a street or road, a day of the week, or a specific date.

You'll find the envelope on the table.

I prefer to live on a mountain.

Harriet lives on Memorial Drive.

Let's go to a movie on Friday night.

I'll start my new job on September 18.

- *At* indicates a specific address or location or a specific time.

I live at 100 Main Street.

You'll find the snowshoes at the Army-Navy Store.

I'll meet you at your favorite restaurant.

I'll see you at 7:30 p.m.

At midnight, Cinderella turned into a pumpkin.

ACTIVITY 4: Use *in, on,* and *at* in Sentences

Fill in the blanks in each of the following sentences, using *in, on,* and *at* correctly.

EXAMPLE I arrived ___at___ the party a few minutes early.

1. Calvin is always ready to leave the house _______ 7:15 a.m.
2. Professor Chen's office is _______ the Physical Sciences building.
3. Please don't leave your shopping bags _______ the floor.
4. There is a telephone _______ the kitchen.
5. We live _______ an apartment but are looking for a house to buy.
6. Elliot is paid _______ the first and fifteenth of the month.
7. Your lunch break is _______ 1:00.
8. The ice cream bars are _______ the freezer _______ the top shelf.
9. Geneva will leave for Padre Island _______ June 5.
10. Like Easter, Passover is celebrated _______ the spring.

ACTIVITY 5: Use *in, on,* and *at* in a Paragraph

Fill in the blanks in the following paragraph, using *in, on,* and *at* correctly.

EXAMPLE I first met Mireille ___at___ the university.

Last summer, I visited my friend, Mireille, who lives _______ Québec City. She and I met _______ Toronto two years ago. I arrived _______ Jean LeSage Airport _______ June 3 _______ 3:30 _______ the afternoon. That evening, she took me to dinner _______ a bistro _______ the Old City. The moonlight sparkled _______ the surface of the Saint Lawrence River. I stayed with Mireille for five days. While I was there, we made plans to see each other again _______ the fall. We plan to stay _______ a small hotel _______ Victoria.

Besides *in, on,* and *at,* the most common prepositions for showing time are *for, during,* and *since.*

- *For* usually refers to an exact period of time that something lasts, a period that has a beginning and an end.

  I went into the army for six years.

  It has been snowing for two hours.

  I've been jogging for three weeks.

- *During* usually refers to an indefinite period of time in which something happens.

  Several times during the hike I stopped to catch my breath.

  I plan to climb Mount Everest sometime during the summer.

  It hailed during the night.

- *Since* usually refers to a period of time that has passed between an earlier time and the present.

  I've gained weight since the holidays.

  Since last spring, Nicola has been working at the zoo.

  Pete's been so happy since quitting smoking.

ACTIVITY 6: Use *for, during,* and *since* in Sentences

Fill in the blanks in each of the following sentences, using either *for, during,* or *since* correctly.

EXAMPLE I visited my mother __during__ spring break.

1. Madeline has been a vegetarian _________ thirteen years.
2. _________ he turned eighteen, Trent has been living on his own.
3. The telephone rang _________ dinner.
4. I haven't seen Benny _________ three weeks.
5. Advertisers make special commercials to show _________ the Super Bowl.
6. After taking the pills, you should not eat _________ two hours.
7. The air conditioner runs nonstop _________ the hottest weeks of summer.

8. Somebody in the audience started coughing ________ the performance.
9. Caronne has been feeling sick ________ last night.
10. Mr. Jensen will be out of town ________ five days.

ACTIVITY 7: Use *for, during,* and *since* in a Paragraph

Fill in the blanks in the following paragraph, using either *for, during,* or *since* correctly.

EXAMPLE Karate has been popular in the United States ___for___ many years.

Anthony has been practicing karate ________ seven years, ________ he was twelve years old. ________ the school year, he trains three days a week, and ________ vacations, he trains nearly every day. He intends to practice this martial art ________ the rest of his life.

HOW TO Learn to Use Prepositions

- Learn the rules for the prepositions that have rules, such as *in, on,* and *at* and *for, during,* and *since.*
- Pay attention to how prepositions are used when you are listening to others or reading books, magazines, or newspapers.
- Keep a list of expressions that contain prepositions. Use index cards or a small notebook so you can refer to the list wherever you are.

D. OMITTED OR REPEATED SUBJECTS

In English, every sentence has a subject and a verb. The *subject* tells who or what is doing the action; the *verb* expresses an action or a state of being.

For more help with subjects, turn to pp. 474–80.

Omitted Subjects

The subject of a sentence must be stated, even when the meaning of the sentence is clear without its being stated.

INCORRECT Want to get my degree in mechanical engineering.

CORRECT *I* want to get my degree in mechanical engineering.

INCORRECT My sister loves to read. Goes to the library twice a week.

CORRECT My sister loves to read. *She* goes to the library twice a week.

A dependent clause is sometimes called a subordinate clause. *Learn about subordinate clauses on pp. 523–24.*

The subject of a dependent clause must also be stated. A *dependent clause* contains a subject and verb but can't stand alone as a sentence because it begins with a subordinating conjunction (such as *because* or *although*) or a relative pronoun (such as *who, that,* or *which*).

INCORRECT I already knew that wanted to major in math.

CORRECT I already knew that *I* wanted to major in math.

INCORRECT I threw the package away because was empty.

CORRECT I threw the package away because *it* was empty.

English sentences and dependent clauses often begin with the word *it* or *there* followed by a form of *be,* as in *it is, there is,* and *there were.* In such a sentence or clause, the *it* or *there* acts as a kind of subject and can't be omitted.

INCORRECT Is too late to hand in the paper.

CORRECT It is too late to hand in the paper.

INCORRECT Are three bottles on the shelf.

CORRECT There are three bottles on the shelf.

ACTIVITY 8: Add Missing Subjects to a Paragraph

Using the preceding guidelines, add a subject in each place where one is missing in the following paragraph.

EXAMPLE ~~A~~re several different kinds of friends. (There inserted: "There are several different kinds of friends.")

Every Friday evening, a group of us meet at a café. Enjoy the time we spend together. Formerly, we went to bars. Then, my friend Cassie developed a problem with alcohol because was going to bars too often. We decided to stop drinking as a group. Is still fun sometimes to go to clubs to dance and to meet new people. Is a strange connection between dancing and alcohol.

Repeated Subjects

Be careful not to repeat a subject that has already been stated earlier in the sentence.

INCORRECT The lady in the store *she* was rude.

CORRECT The lady in the store was rude.

(The pronoun *she* repeats the subject *lady.*)

INCORRECT Some people *they* like to go to parties.

CORRECT Some people like to go to parties.

(The pronoun *they* repeats the subject *people.*)

ACTIVITY 9: Identify Repeated Subjects

Draw a line through the repeated subjects in the following paragraph.

EXAMPLE The people in the class ~~they~~ decided to postpone the test.

The members of my fraternity we decided to give holiday presents to children in local hospitals. Cliff and Rodney, who suggested the project in the first place, they contacted businesses for contributions. Andre, whose family owns a discount store, he was able to purchase toys at wholesale prices. Several members with trucks and vans they delivered the gifts to hospitals. All of us who worked on this charitable project we enjoyed watching the children open their presents.

E. WORD ORDER

In English, the basic word order of a sentence is *subject, verb, object.*

S V O
Jordan ironed the dress.

Adjectives and adverbs are placed close to the words they modify.

S V O
Jordan quickly ironed the blue dress.

Adjective Placement

In English, adjectives almost always come before the noun they modify.

See pp. 514–15 for more information about adjectives.

An *important* thing to remember is to stop at stop signs.

George prepared to take the *difficult* test.

Julie bought the *red* motorcycle.

In addition, different kinds of adjectives appear in a particular order. Though exceptions exist, this order is usually followed:

articles and pronouns: *a, an, the, my, your*
words that evaluate: *ugly, handsome, honest, appealing, flavorful*
words about size: *big, small, large*
words about length or shape: *small, big, round, square, wide, narrow*
words about age: *old, young, new*
words about color: *red, blue, yellow*
words about nationality: *Irish, Mexican, Canadian, Chinese*
words about religion: *Muslim, Buddhist, Protestant, Jewish*
words about the material of the noun: *wooden, glass, brick, adobe, stucco*
nouns used as adjectives: *bathroom floor, track team*

Finally, the noun goes last: *book, car, movie, church, bench, computer.*

The handsome old house sat at the top of the hill.

My German Catholic grandmother died last year.

The square wooden jewelry box sat on the table.

HOW TO Decide Whether to Use Commas between Adjectives

How do you decide whether you need a comma between two or more adjectives? If you can place *and* between the adjectives and the sentence still makes sense, then you need the comma.

Suppose you want to write this:

The tall fragile rosebush was blooming.

Do you need a comma between *tall* and *fragile*? Yes, because "the tall *and* fragile rosebush" makes sense.

The tall, fragile rosebush was blooming.

ACTIVITY 10: Revise Sentences to Use Adjectives Correctly

Revise each of the following sentences so that the adjectives are placed correctly and commas are used between them where necessary.

EXAMPLE Please hand me the brown big box.

Please hand me the big brown box.

1. We bought the leather sofa most comfortable.

____

2. Curtis promised to throw out his plaid old pajamas.

____

3. The dark Belgian delicious chocolates were a gift.

____

4. A spotted big snake crawled under the house.

____

5. The car little red fit in the parking space.

____

6. After the movie, Marisol remembered her assignment boring and difficult.

____

____

7. I gave the cheerful friendly child a cookie.

____

8. His leather black beautiful jacket was ruined.

____

9. We admired the aluminum elegant animal sculptures.

____

10. My grandmother recited a Jewish short prayer over the candles.

____

ACTIVITY 11: Add Adjectives Correctly

In each of the following sentences, add the number of adjectives indicated in parentheses in the space provided. Use commas as necessary.

EXAMPLE A curved stone path led to the house. (2)

1. I wanted a ________________ car. (2)
2. Smoking is a ________________ habit. (2)
3. The sight of the ________________ tacos made my mouth water. (3)
4. Linda wanted to take one of the ________________ puppies home with her. (2)
5. The ________________ sweater fit Ivan perfectly. (2)
6. Whenever Kevin wanted to quit school, he remembered his ________________ parents back home. (2)
7. To be accepted into the program, I had to pass a ________________ exam. (2)

8. Eunice refused to climb the ______________ steps. (3)

9. Last year, I dated a ______________ student. (2)

10. Our assignment was to read a chapter in our ______________ ______________ textbook. (3)

Adverb Placement

Adverbs that modify verbs can appear at the beginning or end of a sentence, before or after the verb, or between a helping verb and the main verb. Most often, the adverb appears as close as possible to the verb.

More information about adverbs is available on pp. 515–16.

Hurriedly, we escaped out the back door.

The dog scratched *frantically* against the window.

Abner *eagerly* wrote the letter.

My brother has *often* stayed out after midnight.

Do not put an adverb between a verb and its direct object. A direct object receives the action of the verb.

INCORRECT Li put quickly the package on the table.

CORRECT Li quickly put the package on the table.

INCORRECT The hairdresser cut carefully my hair.

CORRECT The hairdresser carefully cut my hair.

ACTIVITY 12: Place Adverbs Correctly

Revise the following paragraph, adding at least one adverb to each sentence.

EXAMPLE Many students ^impatiently^ wait in long lines during late registration.

Some students complain to the people around them about the lack of classes. Other students, who had to bring their children, make sure the kids don't run around the building screaming. A few students laugh with their friends. Many students check their watches and wonder how long they can wait. Everyone wishes the lines were shorter.

F. VERBS

To learn more about verbs, turn to pp. 480–90.

A *verb* expresses an action (*smile, work, hit*) or a state of being (*be, seem, become*). Depending on your language background, verbs in English can be particularly challenging to master. This section will help you correctly use verb tenses, helping verbs, and verbs followed by gerunds and infinitives.

Verb Tense

The *tense* of a verb indicates the time in which the action or condition that the verb expresses took place. The three basic tenses in English are the *simple present, simple past,* and *simple future.* These must be distinguished from the *present perfect, past perfect, future perfect, present progressive, past progressive,* and *future progressive* tenses.

Simple Present Tense. The simple present tense shows an action or a condition that is taking place at the time it is mentioned. The simple present can also show an action or a condition that occurs repeatedly or one scheduled to occur in the future. Except for *be* and *have,* the simple present uses the base form of the verb (*swim, work*), with an *-s* or *-es* added if the subject is a singular noun or *he, she,* or *it.*

Jamilla *seems* depressed recently.

Pierre *studies* at least five hours a day.

I *drive* my daughter to school every weekday morning.

The new store *opens* next week.

For a list of common irregular verbs and their past-tense forms, see p. 489.

Simple Past Tense. The simple past tense indicates an action or a condition that began and ended in the past. Except for irregular verbs like *go* or *teach,* the simple past consists of the base form of the verb with *-ed* added to the end.

Yesterday I *passed* my driver's test.

When he *was* a student, he *walked* wherever he *had* to go. (The action of walking happened more than once in the past, but it's not happening now.)

Future Tense. The future tense shows an action or a condition that will take place or will probably take place. The future tense requires the use of *will* or *be going to* followed by the base form of the verb.

I *will spend* next summer in New York City.

These economic conditions *are going to continue* indefinitely.

Present Perfect Tense. The perfect tenses show a completed action or condition. They are formed using the past participle of the verb and the appropriate form of *have*.

The present perfect tense shows an action or a condition that began in the past and that either is now finished or continues into the present. Unlike with the past tense, the specific time of the action or condition is not given. To form this tense, use *has* or *have* followed by the past participle. Except for irregular verbs, the past participle consists of the base form of the verb with *-ed* added to the end.

Alex *has cooked* the dinner.

The lawyers *have argued* their case.

For a list of common irregular verbs and their past participles, see p. 489.

When the present perfect expresses an action or condition that began in the past and continues into the present, it usually is used with an expression of time beginning with *since* or *for*.

Susan *has played* the trumpet since she was a child.

(Susan has played in the past and continues to play in the present.)

They *have been* in Seattle for three years.

(They went to Seattle in the past, and they are still there.)

Past Perfect Tense. The past perfect tense indicates an action or a condition occurring in the past before another time in the past. To form this tense, use *had* and the past participle of the verb.

I *had learned* the formulas by the day of the test.

They *had smelled* smoke before they saw the fire.

Future Perfect Tense. The future perfect tense indicates a future action or condition that will end by or before a specific future time. To form this tense, use *will have* and the past participle of the verb.

By next Tuesday, I *will have finished* all my classes for the semester.

Heather *will have left* the office before you get there.

Present Progressive Tense. The progressive tenses show a continuing action or condition. They are formed using the present participle (the *-ing* form of the verb) and the appropriate form of *be*.

The present progressive tense indicates an action that is happening at the time it is mentioned or an action that is scheduled to happen in the future. To form this tense, use *am, is,* or *are* and the *-ing* form of the verb.

Eduardo *is helping* us move the furniture.

We *are leaving* for the beach tomorrow.

Past Progressive Tense. The past progressive tense shows an action or a condition that continued for some time in the past and is now over. To form this tense, use *was* or *were* and the *-ing* form of the verb.

Over the summer I *was spending* my money mostly on food.

Last night the sick man's words *were becoming* very faint.

Future Progressive Tense. The future progressive tense indicates a continuing action or condition in the future. To form this tense, use *will be* and the *-ing* form of the verb.

The judge *will be hearing* your case soon.

By next week you *will be feeling* better.

ACTIVITY 13: Identify Verb Tenses

Identify the verb tense in each of the following sentences.

EXAMPLE The cake *will be* ready tonight. ___future___

1. Julian *has completed* all the prerequisites. ________
2. You *have wasted* the whole semester. ________
3. Before getting married, Bill and Jenny *had decided* to move to Colorado. ________
4. Last week, I *was recovering* from surgery. ________
5. The tomatoes *will be ripening* next week. ________
6. They *work* at City Hall. ________
7. *Will* Marcie *compete* in the next essay contest? ________
8. They *have taken* all morning to buy groceries. ________
9. Wayne *drank* an entire pitcher of iced tea. ________
10. Dolores *is talking* to her doctor. ________

ACTIVITY 14: Use Verb Tenses Correctly

For each of the following sentences, write the required verb tense of the verb in parentheses.

EXAMPLE You ___had been___ (be) doing very well in that class until now. *(past perfect)*

1. I ______________ (do) my best to make you happy. *(present progressive)*
2. Lillian ______________ (whisper) her secret to Josie. *(past)*
3. The children ______________ (play) for an hour. *(present perfect)*
4. Hans ______________ (be) here tomorrow. *(future)*
5. We ______________ (hire) a DJ for the party. *(future)*
6. The sales associate ______________ (consult) the manager before lowering the price. *(present)*
7. The procedure ______________ (work) more effectively last year. *(past progressive)*
8. Before the concert, the advertisements ______________ (say) the tickets would be thirty-five dollars apiece. *(past perfect)*
9. The senator ______________ (decide) to run for reelection. *(present perfect)*
10. Fred ______________ (take) the children to the circus. *(present perfect)*

Helping Verbs

A *helping verb* is a verb that is used with another verb, called the *main verb,* to create a phrase that acts as a verb in a sentence. Sometimes, such a phrase includes two or even three helping verbs in addition to the main verb. Helping verbs are used for a number of different purposes, including to form the future, the perfect, and the progressive tenses and the passive voice; to ask questions and make negative statements; and to show that something is possible or required.

See p. 481 for more information about helping verbs.

Micah has left the room. (*Has* is the helping verb; *left* is the main verb.)

You must wait for the train to leave the station. (*Must* is the helping verb; *wait* is the main verb.)

I have been sitting here for two hours. (*Have* and *been* are the helping verbs; *sitting* is the main verb.)

Modals. Some helping verbs, known as *modals,* are used only as helping verbs:

can	might	should
could	must	will
may	shall	would

When using a modal in a sentence, use the base form of the main verb after it unless the modal is followed by another helping verb.

Luisa *might travel* to Thailand.

My sister *would sing* if she could read music.

Rupert *can carry* the suitcase.

Carlos *could have been* a better candidate.

Our chorus *may be performing* in New York next year.

Unlike other helping verbs, a modal does not change form to agree in number with the subject, and neither does the main verb that follows it.

INCORRECT He wills leave.

INCORRECT He will leaves.

CORRECT He will leave.

ACTIVITY 15: Identify Modals

Circle the modals in the following paragraph.

EXAMPLE Friends (should) help each other out.

Three of my best friends are leaving town next week. Frank is going to Los Angeles, where he will begin his career as a movie editor. He should be able to find a job quickly. Janice is moving to Chicago in order to attend medical school. She might be able to afford her own apartment, should she be able to find one. Finally, Leroy is going to New York. Because he has little money saved up, he must find a job right away.

Do, Does, Did. Like modals, the helping verbs *do, does,* and *did* are followed by the base form of the verb. These verbs are used

- to ask a question:

  Do you want to dance?

  Did my brother pick up his suit?

- to make a negative statement (when used with *not*):

  I did not request this car.

  Sammy does not eat broccoli.

- to emphasize a main verb:

  Once again, I do appreciate the gift.

  She does look beautiful.

Unlike modals, the helping verbs *do* and *does* change in number to agree with the subject of the sentence.

INCORRECT He do not enjoy watching football.

CORRECT He does not enjoy watching football.

Have, Has, Had. The helping verbs *have, has,* and *had* are used to indicate the perfect tenses. *Have* and *has* change form to agree in number with the subject.

INCORRECT They has broken all the good plates.

CORRECT They have broken all the good plates.

Forms of Be. Forms of the verb *be — be, am, is, are, was, were, been* — are used as helping verbs for two purposes. Together with the present participle of the main verb, they are used to indicate the progressive tenses.

I am taking calculus this year.

The birds were singing in the tree near my window.

Together with the past participle of the main verb, forms of *be* are used to indicate the passive voice, in which the subject doesn't perform the action of the verb but receives the action. Here are some examples.

Find out more about the passive voice on pp. 572–73.

Jonathan was hit by the flying glass.

The book was written by Tom Wolfe.

Parts of the city have been closed by the chief of police.

ACTIVITY 16: Use Helping Verbs

In each of the following sentences, fill in the blank with an appropriate helping verb followed by the correct form of the verb in parentheses.

EXAMPLE After our argument, my brother did not speak (speak) to me for two years.

1. Nobody ____________ (see) Caroline for the past few weeks.
2. Barney ____________ (paint) the kitchen last Saturday.
3. Until Halloween, the weather ____________ (be) pleasant.
4. With this excellent progress, you ____________ (convince) me that you are motivated.
5. For three years, I ____________ (accept) these strict rules.
6. Until she took organic chemistry, Aunt Lucy ____________ (want) to be a doctor.
7. To my surprise, Angel ____________ (win) a spelling bee when he was in the fifth grade.
8. Johnny Depp ____________ (act) in many unusual roles.
9. To be independent in many rural areas, you ____________ (own) your own car.
10. Shawna ____________ (work) at McDonald's while she takes college classes.

ACTIVITY 17: Use Helping Verbs in a Paragraph

In the following paragraph, fill in each of the blanks with an appropriate helping verb followed by the correct form of the verb in parentheses.

EXAMPLE Elyse should thank (thank) her family for their support.

Later today, at the graduation ceremony, Elyse ____________ (receive) her diploma from the university. She began her studies at the age of forty, after she ____________ (work) for many years. Since then, she ____________ (struggle) to earn her degree. Many obstacles ____________ (interrupt) her education, mostly health and financial difficulties. However, nothing

_______________ (stop) her from reaching her goal. Indeed, she _______________ (graduate) with honors. Throughout these difficult and rewarding years, her family _______________ (remain) her first priority. She _______________ (celebrate) tonight among her loved ones.

Verbs Followed by Gerunds or Infinitives

A *gerund* is a form of a verb that ends in *-ing* and is used as a noun.

I enjoy *walking.*

Cooking is his favorite hobby.

In contrast, an *infinitive* is the base form of a verb with the word *to* in front of it.

I decided *to stop* my car.

I went home *to wash* my clothes.

The following verbs can be followed by either a gerund or an infinitive without changing the meaning of the sentence.

begin
stand
continue
hate
like
love
start

I started *to like* him right away.

I started *liking* him right away.

With other verbs, the meaning changes depending on whether they're followed by a gerund or an infinitive.

She stopped *smoking* cigarettes.

(She gave up the habit of smoking.)

She stopped *to smoke* a cigarette.

(She paused so she could light up a cigarette.)

George remembered *to buy* the gift.

(George had planned to buy the gift and did so.)

George remembered *buying* the gift.

(George recalled the act of purchasing the gift.)

The following verbs may be followed by a gerund but not by an infinitive:

admit	escape	quit
appreciate	finish	recall
avoid	imagine	resist
deny	miss	risk
discuss	practice	suggest
enjoy	put off	tolerate

Jonah denied *witnessing* the car accident.

My father missed *opening* the presents.

These verbs may be followed by an infinitive but not by a gerund:

agree	expect	mean	promise
ask	have	need	wait
beg	hope	offer	want
decide	manage	plan	wish

She planned *to take* the 7 a.m. flight.

Fred asked *to leave* the room.

ACTIVITY 18: Use Verbs Plus Gerunds or Infinitives Correctly

Complete each of the following sentences with the gerund or infinitive form of the verb in parentheses, whichever is correct.

EXAMPLE Lucy enjoyed ___seeing___ (see) her parents.

1. We decided ____________ (take) the scenic road to the lake rather than the freeway.
2. Theodore can't stand ____________ (wait) for an elevator, so he always takes the stairs.
3. April decided ____________ (attend) the community college before transferring to a university.

4. Ward denied ____________ (be) my secret admirer.
5. Nora practiced ____________ (drive) in a parking lot before she went on the road.
6. Chester started ________________ (collect) fossils when he was in high school.
7. The teens expected ____________ (receive) a reward for returning the lost wallet.
8. Dorcas imagined ____________ (win) the lottery.
9. Students resist ____________ (use) the university library.
10. My little sister continues ________________ (bother) me when my friends visit.

ACTIVITY 19: Write Sentences Using Verbs Plus Gerunds or Infinitives Correctly

Complete each of the following sentences with a gerund or an infinitive, as well as other words if necessary.

EXAMPLE Because of her age, my daughter avoided taking the test.

1. Tomorrow, Richie will finish ________________________.
2. Whenever possible, I avoid ________________________.
3. My children love ________________________.
4. You do not need to beg ________________________.
5. Sheila only pretended ________________________.
6. A busy student certainly appreciates ________________________.
7. I made a New Year's resolution to quit ________________________.
8. I never succeed when I try ________________________.
9. In one hour, Maurice will start ________________________.
10. My parents hope ________________________.

Two-Part Verbs

Many verbs in English consist of two words. Here are some of the most common ones:

ask out	clean up
break down	drop in
call up	get along
give up	pick up
help out	play around
keep up	put together
leave out	shut up
make up	wake up

Be careful not to leave out the second word of such verbs.

INCORRECT Susan picked her room.

CORRECT Susan picked up her room.

INCORRECT When buying gifts, James left his cousin.

CORRECT When buying gifts, James left out his cousin.

ACTIVITY 20: Use Two-Part Verbs Correctly

For each of the following sentences, complete the two-part verb. Refer to the list above.

EXAMPLE Let me help you clean ___up___ the kitchen.

1. Professor Zindell wants us to drop ________ for a visit whenever we wish.
2. Please pick ________ your dirty clothes before you go to sleep.
3. The cat and dog get ________ very well.
4. Whenever I make that fruit salad, I always leave ________ the bananas.
5. Children always want to help ________ in the kitchen when they are too young to be useful.

ACTIVITY 21: Add Two-Part Verbs

Use a two-part verb to complete each of the following sentences. Refer to the list above.

EXAMPLE Roland ___called up___ his girlfriend on his cell phone.

1. Mary Alice has ______________ a professional wardrobe using a few basic garments.
2. I ______________ my mess so well that nobody knew that I had made one.
3. Yesterday, Jim ______________ a story to amuse the neighbor's children.
4. The truck always ______________ in hot weather.
5. If you do these assignments, you will be able to ______________ your classmates.

Participles Used as Adjectives

The present participle and past participle of verbs that refer to feelings or senses are often used as adjectives. Such verbs include the following:

interest	excite	fascinate	charm
disappoint	bore	tire	embarrass
disturb	encourage	frighten	confuse

When the adjective refers to a person or an animal *having* the feeling, use the past participle form, the one that ends in *-ed*.

The *frightened* cat jumped on the shelf.

The student was *bored*.

The *confused* child began to cry.

When the adjective refers to a thing or person *causing* the feeling, use the present participle form, the one that ends in *-ing*.

The *frightening* movie scared the children.

The book was *boring*.

The *confusing* message was not conveyed.

INCORRECT I was interesting in the show.

CORRECT I was interested in the show.

INCORRECT The story was excited.

CORRECT The story was exciting.

ACTIVITY 22: Use Participles as Adjectives

Complete each of the following sentences with the correct participle of the verb in parentheses.

EXAMPLE I was ___encouraged___ (encourage) by the positive reviews of my show.

1. I was __________ (fascinate) by the butterfly collection.
2. The butterfly collection was __________ (fascinate).
3. Jane, who was __________ (embarrass) by all the attention, wanted to be left alone.
4. The children's play was __________ (charm).
5. I have never seen such a __________ (disturb) collection of artwork in my life.
6. The spectators enjoyed the __________ (excite) fireworks display.
7. Frankly, I found the speech rather __________ (tire).
8. The __________ (disappoint) viewers turned off the television.
9. I am __________ (charm) to meet you.
10. When will this __________ (embarrass) display of affection end?

Acknowledgments

B.C., "Homeless in Prescott, Arizona" from *I Thought My Father was God and Other True Tales from NPR's National Story Project,* edited by Paul Auster and Nelly Reifler. Copyright © 2001. Reprinted by permission of the Carol Mann Agency.

Lara Flynn Boyle, excerpt from "My Favorite Day in Chicago," an interview with Mark Seal from *American Way,* July 15, 2000. Reprinted by permission of Mark Seal.

Jane Brody, excerpt from "The Hangover" from *Jane Brody's Nutrition Book*. Copyright © 1981 by Jane E. Brody. Used by permission of W. W. Norton & Company, Inc.

Gavin de Becker, "Why I Fight Abuse" from *Protecting the Gift*. Copyright © 1999 by Gavin de Becker. Used by permission of The Dial Press/Dell Publishing, a division of Random House, Inc.

Marshall Glickman, "Money and Freedom." Copyright © 1987 by Marshall Glickman. Reprinted by permission of the New York Times Company.

Pete Hamill, excerpt from "Crack and the Box" from *Esquire,* May 5, 1990. Copyright © 1990 by Pete Hamill. Reprinted by permission of International Creative Management, Inc.

Institute for Children and Poverty, excerpt from "The Age of Confusion: Why So Many Teens Are Getting Pregnant, Turning to Welfare and Ending Up Homeless," April 1996. Reprinted by permission of the Institute for Children and Poverty.

Rebecca Thomas Kirkendell, excerpt from "Who's a Hillbilly?" from *Newsweek,* November 27, 1995. Copyright © 1995 Newsweek, Inc. All rights reserved. Reprinted by permission.

Steven Muller, "Our Youth Should Serve" from *Newsweek,* 1978. Reprinted by permission of the author.

Anna Quindlen, excerpt from "Put 'Em in a Tree Museum" from *Newsweek,* August 23, 2004. Copyright © 2004 by Anna Quindlen. Reprinted by permission of International Creative Management, Inc.

Patricia Raybon, "A Case of Severe Bias" from *Newsweek,* October 1989. Copyright © 1989 by Patricia Raybon. Reprinted by permission of the author.

Wilbert Rideau, "Why Prisons Don't Work" from *Time,* March 21, 1994. Copyright © 1994 by Wilbert Rideau. Reprinted with the permission of the author, c/o The Permissions Company, PO Box 604, Mount Pocono, PA 18344. All rights reserved.

Mike Rose, excerpt from "I Just Wanna Be Average" from *Lives on the Boundary: The Struggles and Achievements of America's Underprepared*. Copyright © 1989 by Mike Rose. All rights reserved. Reprinted with the permission of The Free Press, a Division of Simon & Schuster Adult Publishing Group.

Charles Smith, "Running Out of Money Before Graduation" from *Black Issues in Higher Education,* June 7, 2001. Reprinted with permission from Black Issues In Higher Education, www.blackissues.com.

Sam Smith, excerpt from "The Luddites at Microsoft: Making Machines That Smash Themselves" from *Progressive Review,* January 28, 2004. Published at prorev.com. Reprinted by permission of the author.

Sarah Stage, "Better Living Through Electricity" from *The American Promise, 3e* by James Roark et al. Copyright © 2005 by Bedford/St. Martin's. Reprinted by permission of Bedford/St. Martin's.

Steve Tesich, excerpt from "Focusing on Friends" from *The New York Times,* December 4, 1983. Reprinted by permission of Nadja Tesich.

Neely Tucker, excerpt from *Love in the Driest Season: A Family Memoir*. Copyright © 2004 by Neely Tucker. Used by permission of Crown Publishers, a division of Random House, Inc.

E. B. White, "The Three New Yorks" from *Here Is New York*. Copyright © 1949 by E. B. White. Reprinted by permission of International Creative Management, Inc.

Jan Zeh, "The 'Golden Years' Are Beginning to Tarnish" from *Newsweek,* August 2, 2004. Copyright © 2004 Newsweek, Inc. All rights reserved. Reprinted by permission.

Photo Credits

p. 2, © Susie Fitzhugh Photographer; p. 16, © Reuters NewMedia Inc./CORBIS; p. 48, © Joseph Sohm; ChromoSohm Inc./CORBIS; p. 70, © Rupert Daniel Ullman/Design Conceptions; p. 92, © Art on File/CORBIS; p. 114, © Susie Fitzhugh Photographer; p. 136, © Bob Daemmrich/The Image Works; p. 160, © Susie Fitzhugh Photographer; p. 184, © Joel Gordon; p. 206, © Joel Gordon; p. 230, © Joel Gordon; p. 254, © Susie Fitzhugh Photographer; p. 284, © Susie Fitzhugh Photographer; p. 314, © Susie Fitzhugh Photographer; p. 344, © Mark L. Stevenson/CORBIS; p. 376, © Joel Gordon; p. 412, © StephanieFelix Photography; p. 424, © Jean-Claude Lejeune; p. 434, © Bill Lai/The Image Works; p. 444, © Frank Pedrick/The Image Works.

Index

A QUICK REFERENCE TO EDITING SYMBOLS

adj	adjective error 514, 645
adv	adverb error 515, 648
awk	awkward wording
cap	capital letter needed 626
coord	correct coordination in sentence 309, 338, 517
cs	comma splice 87, 561
dm	dangling modifier 225, 569
frag	sentence fragment 65, 548
jar	avoid jargon
lc	use lower-case letter 626
mm	misplaced modifier 225, 566
no cap	no capital 626
pass	avoid passive voice 155, 572
prep	preposition error 475, 639
pr agr	pronoun agreement error 202, 511
ref	error in pronoun reference 248, 509
rep	repetitious 179, 581
r-o	run-on sentence 109, 554
-s	*s* needed at the end of word
sp	spelling error 584
sub	correct subordination in sentence 370, 404, 522
s-v agr	error in subject-verb agreement 132, 490
trans	transition needed 42
v or vb	verb error 480
vt	shift in verb tense 486
w	too wordy 179, 582
ww	wrong word 578
¶	begin new paragraph 18, 469
?	meaning unclear
√	good idea or expression
x	error marked or crossed out
^	insert
℘	delete